MACROMEDIA® FLASH™ MX 2004 GAME DESIGN DEMYSTIFIED

JOBE MAKAR
BEN WINIARCZYK

macromedia® PRESS

Macromedia® Flash™ MX 2004 Game Design Demystified
Jobe Makar and Ben Winiarczyk

Published by Peachpit Press, a division of Pearson Education, in association with Macromedia Press.

Peachpit Press
1249 Eighth Street
Berkeley, CA 94710
510/534-2178 * 800-283-9444
510/524-2221 (fax)

Find us on the World Wide Web at: **http://www.peachpit.com**
http://www.macromedia.com
http://www.gamebook.net

Senior Acquisitions Editor: Linda Bump Harrison
Development Editor: Chris Zahn
Senior Project Editor: Kristy Hart
Copy Editor: Ben Lawson
Interior Design: Mimi Heft
Compositor: Molly Sharp
Cover Design: Aren Howell
Index: Lisa Stumpf

Notice of Rights

Trademark Notice

Notice of Liability

ISBN: 0-7357-1398-7

9 8 7 6 5 4 3 2 1

Printed and bound in the United States of America

Acknowledgments

Jobe's Acknowledgments

This book is the product of the hard work of many people. Ben, it has been a pleasure collaborating with you on this immense project. Your combined talent with programming, art, and writing makes you invaluable! Thank you Linda for keeping us on track and helping us solve some difficult issues. Chris, your edits and helpful comments have shaped this book into something great. Thanks to all the other folks at Peachpit's Indy office who have helped bring this book to fruition: Kristy Hart, Ben Lawson, Lisa Stumpf, Jay Payne, and Stephanie Wall.

As always, I owe much thanks to my colleagues at Electrotank for bearing with me during the writing process, and for continuous useful feedback on the chapters and examples in this book.

Kelly, your support during this long process was just what I needed.

Ben's Acknowledgments

The first edition of this book, *Macromedia Flash MX Game Design Demystified*, was and still is an incredible resource and inspiration for aspiring game developers as well as a comprehensive reference for experienced developers. This book, updated for Flash MX 2004 and ActionScript 2.0, with loads of new games and content, is sure to become the new "must have" book for us game developers, and it is a huge honor to have been given the opportunity to work on this project.

I am extremely grateful to Jobe for asking me to work with him on this book. His technical expertise and the work of Electrotank are impressive and inspiring, and it is an incredible honor to work with him. Thanks Jobe!

ABOUT THE AUTHORS

Jobe Makar

Jobe Makar is the lead programmer and co-owner of Electrotank, Inc. and winner of several international game awards. The creator of over 100 Flash games, Jobe has been working with Flash since version 3. He has authored or co-authored several books on Flash including *Macromedia Flash MX 2004 ActionScript: Training from the Source*. Among his many accomplishments, Jobe was the Lead Programmer at Learnimation when they received four Small Business Innovation Research Awards from the National Science Foundation and the U.S. Department of Education. Jobe currently lives with his wife and entirely too many animals in Raleigh, North Carolina.

Ben Winiarczyk

Ben Winiarczyk is the founder and Creative Director of Blit Inc., a high end, custom game design firm serving such clients as Comedy Central, Sports Illustrated for Kids, and eUniverse. He has designed hit games for *South Park*, *The Man Show*, *The Daily Show*, and *Battleball*. With a background centered on animation and design as well as ActionScripting, he is able to creatively push today's technology to the limit, creating award-winning games and supporting technologies. Ben has been working with Flash since version 3.

About the Technical Reviewer

John Grden

John Grden is a Senior Macromedia Flash Developer for Blitz Digital Studios (BlitzDS.com) as well as founder/owner of AcmeWebWorks.com. Along with moderating one of the largest Macromedia User Lists on the Internet, John spends most of his Flash development time creating some of the most engaging Flash games on the web today. Currently he's re-creating specific games based on a popular movie series' battles and events that are not only available on his site but also at www.TheForce.net. John is certified as a Macromedia Flash Designer, and you can find out what he's been up to at BlitzDS.com or AcmeWebWorks.com.

Contents at a Glance

Introduction xvii

Part I: Getting Started with Flash Game Design

Chapter 1: First Steps 5

Chapter 2: Making a Game Fun 21

Part II: Examining the Nuts and Bolts

Chapter 3: Game Math 43

Chapter 4: Basic Physics 69

Chapter 5: Collision Detection 97

Chapter 6: Collision Reactions 151

Chapter 7: Tile-based Worlds 179

hapter 8: The Isometric Worldview 211

Chapter 9: Level Editors 249

Chapter 10: High Score List 263

Chapter 11: Artificial Intelligence 277

Chapter 12: Efficient Game Graphics 311

Chapter 13: The Sound of Games 331

Chapter 14: Introduction to Multiplayer Games 359

Part III: The Games

Chapter 15: Word Search 381

Chapter 16: Multiplayer Chess 409

Chapter 17: 501 Darts Game 435

Chapter 18: Cone Crazy 453

Appendices

Appendix A: Developer Resources 479

Appendix B: Other Games 489

Index 495

TABLE OF CONTENTS

Introduction xvii

Part I: Getting Started with Flash Game

Chapter 1: First Steps 5

Inspirational Kick-Start 8
Terminology 8
Game Views 8
General Terms 11
Game Genres 13
Flash Limitations 14
Flash Versus Non-Flash Games 14
Infeasible Game Features 16
Points to Remember 18

Chapter 2: Making a Fun Game 21

Understanding the Audience 22
So, Who Is This Audience? 22
Demographics 23
Playback Specs 24
Concept and Flow 27
The Initial Concept 27
Develop the Theme 28
Storyline and Characters 29
Flow 30

Game Basics 31
Scoring 31
Difficulty Levels 32
Health/Lives 33
Bonuses and Power-Ups 33
Easter Eggs 34
Length of play 34
Human Competition 35
Real-Time Multiplayer 35
Challenge/Send to a Friend 35
High Score Lists 35
Saving Game Data 36
Option 1: Flash's Local Shared Object 36
Option 2: Server-Side Database 38
Option 3: Local Files 38
Points to Remember 38

PART II: EXAMINING THE NUTS AND BOLTS

Chapter 3: Game Math 43

Why Learn Trigonometry? 44
The Flash Coordinate System 44
Cartesian Coordinates 45
Angles 48
Anatomy of a Triangle 51
The Pythagorean Theorem 52
The Heart of Trig 55
Sine, Cosine, and Tangent 55
Projection 59
Vectors 62
Points to Remember 66

Chapter 4: Basic Physics 69

Introduction to Physics 70
Speed, Velocity, and Acceleration 71
Speed and Velocity 72
Applying Speed with ActionScript 73
Acceleration 78

Newton's Three Laws of Motion . . . 82
Newton's First Law . . . 82
Newton's Second Law . . . 83
Newton's Third Law . . . 86
Gravity . . . 87
Real Gravity . . . 88
Good-Enough Gravity . . . 89
Friction . . . 90
Real Friction . . . 90
Good-Enough Friction . . . 92
Points to Remember . . . 94

Chapter 5: Collision Detection 97

What Is a Collision? . . . 98
Detection Using *hitTest()* . . . 99
Movie Clip-Movie Clip Collisions . . . 100
Movie Clip-Point Collisions . . . 103
Shape-Point Collisions . . . 107
Detection Using Math . . . 110
Point-Circle Collision Detection . . . 112
Circle-Circle Collision Detection . . . 115
Line-Line Collision Detection . . . 126
Circle-Line Collision Detection . . . 135
Point-Rectangle Collision Detection . . . 142
Rectangle-Rectangle Collision Detection . . . 145
Collision Detection with Advanced Shapes . . . 147
Points to Remember . . . 148

Chapter 6: Collision Reactions 151

Bouncing Off the Walls . . . 153
Object-Wall Reactions . . . 153
Circle-Line Reactions . . . 159
Conservation of Momentum and Energy . . . 162
Review: What Are Momentum and Energy? . . . 163
The Conservation Laws . . . 164
Applying the Conservation Laws . . . 165
Rectangle-Rectangle Reactions . . . 167
Circle-Circle (Billiard-Ball) Reactions . . . 169
Points to Remember . . . 177

Chapter 7: Tile-Based Worlds 179

Introduction to Tiles 180
Design Considerations 182
The View 182
Seamless Tiles 183
Scale 184
Tile Creation and Management 185
Creating the Grid and Storing Information 185
Selective Processing 189
Identifying the Tile 190
Getting the Position Within the Tile 193
Tile-Independent Objects 194
Creating Objects 194
Managing Objects 195
Destroying Objects 196
Altering the World 196
Adding a Character to the World 197
Defining Worlds with XML 203
Points to Remember 208

Chapter 8: The Isometric Worldview 211

Introduction to Isometrics 212
A Technical Look at Isometrics 215
The Orientation of the Isometric World 215
Placing an Object in the Isometric World 220
Z-Sorting 229
Deconstruction of a Simple World 234
Points to Remember 246

Chapter 9: Level Editors 249

Introduction to Level Editors 250
An Example Level Editor and Game 251
The Game 251
The Editor 252

The Class Files 255
Creating an Enhanced Executable 256
Flash Studio Pro 257
The ActionScript 260
Points to Remember 261

Chapter 10: High Score List 263

Administration of the High Score Lists 265
The List in Action 268
The User-Interface Frames 268
The *HighScoreList* Class 269
The Frame ActionScript 271
Points to Remember 274

Chapter 11: Artificial Intelligence 277

Types of AI 278
Homegrown AI 281
Rules for Controlling Characters 282
Drawbacks and Solutions 284
Enemy ActionScript 284
The Perfect Maze 288
Rules for the Perfect Maze 289
Using ActionScript to Create the Perfect Maze 290
Visual Implementation of the Perfect Maze 295
Pathfinding Algorithms 295
The A* Algorithm 297
Points to Remember 308

Chapter 12: Efficient Game Graphics 311

Vector Versus Bitmap 312
Vector Graphics 312
Bitmap Graphics 314
Various File Types 315

Compression 317
Compression Schemes 318
Using Flash's Compression Settings 320
Special Considerations with Lossy (JPEG) Compression 321
Performance 322
Optimize Your Images 322
Optimize Your Code 325
Loading Graphics at Run-Time 326
Points to Remember 327

Chapter 13: The Sound of Games 331

Why Sound Is Important 332
Managing Sound Effects 334
Sound Placed on Frames 334
Sound Controlled with ActionScript 338
Creating Sound Effects 345
Setting Up 346
Recording 347
"That's Not the Right Sound!" 347
Creating Music Loops 350
Drum Loops 350
Editing and Preparing Audio Loops 352
Points to Remember 355

Chapter 14: Introduction to Multiplayer Games 359

The Human Element 360
Computer-Based Multiplayer Games 361
Socket-Servers 361
Turn-Based Multiplayer Games 363
Real-Time Multiplayer Games 364
ElectroServer 3 367
A Basic Chat Application 370
The *ElectroServer* Class 370
The Chat 371
Playing a Multiplayer Game 375
Points to Remember 376

PART III: THE GAMES

Chapter 15: Word Search 381

Game Overview 382
Game Logic 387
Choosing a Category 387
Generating the Grid 391
Detecting a Choice 402
Points to Remember 406

Chapter 16: Multiplayer Chess 409

Game Rules 410
Multiplayer Aspects of the Game 414
Game Code 417
Multiplayer Logic 418
Game Logic 426
Points to Remember 433

Chapter 17: 501 Darts Game 435

Game Overview 436
Game Play 436
Scoring 436
Game Logic 438
Before the Game 438
Playing the Game 440
After the Game 449
Points to Remember 450

Chapter 18: Cone Crazy 453

Game Overview 454
Game Logic 454
Before the Game 454
Setup 455
Constructing the World 460

Adding the Player Car 462
Playing the Game 463
After the Game 474
Points to Remember 475

APPENDICES

Appendix A: Developer Resources 479

General Game Resources 480
On the Web 480
Books 480
AI 481
On the Web 481
Books 482
Isometric 482
On the Web 482
Books 483
Math 483
On the Web 483
Books 484
Physics 484
On the Web 484
Books 484
Audio Resources 485
Sound Libraries 485
Drum Machines 486
Audio-editing Software 486

Appendix B: Other Games 489

3D_race 490
Arkanoid 490
Asteroids 490
Car 490
Cards 490
Fox and Geese 491
Invaders 491

Iso_maze 491
Pac-Man 491
Projectile_motion 491
RaiseTheBlocks 492
Robust_tracing 492
Shared_object_highscore_list 492
Ship 492
Shuffle_deck 492
Tic_tac_toe_ai 493
Tile_boat 493
Worms 493

Index 495

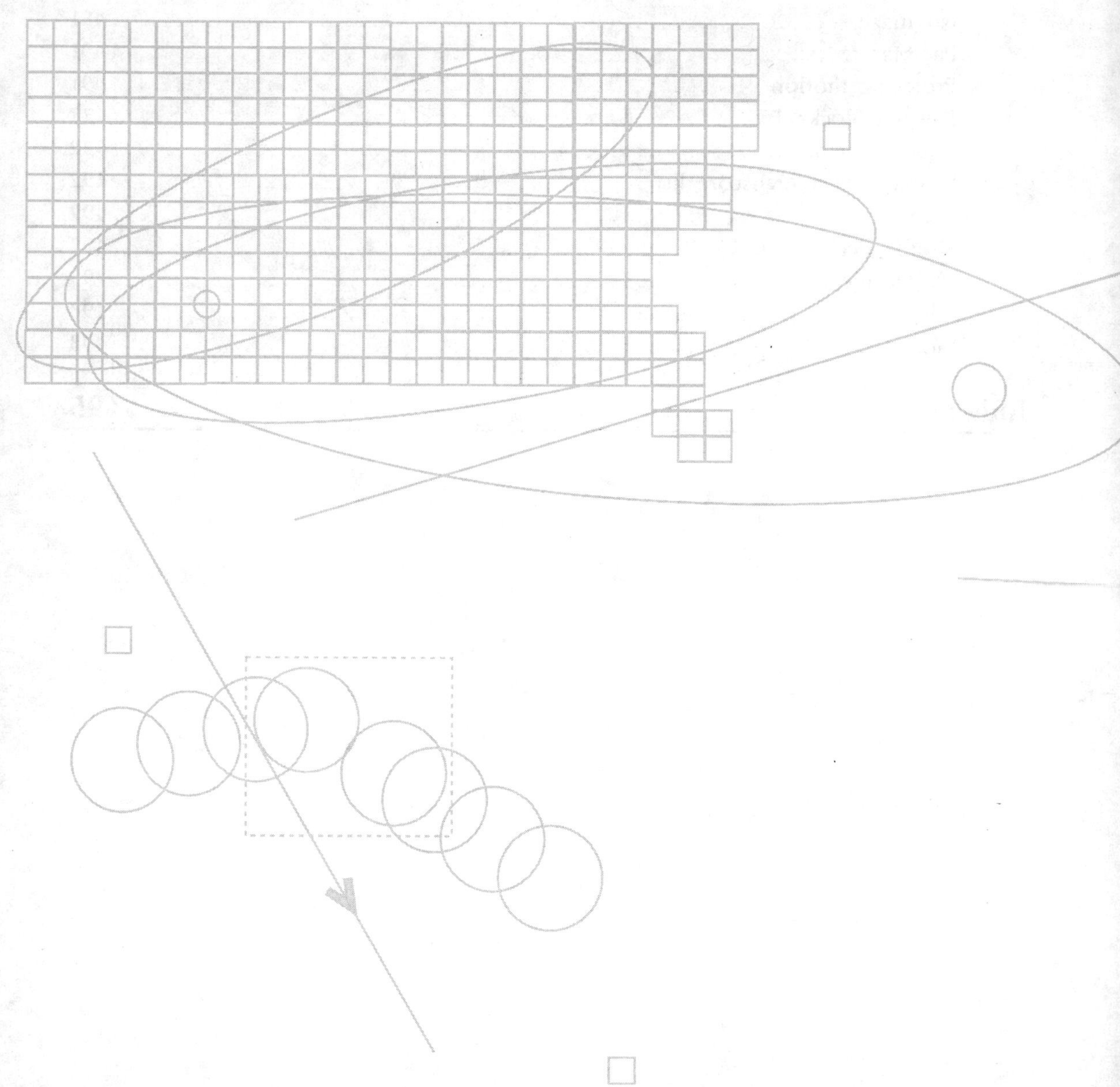

INTRODUCTION

We are back with a grand revision for Flash MX 2004! This book brings with it the great concepts and files brought together for the previous edition, but updated to ActionScript 2.0. In addition, we have created and dissected four brand new games and added new content on real-time multiplayer games, graphics, making games fun, and object-oriented programming.

This book brings you into the world of game development—specifically, game development in Flash MX 2004 using the power of ActionScript to help you automate, repeat, change, anticipate, and govern the actions of games, from a simple game to a complicated real-time multiplayer game. It is in no way a basic Flash tutorial, and a fair amount of familiarity with Flash is assumed, without which you might have a hard time navigating the terrain.

If you're new to Flash gaming, you'll acquire the knowledge and techniques to build your own games and a good sense of the overall process and its pitfalls.

If you aren't new to gaming, you'll be able to see what you can do better (or worse) by using Flash, and you'll still come away with the knowledge and techniques necessary to build Flash games.

A book about games wouldn't make any sense without source material—would you rather learn how to create a platform game by hearing about it or by playing through example files?—and this book is no exception. Each chapter is accompanied by Flash movie files and sometimes other supporting format files to emphasize and describe the point at hand and enable you to see the function in action.

We welcome your input on this book; you can send Jobe Makar feedback at jobe@electrotank.com and Ben Winiarczyk at ben@blitinteractive.com. We also encourage you to visit GameBook.net (www.gamebook.net), the web site for this book, for updates, innovations, and inspiration.

WHY FLASH?

Macromedia Flash is many things to many people. In its few years on Earth so far, it's been an animation tool, a web site creation program, an application development program, and now a game development platform. In Part I, "Getting Started with Flash Game Design," of this book, you'll hear more about Flash's strengths and weaknesses in this area, and in the course of this book, you'll be able to see some of the many things it can help you achieve.

System Requirements

The system requirements for both Windows and Macintosh are identified here.

Windows

- 600 MHz Intel Pentium III processor or equivalent
- Windows 98 SE, Windows 2000, or Windows XP
- 128 MB RAM (256 MB recommended)
- 275 MB available disk space

Macintosh

- 500 MHz PowerPC G3 processor
- Mac OS X 10.2.6
- 128 MB RAM (256 MB recommended)
- 215 MB available disk space

HOW TO USE THIS BOOK

This book introduces you to the world of online gaming, shows where Flash fits into the larger universe of online gaming, shows what it is and isn't good for, and goes into great detail on how to create games using Flash.

Game development isn't all fun and games. It requires a lot of planning, projecting, and imposing logical structures on information. Part I introduces you to the general world of gaming, its terminology, and its basic genres. The chapters in Part II, "Examining the Nuts and Bolts," move through the important concepts that underlie the actual game creation. Although they are not exactly in linear succession, these chapters proceed from the most fundamental of gaming tools (such as trigonometry) to the more complex topics such as collision reactions and the use of artificial intelligence to add complexity and interaction to your games. In the latter portion of Part II, we introduce chapters on enhancements such as fine-tuning graphics for your games, creating optimal soundtracks, and using high score lists. We end Part II with a chapter introducing multiplayer games. Wherever you start reading, we'll keep you apprised of what you might need to refer to elsewhere to be sure you are getting the most out of the material.

In Part III, "The Games," of the book, armed with the knowledge you've amassed in the several hundred pages leading up to it, you'll work directly with complete games and see exactly what went into them. You'll even see ways you can improve them on your own!

The appendices will help you find additional resources for game design and provide you with many additional game source files.

We use the following icons to call attention to special sections:

This indicates helpful suggestions—advice that will help you get the most out of the subject at hand.

This means "Pay attention: important stuff here!"

This indicates that you should open a designated file from the CD to follow along with the text.

These suggest another idea you might want to try in addition to the main point that's being made.

This arrow refers you to a related section of the book where the same topic is discussed in more detail.

This symbol warns you of the pitfalls or disadvantages you may encounter in the process being discussed.

THE CD-ROM COMPONENT

The accompanying CD-ROM includes all the example and supporting files necessary to dissect and understand the games discussed in this book. The files are organized by chapters. There are also trial versions of ElectroServer 3, Flash Studio Pro (for Windows only), and Macromedia Flash MX 2004, as well as additional games and game-related files that are not actually dissected in Part III but that you can dig into yourself.

PART I:

Getting Started with Flash Game Design

Chapter 1
First Steps 5
Inspirational Kick-Start 8
Terminology 8
Game Genres 13
Flash Limitations 14
Points to Remember 18

Chapter 2
Making a Fun Game 21
Understanding the Audience 22
Concept and Flow 27
Game Basics 31
Human Competition 35
Saving Game Data 36
Points to Remember 38

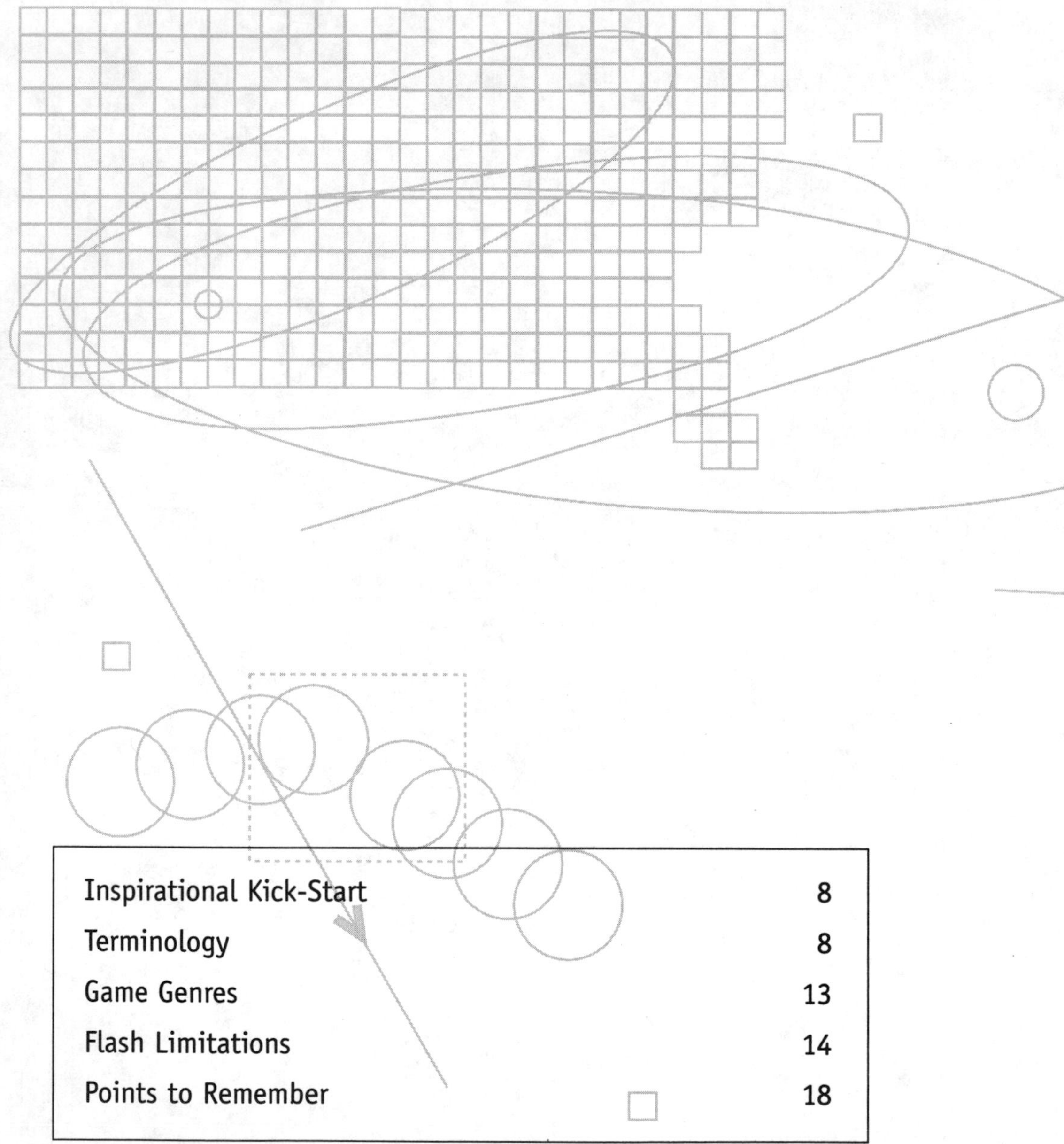

Inspirational Kick-Start 8

Terminology 8

Game Genres 13

Flash Limitations 14

Points to Remember 18

CHAPTER 1

FIRST STEPS

SO YOU WANT TO MAKE FLASH GAMES? WELL, THIS IS A GREAT STARTING place. If you're completely new to game design, the whole idea can seem overwhelming. You may have a great idea for a game, but building an actual game from it is another story—setting up for multiple players, 3D motion, and so on. Don't worry—we've all felt that way. And we're here, after all, to demystify the process.

We'll proceed one step at a time. Before you jump in and start making games, I'll introduce you to some general game-world concepts and terminology.

In this chapter, to orient you for your trip into game design, we will discuss the most common Flash game genres, their terminology, and Flash's capabilities as a game-development environment.

Pictured here are some of the games that you'll know—literally inside and out—when you're done reading this book. They include a) Word Search, b) Multiplayer Chess, c) 501 Darts, and d) Cone Crazy.

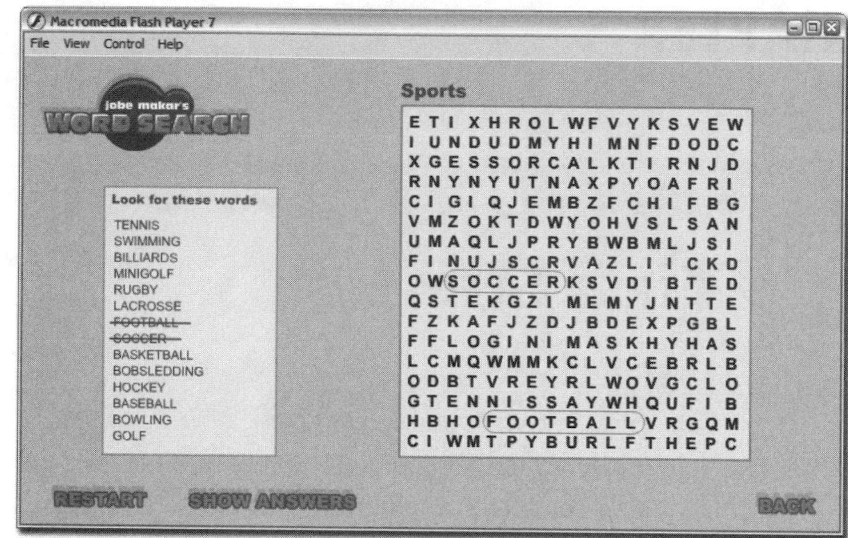

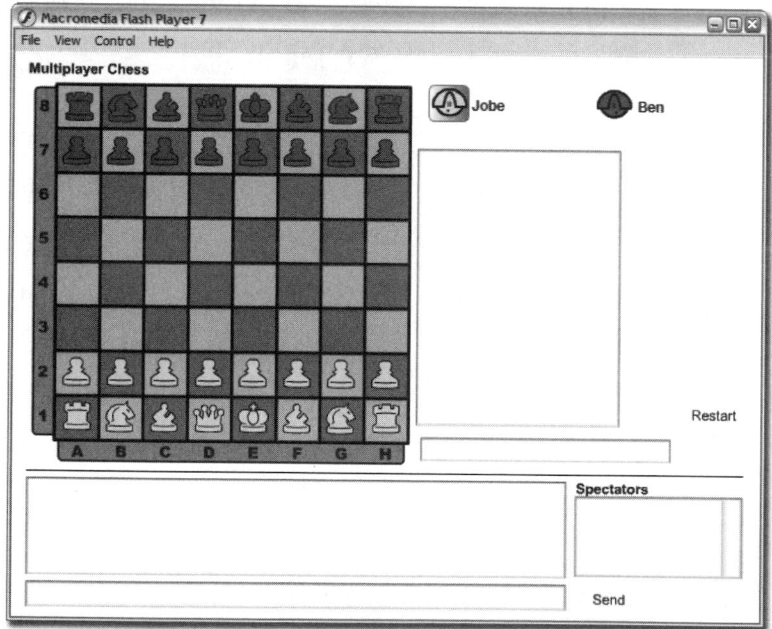

Macromedia Flash Player 7
File View Control Help
YOUR BEST
58
THROWS
27
POINTS LEFT:
58
501 DART CHALLENGE

Macromedia Flash Player 7
File View Control Help
cone crazy
180

Inspirational Kick-Start

Flash is an incredible authoring tool. With it, you can create rich web pages, advanced applications, and, of course, games. As a Flash game developer, you can create amusements as simple as tic-tac-toe or as complicated as a real-time multiplayer game. Imagine what it would be like to think of an amazing game idea (which you may have already done) and then sit down at your computer and actually build it. With Flash, this process can be very easy, and you don't need a degree in computer science to do it! You will learn how to tap into the logic you already possess (common sense) and apply it with ActionScript (the programming language used in Flash).

What kinds of games are possible in Flash? Take a look at some of the games that are dissected and explained in detail in the third section of this book, Part III, "The Games." (The source files for these games are provided on the accompanying CD-ROM.) All the information and techniques needed to make games like these are covered in this book. Soon you will be making your own!

Terminology

What do you think of when you see the word *isometric? Tile-based? Avatar?* Don't worry, there's no need to run for your dictionary. Upon entering the world of game development, you'll find that, as with all specialized fields, many descriptive terms are commonly used when talking about games. It is important to understand, or at least have some idea of, what a word means when you run across it in this book. Most of these terms will be described in more detail in later chapters, but here's an overview to get you started.

Game Views

A *game view* is the player's perspective in the game. Is the player seeing everything through a character's eyes or from above? Each of the possible views has its own name. The game view is sometimes referred to as the *point of view*. Each game view is discussed in this section.

3D—This generic term encompasses almost all possible views of any game that is not two-dimensional. Specific types of popular 3D views have their own terms (listed next). Almost all the most popular store-bought computer games (such as *Unreal Tournament*; see Figure 1.1) use a 3D view. Although we will not be using a generic 3D engine in this book, we will be using a specific 3D view, *isometric*.

FIGURE 1.1
Unreal Tournament utilizes the 3D view (Courtesy of Epic Game, Inc.).

Chase—This type of 3D *camera* view is popular in some sports games, such as hockey and football. The camera (that is, what you see) follows the character or the action and may even swing around to get the best angle. This game view will not be used in this book.

First person—This view is what it would be like to see the environment from the character's point of view. First-person-view games are very popular in shoot-'em-up games such as *Quake, Half-Life,* and *Unreal Tournament*. Programming a Flash game to use a first person view can be a very difficult task and requires advanced 3D programming techniques not covered in this book, and consequently we will not use this view in any games in this book.

Isometric—This is one of the most widely used 3D views. You may have seen this view in games such as *Diablo* (see Figure 1.2) or Electrotank's *Mini Golf*. It is used frequently because it enables you to get away with graphical tricks that reduce the work of both the programmer and the graphic artist. We will discuss this in detail in Chapter 8, "3D Isometric Worldview."

FIGURE 1.2
Diablo exemplifies the isometric view (Courtesy of Blizzard Entertainment®).

Side—This type of view lets you see what is happening from the sidelines. You may have seen this view in games such as *Super Mario Brothers* or *Donkey Kong*. Side views are very popular in platform games and are almost always two-dimensional. This view is used in *Ice World*, which is shown in Figure 1.3 and dissected in Chapter 16, "Multiplayer Chess."

FIGURE 1.3
Ice World provides a good example of the side view (Courtesy of Electrotank, Inc.).

Third person—This term describes any view that isn't either first person or seen through another character's eyes. Most of the views listed in this chapter, such as the isometric view, are third-person views.

Top down—The top-down view, which is a third-person view, shows you the game area as seen from above, the way a bird would see it. This view is popular for games like the original *Zelda* and for many puzzle games like *Minesweeper*. Figure 1.4, of course, is *Pac-Man*.

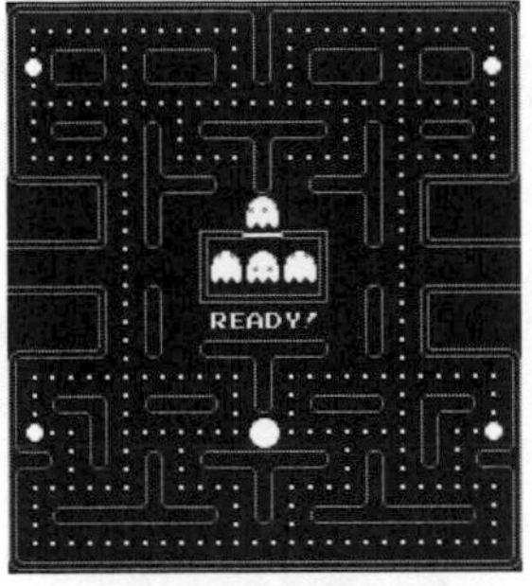

FIGURE 1.4
Pac-Man clearly uses a top-down view.

PAC-MAN® ©1980 Namco Ltd., All Rights Reserved. Courtesy of Namco Holding Corp.

General Terms

Here are some commonly used game development terms that you should know.

Algorithm—An algorithm is a logical process by which a problem can be solved or a decision made. An algorithm can be represented in a programming language, but it is more abstract than that. For instance, you can create a process to sort a list of names. This process is an algorithm and can be expressed with ActionScript or any other programming language.

Artificial intelligence (AI)—This refers to an algorithm or set of algorithms that can make decisions in a logical way. For example, the AI routine for a bad guy in a game might let him figure out how to find you. Another use of AI is to have a maze or puzzle be solved automatically.

Avatar—Some chat rooms are designed to enable users to have graphical representations. These are called *avatars,* and the chat is often referred to as an *avatar-chat.*

Client—In the application and gaming sense, *client* refers to the person playing the game or chatting or the machine that is being used to do so. If there are 100 people in a chat, then there are 100 client machines connected to the chat.

Collision detection— Also called *hit detection,* collision detection is the act of noting the intersection of two objects. This can be something as simple as determining if the mouse pointer is over a button or as complicated as detecting the overlap of two moving objects.

Collision reaction—This is what happens after a collision has been detected. The term is usually used when talking about physical reactions, such as two billiard balls colliding and moving apart, or a ball bouncing off the ground.

Console—A computer designed for the sole purpose of playing video games. Among the console manufacturers are Microsoft, Nintendo, and Sony. Popular console gaming platforms are Sony Playstation 2, Nintendo GameCube, and Nintendo Game Boy.

Map—An area that defines the world of the game.

Multiplayer Server—Also known as a *socket server* or *multi-user server*, a multiplayer server is what makes multiplayer games and chats possible in Flash. It is an application that runs on a remote computer and handles routing information to connected computers.

Real-time—Unlike *turn-based* games, in real-time games you can make a move whenever you like.

Render—To *render* is to draw an object to the screen. This term is most often used in reference to 3D games: The 3D engine calculates where a projectile should be and then renders it.

Source code—Also known as *source*, source code is the original work created by a developer. Source code is compiled, or published, into a new file. This compiled file is what users will see, not the source itself. In Flash, the source is a .fla (or FLA) file, and its published version is a .swf (or SWF) file. The .swf file contains only a fraction of the information in the .fla file. This serves to protect the author's work so that another person cannot take the source. This book's accompanying CD-ROM contains the source for many games.

Although the FLA source file is the only file type that can be compiled into an SWF file, it can pull in other types of Flash files during compilation. These files include external ActionScript files (which are text files containing ActionScript) and FLV files.

Sprite—This is an object that can, internally, change how it is displayed. In Flash, a movie clip can be a sprite. Take a character that can walk and jump, for example—one movie clip can contain all the needed animations (walk cycle, jump cycle, and so on).

Turn-based—This refers to a restriction on when you, the game player, can make a move. For instance, chess is a turn-based game; rather than make a move whenever you want, you must wait for your turn. Many multiplayer games are set up this way, as we will see later in the book.

Vector graphics—Notable for their small file sizes and scalability, vector graphics are defined by sets of mathematical points. Flash uses this graphics format to great advantage.

World—This is a general term that refers to an entire game environment.

Game Genres

A *game genre* is a type or category of game. As with movies, there are many game genres, and they are often hard to classify. Some games may fit in more than one genre. Here's a list of the most popular genres.

Action—An action game has moving objects and focuses on your timing, reflexes, hand-eye coordination, and quick thinking to achieve a good score. Most games have some action in them but aren't necessarily considered "action games." *Space Invaders* and *Half-Life* are good examples of action games.

Adventure—Often confused with RPGs, adventure games let you control a character in an environment while the story is discovered. Unlike what happens in an RPG, your actions do not affect your character's overall abilities. Examples of adventure games range from Super Mario Brothers to the games in the King's Quest series.

Casino—One of the most popular genres to play on the Internet is casino (that is, gambling) games, such as Poker and Roulette.

Educational—In an educational game, the goal is to educate the player. This game can also be a part of another genre; for instance, you can have an educational puzzle game.

First-person shooter—This style of game lets you see a world through the character's eyes as you run around and try to shoot anything that moves. Typically the action in these games takes precedence over the story.

Puzzle—A puzzle game, also called a *logic game,* challenges your mind more than your reflexes. Many puzzle games are timed or limit the amount of time in which you can make a move. Games such as *Tetris* and *Sobokan* are good examples of puzzle games. Puzzle games also include some classics such as *Chess* and *Checkers*.

Sports—A sports game is an action game with rules that mimic those of a specific sport. For instance, *NHL 2004*, by Electronic Arts, is an ice hockey sports game.

Role-playing game (RPG)—An RPG is a game in which you, the game player, control a character in its environment. In this environment, you encounter other beings and interact with them. Depending on your actions and choices, the character's attributes (such as fighting ability, magical powers, and agility) change, and so may the story. *Baldur's Gate* is an RPG.

Strategy—This type of game focuses on your resourcefulness and deal-making ability as you try to build and/or run something. In some games, your goal is to successfully build and run a city; in others, what you have to build or run can be anything from an army to a roller coaster. Obvious examples here include about any of the *Sim City* derivatives or *Roller Coaster Tycoon*.

FLASH LIMITATIONS

Like all software applications, Flash games have limitations. Macromedia has added an amazing number of new features and capabilities to Flash with each release, but it can't do everything (yet). In this section I talk about the major advantages and disadvantages of using Flash to develop games, and I discuss certain types of games that are not easily workable in Flash.

Flash Versus Non-Flash Games

Although I'd like to tell you that Flash can outperform all other game-development platforms with its hands tied behind its back, that's just not the case. There are many reasons to choose Flash for game development, and there are many other reasons not to choose Flash. In this section we discuss the major reasons for both.

The Pros of Using Flash for Game Development

Not surprisingly, as I've put a lot of time and effort into Flash game development, I'll list the benefits first.

Web deployment—Because Flash files are designed to be viewed in web pages, Flash is a good choice if you want your game to be available on the Internet.

Device deployment—Flash files are supported on an increasing number of devices, such as set top boxes, cell phones, PDAs, and even watches! Because Flash is supported, so too are Flash games, which is an exciting prospect for Flash game developers.

Small file size—Flash makes use of vector graphics and compressed sound files, so a Flash game's final file size can be exponentially smaller than those of games developed on other platforms.

Plug-in penetration—The plug-in that's required for viewing Flash files in a web page comes with all major browsers. More than 98 percent of people on the Internet worldwide can view Flash content. The exact penetration for each version of the plug-in is listed on the Macromedia web site (go to `www.macromedia.com/software/player_census`).

Server-side integration—Flash games can talk to the server seamlessly. Using Flash's built-in features, you can communicate with server-side applications that make chats, multiplayer games, and high score lists possible.

File sharing between programmer and graphic artists/designers—With Flash, programmers and graphic artists can collaborate using the same source files. This is rare in game development.

Ease of use—Perhaps one of the most attractive reasons for choosing Flash is that you can learn the program and start creating games in a very short time. With other languages, it could take years!

The Cons of Using Flash for Game Development

As I already mentioned, some strong reasons also exist for not choosing Flash as your development platform. It's important to know them as well before you get started and encounter unpleasant surprises.

Performance—Macromedia spent thousands of hours making the required Flash plug-in for the web as small as possible so that the maximum number of people could download it easily. But that required some sacrifices, and the major one was performance. Even though the latest Flash Player (version 7) executes code two to ten times faster than the previous player, Flash underperforms virtually all other game-development platforms in speed of code execution and graphics rendering. On the other side of the fence, game-development platforms such as Macromedia Director and WildTangent perform very well but have enormous plug-ins. As a result, few people can view such content without being forced to download the plug-in in addition to the game.

Lack of 3D support—Flash doesn't provide native support for real 3D engines or for any sort of texture mapping (the act of applying an image to a 3D polygon).

Lack of operating-system integration—When you run your game as a Projector file, Flash cannot easily talk to the local operating system to do things such as browse files on the hard drive. (But this type of integration is possible with the use of third-party software such as Flash Studio Pro, available at `http://www.multidmedia.com`.)

Most of the developers who choose Flash as their game-creation tool do so because they want their games to be available to many people easily on the Internet. If the intention is to have the game available offline on CD-ROM, then Flash is still a choice—just not necessarily the best choice.

Infeasible Game Features

It is much simpler to talk about things Flash cannot do easily than to discuss everything it *can* do. I'll touch on some things here that are very difficult to achieve in Flash or that aren't feasible for another reason. I don't want to say anything is impossible with Flash because there are so many creative people out there with dozens of tricks to make the seemingly impossible possible.

3D Rendering with Texture Mapping

Many people have created 3D engines with ActionScript. A 3D engine is code that can take 3D coordinates and map them onto your screen. Although these engines actually manipulate coordinates in 3D space and then map them correctly back onto a 2D screen, there are two major limitations:

Texture mapping—You cannot map textures (bitmap images) onto an object in Flash. As I have already mentioned, many people make creative attempts to get around program obstacles like this one. Some people have successfully done very simple mapping onto flat surfaces. Nevertheless, this is a limitation. Mapping is not achieved easily and only works in some conditions.

Z-sorting—This refers to the order in which objects appear in front of other objects. In real 3D rendering games, the sorting order is not limited to whole objects but can actually pierce surfaces of objects (if two things happen to be moving through each other). Flash is limited to sorting at the movie-clip level.

Intense Real-Time Calculation

I know this sounds like a vague limitation. But when you're creating a game, it is important (although admittedly difficult) to try to guess how intense the calculations are going to be. For instance, a game that has dozens of enemies—who all think for themselves and constantly run around trying to decide what to do next—is an excellent candidate to bog down the computer processor! You'll have to do a lot of testing and experimenting to determine exactly how many of these enemies the computer can handle and still perform well.

This chapter should provide you with a better idea of what types of games exist and which ones are possible in Flash. With this book, you'll learn about all the pieces you need to build a game, from graphics to sound, and you'll see how everything was put together in several finished games. By the end of the book, you should be well on your way to making your own gaming ideas a reality!

Points to Remember

- Flash is a powerful authoring tool that can help you create games from the simple to the extremely complex.
- Flash's strengths and limitations make it ideal for creating some kinds of games and less than optimal for others.
- ActionScript—the programming language used in Flash—is the main tool through which you bring your games to fruition.
- Familiarizing yourself with game genres and terminology is a good first step toward deciding what sorts, and levels, of games interest you as a developer—and will also show you where you need to brush up!
- For reasons of portability, extensibility, integration, file size, and near-universal access, Flash is a good choice for games you'd like to make available on the Internet.
- Flash is easy enough to learn that you can be up and creating games in a very short time.
- A high cost of the small file sizes and accessibility of Flash games is their slow performance relative to games created on virtually all other game-development platforms.
- The Flash Player has serious limitations with respect to 3D. It is a 2D environment in which certain levels of 3D can be simulated.

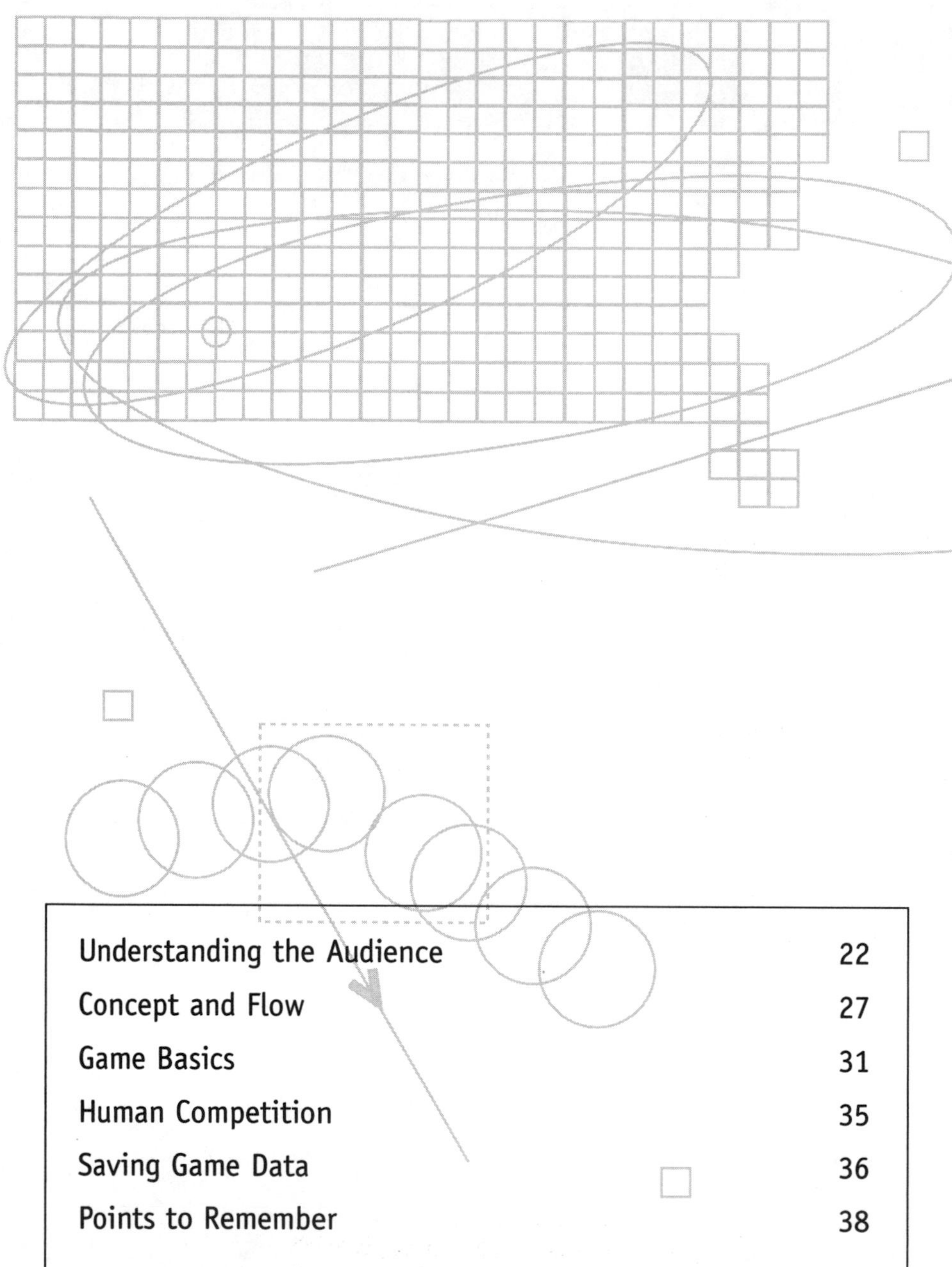

Understanding the Audience 22

Concept and Flow 27

Game Basics 31

Human Competition 35

Saving Game Data 36

Points to Remember 38

CHAPTER 2

MAKING A FUN GAME

YOU MIGHT THINK THAT MAKING A FUN GAME STARTS WITH THE ACTION. Not so. The word "fun" is a very subjective term. What different people find fun can vary wildly from one person to the next, so understanding who will be playing is the first step. Then there are some fundamental steps to planning out your game and all the supporting interactivity that you need to effectively deliver it to your audience. For the game itself, you'll need some basic ingredients as well. In this chapter, we'll discuss all the aspects that go into making a fun game. We'll start at the beginning with the audience.

UNDERSTANDING THE AUDIENCE

The first step in designing a hit game is to understand the target audience. These are the people that you (or your client) want to play the game. As a game designer, it is your mission to create a game that is not only enjoyable to that group but also easily playable by that group. Overly complicated controls or intricate storylines will be likely to confuse and discourage a younger audience. Likewise, games with intense graphics that require high-end machines most likely will not be playable by the less savvy group in your parents' age bracket.

Even the coolest game ever created can turn into a miserable experience for a user if he or she can't figure out how to play or even start the game. Essentially, in order for a game to be fun, it has to be easy to get into and play. Be careful not to design above the audience. Make your game very easy to understand and control and make the objectives obvious.

It is important to realize that the majority of people who will be playing your game may not be as technically aware or as game savvy as you are. Most people playing your game for the first time will not give it more than a couple of seconds if it is difficult to figure out.

So, Who Is This Audience?

If you are developing a custom game for a client or sponsor, they will most likely have done the research and can tell you exactly which groups they are targeting.

For instance, a client may request a game specifically targeted to girls age 6–12. Right away, we know that we aren't going to be proposing something akin to a first person shooter game. We would be more likely to propose a very cute, cartoon-style game such as *Mystery Date*.

If you are developing a game to be placed on a game web site, you can ask your contact at that site for a breakdown of the site's user demographics. Most sites will make this information available to you if you are going to be providing content for them.

These are very important questions to ask BEFORE getting started. To really push the envelope and develop a hit game that people will come back to play again, you need to understand who is going to be playing and with what equipment.

Let's discuss some facets of the target audience.

Demographics

Demographics is a science to advertisers. Basically, it is the statistical study of the attributes of a section of the population. Most demographic studies delve deep into very specific aspects of a group, such as household income, number of children, eating habits, and so on. These specifics don't concern us much; we are going to be most interested in the biggies, age group and gender.

Age Group

The age group of your audience is probably the most important demographic factor to consider. A child will approach your game with a very different mindset than an adult. Advertisers have been segregating the population into age brackets since before anyone thought of creating a computer game. The breakdowns can get very specific and overlap in many cases, but here are a few broad groups to consider.

- Kids 6–12
- Tweens 9–14
- Teens 12–17
- 12–24
- 18–24
- 18–34
- 25–34
- 35–44
- 45–55
- 55+

In my experience, it is always best to aim a bit low in your range. Adults can more easily relate to younger material than kids can relate to more sophisticated material.

Gender

Coupled with the age of your audience is their gender. Boys, girls, men, and women all have different views and may consider different games to be fun. The browser-based game market pretty much seems to be split evenly with women slightly higher in numbers. That is not to say that no market exists for blood and guts games of destruction and mayhem, but because the majority of Internet game players are female and might appreciate a less violent storyline, don't neglect to consider the lighter side of things when trying to target a broader range of people.

To get a good idea of what kind of content the different groups might be interested in, look to the great American pastime, television. Networks have a lot more time and resources to invest in targeting an audience than you do. Find some shows that your target might watch and then take note of the style of the program and the commercials that play on it. You should be able to get a pretty good idea of what that group would find interesting.

Playback Specs

What kind of machine is the intended audience likely to have? What operating system and browser version will they be playing your games with? Make sure your game will work on a broad range of systems. Not everyone updates his or her computer every time some new technology is released.

This is a really important aspect to keep in mind. I have seen games that look like they are going to be amazing but do not perform well enough to provide any fun game play.

Fortunately, the big advantage of using Flash is that it takes a lot of the guesswork out of the equation because Macromedia was kind enough to make the Flash Player browser plug-in work fairly consistently across different operating systems and browser types. Notice I said "fairly consistently." Some unexpected exceptions always crop up, especially when dealing with server-side technologies and passing data back and forth. Different server configurations may handle data in different ways; for example, some may require more attention to the format of the data you are passing than others. Case sensitivity, relative URLs, and special characters are common hang-ups and should be tested with a server configuration that matches the hosting environment.

With platform and browser concerns out of the way, the most important aspects of the playback environment for game designers are the computer speed, Flash version, and screen size.

Keep an old machine lying around that you can use for testing your games. If possible, find one at least one year old with an out-of-date everything, last-generation processor, and not nearly enough RAM. This is closer to the machine on which people will be trying to play your games.

Computer Speed

How fast will the playback system be? This is pretty important, considering that the smoothness of movement in a game with motion is vital to the overall user experience.

If your game is a word game, puzzle, or a memory match-style game, this is less of a concern, but let's face it, you probably want to make an action game. Action games call for fast-moving graphics, sounds, and intense calculations to run smoothly, so you have to make sure the playback machines are up to it. Do frequent testing on your ideas to make sure you are not taxing the machine too much.

Look for tips on getting the most out of the available computer speed in Chapter 12, "Efficient Game Graphics."

You can use many tricks to optimize your game. These tricks come from two schools of thinking—more efficient code and more efficient graphics. Do them both.

Flash Version

Each new version of Flash offers more and more cool features and power to help you create more and more cool games. Flash MX 2004 offers the most powerful feature set to date, but be aware of the lag in what is available to you as a developer and what the majority of people will have.

TABLE 2.1 **Macromedia Flash Player Version Penetration**

Worldwide Ubiquity of Macromedia Flash by Version - June 2003
(NPD Online - Worldwide Survey)

	Flash 2	Flash 3	Flash 4	Flash 5	Flash 6
US	97.4%	97.3%	97%	94.8%	86.3%
Canada	97.5%	97.3%	96.8%	95.8%	86.9%
Europe	97.7%	97.7%	97.5%	97.1%	87.2%
Asia	96.1%	95.3%	94.2%	92.6%	82.7%

Screen Size

Another important factor that is often overlooked is the size of the display screen. Most of us have giant display screens when developing, and it is easy to forget that the players that will be playing your game will often be viewing on a smaller display screen and will be using a web browser that significantly cuts down on the available space. For example, a common screen size of 800×600 running the IE 6 browser will have an approximately 780×436 available screen space for all the site content (see Table 2.2 and Figure 2.1). If the site has a navigation frame or banner space, the space for your game will be even smaller.

TABLE 2.2 **Common Screen Resolutions as of July 2003**

	800×600	1024×768+
Percent Usage	44%	49%
Max Available Space	780×436	1004×604

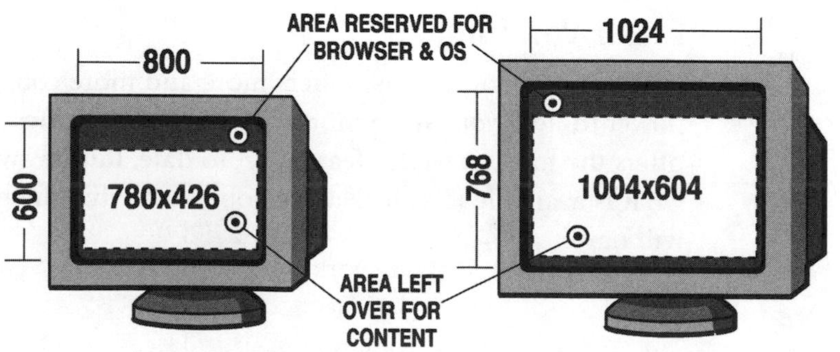

FIGURE 2.1
Usable space for two common screen sizes.

Keep your game small enough so that the user does not have to mess with browser scrolling or settings to play. People tend to get very aggravated if any Internet content requires them to change their desktop settings in any way.

Concept and Flow

Ok, now that we've discussed all the boring fundamentals, let's start discussing the game design itself.

There are many genres or types of games that you could make, as mentioned in Chapter 1, "First Steps." You probably will get around to creating games or at least experimenting with most of them over the coming years, but each time you start a new project, regardless of the genre you have chosen, it is important to begin with a solid, well thought out concept.

You might have the urge to just open up Flash and start coding, so keep this in mind: No matter how small or simple the game might seem in your mind's eye, planning out the game play and supporting interactivity such as loading, setup, and help screens, improves the overall game experience for the user and can spare you a lot of headaches during development. It is very easy to overlook some vital game elements when developing without a plan, which could prove to be ten times more difficult to add later in the developmental process.

Let's go through the steps in the design process.

The Initial Concept

Start with the game concept. This includes the genre of game you'd like to create, the game's target audience, and an overall feeling of what you want the game to be like. Take what you learned about your target audience and tailor the game plan to fit.

For instance, if you are making a simple shooter-style game, the concept that would work best for one demographic would be a lot different than the concept that would work best for another. Boys in the 6–12 age range might respond well to a robotic warrior laser shootout, whereas adults might prefer something political or ripped from the headlines.

You should be able to condense your concept into a single sentence. Let's assume we are planning to create a game to be played on a popular kids' web site with an age range of 6–12. The demographic is split 50/50 boys/girls and the purpose of the game is to attract traffic to the site. In keeping with our classic shooter idea that we'll develop further throughout the rest of this chapter, our concept treatment might go something like this:

"Western style, comedic point-and-click shooter game where kids challenge each other for bragging rights and high scores."

Sounds pretty basic, right? Remember, this is just a starting point for us to build on, so let's do just that and start by developing the Wild West theme.

TIP

When beginning to develop the game concept, it is important to keep in mind the limitation of your skills as well as the limitations of the playback environment of your target audience. Designing outside of these limits can result in a game that is either simply not playable by the intended audience or a game that never actually gets finished because some elements were too difficult for you to accomplish.

Develop the Theme

Most memorable games have at least some hint of a theme or storyline to grab and hold the user's attention. A good title for the game goes along with the theme and also gives you a much more memorable game.

The difference between a cool game and a cool game that people talk about is a good theme. If you can get people talking about your game and telling their friends, it will help set up the purpose of the game and can set one shoot 'em-up game apart from another.

Imagine a game where you are clicking on red dots with your mouse to see how many you can click on before time runs out. Now imagine a game where you are a sharpshooter in the Wild West, and you have to shoot as many bottles as possible out of the air without missing to prove your claims to be the best in the West. Old-time piano music and cowboy commentary complete the effect: "Nice Shootin' Partner!"

These are virtually the same basic shooter games and offer the same playability, but you can bet your guns that the Wild West game will be much more fun to play. Games are generally more fun to play if they offer a purpose to the player. If something is at stake and the pressure is on, people will have more fun playing.

Storyline and Characters

Expanding on the theme by developing a storyline and characters to support your game is a very effective way to add appeal and value to your game. Sometimes you might want to develop the theme even further and really set up a story that brings the user into the game.

Let's take our Wild West theme and wrap a storyline with characters around it.

Your storyline does not have to be complicated or even visually represented. Just an interesting mission statement before play can do the trick.

The main character is a dusty but law-abiding gunslinger named Wild [Inset Player Name Here]. Let's go with William for this scenario. Wild William is in a saloon arguing with a man in a black hat about who is the better shot. The man in the black hat challenges Wild William to shoot 99 bottles tossed into the air without missing more than 5. If he succeeds, the man in black promises to drink an entire bottle of the hottest red pepper sauce in the West. If our friend Will fails, then he'll be drinking the sauce.

This leads us into the game. Now the player can relate to the characters and will likely have a lot more fun shooting bottles out of the air with his or her honor on the line.

After play, jump to a quick animation showing the looser gulping down the sauce and making some comical scene. You can take this a step further and create a few endings. People will play again and again just to see how the user will react to the hot sauce.

When you have your ideas together, you create a simple storyboard illustrating the sequence. A storyboard is really just a few drawings that describe the action. This will start to bring your ideas to life and will help others visualize the story.

Figure 2.2 presents an example of part of our story in storyboard format.

FIGURE 2.2
Storyboarding.

Flow

Now that you have your ideas down, make sure your game flows from setup through the game to whatever screens you have in there after play.

Plan all this out ahead of time so that your end product has continuity (see Figure 2.3). Make sure you account for the following:

- **Loading Screen**—This displays the loading status of your media. This can also contain some graphics to help set up the theme.
- **Welcome Screen**—The game should hold on this screen after loading. This is where the user is presented with the story or mission and is prompted to play the game.
- **How to Play/Help**—Include a screen containing the instructions and controls for the game. This may be incorporated into the Welcome Screen or into a separate, always-available pop-up screen.
- **The Game**—This is the playable game.
- **Game Over**—This is the conclusion to the game. Player will see the outcome here. This screen should also contain a prompt for the user to play again.

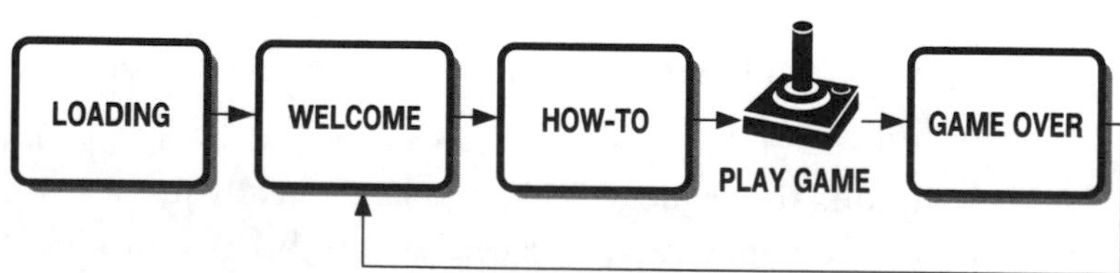

FIGURE 2.3
Plan the flow.

Also, if your game is going to have multiple levels, modes, or special features during play, plan these out too. Nothing is more frustrating than trying to add a forgotten feature or screen after the fact, only to find that your code doesn't accommodate the change easily. This can lead to a very clunky and unprofessional game experience.

Game Basics

Now we are on the way to making a great game. We've discussed all the ingredients that create the framework for the playable part of the game; now let's discuss the game itself and what basic ingredients we should include to make it well-rounded.

Scoring

People love to get points. Point systems in games should serve as some kind of measurement of how the users are doing, something to compare to or compete with their friends. Reward people for doing well and for taking chances during play. It is important to explain how the scoring system works during the game set-up screens. This gives players the information they need to make split decisions during play, provides some anticipation, and overall makes for a more fun game.

The scoring matrix should be adjustable during development and finalized during the testing process. It is very difficult to tell when you are developing just how quickly you can accumulate points.

As a general rule, set up the scoring matrix to give the player a steady stream of easy, small point awards just for playing and then have larger point values for accomplishing difficult tasks or taking chances. As difficulty increases, these bonus points should get more attractive.

Scoring is your tool as a game developer to tempt the player to take chances, try new paths or moves, and keep things interesting.

Difficulty Levels

Games are more fun to play if the difficulty ramps up as you go. Many players are likely to have never played the game before. First levels should be fairly easy to complete with no prior experience. If a first-time player dies right away, he or she is likely to give up and go play something else.

The first level should introduce the player to all the controls and features of the game and demonstrate the basic skills that will be needed in later levels. Each level from there should be more and more difficult to complete. This allows players to improve or get further the more they play, which keeps them coming back.

In addition to ramping up the difficulty from one level to the next, ramp up the difficulty toward the end of each level. This is an effective trick in getting the replay. If a player can see that he or she is nearing the end of a level and then doesn't make it, the player is more likely to try again because he or she was "so close" to the end of the level.

It also adds a lot of fun to the game overall if you name the levels and tie them into the game theme. If a user is talking about your adventure game to a friend, it sounds more fun to say "I made it to the Jungle of Death!" rather than "I made it to level 3."

Figure 2.4 shows an example of a five-level game difficulty ramp.

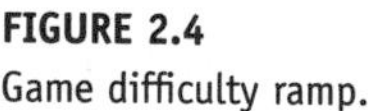

FIGURE 2.4
Game difficulty ramp.

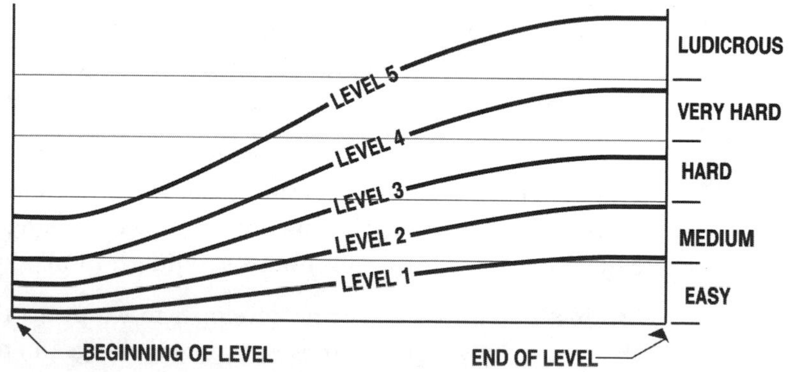

Keep difficulty levels and scoring adjustable. After you have finished development, you'll want to watch some friends and family play your game. Don't tell them anything about the game beforehand and just observe how they play and how difficult it is for them. Keep in mind that this game is your idea, and you know what to expect. A first timer might have a much harder time starting out than you might think. I find that nine times out of ten, the game needs to be adjusted and made a bit easier after testing.

Health/Lives

The game can't last forever. Lives help you regulate the play time, and they give the player multiple chances to improve. This could be anything from a health meter in a fighting game to misses in a shooting game or lives in an arcade-style game. Let people fail a few times before you call the game over.

If your game has multiple levels, each new life should start the player back at the beginning of the level the player was on when he or she died. If you make players start at the beginning of the game each time, they can become very discouraged and may not want to try again.

Typically, you'd allow a player three lives. This is what people are most familiar with and provides for an ideal length of game.

If using lives, set your life display up so that you decrease the number of lives at the beginning of play. If you start with three, then remove one (the one you are playing with currently) before play. This way, players will know they are playing with their last life if there are no more available in the life meter.

Bonuses and Power-Ups

Another effective way to increase the fun of a game is to add in a few bonuses or power-ups throughout each level. A power-up is a term generally used to refer to an extra goody found in a game, such as health, an extra life, or just about anything special. This adds some excitement to the game as players discover these things and use them to gain points or an advantage in the game.

Bonuses and/or power-ups can be used with any style of game. For instance, if you are creating a racing game, a power-up object in the road might provide the car with a boost of super-speed. For a shooter-style game, a bonus target might appear every once in a while and offer some extra points.

Bonus objects should not be vital to your game. They are really just another tool we have to easily turn up the fun dial a notch or two.

Easter Eggs

Easter eggs are fun little surprises within the game. These can be anything from extra levels to bonuses, extra lives, and so on. Easter eggs are generally secret and meant to be discovered by the player by accident. It could be something as simple as simple as pushing a specific key combination to make the game character do something funny or as complex as doing a series of in-game actions to unlock a special level.

Easter eggs are almost always good surprises. You would not want the game to reward your happy little accident by losing points or game lives.

Length of play

How much time do you expect your game players to invest in one play? It is also important to design your game to last an appropriate amount of time for your audience. You'll want players to have enough time to get through a game without investing their entire afternoon and without getting frustrated that they didn't have time to get into the game.

Most adult web-based game players are playing during the day at work when they are waiting for a meeting to start or needing a quick break to clear their head. Younger players may only have a few minutes after school to get in a quick game or two, not to mention a relatively short attention span. If your game requires a large investment of time, many people may not even bother with it.

The ideal length of time a game should last is arguable. I have found that a game lasting somewhere between two to five minutes per play is just about right. For longer adventure-style games, including a save game feature can help out a lot because people can play as long as they can and then save and come back to continue where they left off later when they have more time. (See "Saving Game Data," later in this chapter).

Human Competition

Competition can be the driving force behind hit games. People do love to waste time and fool around with cool games and gadgets on the Internet, it's true, but what people really love is to compete with themselves and others. If you take a good game and add an element of competition, you'll have a great game. There are many ways to add an element of competition to a game. In the next several sections, we will cover a few.

Real-Time Multiplayer

Real-time multiplayer games offer competition with another player (or multiple other players) in real time. This means you are playing directly against another player.

These types of games require an active Internet connection and a server-side component to function. Real-time multiplayer games are gaining in popularity with increased Internet connection speeds and availability of ready-to-go multiplayer servers such as *ElectroServer 3*.

We have an entire chapter devoted to multiplayer games (see Chapter 14, "Introduction to Multiplayer Games").

Challenge/Send to a Friend

Challenge games require a lot less server-side development but still offer the opportunity for people to compete with their friends. In a challenge game, the first player completes the game and receives his or her score. Then the score is sent to a friend via email as a challenge.

Challenge games differ from multiplayer games in that in a challenge game, both players play the game alone and then the scores are compared. In a multiplayer game, both players play at the same time.

High Score Lists

High score lists are a very effective, passive way to enable competition between users. The simple act of providing a list of the top 10 players for a particular game can add the ever-effective competition factor to a simple, single-player game. This feature has been used on arcade games since the 80s and has not lost its value.

High score lists are not very difficult to set up but will require a server-side component to store the high score data. Basically, each time a player finishes a game, you check the server to see if the score is eligible for the high score list. If so, prompt the user for a first name and then submit it to the server to be included in the list.

The second part of the system retrieves the high score data from the server (perhaps as the game is loading) and displays the top 10 names with scores. Receiving this information before game play starts will fire people up to get their names posted or to knock an adversary off the list (see Chapter 10, "High Score List," for more on high score lists).

Saving Game Data

Enabling users to save their games gives them a good reason to come back and play again. This is especially important for games that require a long investment in time to play or games that take a while to accumulate some kind of in-game status. Also, games that require a lot of setup before play can benefit from this feature to save user-specific setup choices.

There are a few popular options for saving player-specific data; let's explore them.

Option 1: Flash's Local Shared Object

The `SharedObject` class in Flash works much the same way that a browser cookie works. The data is saved locally on the user's machine. When you close the .swf file, the data remains and can be retrieved at a later date. This can be very useful in saving data specific to a single user. But like a cookie, the data will only be available from the machine it was originally saved on.

Using shared objects, you can actually save objects, not just variables or text. A shared object can be any data type in Flash such as arrays, dates, and XML. However, we are limited to data objects. You can save a pathname or

URL that points to a media element, but actual media elements, such as movie clips, MP3s, JPGs, and so on cannot be stored in a `SharedObject`.

Let's examine the process of saving and retrieving game data using the `SharedObject` class.

1. When your game starts running, establish the shared data object. The `getLocal` method of the `SharedObject` class will actually create the new shared object if it does not already exist and then return a reference to it. If it does exist, then it just returns a reference to it.

   ```
   //SET UP THE OBJECT
   var myGameData:SharedObject =
   ➥SharedObject.getLocal("myGameData");
   ```

2. Check to see if any game data has been saved in it. If we find data in the object, we can assume there has been a game saved and invoke any actions needed to provide the user a method to restore the saved game.

   ```
   //CHECK FOR SAVED GAME DATA
   if (myGameData.savedGameData != undefined){
       //YOU HAVE SAVED DATA, GET IT
   var retrievedGameDATA = myGameData.data.savedGameDATA;
   }
   ```

3. Save your data to the saved game object. Use the `flush()` method to actually save the data to the hard drive.

   ```
   //SAVING THE GAME DATA
   myGameData.data.savedGameDATA = currentGameDATA;
   myGameData.data.flush();
   ```

4. If you want to erase this data, simply set it to `null`.

   ```
   //ERASING THE DATA
   myGameData.data.savedGameDATA = null;
   myGameData.data.flush();
   ```

5. That's it. You have a reliable client-side data system.

   For more information on using Flash `SharedObjects`, check out this article on the subject. (`http://www.acmewebworks.com/default.asp?ID=85`)

Option 2: Server-Side Database

Using a server-side database to save game data gives you more options. You can still save all the same user-specific data, but you can also accumulate data about groups of players, game activity, and so on. One big advantage of using a server-side database to save game data is that the data is available from anywhere you can access the Internet. A player might begin a game at home, play a bit more during lunch at work, and then finish later back at home.

Server-side data systems are fairly easy to use but do require access to a database and the capability to run a simple script on the server.

Option 3: Local Files

It is becoming very popular now to take a Flash game and make it into an installable executable file that can be run on a Windows machine. There are several third-party companies that make software which enables a developer to enhance the capabilities of the Flash Player when run as an executable file. One of these added capabilities lets you create files or directories. It is very easy to save data locally as text files.

Why would you use text files over shared objects? Well, if you create an installable game, then when the user wants to uninstall the game, it is much cleaner to remove everything that the game created, even the stored data for a game. If you are storing the data for a game in a text file, then the uninstaller will remove the text file. Uninstallers do not clean up shared objects. Shared objects are best used in browser-based games.

Pretty simple right? You can use these methods to save all sorts of data that pertains to your game, players, and so on, such as game setup decisions, game state, high scores, and so on.

POINTS TO REMEMBER

- Your target audience is the judge of your game and will determine the game's success or failure. Do your best to design according to that group.

- Target your game to a slightly lower playback specification than you assume the players will have.
- Plan out your game BEFORE you begin developing.
- Take the time to develop the theme. Games with themes make a better impression than games without them.
- Don't forget the supporting screens such as Loading, Welcome, How-to, and Game Over.
- Ramp up difficulty during play. Start the game off easy to let the player get familiar with the controls.
- Keep your game to a two to five minute play time if possible. If the game requires a longer play time, consider including a save game feature.

PART II:

EXAMINING THE NUTS AND BOLTS

CHAPTER 3
GAME MATH 43
- Why Learn Trigonometry? 44
- The Flash Coordinate System 44
- Anatomy of a Triangle 51
- The Pythagorean Theorem 52
- The Heart of Trig 55
- Vectors 62
- Points to Remember 66

CHAPTER 4
BASIC PHYSICS 69
- Introduction to Physics 70
- Speed, Velocity, and Acceleration 71
- Newton's Three Laws of Motion 82
- Gravity 87
- Friction 90
- Points to Remember 94

CHAPTER 5
COLLISION DETECTION 97
- What Is a Collision? 98
- Detection Using hitTest() 99
- Detection Using Math 110
- Collision Detection with Advanced Shapes 147
- Points to Remember 148

CHAPTER 6
COLLISION REACTIONS 151
- Bouncing Off the Walls 153
- Conservation of Momentum and Energy 162
- Applying the Conservation Laws 165
- Points to Remember 177

CHAPTER 7
TILE-BASED WORLDS 179
- Introduction to Tiles 180
- Design Considerations 182
- Tile Creation and Management 185
- Selective Processing 189
- Tile-Independent Objects 194
- Adding a Character to the World 197
- Defining Worlds with XML 203
- Points to Remember 208

CHAPTER 8
THE ISOMETRIC WORLDVIEW 211
- Introduction to Isometrics 212
- A Technical Look at Isometrics 215
- Z-Sorting 229
- Deconstruction of a Simple World 234
- Points to Remember 246

Chapter 9
Level Editors 249
Introduction to Level Editors 250
An Example Level Editor and Game 251
The Class Files 255
Creating an Enhanced Executable 256
Points to Remember 261

Chapter 10
High Score List 263
Administration of the High Score Lists 265
The List in Action 268
Points to Remember 274

Chapter 11
Artificial Intelligence 277
Types of AI 278
Homegrown AI 281
The Perfect Maze 288
Pathfinding Algorithms 295
Points to Remember 308

Chapter 12
Efficient Game Graphics 311
Vector Versus Bitmap 312
Various File Types 315
Compression 317
Special Considerations with Lossy (JPEG) Compression 321
Performance 322
Loading Graphics at Run-Time 326
Points to Remember 327

Chapter 13
The Sound of Games 331
Why Sound Is Important 332
Managing Sound Effects 334
Creating Sound Effects 345
Creating Music Loops 350
Points to Remember 355

Chapter 14
Introduction to Multiplayer Games 359
The Human Element 360
Computer-Based Multiplayer Games 361
ElectroServer 3 367
A Basic Chat Application 370
Playing a Multiplayer Game 375
Points to Remember 376

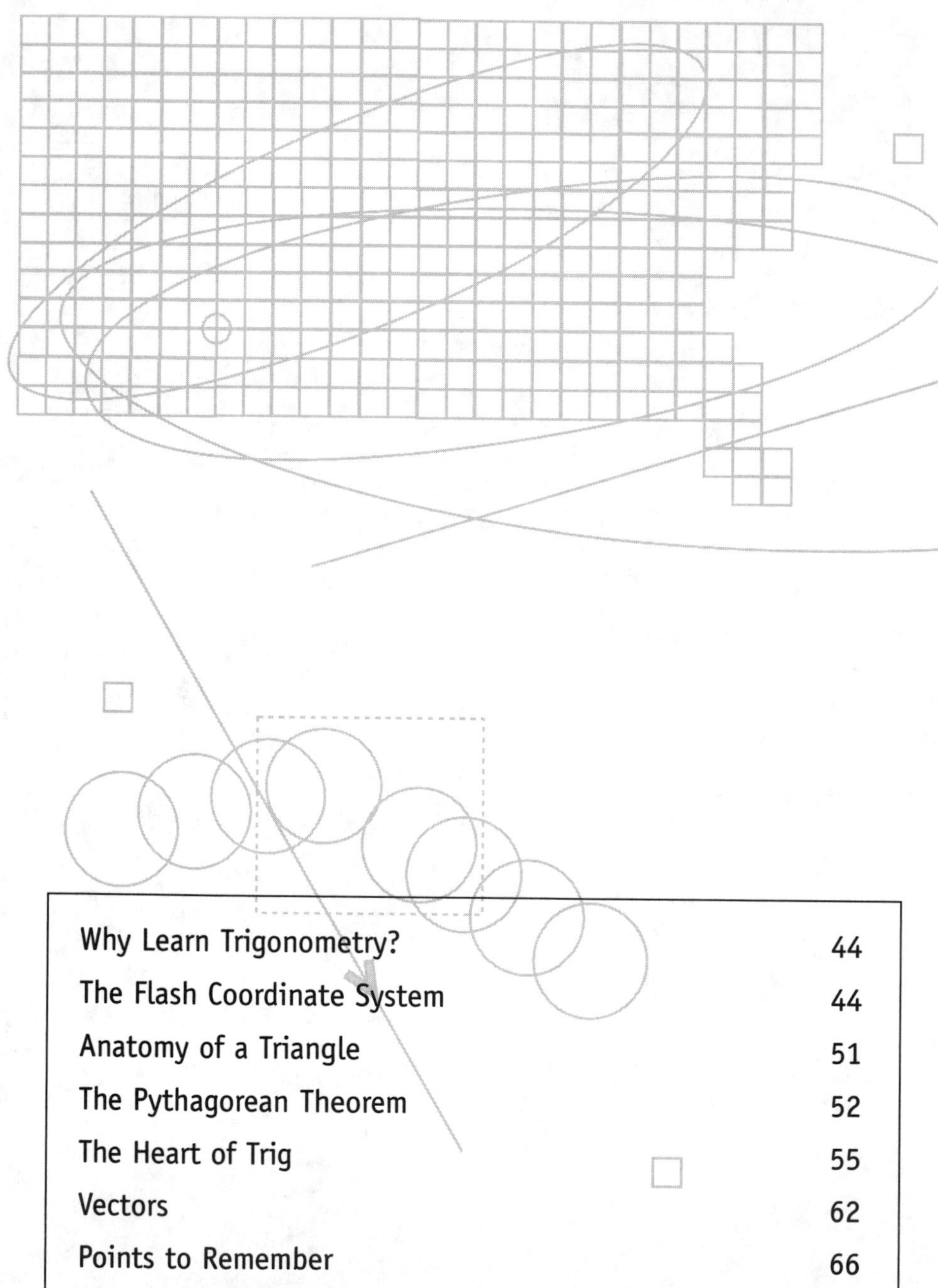

Why Learn Trigonometry? 44

The Flash Coordinate System 44

Anatomy of a Triangle 51

The Pythagorean Theorem 52

The Heart of Trig 55

Vectors 62

Points to Remember 66

CHAPTER 3

GAME MATH

FOR THOSE OF YOU WHO DON'T REMEMBER THIS FROM SCHOOL, TRIGONOMETRY is the branch of mathematics that deals with the relationships between the sides and angles of triangles. In this chapter we're going to cover the basics of trigonometry, which should handle almost every need you'll have. However, if you would like to learn more about this subject, see Appendix A, "Developer Resources," for book suggestions.

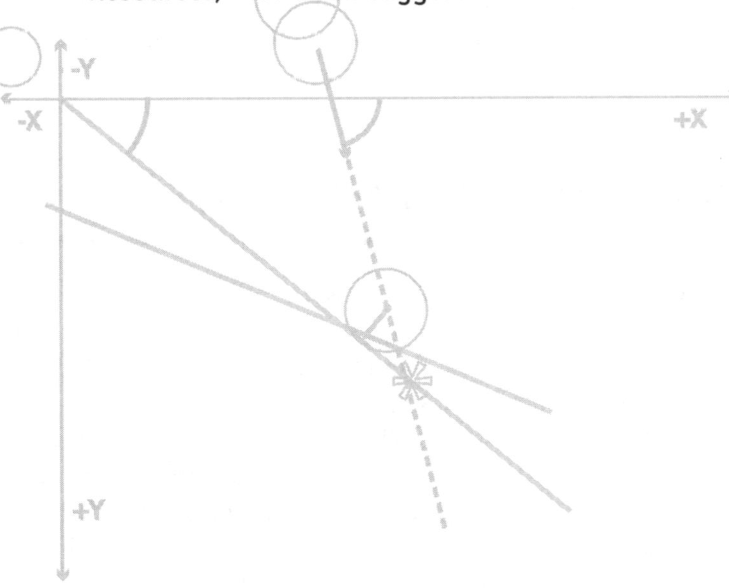

Why Learn Trigonometry?

When programming a game, you'll often need to do things such as finding the distance between two points or making an object move. (In fact, *very* often!) Here are a few examples:

- Rotating a spaceship or other vehicle
- Properly handling the trajectory of projectiles shot from a rotated weapon
- Calculating a new trajectory after a collision between two objects such as billiard balls or heads
- Determining if a collision between two objects is happening
- Finding the angle of trajectory (given the speed of an object in the *x* direction and *y* direction)

You are going to use trigonometry within ActionScript to complete these (and many other similar) tasks. Although you may not need to do so in every single game, the requirement for trigonometry can pop up in any genre. In this chapter I'll discuss the major uses of trigonometry in Flash and how to apply them.

The Flash Coordinate System

The coordinate system used in Flash is called the *Cartesian coordinate system*. (This may sound vaguely familiar to you from math classes, and if so, the information here should be a simple review.) Understanding how the Cartesian coordinate system is set up and how to use it is very important for a game developer. Why, exactly? Because in your games you will be creating and moving objects around the screen, using ActionScript to tell an object which coordinates to move to. To write ActionScript that does this, you must have an understanding of the coordinate system. In this section, I'll (re)acquaint you with this all-important grid. We'll also discuss how the Flash coordinate system measures angles.

Cartesian Coordinates

The Cartesian coordinate system is grid-based (made up of many equal-sized imaginary squares), with a horizontal axis called the *x-axis* and a vertical axis called the *y-axis* (see Figure 3.1).

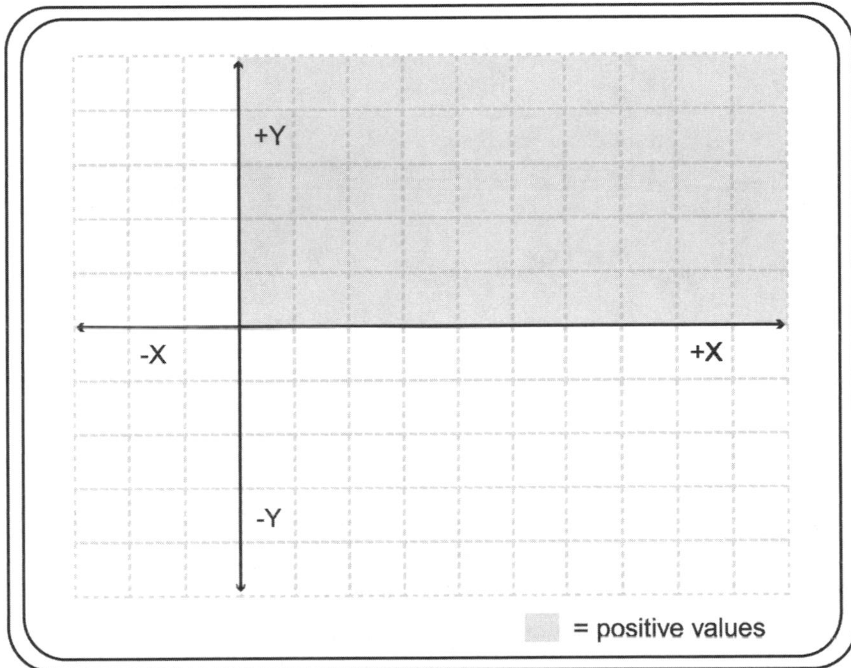

FIGURE 3.1
The Cartesian coordinate system.

The way we look at this grid in Flash positions the negative side of the *y*-axis higher than the positive side (see Figure 3.2).

Actually, there is no difference at all between the two coordinate systems you've just seen. What *is* different is how we are observing them. If you stand on your head to view an object, then only the way you are observing it has changed, not the object itself. That is what's happening here. In math class, you observed the coordinate system one way; in Flash, you observe it upside-down and backward.

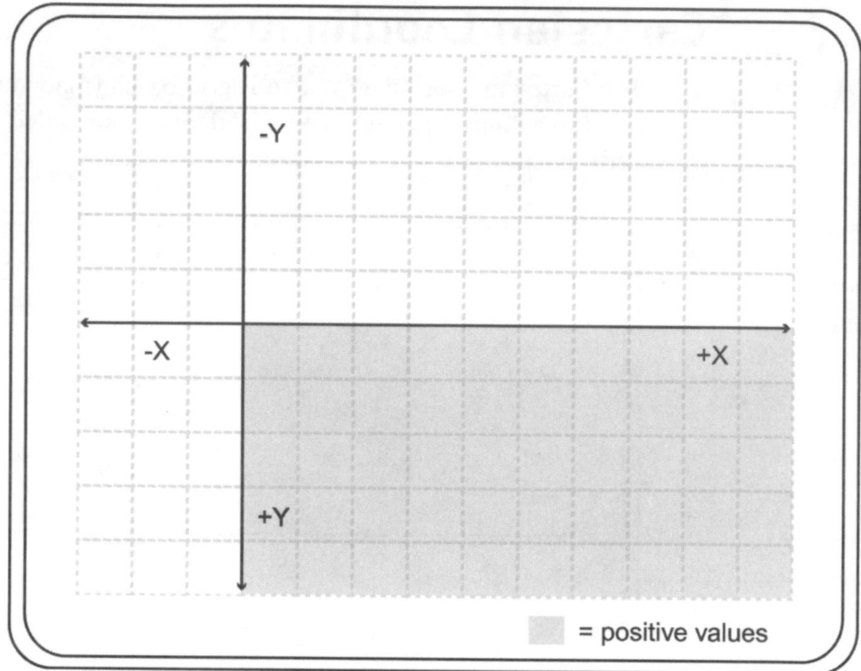

FIGURE 3.2
The Flash version of the Cartesian coordinate system.

Most computer programs use the same orientation of the coordinate system as Flash. If you have a window open on your computer, you can grab a corner to resize it. The contents of the window may resize, or perhaps the amount of content shown changes. But what does *not* change is the upper-left corner of the window. That corner is designated as the *origin*—the point where the *x*-axis and *y*-axis cross. All the contents are contained within the +*x* and +*y* quadrant (see Figure 3.3). If the origin was always, say, in the center of the screen, then as you resized the window, the coordinates of every element in your window (images or movie clips) would change. A top-left-origin coordinate system is a great convenience.

A Cartesian coordinate is a set of two numbers that describe the position of a point. In math, the two numbers in the coordinate are usually grouped in parentheses, like this: (4, 8). The 4 represents a distance along the *x*-axis, and the 8 represents a distance along the *y*-axis (see Figure 3.4).

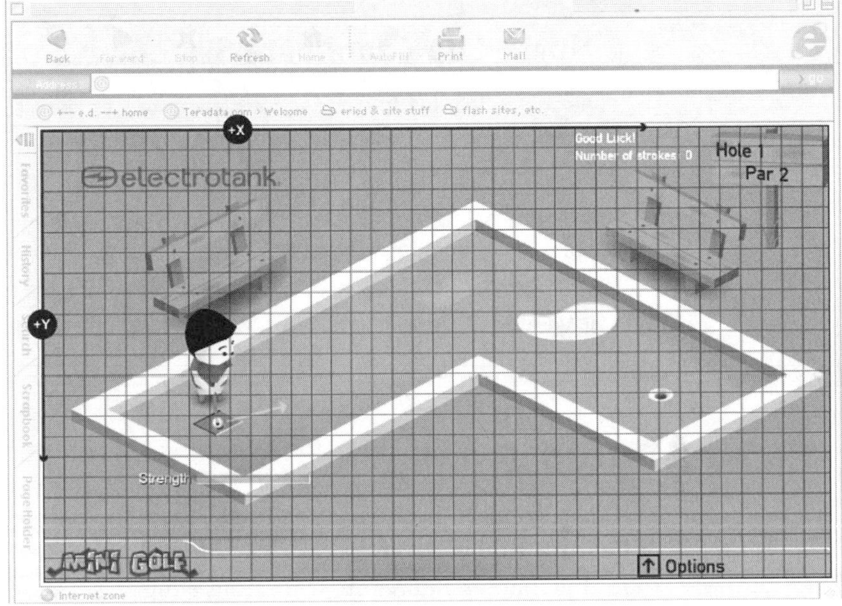

FIGURE 3.3
All the contents are contained within the *+x* and *+y* quadrant.

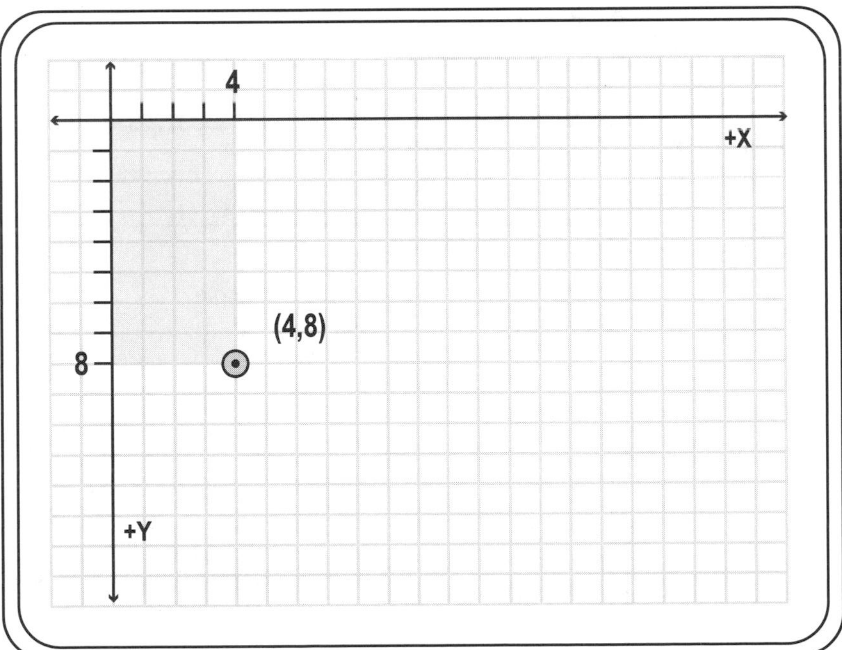

FIGURE 3.4
Graphical representation of the point (4, 8).

Movie-Clip Coordinate Systems

As you've learned in this section, the origin of Flash's coordinate system is the upper-left corner of the Flash movie. Every individual movie clip also has its own coordinate system (called a *relative coordinate system*). The origin for movie clips is called, in Flash terminology, a *registration point*. At this point in the book, it is only important to know that movie clips contain their own coordinate systems. In later chapters, we will make use of these movie clip coordinate systems.

Angles

Angles are used in two ways in Flash: They are used to rotate objects, and they are used with the trigonometric functions that will be discussed later in this chapter. But before you can use angles to do anything, you need to understand how they are measured in the Flash coordinate system.

Positive angles are measured from the *x*-axis, rotated in a clockwise direction, and with a fixed point at the origin (see Figure 3.5).

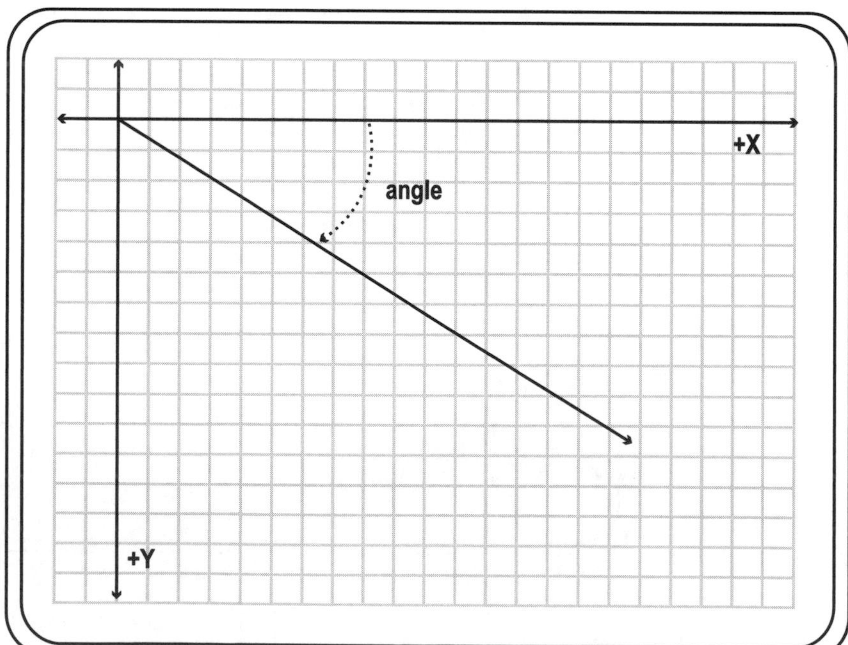

FIGURE 3.5
Graphical representation of an angle.

Angles are measured in *degrees* and can have a value of 0° to 360°. The entire coordinate system is made up of four quadrants separated by the axes. Each quadrant covers 90° (see Figure 3.6).

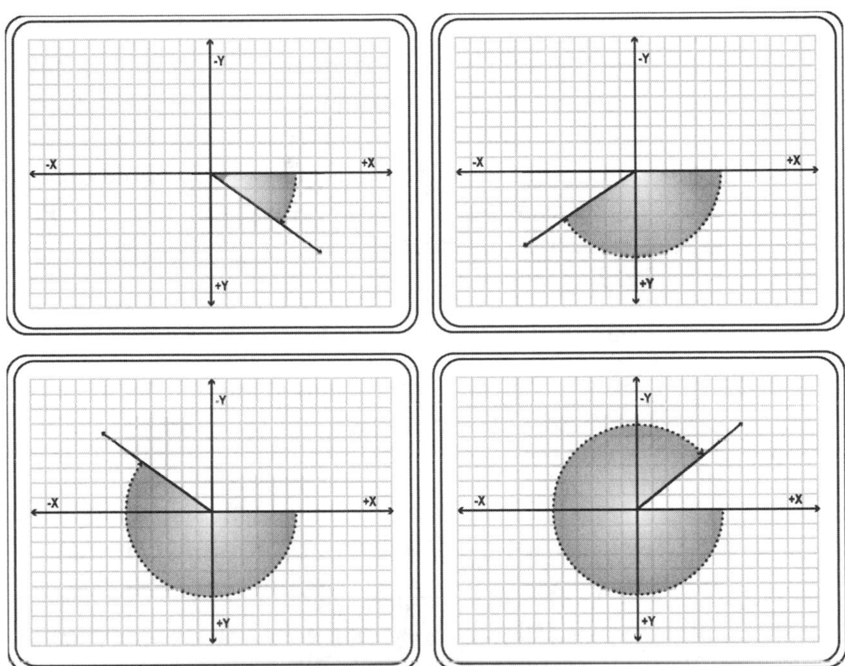

FIGURE 3.6
Angles in each of the four quadrants.

More on Angles

Angle measurements are *repeating*—that is, you can never have an angle greater than 360°. So let's say you have an object that may have actually rotated 720°—two full rotations. That is possible, of course, but its orientation is still 360°. (You determine the end orientation of an angle by subtracting 360 from the total number until it becomes less than or equal to 360.)

Negative angles are also possible. But that description doesn't mean the angle itself is negative or inverted (that wouldn't make any sense). The negative number merely tells you that the angle was measured counterclockwise from the *x*-axis.

You are familiar with things being represented in different ways. For instance, distance can be represented in miles or kilometers, and power can be represented as horsepower or watts. The same thing applies to angles. In addition to degrees, another common way to measure angles is in *radians*. One full rotation is 2π radians. With degrees, we know that one rotation is 360°, so each quarter rotation is 90°. Likewise, with radians, because a full rotation is 2π, each quarter rotation is $\pi/2$. For those who may not remember, π (*pi*, or `Math.PI` in ActionScript) is a special number in math, representing the ratio of the circumference of a circle to its diameter. Rounded to two places, it is 3.14. Pi can be accessed in Flash by using `Math.PI`. For example, here is a way to create a variable that has the value of *pi*:

```
var myPI:Number = Math.PI;
```

So why do you need to know about radians? Because everything you do in Flash with angles—with one exception—needs to be expressed in radians.

Radians as a Unit of Measurement

Unlike degrees, which are arbitrary, radians form a "natural" unit of measurement. The word *natural* here means a unit that (through the use of mathematical theory) has been found convenient and logical. That's probably why mathematicians, physicists, and programmers like radians better and use them almost exclusively.

The only time you can use degrees directly in Flash is when you're changing the `_rotation` property of a movie clip. However, human nature and habit being what they are, it is very common (and perfectly acceptable) to work with degrees in ActionScript and then convert from degrees to radians just before you need to use the angle. Converting degrees to radians or radians to degrees is easy (see Figure 3.7).

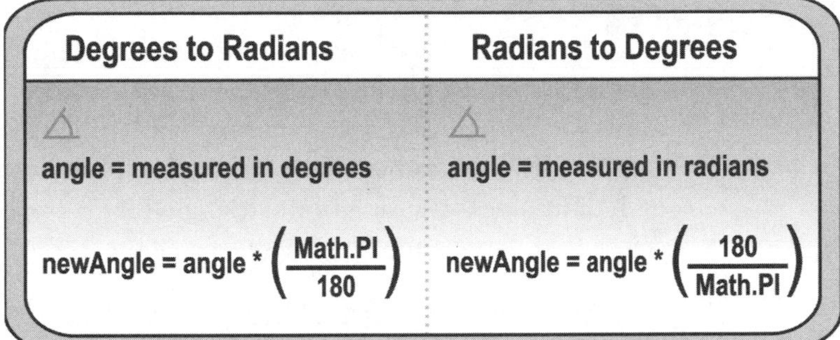

Degrees to Radians
Radians to Degrees
angle = measured in degrees
angle = measured in radians
newAngle = angle * (Math.PI / 180)
newAngle = angle * (180 / Math.PI)

FIGURE 3.7
Conversion formulae for degrees to radians and radians to degrees.

Anatomy of a Triangle

Trigonometry, as I've said, is based on the relationships of the sides of a triangle to its angles. Before we get into the heart of trigonometry, let's refresh your memory on the basics of triangles and how they fit into the coordinate system.

Triangles are made up of three line segments joined in three places. Each joint is called a *vertex*. In a triangle, there are three angles, one formed at each vertex (see Figure 3.8). These three angles must always total 180° (or π radians). As you may remember from geometry class, there are descriptive names associated with certain types of triangles, such as *isosceles, scalene, equilateral,* and *right*. We are only going to concern ourselves with one of these—the right triangle.

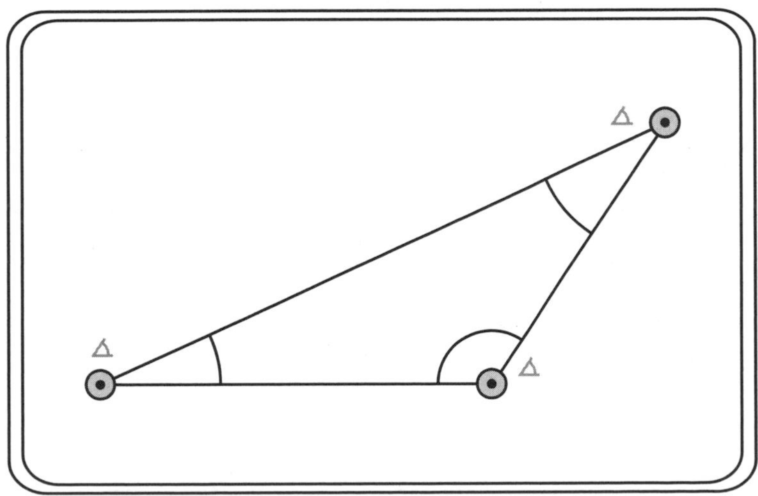

FIGURE 3.8
Triangles are made up of three angles, one formed at each vertex.

A right triangle is any triangle that has a 90° angle. The right triangle is a very useful tool for us because two of its sides fit nicely into the Cartesian system we use in Flash—one of them along the *x*-axis and another along the *y*-axis. (No other type of triangle can claim this!) Because of this, it is generally easier to gain information about the length of its sides. The side of the triangle that is opposite the 90° angle has a special name—the *hypotenuse* (see Figure 3.9).

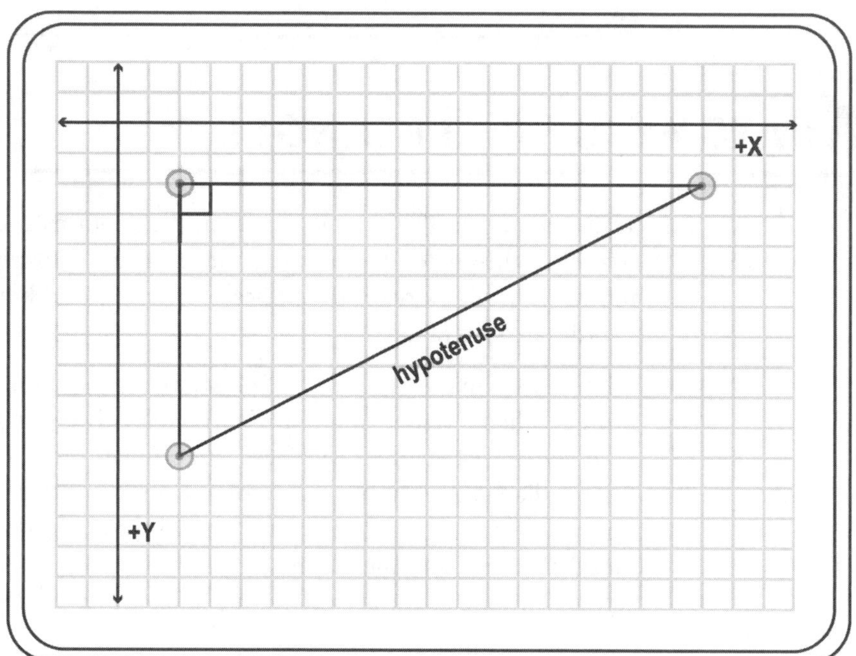

FIGURE 3.9
The side opposite the right angle is called the hypotenuse.

The Pythagorean Theorem

Named after the Greek philosopher Pythagoras, the Pythagorean theorem states a simple but powerful relationship between the sides of a right triangle: *The square of the hypotenuse of a right triangle is equal to the sum of the squares of the remaining two sides.*

So, given a triangle with sides of length *a*, *b*, and *c* where *c* is the hypotenuse (see Figure 3.10), the theorem reads $a^2 + b^2 = c^2$.

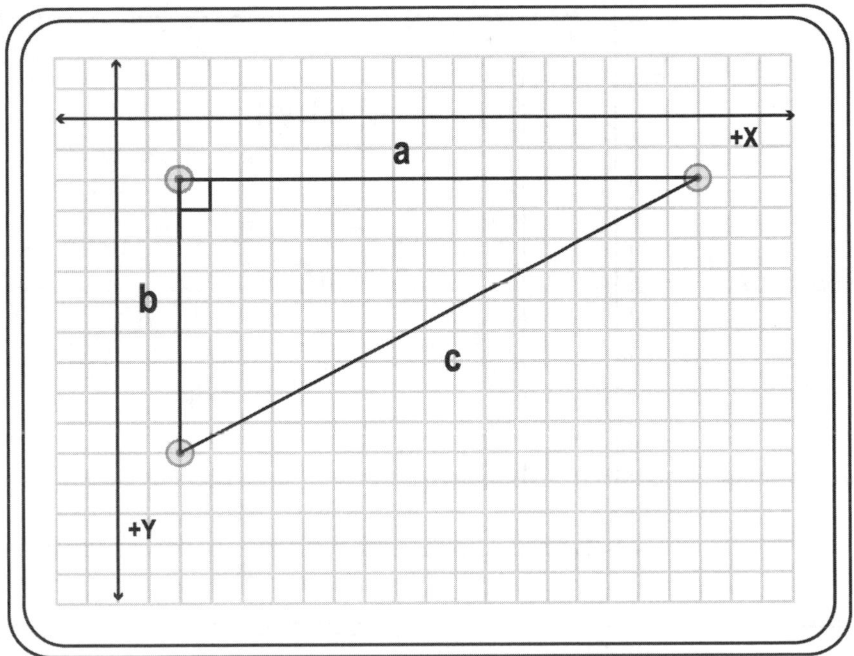

FIGURE 3.10
A right triangle with the sides labeled *a*, *b*, and *c*.

Now that you know (or have finally remembered!) this simple relationship, let's see how you can use it to find the distance between two points. Imagine that there is a black ball at the point ($x1$, $y1$) and a gray ball at the point ($x2$, $y2$) (see Figure 3.11). What is the distance between these balls?

You've probably guessed by now where I'm going with this—you can use the Pythagorean theorem to find the distance between these two points. The only conceptual hurdle in this problem is to realize that there exists an imaginary right triangle whose hypotenuse is the line joining the two balls (see Figure 3.12). But if you've been following the discussion to this point, that's probably not too big a hurdle.

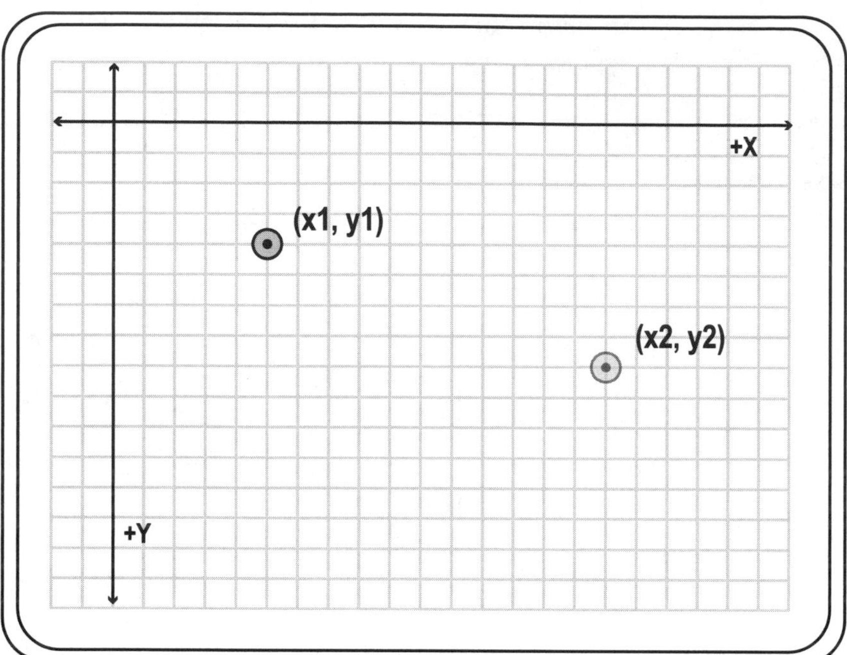

FIGURE 3.11
Finding the distance between two points.

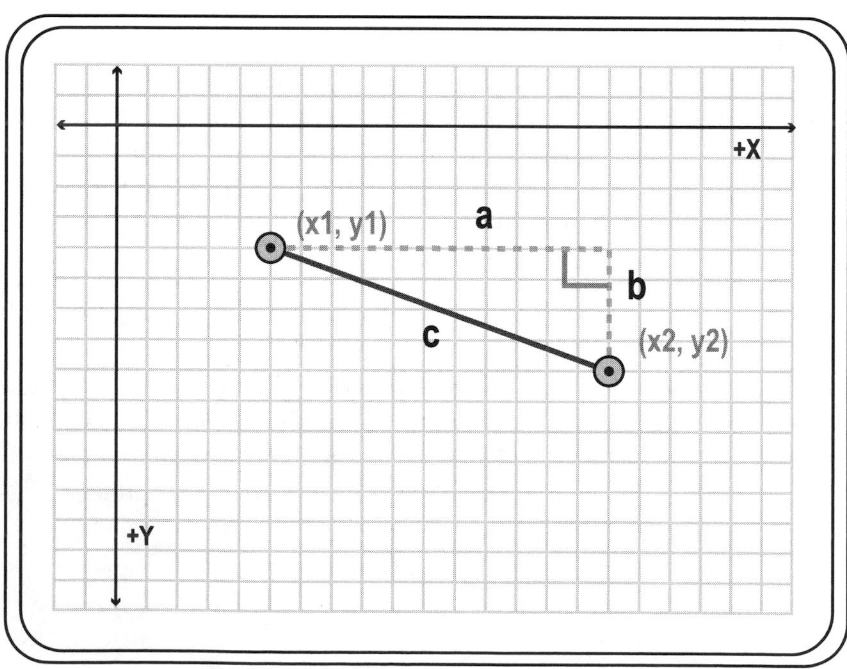

FIGURE 3.12
The imaginary right triangle.

The theorem states that $c^2 = a^2 + b^2$. You'll recall that *c* is the hypotenuse—that is, the value we're looking for to determine the distance between the two points. So we solve this equation for c to get $c=\sqrt{a^2+b^2}$. If we write *a* and *b* in terms of the information we already know, then we can find the value of *c*. The side labeled *a* in Figure 3.12 is along the *x* axis, and its length is *x*2-*x*1. Likewise, the length of side *b* is *y*2-*y*1. Knowing this information, we can write a generic equation that will always give you the distance between any two points:

$$c=\text{distance}=\sqrt{(x_2-x_1)^2 + (y_2-y_1)^2}$$

With this mathematical equation, you can find the distance between any two points in Flash! This useful little "recipe" will come in handy frequently. For instance, you will use it when detecting most types of collisions in your games. In ActionScript, this distance formula would look like this:

```
var Distance:Number = Math.sqrt((x2-x1)*(x2-x1) +
➥(y2-y1)*(y2-y1));
```

The Heart of Trig

Is it all coming back to you yet? I hope so, because here's where we get to the real inner workings of trigonometry—where you can see how it's all going to come together. In this section, we will cover the *sine, cosine,* and *tangent* functions, as well as *projection*. With knowledge of these operations under your belt, you will be able to understand the programming concepts you'll encounter in the following chapters (especially Chapter 6, "Collision Reactions").

Sine, Cosine, and Tangent

Sine, cosine, and tangent are known as *trigonometric functions*. Although what they mean is very simple, many people have trouble understanding them. This conceptual problem happens because it is easy to think that the trigonometric functions give a result by some esoteric or even mystical process. The truth is that these functions just use various ratios of the triangle side lengths to give results. Look at the triangle in Figure 3.13. Notice that we are using *x* and *y* instead of *a* and *b* to label the side lengths. These are more common side names in programming. Notice the angle in the figure labeled *angle*.

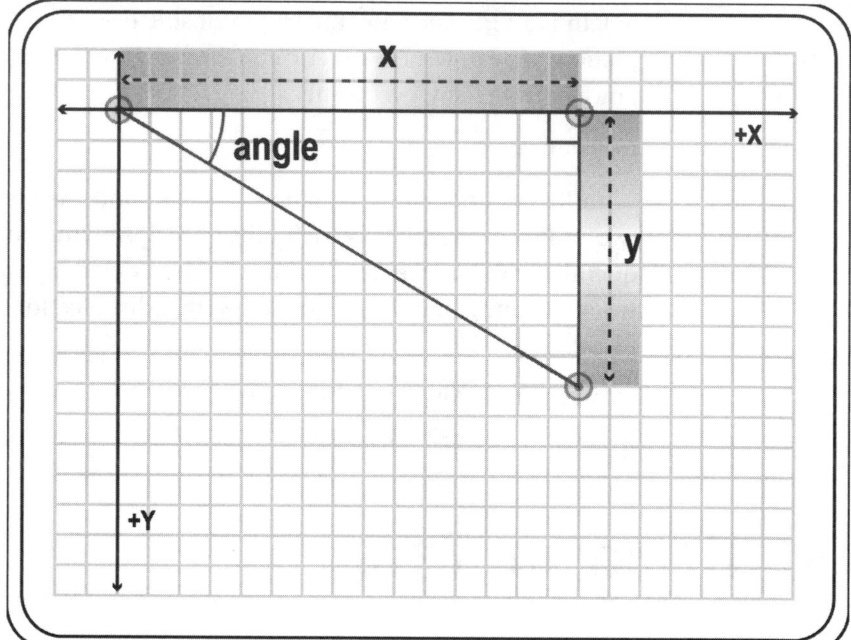

FIGURE 3.13
Triangle with the sides labeled *x* and *y*.

All three of the trigonometric functions are defined by taking ratios of the sides of this triangle. A trigonometric function takes an angle (in Flash it must be measured in radians) and returns a value. For instance, the sine of 45° is .707. To test this for yourself in Flash, here is an ActionScript code snippet you can write:

```
var angle:Number = 45;
var radians:Number = angle*Math.PI/180;
trace(Math.sin(radians));
```

The first line in this code block sets the angle in degrees. The second line converts degrees to radians, and the third line computes the sine and displays the result in the output window.

Table 3.1 lists these "big three" functions, their definitions, which methods of the Math class they correspond to in Flash, and a valid value range that can be returned from these functions.

TABLE 3.1

Trigonometric Functions in Flash

Trigonometric Function	Mathematical Definition	Method in Flash *(Angle is in radians)*	Minimum Result	Maximum Result
Sine	sin(angle)=*y*/*c*	`Math.sin(`*angle*`)`	-1	1
Cosine	cos(angle)=*x*/*c*	`Math.cos(`*angle*`)`	-1	1
Tangent	tan(angle)=*y*/*x*	`Math.tan(`*angle*`)`	Negative infinity	Positive infinity

It wouldn't hurt to commit some simple results of the trigonometric functions to memory. This can help tremendously when debugging a script. Table 3.2 shows some simple values for you to remember, should you choose to.

TABLE 3.2

Trigonometric Equivalents

Typical Angles in Degrees	Sine	Cosine	Tangent
0	0	1	0
45	0.707	0.707	1
90	1	0	Infinity
180	0	-1	0

Because you are able to calculate the sine, cosine, and tangent of an angle, it makes sense that there would also be some way to go from a number back to an angle. There is a set of functions for this, called the *inverse trigonometric functions*: *inverse sine*, *inverse cosine*, and *inverse tangent*. Some people use the term *arc* (as in *arcsine)* rather than *inverse*. Table 3.3 contains a list of the available inverse trigonometric functions.

TABLE 3.3 **Inverse Trigonometric Functions**

Inverse Trigonometric Function	Method in Flash	Description
Inverse sine	`Math.asin(`*number*`)`	Returns the angle whose sine is equal to the number
Inverse cosine	`Math.acos(`*number*`)`	Returns the angle whose cosine is equal to the number
Inverse tangent	`Math.atan(`*number*`)`	Returns the angle whose tangent is equal to the number
Inverse tangent2	`Math.atan2(`*y*`, `*x*`)`	Returns the angle whose tangent is equal to *y*/*x*

The inverse trigonometric functions take a number as an input parameter and return an angle in radians. To convince yourself of how this works, try this example in Flash:

```
var input:Number = .707;
trace(Math.asin(input)*180/Math.PI);
```

The first line sets a variable called `input` with a value of `.707`. The second line uses the inverse sine method of the `Math` class (which returns an angle in radians) and then converts it to degrees. The result is traced in the Output window (see Figure 3.14) and should be very close to 45°. (It is not exactly 45° because the true sine of 45° has many more decimal places than .707.)

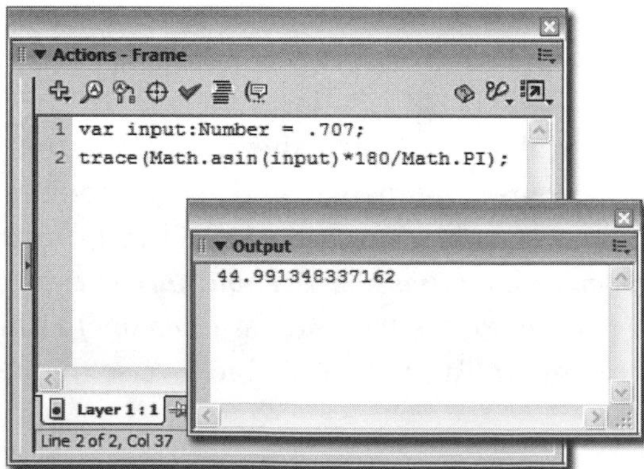

FIGURE 3.14
The result in the Output window.

Projection

The word *projection* in the context of trigonometry means to project a quantity (such as distance or velocity) onto the *x*-axis and *y*-axis. Using what you'll learn in this section will help you when building games. For an example of what projection can help you accomplish, open the file shooter.fla in the Chapter03 folder on the CD-ROM. In this file, a ship rotates to point toward your mouse (see Figure 3.15). When you click anywhere on the movie's Stage, a projectile fires from the nose of the ship. The velocity of the projectile points toward your mouse (or at least to the place where your mouse was when you clicked it). For this movement to be programmed in Flash, the velocity must be projected along the *x*-axis and *y*-axis.

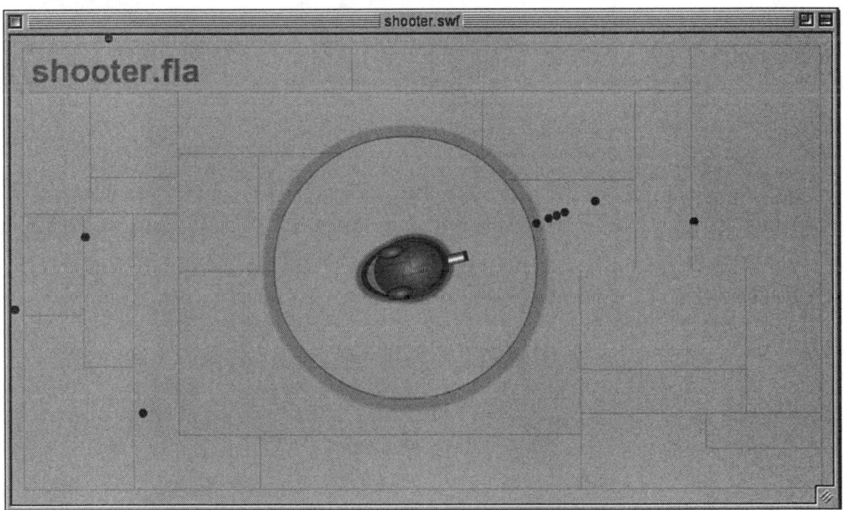

FIGURE 3.15
Shooter.fla.

The programmatic movement seen in shooter.fla is not covered until Chapter 4, "Basic Physics."

Imagine a diagonal line of length *len* drawn in Flash at angle *ang*. A piece of this line extends along the *x*-axis and another piece of it along the *y*-axis. If the angle were 0°, then the line would extend only along the *x*-axis. If the angle were 90° then the line would extend only along the *y*-axis. With any other angle, the line extends both in the *x* direction and the *y* direction. (Put another way, no two coordinates on the line have the same *x* or *y* value. A horizontal line always has the same *y* value for all its coordinates. A vertical line always has the same *x* value for all its coordinates. A diagonal line never repeats an *x* or *y* coordinate.) If you were to draw a right triangle from this diagonal line, then the two other sides of that triangle would be the pieces that extend along the *x*-axis and *y*-axis.

Finding the length of either (or both) of those pieces by using the values *ang* and *len* (see Figure 3.16) is called *projection*. These values are found by using the trigonometric functions that we've already discussed above.

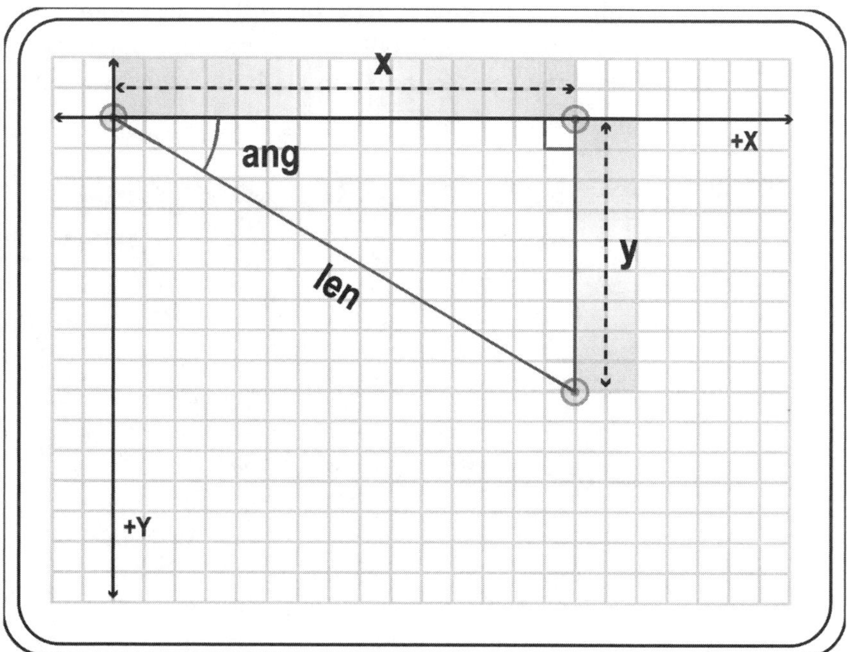

FIGURE 3.16
The values *ang* and *len*.

As seen in the previous section:

```
cos(angle)=x/c
```

In the example here, *angle* is replaced with *ang* and *c* with *len*. So:

```
cos(ang)=x/len
```

To find the projection of *len* along the *x*-axis, we solve the equation for *x*:

```
x=len*cos(ang)
```

Or with ActionScript:

```
var x:Number = len*Math.cos(ang);
```

To find the *y* projection, we use:

```
sin(ang)=y/len
```

And solve for *y*:

```
y=len*sin(ang)
```

Which converts to this in ActionScript:

```
var y:Number=len*Math.sin(ang);
```

Think of projection like a shadow cast from an object onto the floor or a wall (see Figure 3.17). For the example given in this section, first we would imagine a light source coming from below to cast a shadow on the *x*-axis. The length of the shadow cast from the line on the *x*-axis is the same as the projection we would calculate using trigonometry. Next we would imagine a light source coming from far off to the right shining left. The shadow cast on the *y*-axis is equal to that which we would calculate using trigonometry.

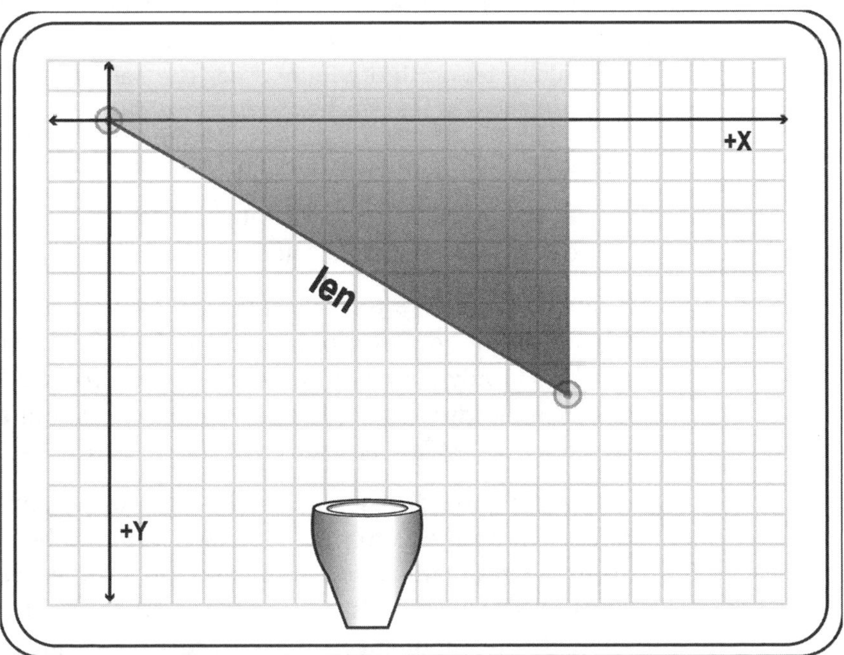

FIGURE 3.17 Projection as a shadow.

Vectors

A vector is a mathematical object that has both magnitude (a numeric value) and direction. Velocity is a vector because it has both magnitude and direction. For example, a velocity of 33 kilometers per hour (kph) southeast has a magnitude of 33 and a direction of southeast. Speed is not a vector, and direction is not a vector, but speed and direction together, modifying the same object, form a vector. Here are some other examples of vectors.

> **Vector Versus Vector**
>
> Note that mathematicians also use the term *vector* to refer to what programmers ordinarily call an array. Just keep in mind that in this book, the word vector is used to refer to the mathematical object, which represents more of a physics definition of the word vector.

- **Displacement** can be a vector when describing the location of one point with respect to another point (whether those points represent two objects, or one object in motion). For example, "New York is 500 miles north of Virginia" or "The ball rolled 3 feet to the left."
- **Force** can be a vector because the gravitational force that pulls you toward the earth has both a magnitude and a direction.
- **Rotation,** when modified with a direction, is a vector. Think of a clock hand rotated 90° clockwise.

Graphically, a vector is usually represented as an arrow (in other words, if you had to show a vector in a graph, that's how you'd sketch it). Mathematically, a vector's direction is often specified by an angle. To use the example given above, "33 kph southeast" may alternatively be described as "33 kph at 45 degrees" (see Figure 3.18).

In Flash, vectors are used primarily with physics applications. This is because multiple vectors (of the same type) can be added together to form one resultant vector. Adding vectors is called *superposition*. For example, if a balloon is floating in the air, several forces are being exerted on it simultaneously (see Figure 3.19), such as force from the wind, gravitational force, and a buoyant force (that is, the force that is pushing the balloon up). With three forces acting on one balloon, it might be difficult to figure out what the balloon will do. Will it rise or will it fall? Using superposition, you can add the vectors together to find the resultant vector (and determine the balloon's next move). One vector is much easier to work with than three.

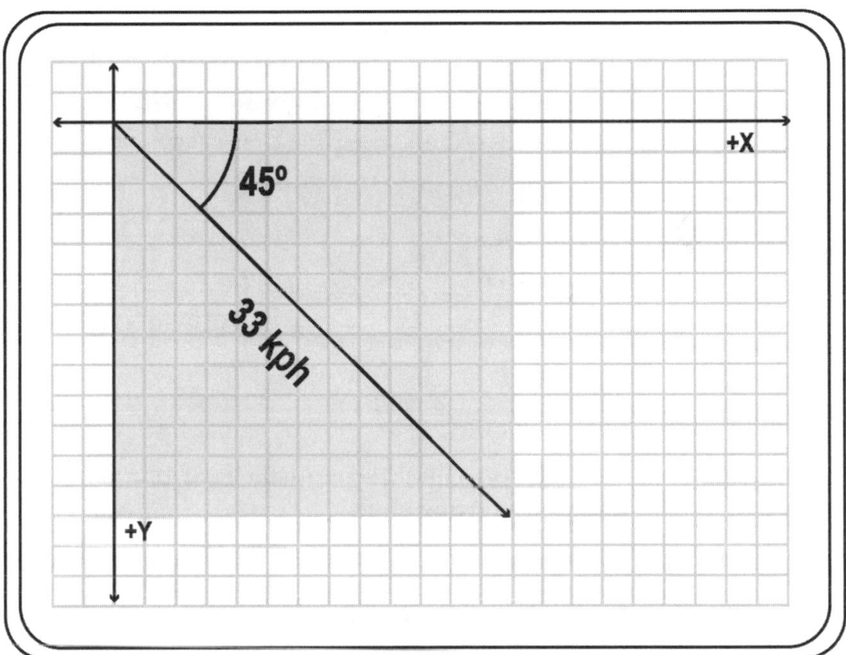

FIGURE 3.18
A vector's direction can be specified by an angle.

Vectors can be divided up into *x* and *y* components (in this context, the word *components* refers to pieces). This is called *resolving* a vector. You already did this same thing in the "Projection" section. Resolving a vector is nothing more than projecting it along the coordinate system axes. To add vectors together, you must:

1. Resolve all the vectors into their x and y components. Those pieces are the remaining two sides of the right triangle.
2. Add all the x components together.
3. Add all the y components together.

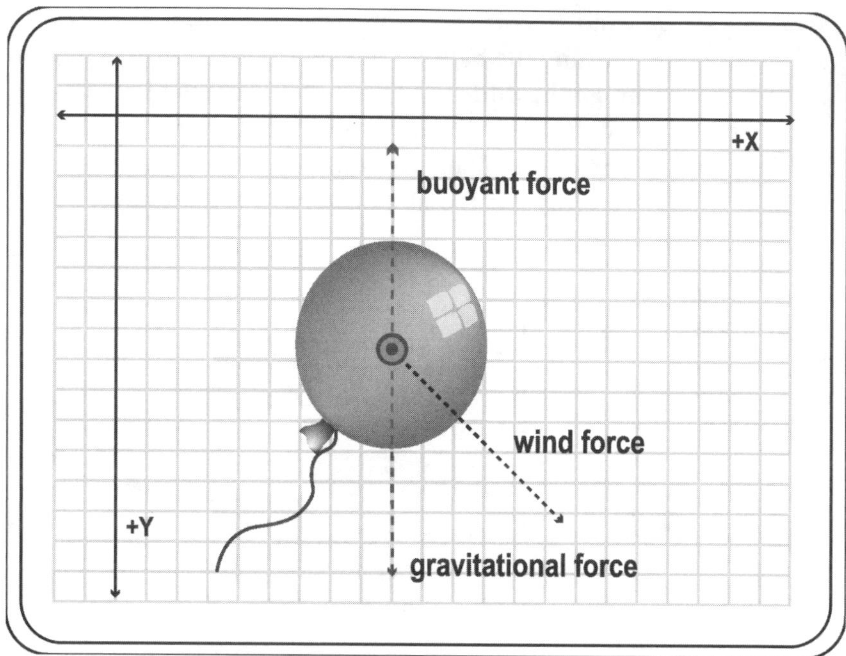

FIGURE 3.19
Three forces acting on a balloon.

Let's use the example we started above. Imagine a balloon in the air with three forces acting on it:

- A gravitational force with a magnitude of 10 at an angle of 90°.
- A buoyant force with a magnitude of 8 at an angle of 270°.
- A wind force with a magnitude of 5 at an angle of 45°.

To add the vectors together (looking back at our three-step checklist), the first step is to resolve each vector into its components.

What follows is the balloon example we've been using, written in ActionScript. Nothing will appear on the screen; this is purely a mathematical exercise to introduce you to the role of ActionScript in this process. Later in the book, after I've introduced you to the other concepts necessary to understanding them, we'll delve into many more practical examples.

In the code below, I've used the number 1 appended to the ends of all variables associated with the gravitational force, 2 for the buoyant force, and 3 for the wind force. (The lines that begin with // are comment lines, for information only.) To try this ActionScript yourself, open the

Actions panel in Flash and enter the ActionScript below, or open the force_example.fla file from the Chapter03 folder on the CD-ROM.

```
//Gravitational force
var angle1:Number = 90;
var magnitude1:Number = 8;
//Buoyant force
var angle2:Number = 270;
var magnitude2:Number = 10;
//Wind force
var angle3:Number = 45;
var magnitude3:Number = 5;
//Resolve the vectors into their components
var x1:Number = magnitude1*Math.cos(angle1*Math.PI/180);
var y1:Number = magnitude1*Math.sin(angle1*Math.PI/180);
var x2:Number = magnitude2*Math.cos(angle2*Math.PI/180);
var y2:Number = magnitude2*Math.sin(angle2*Math.PI/180);
var x3:Number = magnitude3*Math.cos(angle3*Math.PI/180);
var y3:Number = magnitude3*Math.sin(angle3*Math.PI/180);
```

Notice the `Math.PI/180` factor in each line of ActionScript above. Remember that the trigonometric functions only work with angles measured in radians. This factor converts the angle from degrees to radians.

The next two steps are to add all the *x* components and *y* components together to form two resultant vectors:

```
//Add the x pieces
var x:Number = x1+x2+x3;
//Add the y pieces
var y:Number = y1+y2+y3;
```

You now have the sum of all the forces in the *x* direction and the sum of all the forces in the *y* direction. Add these two lines of ActionScript to display the result in the Output window:

```
trace("Force in the x direction="+x);
trace("Force in the y direction="+y);
```

When you test the SWF file, you will see that the force in the *y* direction is 1.53. Because this number is greater than 0, the balloon will be forced to move toward the ground. The force in the *x* direction is 3.53. This means that the balloon will be forced to move to the right.

Still Lost? There Is Hope!

To many people, math is a dry subject. It is understandable if, when you've finished this chapter, you feel like you have grasped only part of it. Everything will make more sense when you start to see the practical uses of the math you've seen here, and the concepts will become more solidified in your mind. It may make sense for you to reread parts of this chapter when you start to use trigonometry in your games.

With the concepts and techniques in this chapter, you are adding practical skills to your programming toolkit. You will find that these things will come in handy frequently. We will revisit vectors and explore more examples of vector uses in the chapters on physics and collision reactions.

POINTS TO REMEMBER

- Trigonometry is the branch of mathematics that deals with the relationships between the sides and angles of triangles.
- In game programming, trigonometry is used to help determine trajectories, distances, and deflection after a collision, to name a few of its functions.
- Flash uses the grid-based Cartesian coordinate system to identify, place, and move objects.
- By default, the registration point of a Flash movie clip is the upper-left corner of Stage or movie.
- The unit of measurement that Flash uses for angles is not degrees, but radians. You can easily convert from one unit of measurement to the other to work in a more familiar manner. The one exception to having to use radians in Flash is when you're changing the `_rotation` property of a movie clip.
- You can use the Pythagorean theorem to find the distance between two points.

- The trigonometric functions sine, cosine, and tangent use various ratios of the triangle side lengths to determine values and, used inversely, to deliver results as angles.
- A vector is a mathematical object that has both magnitude (a numeric value) and direction. For example, velocity is a vector because it has both magnitude and direction. A vector can be divided up into x and y components to project it along the axes of the coordinate system. This is called *resolving* a vector.

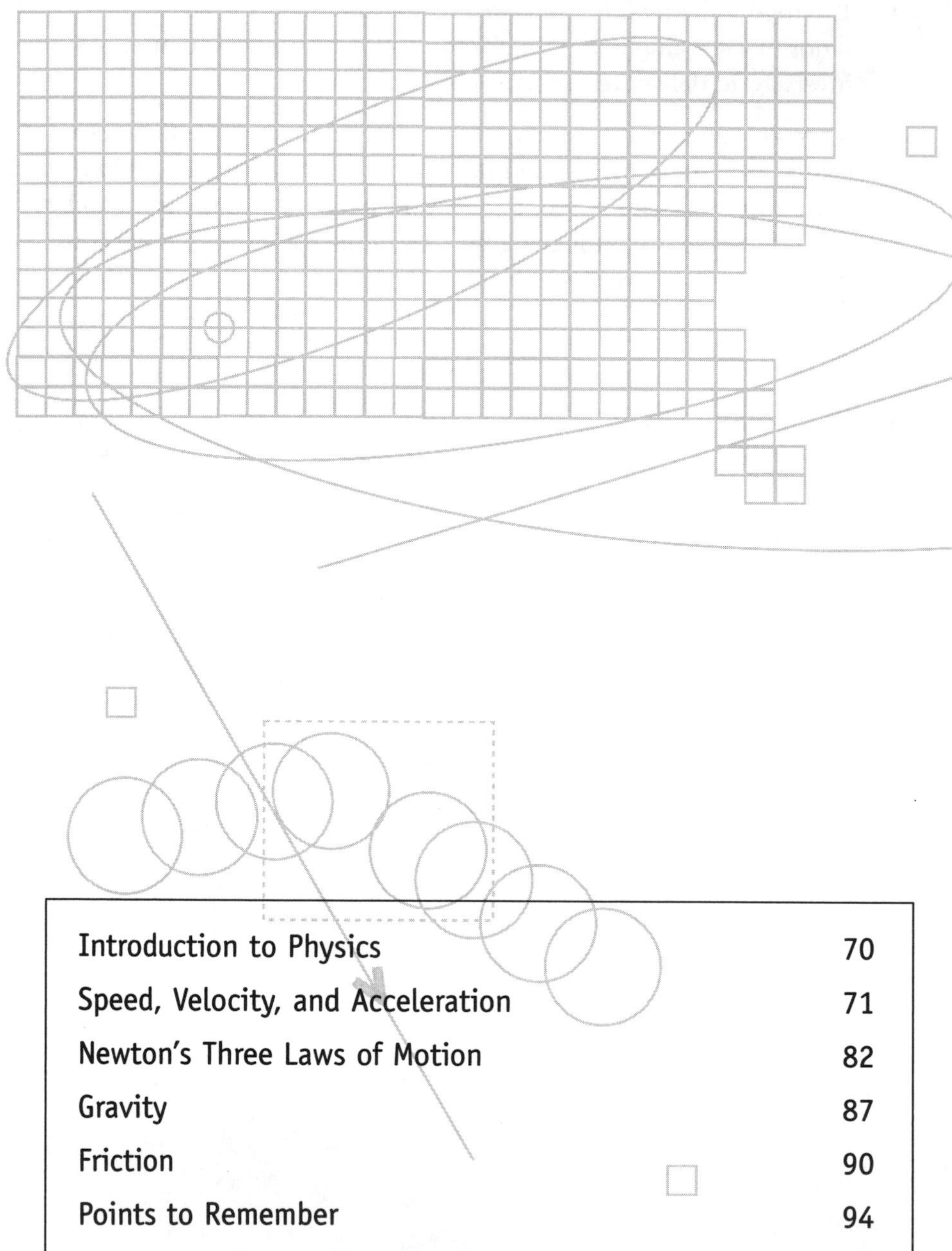

Introduction to Physics	70
Speed, Velocity, and Acceleration	71
Newton's Three Laws of Motion	82
Gravity	87
Friction	90
Points to Remember	94

CHAPTER 4

BASIC PHYSICS

HAVE YOU EVER WONDERED HOW TO ADD GRAVITY TO A GAME, OR EVEN HOW to make a movie clip move around the screen? Understanding basic physical laws and how to apply them is the key to creating dynamic realism in games. In this chapter, you will learn some of the most fundamental physics concepts, such as gravity and friction, and how to apply them in Macromedia Flash using ActionScript.

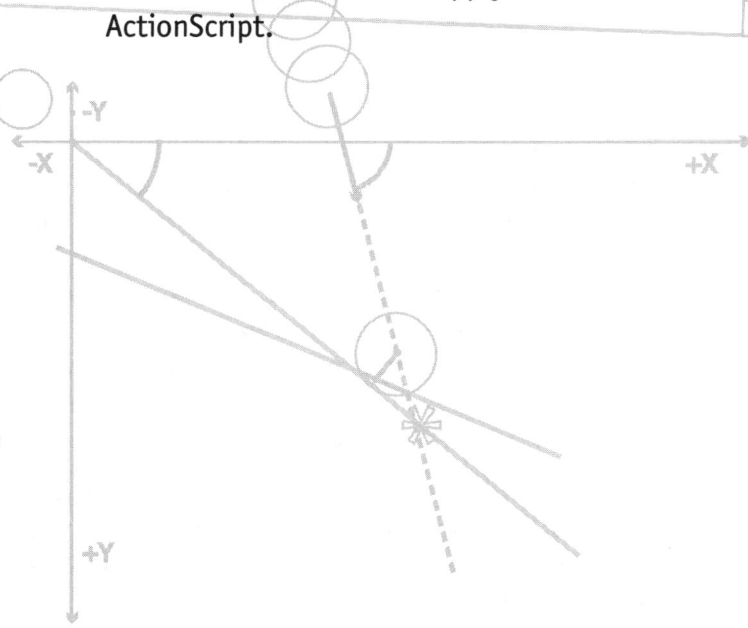

Introduction to Physics

For some reason, people often fear physics or feel that it's unapproachable. When I was in college and the fact that I was a physics major came up in conversation, I would inevitably get one of three odd looks. The first one implied that I had just sprouted another head; the second appeared as if the person had a sour taste in his or her mouth; the third (my favorite) was a consoling glance that said, "I am so sorry." I'm not sure what caused this general feeling about physics, but rest assured that in this chapter, we will allay those fears.

Physics is the branch of science that studies and describes the behavior of objects in nature on the most fundamental level. Here are some interactions and occurrences that physics is used to describe:

- An object falling to the ground (remember Isaac Newton and his apple)
- The effect of an electron on a proton
- Electrical current
- The motion of the planets

Many fields of specialized study exist within physics, and some areas of physics are very difficult to learn. Fortunately for us, Flash requires us to learn only the basics of the easiest-to-learn type: classical mechanics. Classical mechanics is the one area of physics where it is easy to conceptualize what is happening, or what should happen, in a simple situation. For instance, if you have a ball on a hill (see Figure 4.1), you don't need an advanced degree in science to tell you that the ball will roll down the hill—common sense should suffice. (In other areas of physics, it can be difficult to predict what will happen just by looking at the situation.)

In this chapter, we will discuss the basic concepts of speed, velocity, and acceleration, as well as Newton's laws, gravitation, and friction. We will not cover conservation of energy or momentum until Chapter 6, "Collision Reactions." This is because we are trying to introduce topics and concepts in a somewhat linear fashion. Conservation of energy and momentum are concepts that apply after a collision of objects occurs, and we have not yet reached that point.

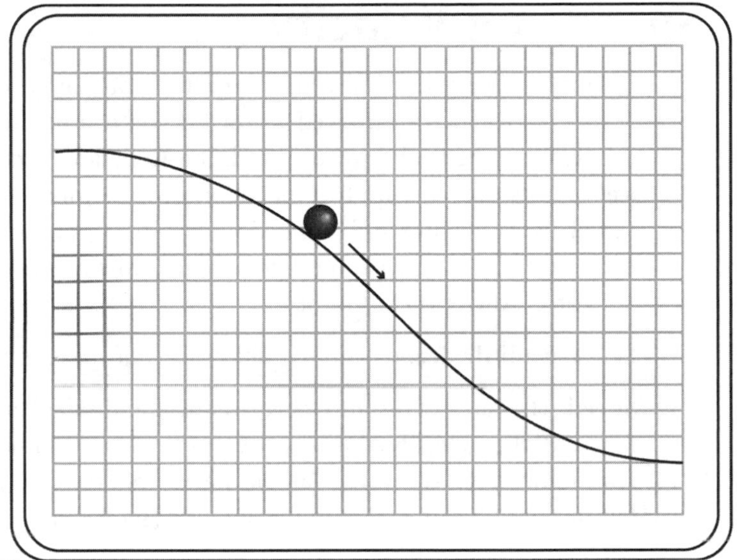

FIGURE 4.1
Many principles of physics are common sense.

One more thing to note before we jump in: I'm going to be making some distinctions between *real* physics and *good-enough* physics. Real physics concerns the motion and reactions that can be described by real physics equations. Everything initially discussed in this chapter is real physics. However, in some situations, the real physics equations may be a little too intense for Flash to calculate frequently. As it turns out, they can be replaced with vastly simplified equations that give good-enough results. We will discuss two of the most commonly used "good-enough" physics substitutes in the "Gravity" and "Friction" sections.

Speed, Velocity, and Acceleration

You may not know the difference between speed and velocity, but you probably have at least some idea of what speed, velocity, and acceleration are. In this section, I'll introduce you to these concepts and point out the differences between them.

Speed and Velocity

Velocity is a vector; speed is the magnitude of that vector. In Chapter 3, "Game Math," we introduced vectors. If you're a linear reader, this concept may be fresh in your mind. But to review, vectors are mathematical objects that contain two pieces of information: a magnitude (also called a *scalar* value) and a direction. For instance, the velocity 30 kilometers per hour (kph) southeast is a vector. Its magnitude (the speed) is 30, and its direction is southeast.

Let's dig a little deeper into the definitions of these important concepts.

Speed: The ratio of distance covered and the time taken to cover this distance. Mathematically, this is written as the equation *speed = distance/time*. For example, if a car travels 30 kilometers in 2 hours, then its speed is 30 kilometers/2 hours = 15 kilometers/hour (see Figure 4.2).

FIGURE 4.2
Speed defined.

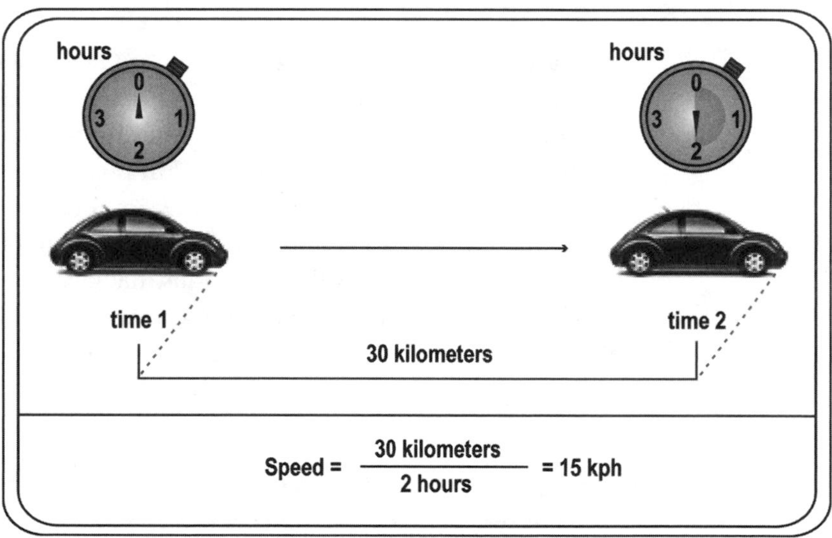

As defined previously, speed is distance divided by time. When you read "15 kilometers/hour," you say "15 kilometers per hour."

Velocity: A vector formed by combining speed with a direction.

Now let's see how to use this concept of speed and velocity to find the distance traveled in a certain amount of time. If we know the speed at which a car is traveling, how do we know how far it has traveled in, say, 3 hours? Previously, we said:

```
speed = distance/time
```

By doing simple algebra (multiplying both sides by *time*), we arrive at this equation:

```
distance = speed*time
```

With this equation, we can find how far a car (or any object) traveled if we know its speed and the amount of time it moved. In the same way, if we know how far the car traveled and the speed of the car, then we can calculate the travel time using the final permutation of this equation:

```
time = distance/speed
```

Applying Speed with ActionScript

So now you understand what speed and velocity are, and you understand that if you know any two of the following variables—speed, distance, or time—you can find the remaining value. In many games, you need to program movie clips (such as a ball, a car, or a rocket ship) to move. So how do you apply speed to a movie clip? You are about to find out.

We have been talking and thinking about speed as being measured in units of distance/time (distance divided by time). But Flash is not a time-based environment—it is a frame-based environment. To Flash users, one frame can be assumed to be one unit of time. So (as you'll see on your screen if all goes well), it is acceptable for us to replace every occurrence of a time variable in equations with a variable for frames. For instance, if *distance = speed×time*, then the new form is *distance = speed×frames*. (In other words, speed is no longer 10 miles/hour, it's 10 units/frame.) In Flash, we are going to change the definition of speed by replacing time with frames. So let's look at our definition of speed again, this time with our new twist:

Speed: The ratio of distance covered and the frames taken to cover this distance. Mathematically, this is written as the equation *speed = distance/frames*. For example, if a movie clip travels 30 units in two frames, then its speed is 30 units/2 frames = 15 units/frame.

As seen in this new definition, the unit of distance measurement is not meters but simply units, or pixels. (I prefer to use the word *unit* because if the Flash movie is scaled to a larger or smaller size, then unit is the only word that still applies.) At a scaled size, the pixel dimensions do not change, but the unit dimensions do.

To see a simple application of speed, open up car1.fla in the Chapter04 directory on the CD-ROM (see Figure 4.3). Notice that the frame rate has been set to 30 frames per second (fps) to ensure smooth playback. On the Stage, you'll see one movie clip with an instance name of `Car`. There are a few lines of ActionScript on frame 1 of the Actions layer that read as follows:

FIGURE 4.3
car1.fla.

Throughout the rest of the book, you'll see that I call all x direction speeds xmov and all y direction speeds ymov, or some variation of these basic names (such as tempxmov or xmov1).

```
var xmov:Number = 3;
_root.onEnterFrame = function() {
      car._x += xmov;
};
```

Line 1 sets a variable for the speed called xmov with a value of 3. Line 2 sets up an onEnterFrame clip event. All the actions listed within an onEnterFrame event are called one time in every frame. Line 3 is where we apply the speed to the object. It takes the current position of the car (car._x) and adds the value of the speed to it. Remember that the speed is units per frame, so a speed of 3 means that we will move the car along the *x*-axis three units in every frame.

Using the Best Frame Rate—30 fps

When making objects move around the screen using ActionScript, it is appropriate to consider your frame rate. The default frame rate in Flash is 12 fps. The human eye is fooled into thinking that objects are continuously moving when they are really just appearing at different places. Raising the frame rate increases the number of appearances per second, which makes for smoother-looking motion and fools the eye more successfully. The Flash Player will try hard to meet the frame rate at which you set your SWF, but if the processor speed combined with the intensity of your ActionScript is too much for the computer running the SWF, then the frame rate will go down while the movie is playing. So the key is to find a good frame rate that most computers can maintain at the intended speed. Through much experimentation and real-world experience, I have found that 30 fps works well for all games.

When you generate an SWF file to test this movie, you will see the car move relatively smoothly. Actually, the car is being redrawn in a new position 30 times per second. In that way, it's a lot like one of those flip books you might have had when you were a kid, with static images giving the illusion of movement. The frame rate is the vehicle (no pun intended) through which we trick the human eye into seeing what appears to be a continuously moving car, although the movement is actually happening in discrete chunks.

ActionScript Review: +=

The operator +=, used in the previous ActionScript example, is a shortcut that means "take what is on the left, add what is on the right, and then replace the original value with the result." For instance:

```
var x:Number = 2;
x += 3;
```

Now x has a value of 5. Alternatively, the second line could have been written as:

```
x = x + 3;
```

Now, what if you want to make this car move in two directions at once? To see how to add a second dimension, *y* speed, open car2.fla. This FLA file has the same setup as the previous example. The only difference is in the ActionScript. Open the Actions panel to view the ActionScript on frame 1.

```
1    var xmov:Number = 3;
2    var ymov:Number = 2;
3    _root.onEnterFrame = function() {
4        car._x += xmov;
5        car._y += ymov;
6    };
```

This differs from the ActionScript in the previous example by two lines of code. Line 2 defines a variable to represent the speed in the *y* direction, and line 5 controls the placement of the car by adding the value of ymov to the car's *y* position. This is done 30 times a second, so the result is what looks like a moving car (see Figure 4.4).

You may have already picked up on a visual problem in this case, though. The car is moving diagonally, but it's facing horizontally. To see how to get the car to face the correct direction, open car3.fla. You will notice that, once more, there are two new lines of code just before the onEnterFrame event. They are

```
var angle:Number = Math.atan2(ymov, xmov)*180/Math.PI;
car._rotation = angle;
```

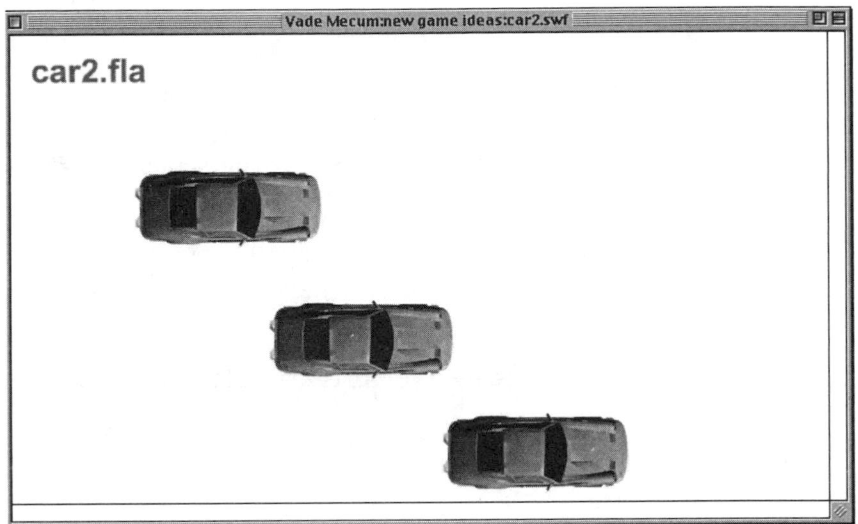

FIGURE 4.4
The car appears to move.

In short, line 1 calculates the angle that the car should be rotated, and line 2 rotates the car. Summoning up what we discussed in the previous chapter (remember trigonometry?), we know that we can use two sides of a right triangle to find the angle made by the trajectory of the car with the *x*-axis. The key is to think about the horizontal and vertical sides of the triangle as the ones made by `xmov` and `ymov`, respectively.

Before rotation, the car forms an angle of 0° with the *x*-axis. We must figure out how much the car needs to be rotated in order to point in the direction in which it is moving. Knowing the *x* side length (the x speed) and the *y* side length (the y speed), we can find the angle using the inverse tangent `Math.atan2()`. This returns an angle in radians—the angle we'll use to rotate the movie clip. To do this, we must use the `_rotation` property. Simple enough—but just to keep things interesting, the `_rotation` property only accepts angles in degrees! That's what's going on in line 1; we're converting the angle into degrees by multiplying by the conversion factor `180/Math.PI`.

For a slightly more advanced practical example, see shooter.fla in the Chapter04 directory on the CD-ROM.

Acceleration

Put quite simply, acceleration occurs whenever the velocity changes. Remember that velocity contains a speed and a direction, so if the speed *or* the direction of something changes, then it has accelerated.

Acceleration, like velocity, is a vector. It has a magnitude and a direction. More specifically, it's a vector with a magnitude that is 1) the ratio of the difference in velocity and the difference in time over which this difference occurred, and 2) the direction in which the acceleration occurred.

```
Acceleration = (velocity2 - velocity1)/(time2 - time1)
```

where *velocity2* is the velocity at *time2*, and *velocity1* is the velocity at *time1*. The units of acceleration are measured as distance/time^2 (see Figure 4.5).

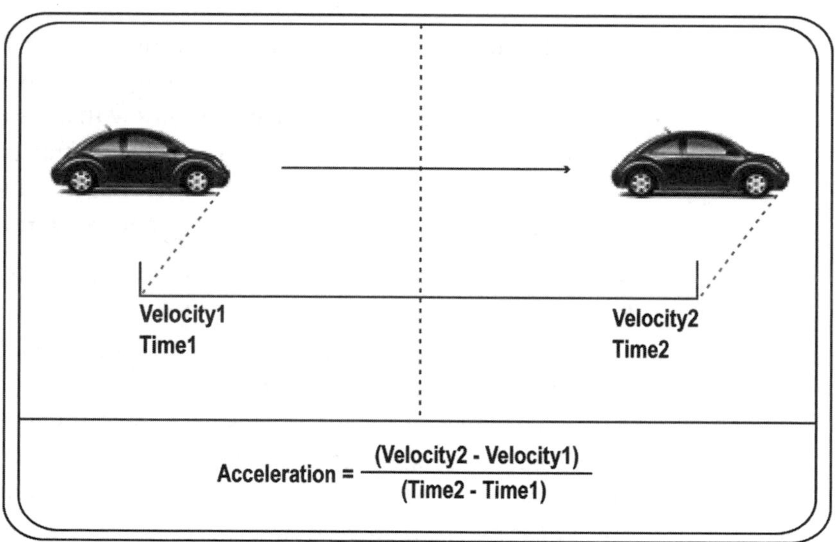

FIGURE 4.5
Acceleration.

If you know the acceleration of an object and its current velocity, then you can find or project the velocity of that object at any time in the future. Here is the equation to do this:

```
velocity_future = velocity_now + acceleration*time
```

The quantity *time* in this equation is how far into the future you are looking. Remember that both velocity and acceleration are vectors. In Flash, we must resolve vectors into their *x* and *y* components before we can use them. After we find the *xspeed, yspeed, xacceleration,* and *yacceleration* (using the techniques used in Chapter 3 and reintroduced earlier in this section), then we can write the following equations:

```
xspeed_future = xspeed_now + xacceleration*time
```

and

```
yspeed_future=yspeed_now + yacceleration*time
```

If you know the current position and velocity of an object, then you can find its position at any time in the future by using the following equations:

```
xposition_future = xposition_now + xspeed_now*time +
➥1/2*(xacceleration)*time²
```

and

```
yposition_future = yposition_now + yspeed_now*time +
➥1/2*(yacceleration)*time²
```

Applying Acceleration with ActionScript

The equations you've just been looking at may seem messy, but their application in Flash is quite easy. Remember that we can replace *time* with *frames* in all our equations. We will always be calculating new values for just one frame later. This is good news for us because it means we can replace the time with 1 everywhere. Using that trick, we can rewrite the four *x*- and *y*-component equations shown in the previous section.

For future speed:

```
xspeed_future = xspeed_now + xacceleration
```

and

```
yspeed_future = yspeed_now + yacceleration
```

For future position:

```
xposition_future = xposition_now + xspeed_now +
➥1/2*(xacceleration)
```

and

```
yposition_future = yposition_now + yspeed_now +
➥1/2*(yacceleration)
```

As you probably know, you cannot add two quantities that have different units. For instance, 10 meters plus 12 ounces makes…no sense. In these equations, we appear to be adding quantities that have different units (with apologies to any physicists, mathematicians, and engineers out there). What happened is that we dropped the frame variable from the equations. We're getting away with this because we assumed the value of the frame variable is always going to be 1 (see the previous paragraph), and because multiplying anything by 1 gives a result of the original value (3×1 = 3), then we just left out that factor. So if you were concerned about the units, you can now rest assured that things are consistent.

After all this theoretical discussion of acceleration, now it's time to apply it within the context of your games. To use acceleration in programming, here is what you should do.

1. Create a variable to contain the acceleration. For instance:

   ```
   var ace:Numberl = 2
   ```

2. Create initial velocity variables for the *x* and *y* directions. For instance:

   ```
   var xmov:Number = 0;
   var ymov:Number = 0;
   ```

3. When acceleration should be applied (such as when a certain key is being pressed), modify the speed. For instance:

   ```
   xmov += accel;
   ymov += accel;
   ```

4. For every frame, set the new position of the object.

   ```
   car._x += xmov;
   car._y += ymov;
   ```

Open up car4.fla from the Chapter04 directory on the CD-ROM. This is the next evolutionary step in the chain of car examples in this chapter. Here, the car starts with a slow initial speed and accelerates when the up arrow key is pressed. (As you might expect, when the down arrow key is pressed, the car decelerates.) Here is the ActionScript that accomplishes this.

```
var xmov:Number = 1;
var ymov:Number = 1;
var accel:Number = 2;
```

```
4     var angle:Number = Math.atan2(ymov, xmov)*180/Math.PI;
5     car._rotation = angle;
6     _root.onEnterFrame = function() {
7           if (Key.isDown(Key.UP)) {
8                 xmov += accel;
9                 ymov += accel;
10          } else if (Key.isDown(Key.DOWN)) {
11                xmov -= accel;
12                ymov -= accel;
13          }
14          car._x += xmov;
15          car._y += ymov;
16    };
```

Line 3 initializes the acceleration variable. Other than that, the only differences between this example and car3.fla are in lines 7–13. That's where the ActionScript dictates that if the up arrow key is pressed, then the xmov and ymov variables are increased by the value of the accel variable. If the down arrow key is pressed, then the xmov and ymov variables are decreased by the value of the accel variable.

ActionScript Review: *Key* class

The Key class lets you get information about the status of the keyboard. You can use this class to find out which key was pressed last, if a certain key is down now, if a certain key is toggled, and more.

The method of the Key class we will use most often for the games in this book is Key.isDown(keyCode), to detect which keys have been pressed by a user. (As you can imagine, capturing "key events" is going to be an important function in controlling games.) For example, Key.isDown(Key.LEFT) returns a Boolean value of true if the left arrow key is pressed, or a value of false if it is not. In a game where I want a character to move to the left every time the user presses the left arrow button, I check for this situation in every frame.

Every key on the keyboard has a corresponding numeric key code that must be passed in to get a result, but some of the keys have premade "verbose" shortcuts that you can also pass in. The ones we will use most frequently are Key.UP, Key.DOWN, Key.LEFT, Key.RIGHT, Key.SPACE, and Key.SHIFT.

Newton's Three Laws of Motion

A chapter about physics would not be complete without discussing Newton's three laws of motion. Sir Isaac Newton (1642–1727), a brilliant physicist and the father of calculus, developed—among other things—three fundamental laws of motion. Only one of these laws, the second, will we actually apply with ActionScript. However, we will discuss all three because knowledge of these "basic" facts may help you to solve some programming problems within your games.

Newton's First Law

At some point in your life, you may have heard something to the effect of, "A body at rest tends to stay at rest; a body in motion tends to stay in motion." Although this is not a complete description, it is the gist of Newton's first law of motion. This law is best understood with the concept of *systems*. A system is anything—any entity, whether it contains one or one million objects—you want to study. For instance, a baseball can be a system. A roomful of people can be a system (as can the room itself, if that's what you're studying). Even an entire planet can be a system.

For the sake of understanding this law, let's take the example of an astronaut floating with no velocity in space (see Figure 4.6). No matter what he does, he cannot move his *center of gravity* (a point by which you can measure his real position). He can kick his legs and wave his arms, but his velocity is not going to change. There is only one possible way he could move from that position: He'd need to have another system apply a force to him, such as gravity from a planet. With this example in mind, let's take a look at Newton's first law:

The velocity of a system will not change unless it experiences a net external force.

This law does not directly apply to your Flash applications. However, understanding it can help you if you find yourself struggling through conceptual programming problems.

FIGURE 4.6
The astronaut cannot move himself.

Newton's Second Law

Newton's first law assumes a system that will not change its velocity unless a net external force is applied to it. That begs the question, what is the acceleration (change in velocity) when a net external force *is* applied? Newton's second law answers this question.

The acceleration of an object is inversely proportional to its mass and proportional to the net external force applied.

Mathematically, this is written as follows:

```
net force = mass*acceleration
```

or, as most people see it:

```
F = m*a
```

where *F* is force, *m* is mass, and *a* is acceleration. The net force is the sum of all the force vectors.

This is an immensely handy equation. You can sum all of the forces acting on an object (the net force), and from that sum determine its acceleration. What does this mean for you, and when would you need it? It means that when you have found the acceleration of an object, you can use it with the equations of motion to move the object around on the screen.

As an example, open balloon.fla from the Chapter04 directory on the CD. In this file, I've applied two forces to a balloon of mass = 1: a gravitational force of 30 (its weight) and a buoyant force of -31 (the force that makes a helium balloon rise) (see Figure 4.7).

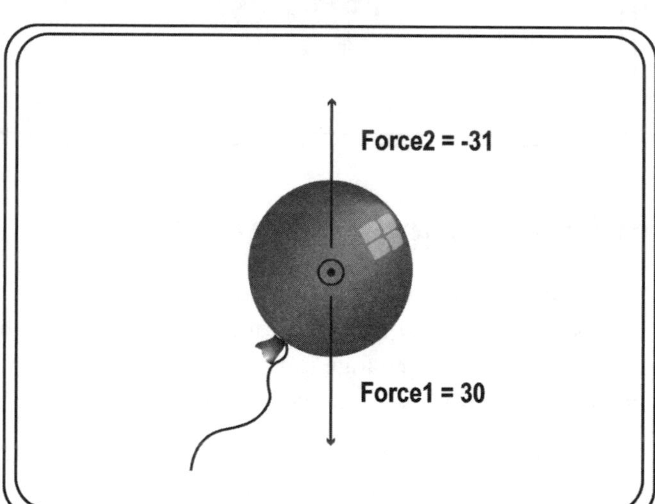

FIGURE 4.7
A balloon with two forces applied.

Notice that the buoyant force is a negative number. This indicates that the force is pointing in the -*y* direction (also known as "up"). The goal is to code this in such a way that the balloon moves in the correct direction. To move the balloon, we need to know its acceleration. To find its acceleration, we use Newton's second law. The simple process to find the acceleration is as follows:

1. Sum all of the forces. In this case, *netForce* = *force1* + *force2*.
2. Solve for the acceleration. Because *netForce* = *mass***accel*, then *accel* = *netForce*/*mass*.

Let's take a look at the ActionScript for the single movie clip in this file (in the Actions layer):

```
1    var ymov:Number = 0;
2    var mass:Number = 1;
3    //weight, the downward force
4    var force1:Number = 30;
5    //bouyancy, the upward force
6    var force2:Number = -31;
7    //total force
8    var netForce:Number = force1+force2;
9    //Newton's second law applied to find the acceleration
10   var yaccel:Number = netForce/mass;
11   _root.onEnterFrame = function() {
12          ymov += yaccel;
13          balloon._y += ymov;
14   };
```

The first thing you'll notice is that all the forces are only in the *y* direction. That means we only need to deal with movement in the *y* direction. In line 2, we set the mass variable. (I've just chosen an arbitrary value of 1.) We then define force1 and force2. In line 8, the forces are summed to arrive at a net force. We then apply Newton's second law in line 10. After the acceleration is found in line 10, everything else deals with moving the object and should be familiar from the section "Speed, Velocity, and Acceleration."

When you test the movie, you can see that because the buoyant force has a greater magnitude than the gravitational force, the balloon floats up.

I hope you can see the power of this law. With it, you can create a complicated situation with an unlimited number of forces acting on an unlimited number of objects. By summing the forces on an object, you can find its acceleration. Even if the situation is complex, the math remains simple—you just keep applying it to the parts until you have solved for all the variables.

Terminal Velocity

In the rising-balloon example we've been using in this section, the balloon accelerates with no upper limit. This means that the balloon will rise faster and faster and will never reach a maximum velocity (except the speed of light, of course). In real life, we know that we are surrounded by atmosphere and that the atmosphere must have a certain amount of effect on us. As a balloon rises, you know it's going to encounter wind resistance (from the atmosphere), which will oppose (or at least affect) its acceleration. No simple equation exists to calculate the force of the wind resistance because it depends on several factors. What you should know, though, is that eventually the wind-resistance force will be so large that the sum of all the forces on the balloon will be 0, and then no further acceleration will take place. At that point, the balloon is traveling upward at its maximum velocity. This is called *terminal velocity*. In games, such as some of those presented later in this book, it's good to set an upper limit to the speed of your objects so they can't move so fast that you can't keep up with them. This upper limit is, of course, subjective, and depends on the game, the object, and the frame rate.

We will add our own terminal velocities just by using simple `if` statements to see if the velocity is too great.

How fast is too fast? An object is moving too fast when game play is no longer fun!

Newton's Third Law

You probably don't think much about physics as you move through your everyday activities, but those activities actually afford lots of examples and physics "problems" to ponder. Here's one: When you sit on a chair, you don't fall through it. Why not? Because while you are exerting a force on the chair (your weight), the chair is also exerting a force on you in the opposite direction. You may have heard of Newton's third law:

For every action, there is an equal and opposite reaction.

Action: You apply a force to a chair by sitting on it. Reaction: The chair exerts a force on you equal to that of your weight but opposite in direction (see Figure 4.8).

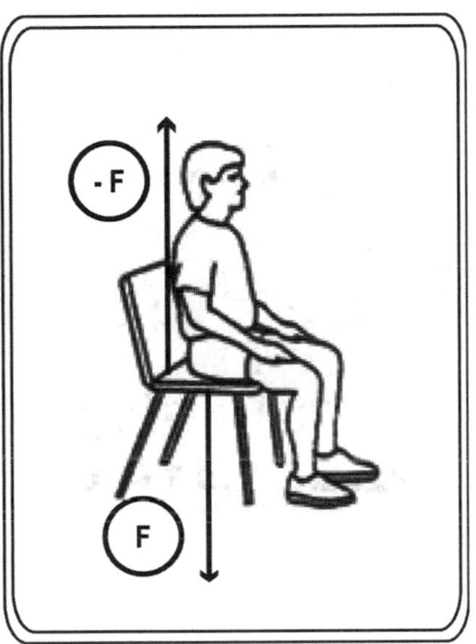

FIGURE 4.8
You exert force on the chair, and the chair exerts force on you.

If you're like most people, you are probably now trying to imagine a situation where this does not hold up. But you can't! Try this one on for size: If a baseball is falling toward the earth, the earth is applying a force (its weight) to the baseball. What you may not have realized is that the baseball is applying an equal but opposite force on the earth. The result is that the ball and the earth accelerate toward each other (yes, the ball does move the earth—however small the amount may be).

As with Newton's first law, there is no immediate application of this law in your physics programming. However, if you are trying to code something physical in Flash that is not discussed in this book, then figuring out the logic involved may be easier with the help of this law.

Gravity

Gravitational forces are what keep you on the ground and the planets in motion around the sun. Newton postulated that every particle in the universe exerts a force on every other particle in the universe. Massive bodies, such as planets, have an enormous number of particles. All of these particles attract each other and attract you as well. In this section, we're going to discuss two ways to treat gravity mathematically: the "right" way and the "good-enough" way.

Real Gravity

The gravitational force experienced by two objects is calculated by using the equation

```
F = G*(mass1*mass2)/distance²
```

F is the force felt by either object (remember Newton's third law—equal but opposite). The value G is called the *constant of universal gravitation*. For mathematical reasons having to do with absorbing constants into other constants (I hope you'll take my word for this one), we can just assume that G has a value of 1. The value *distance* is the distance between the centers of the two objects (see Figure 4.9).

FIGURE 4.9
Real gravity.

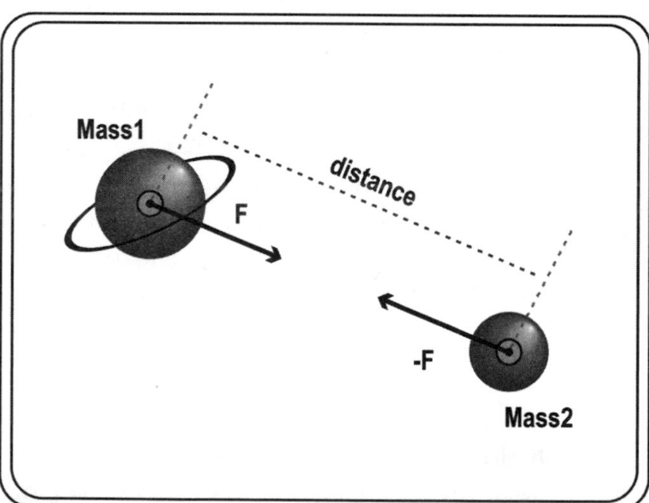

You are most likely never going to need to apply this realistic treatment of gravity in your games. However, if you would like to see a working example of this in Flash, then take a look at a Flash 5 experiment of mine in realGravity.fla in the Chapter04 directory. The ActionScript in realGravity.fla handles collision detection, collision reaction, and gravity.

Good-Enough Gravity

As I mentioned at the beginning of this chapter, sometimes a simplified formula will do for our gaming purposes as well as the complicated, "real" physics that I paid a lot of money to learn about in graduate school. We have come to one of those times now. If you've been worrying about having to work through the gravity equations, you'll be happy to hear that an easy way exists to add a gravity effect to your games: Simply come up with a value for gravity—let's say 2—and then add that value to your *y* velocity in every frame.

To see an example of this, open bounce.fla in the Chapter04 directory on the CD-ROM. In this file, I've affected a ball's velocity using faked gravity. I've also added a simple collision-detection trick so that the ball doesn't fall through the floor (we'll talk more about that in Chapter 5, "Collision Detection" and Chapter 6, "Collision Reactions"). Here is the ActionScript:

```
1     var ymov:Number = 0;
2     //set gravity
3     var gravity:Number = 2;
4     _root.onEnterFrame = function() {
5           ymov += gravity;
6           ball._y += ymov;
7           if (ball._y>400) {
8                 ball._y = 400;
9                 ymov *= -1;
10          }
11    };
```

As you can see in line 5, gravity is used to change the ball's velocity in the same way that acceleration was used to do this. In lines 7 through 10, we check to see if the ball is below 400 (which is the height of the floor on the Stage in this movie). If so, then it is off the screen, and we set its position back to 400 and reverse the *y* velocity, ymov. The final result is a ball that bounces in place.

Friction

Why do objects slow down? Because they are losing energy. Objects that slow down from the interaction with another object lose energy through heat. This heat is caused by the interaction between the two materials. If this sounds familiar, it probably should—what we're talking about here is friction.

Put in more technical terms, a frictional force is one that opposes the direction of motion and is caused by the interaction between two materials. Kinetic energy—the energy associated with the momentum of an object—is lost as heat from the friction, and the object slows down. For instance, when you are driving your car and slam on the brakes (OK, even if you don't actually slam them), the car uses friction to its advantage and slides to a stop. If you then feel the temperature of the tires, you will notice that they are hot. (We'll discuss kinetic energy further in Chapter 6.)

In Flash MX, there are two ways to treat friction: the right way and the good-enough way. In this section, we'll discuss both.

Real Friction

If you slide an object to the right across the floor, then a frictional force points to the left, opposing the velocity vector (see Figure 4.10). The velocity of the box will approach 0 with a constant deceleration. The equation for sliding friction is

```
F = u*mass*gravity
```

The quantity *mass*gravity* is the weight of the object. So the greater the object's weight, the greater the friction that will oppose the motion of the sliding object. The *u* factor is known as the *frictional coefficient* (also sometimes called the coefficient of sliding friction).

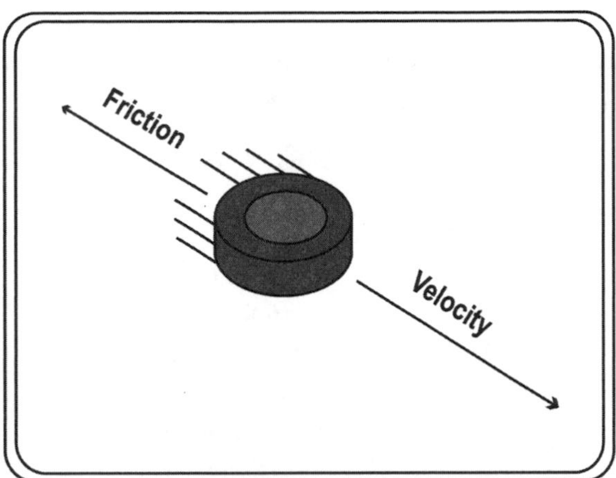

FIGURE 4.10
Frictional force.

A frictional coefficient is a numerical value between 0 and 1. In real life, this factor is found by experimentation and is different for each surface-object interaction. For instance, a wet ice cube on a rubber floor may have a very low frictional coefficient (.01), whereas a tennis shoe on the same floor may have a higher frictional coefficient (.2). In ActionScript, you can simply choose a value for *u* depending on the type of surface you are dealing with.

Using Newton's second law, we can determine the deceleration due to friction:

```
F = mass*accel = u*mass*gravity
```

Canceling out the *mass* on both sides, we get:

```
accel = u*gravity
```

This *accel* variable will be used with the velocity equations we have been working with. Here are the steps you use to apply friction:

1. Find the acceleration due to friction using the equation *accel=u*gravity*.

Remember that negative acceleration is deceleration.

2. Apply the *accel* value to the velocity in every frame (just as we have been doing with acceleration) until the velocity reaches 0.

Stop applying the variable when the velocity reaches 0. If you don't, the object will actually move in the opposite direction.

To see this in action, open roll.fla in the Chapter04 directory. In this file, we have a ball moving in the *x* direction. It is slowed to a stop by friction. Here is the ActionScript used:

```
1	var xmov:Number = 10;
2	var gravity:Number = 2;
3	var u:Number = .2;
4	var accel:Number = u*gravity;
5	_root.onEnterFrame = function() {
6		if (Math.abs(xmov)>=Math.abs(accel)) {
7			if (xmov>0) {
8				xmov -= accel;
9			} else if (xmov<0) {
10				xmov += accel;
11			}
12		} else {
13			xmov=0;
14		}
15		ball._x+=xmov;
16	};
```

In line 1, we give the ball an initial velocity so that it has something to slide to a stop from. We then define a gravity variable and the friction constant `u`. In line 4, we use the gravity and the friction constant to find the value of the acceleration due to the friction. The `if` statements in the `onEnterFrame` event are there to make sure that we either add or subtract the acceleration correctly (depending on the direction of motion). The `if` statement also controls what happens to the ball if the velocity is less than the acceleration; if that is true, then in the next frame, the ball should be stopped.

Good-Enough Friction

Although the method discussed in the previous section is the correct way to handle frictional forces, it can be a little confusing and clunky with all those `if` statements. Here is a faster and easier way to handle friction and achieve a very similar look.

1. Choose a number between 0 and 1. Let's call this number the decay.
2. Multiply the decay by the velocity in every frame.

That's it!

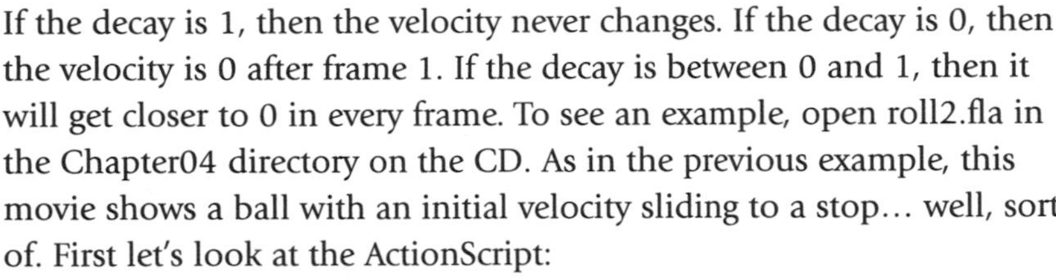

If the decay is 1, then the velocity never changes. If the decay is 0, then the velocity is 0 after frame 1. If the decay is between 0 and 1, then it will get closer to 0 in every frame. To see an example, open roll2.fla in the Chapter04 directory on the CD. As in the previous example, this movie shows a ball with an initial velocity sliding to a stop... well, sort of. First let's look at the ActionScript:

```
var xmov:Number = 10;
var decay:Number = .95;
_root.onEnterFrame = function() {
      xmov *= decay;
      ball._x += xmov;
};
```

As you can see, this is a much simpler way to treat friction (which probably explains why it's also the most commonly used method). The result is a ball that slides from an initial velocity to almost 0 velocity. It is important to note that no matter how many times you multiply a non-zero number by a non-zero number, you will never get zero. This one of the pitfalls of using this method. Later in the book, when we get into some more specific situations with velocity, we will discuss some ways to make the ball stop when a minimum velocity is reached.

To sum up the differences between real friction and good-enough friction, as shown in the examples in the previous sections, the correct frictional implementation decreases the velocity linearly—that is, by the same amount in every frame. The good-enough method decreases the velocity by a percentage of the current velocity—a nonlinear decrease. In most circumstances, the difference between these is not going to be worth the amount of coding you'd have to put into the ActionScript to arrive at the "correct" implementation.

This chapter introduced topics that will be used frequently throughout the book, including velocity, acceleration, gravity, and friction. So don't think you've read the last on physics; you will learn more about physics in Chapter 6.

POINTS TO REMEMBER

- Physics is the study of the behavior of objects in nature on the most fundamental level.
- Understanding basic physical laws and how to apply them is the key to creating dynamic realism in games.
- Velocity is a vector formed by combining speed with a direction.
- Acceleration—also a vector—occurs whenever the velocity changes.
- If you know the acceleration of an object and its current velocity, you can find or project the velocity of that object at any time in the future.
- Although in the real world we generally think of speed as being measured in units of distance/time, in Flash we think of speed as being measured by frames. So Flash users usually assume one frame to be one unit of time.
- When looking for the balance between creating smooth-appearing motion and not overtaxing the processors of most computers, 30 frames per second seems to offer the best results.
- The amazingly simple trick for applying "good-enough" gravity to your effects is to come up with a value for gravity and add that value to your *y* velocity in every frame.
- A frictional force is one that opposes the direction of motion and is caused by the interaction between two materials—in other words, it slows something down.
- Kinetic energy—the energy associated with the momentum of an object—is lost as heat from friction, causing an object to slow down.
- "Real" frictional implementation decreases the velocity linearly; "good-enough" friction decreases the velocity by a percentage of the current velocity (nonlinearly).
- In most circumstances, the difference between "real" frictional implementation and "good-enough" frictional implementation is not going to be worth the amount of coding you'd have to put into the ActionScript to arrive at the "correct" implementation.

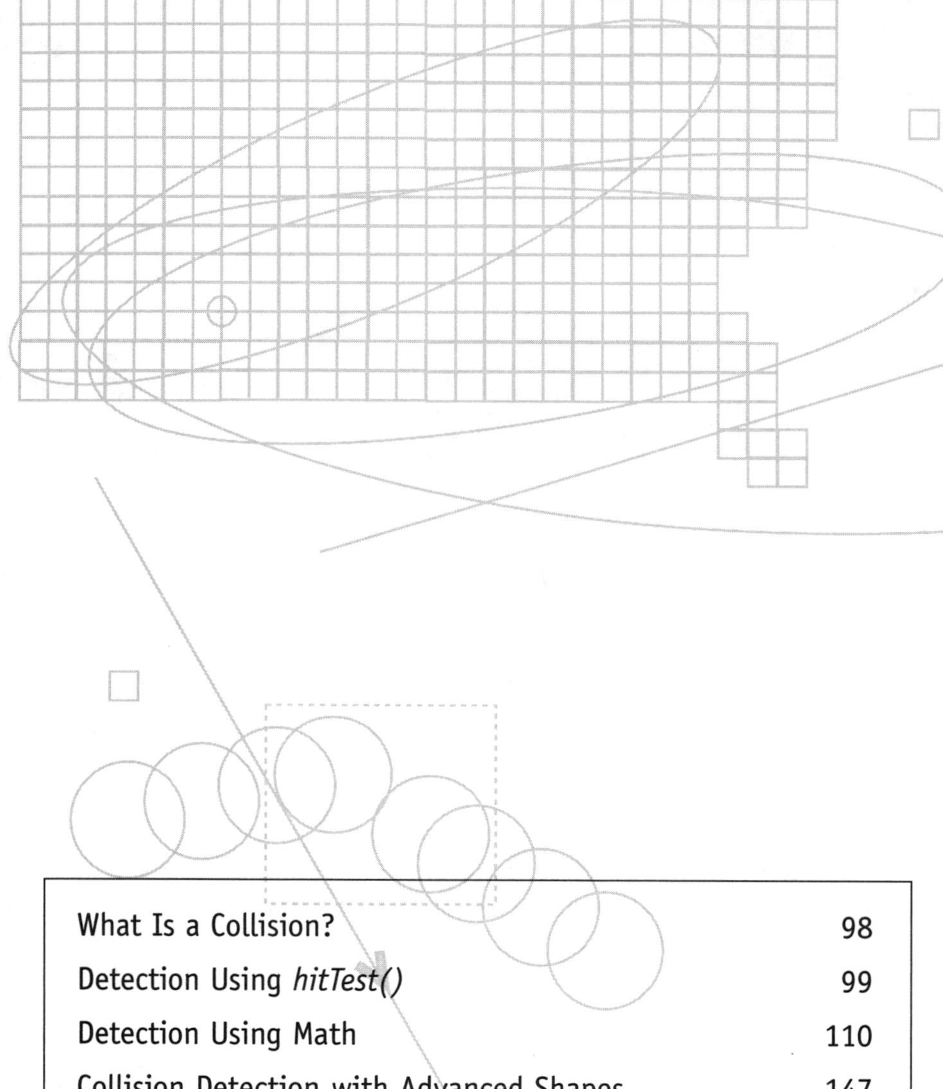

What Is a Collision? 98

Detection Using *hitTest()* 99

Detection Using Math 110

Collision Detection with Advanced Shapes 147

Points to Remember 148

CHAPTER 5

Collision Detection

When you're playing a computerized game of pinball or a platform game like *Super Mario Brothers*, you probably take it for granted that it has realistic-looking reactions. In pinball, the ball gets hit by the flippers and zooms away; in a platform game, the character lands on a platform or falls to the ground. One important thing must happen before any of these realistic reactions can take place: A collision must occur and be detected. (OK, that's *two* things.) When the collision is detected, a reaction can take place—we'll get into that in the next chapter. In this chapter, we'll discuss the ins and outs of collision detection, using both `hitTest()`, a method of the `MovieClip` class that is sometimes useful for this purpose, and math, which is where the real power lies. We will also address the limitations of collision detection in Macromedia Flash and how you can get around them.

What Is a Collision?

Before learning how to program collision-detection scripts, it is important to understand what a collision is. I know what it sounds like—something big and crashy. Of course in a lot of cases that's true, but for our purposes, we need to get down to a more basic definition. Put simply, a collision happens when two separate shapes share one or more points in space. For instance, imagine two circles touching at their edges, such as two billiard balls resting against each other (see Figure 5.1). These two circles share one point; hence, in physics terms they are *colliding*. Some collisions are simple, such as when the mouse pointer overlaps a movie clip or a button. Other collisions are complicated, such as when a ball bounces off an angled line.

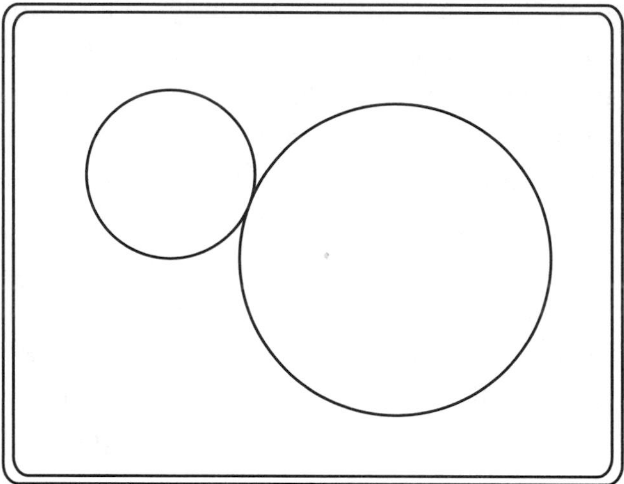

FIGURE 5.1
The two shapes share points, creating a collision.

In this chapter we'll cover several of the most common types of collision detection, including those having to do with intersections or collisions of lines with lines, circles with lines, and rectangles with other rectangles (See Figure 5.2).

As I mentioned earlier, two main types of programmatic collision detection are used in Flash: the use of the `hitTest()` method of the `MovieClip` class and the use of math to determine if a collision has occurred.

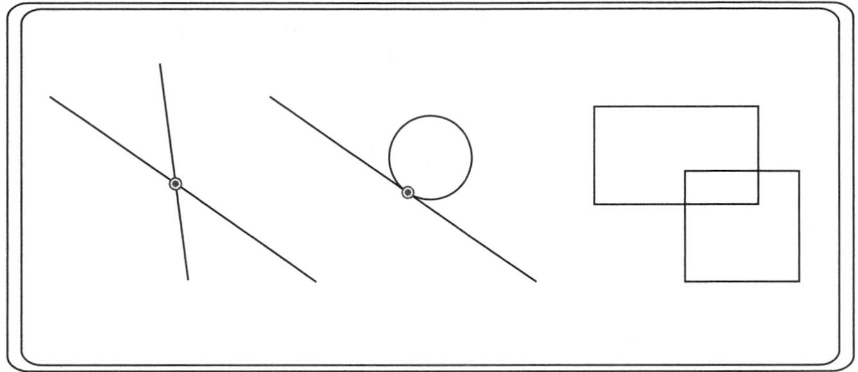

FIGURE 5.2
More collision examples.

As you will see from what follows in this chapter, `hitTest()` has its uses but is vastly inferior to collision-detection scripts that use math. By using math to determine collisions, not only can you determine if a collision is happening, but in some cases you can also tell if a collision is *about* to happen, and at precisely which position this collision will occur. We need this level of precision for some of the more advanced types of games, such as pinball or billiards. But first, let's see what we can wring out of `hitTest()`.

DETECTION USING *HITTEST()*

As you probably know, Flash's `MovieClip` class contains many methods and properties that assist in working with movie clips. When a movie clip is created, either in the authoring environment or with ActionScript, it inherits all the methods and properties of the `MovieClip` class. These methods and properties are then available to this new movie-clip instance.

We can use the `hitTest()` method of the `MovieClip` class to detect collisions in three simple scenarios. But before we discuss these three types of collisions, I'll introduce you to a new term: *bounding box*. Bounding box refers to the imaginary box that encloses everything in a movie clip (see Figure 5.3). If you have a movie clip with a circle in it, then the bounding box for this movie clip is a square that is exactly big enough to fit the circle, with each side of the box touching the circle. Likewise, if you have an irregular shape or multiple shapes within a movie clip, then the bounding box will be made up of a rectangle that touches the uppermost piece in the movie clip, the leftmost piece in the movie clip, the rightmost piece in the movie clip, and the lowest piece in the movie clip.

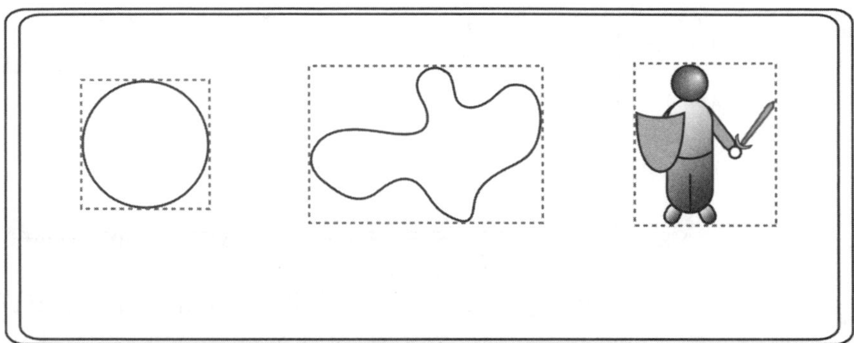

FIGURE 5.3
Bounding boxes are boxes that surround everything in a movie clip.

Now that you have an understanding of the bounding box of a movie clip, we can explain the three types of collision detection that are possible using `hitTest()`.

Movie Clip-Movie Clip Collisions

This type of collision detection determines if the bounding boxes of two movie clips are overlapping. The shapes within the movie clips may or may not be touching, but as long as the two bounding boxes are, then a collision has occurred (see Figure 5.4).

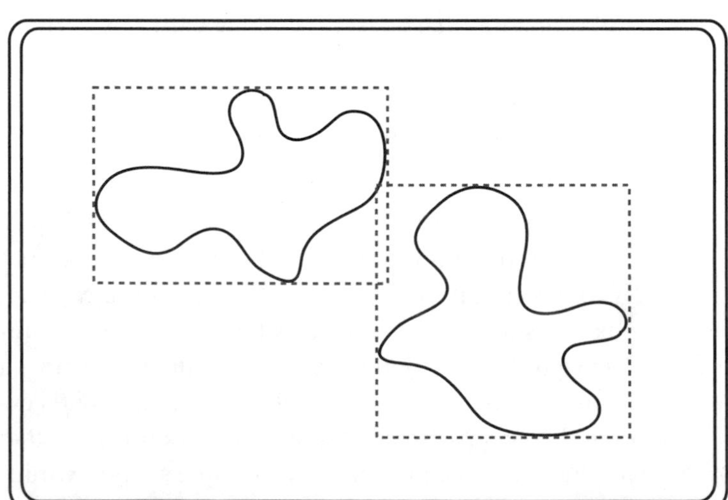

FIGURE 5.4
The bounding boxes touch, so a collision occurs.

Now let's delve into the ActionScript involved. Because `hitTest()` is a method of the `MovieClip` class, it can be applied only to a movie clip (as opposed to any other kind of object, such as a graphic or a text field). Following is the syntax for using `hitTest()` to determine if two movie clips are colliding:

```
myMovieClip.hitTest(target_MovieClip)
```

This line of ActionScript starts with the instance name of a movie clip. After the instance name, the `hitTest()` method is invoked by passing in a parameter. The value of that parameter is the instance name of another movie clip. Translated into English, this line of ActionScript would become a question that would read something like this: "Is the bounding box of `myMovieClip` colliding with the bounding box of `target_MovieClip`?"

When this line of ActionScript is executed, Flash gives you an answer to that question. In English you would expect the answer to be "yes" or "no"; in ActionScript, the answer is `true` (yes) or `false` (no).

Open movieclip_movieclip.fla in the Chapter05 directory on the CD to see an example. In this FLA file we have two movie clips—shape1 and shape2. This file has been programmed so that shape1 will move to the right, and during every frame, it checks to see if a collision occurrs between shape1 and shape2. If a collision is happening, then we simply execute a trace action to indicate that the collision is happening. Here is the ActionScript used.

The trace action is purely for testing and debugging purposes. If you type **trace ("My name is Jobe and I'm a geek.")** in the Flash MX Actions panel and then test the movie, you'll see that message appear in the Output window. Trace actions are only displayed in test-movie mode in the Flash environment, never in a web page or in the stand-alone SWF file.

```
var xmov:Number = 3;
_root.onEnterFrame = function () {
      shape1._x += xmov;
      if (shape1.hitTest(shape2)) {
            trace("They are colliding!!");
      }
}
```

The collision and the result of the trace action can be seen in Figure 5.5.

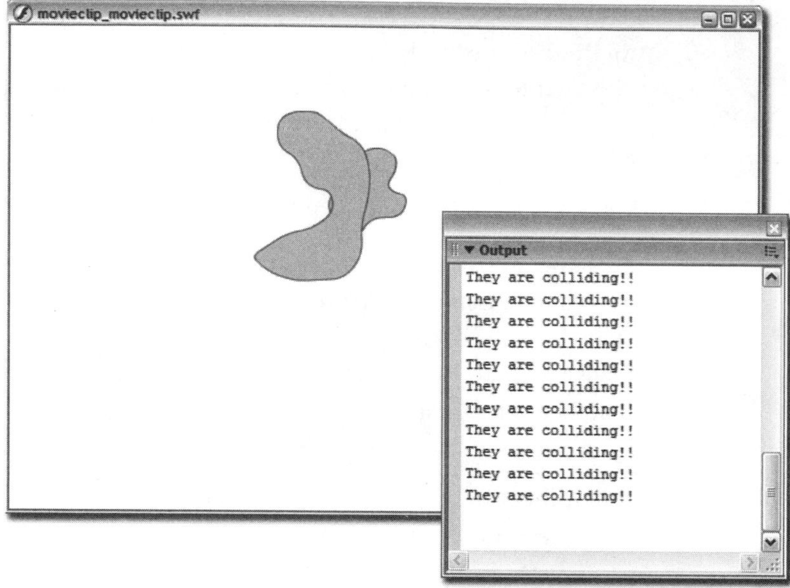

FIGURE 5.5
The results of the trace action can be seen in the Output window.

You can see that we start out moving `shape1` in the same way we introduced in Chapter 4, "Basic Physics"; first a speed variable, `xmov`, is set, and then the position is updated in every frame. We start introducing new ActionScript on the fourth line. This is a conditional statement: If the `hitTest()` method returns a value of `true`, then the condition is fulfilled and the trace action is executed; otherwise nothing happens.

Here is that same conditional statement converted to words: "If the bounding box of `shape1` collides with the bounding box of `shape2`, then put 'They are colliding!!' in the Output window."

For a more practical example, you can check out ball_falling.fla in the Chapter05 directory on the CD. There are two movie clips in this file—ball and floor. Using gravity (as covered in Chapter 4), the ball falls. In every frame, we check for a collision between it and the floor. If `hitTest()` returns a value of `true`, then the velocity of the ball is reversed and the ball goes back up. Generate an SWF to test the file. (The quickest way to do this is to press Ctrl-Enter in Windows or Command-Return on the Mac.) Note that if you run the file for 30 seconds or so, the ball gets stuck in the floor. This is due to one of the limitations of `hitTest()`, which we'll discuss in the "Detection Using Math" section of this chapter.

Movie Clip-Point Collisions

The hitTest() method lets you determine if a point (x, y) is within the bounding box of a movie clip. This can be handy in specific game situations. Usually these are times when the mouse is involved. Simple click-and-destroy–style games make use of this type of collision detection. For example, let's take a balloon game. If the user clicks the mouse when it's positioned over a balloon (see Figure 5.6), then the balloon pops. This is the easiest way to find out if the mouse is over a movie clip without using a button. However, most click-and-destroy games are created with buttons. For that reason, in our opinion, the movie-clip–point method of detection doesn't have many effective uses in games.

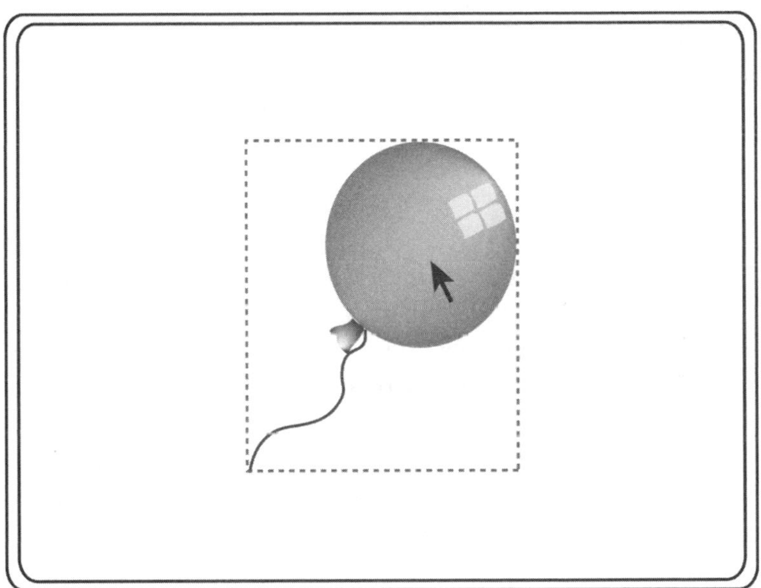

FIGURE 5.6
The mouse pointer over a balloon.

Here is the syntax for using the hitTest() method to determine if a point is colliding with the bounding box of a movie clip:

```
myMovieClip.hitTest(x, y, shapeFlag)
you should show it the way the docs do:
myMovieClip.hitTest(x, y, shapeFlag)
```

And here's the English translation: "Does the point with coordinates of x and y fall within the bounding box of myMovieClip?"

Just ignore the shapeFlag parameter for now. This will be discussed later.

As in the previous section, the answer to this question—that is, the result of the line of ActionScript—is going to be true or false.

To see this in action, open the file balloon_pop.fla from the Chapter05 directory on the CD. You'll see a movie clip containing an image of a balloon on the Stage. This movie clip has an instance name of balloon. The ActionScript on frame 1 in the Actions layer that executes when the mouse is clicked. This script then determines if the mouse is over the balloon clip, and if so, the balloon is "told" to explode. Here is the ActionScript used to accomplish this.

```
1     _root.onMouseDown = function () {
2           var mx:Number = _xmouse;
3           var my:Number = _ymouse;
4           if (balloon.hitTest(mx, my)) {
5                 balloon.play();
6           }
7     }
```

In line 1 of this script, we define a function that will be called when the mouse button is pressed down (and not yet released). When this happens, two variables are set—mx and my—to store the *x* and *y* positions of the mouse. Then, in line 4, we use an if statement to determine if the mouse is within the bounding box of the balloon clip. To satisfy this conditional statement, the statement balloon.hitTest(mx, my) must return a result of true, confirming the "collision" of the pointer and the balloon. If the condition is satisfied, then line 5 is executed, and the movie clip called balloon plays a popping animation (see Figure 5.7).

The popping animation was created inside of the balloon movie clip. The first frame of that movie clip shows the balloon in its unpopped state. The frames after that show the balloon popping. The final frame in the animation is blank.

The idea used in balloon_pop.fla can be extended easily to apply to any number of movie clips. To see such an expanded example, open balloon_pop_many.fla from the Chapter05 folder on the CD. In this file, the number of balloons that will be displayed is controlled by a variable. There's a movie clip in the Library, again called balloon, whose

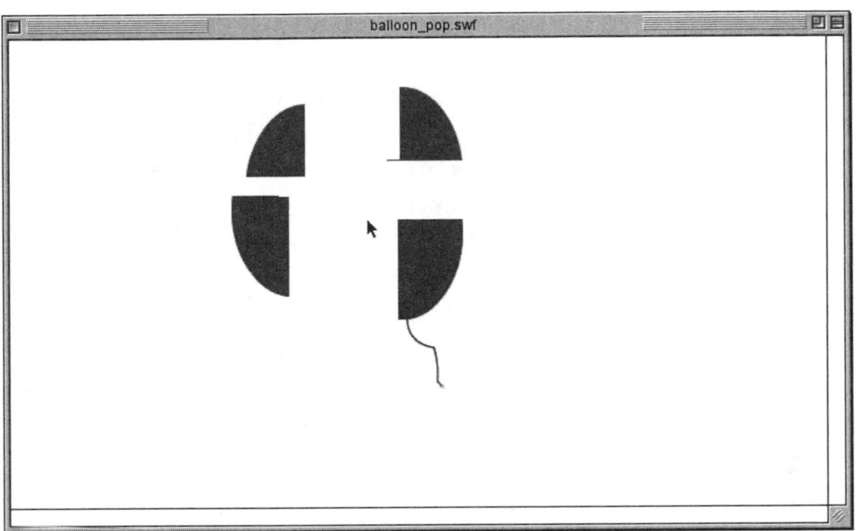

FIGURE 5.7
The balloon pops.

linkage identifier is also named balloon (see the sidebar "ActionScript Review: attachMovie() and Linkage Identifiers" if this is new to you). With the linkage specified, we can attach the balloon clip to the Stage (that is, create new copies of it) as many times as we want. When the mouse button is clicked, we can loop through all the balloons on the screen using ActionScript, performing a hitTest() on each balloon, to determine if there are any collisions between the mouse and the balloon. Here is the ActionScript used in this example.

```
//Number of balloons to be created
var totalBalloons:Number = 10;
//Set the dimensions of the screen so that we can randomly place the balloons
var screenWidth:Number = 700;
var screenHeight:Number = 400;
//Create and place the balloon instances on the stage
for (var i = 0; i<totalBalloons; ++i) {
      var name = "balloon"+i;
      _root.attachMovie("balloon", name, i);
      var x:Number = random(screenWidth);
      var y:Number = random(screenHeight);
      _root[name]._x = x;
      _root[name]._y = y;
}
```

```
15      _root.onMouseDown = function() {
16           var mx:Number = _xmouse;
17           var my:Number = _ymouse;
18           //Loop through all of the balloons looking for
             ➥collisions
19           for (var i = 0; i<totalBalloons; ++i) {
20                var name:String = "balloon"+i;
21                if (_root[name].hitTest(mx,my)) {
22                     _root[name].play();
23                }
24           }
25      };
```

The second line of code above sets a variable called `totalBalloons`. The value of this variable determines how many balloons will be created and placed on the Stage. Lines 4–14 create and place the balloons on the Stage. Lines 19-24 contain an ActionScript loop that checks for a collision with each balloon. The balloons that are created (from lines 4–14) are named sequentially (`balloon0`, `balloon1`, `balloon2`, and so on). In this loop, we dynamically re-create the name of each balloon and use these names to reference the movie clips, checking to see if a movie clip of the same name has a `hitTest()` of `true` with the position of the mouse. For instance, if the loop is on iteration 12, then the name created is `balloon12`. Because the value of name is "balloon12," the action `_root[name]` is equivalent to writing `_root.balloon12`. This is how the references to the movie clips are created dynamically in these loops.

ActionScript Review: *attachMovie()* and Linkage Identifiers

With ActionScript, you can create a new instance on the Stage of a movie clip that is in the Flash file's Library. Many effects are accomplished this way, such as creating an endless supply of bullets from a gun. For ActionScript to pull a movie clip from the Library, the clip must be configured properly. This is very easy. Open the Library panel, find the movie clip you want to make available, right-click (Windows) or Control-click (Mac) it, and select Linkage from the contextual menu. In the Linkage Properties dialog box, make sure the box next to Export for ActionScript is checked, and then type an identifier name. The identifier is how you tell Flash which movie clip you want to attach. Then, to attach a movie clip, simply use the following action:

```
path.attachMovie(linkage_identifier, new_instance_name,
➥depth)
```

For instance,

```
_root.attachMovie("balloon", "balloon2", 2);
```

ActionScript Review: *for* Loops

Loops are an immeasurably helpful ActionScript feature. With them, you can perform the same actions as many times as you want. This is particularly useful for doing the same thing to many movie clips. For instance, if you have pictures on the Stage named picture1 through picture30 and you want to make them all invisible, you can create a simple for loop to do so:

```
for (var i=0; i<=29; ++i) {
        var name = "picture"+i;
        this[name]._visible = false;
}
```

The for loop accepts three parameters. The first parameter (in this case, var i=0) specifies a starting place. The second parameter (i<=29) is a condition that must be fulfilled to continue looping. If this condition is no longer fulfilled, then the loop ends. The third parameter (++i) increments the variable so that the loop will end at some point. If the loop variable is not incremented, then the condition will always be satisfied, and the loop will never end.

Shape-Point Collisions

With the previous two types of collision detection, we saw that a collision happens with the actual bounding box of a movie clip. One other way to use the hitTest() method is to detect a collision between a point and the contents of the movie clip, not just the bounding box, as depicted in Figure 5.8. Imagine a movie clip that contains several separate graphics or shapes. Using the `hitTest()` method, we can tell if a point is colliding with any one of the shapes in this movie clip.

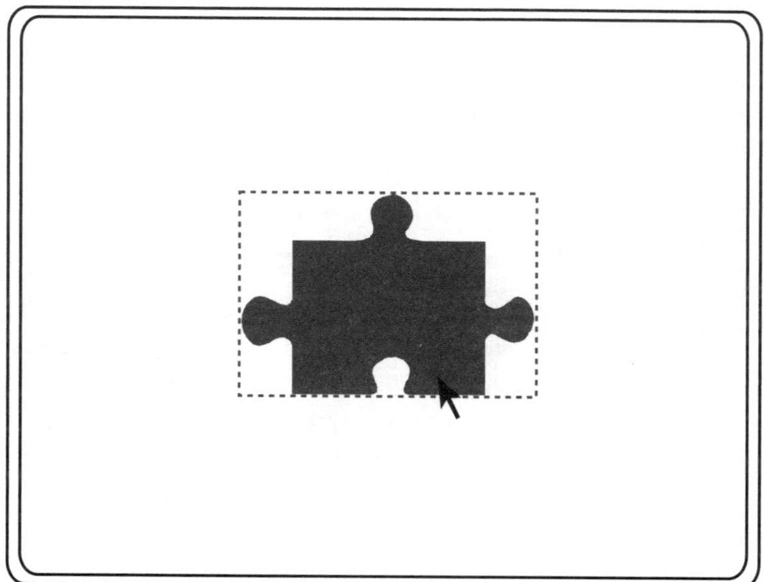

FIGURE 5.8
The mouse interacts with the shape of the puzzle piece.

Here is the syntax used to invoke this type of collision detection:

```
myMovieClip.hitTest(x, y, true)
```

You might immediately notice that this is almost identical to the syntax for the movie-clip–point collision detection, with one change: the addition of the `true` parameter. When that parameter is set to `true`, the `hitTest()` method checks for a collision between the point and the contents of the movie clip. If that parameter does not exist, or if it is set to `false`, then the `hitTest()` method checks for a collision between the point and the bounding box of the movie clip.

To see an example of this, open puzzle_piece.fla in the Chapter05 directory. On the Stage you will see a movie clip with an instance name of piece, containing the shape of a puzzle piece, which happens to be a candid shot of my cat (Figure 5.9). The ActionScript in this movie simply checks for a collision between the mouse and the shape when the mouse is clicked.

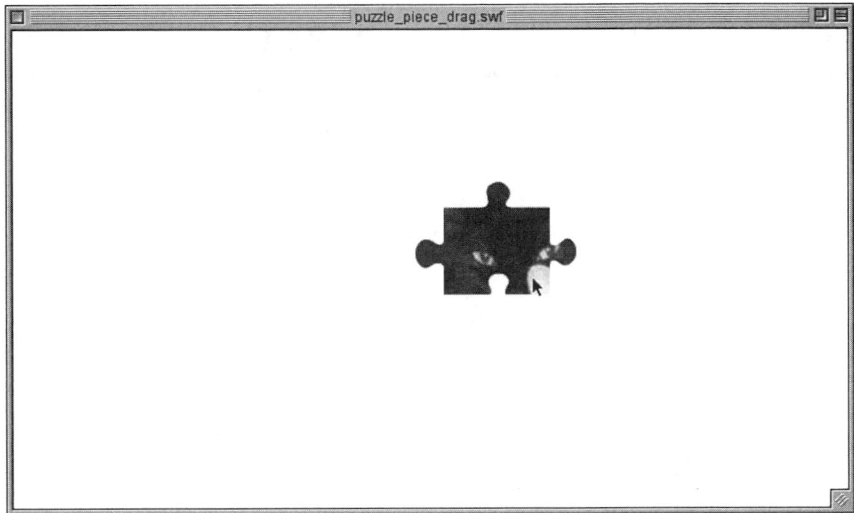

FIGURE 5.9
The puzzle piece containing the cat.

```
1    _root.onMouseDown = function () {
2          var mx:Number =_xmouse;
3          var my:Number =_ymouse;
4          if (piece.hitTest(mx, my, true)) {
5                trace("Meow!");
6          }
7    }
```

The first line of this code defines a function to be called when the mouse button is pressed. When this function is called, it sets two variables, as in our previous examples, to store the position of the mouse cursor. Then, on line 4, a conditional statement checks if the `hitTest()` of the mouse position with the movie clip called piece is `true`. If it is `true`, then a trace action is executed to show you that a collision was detected.

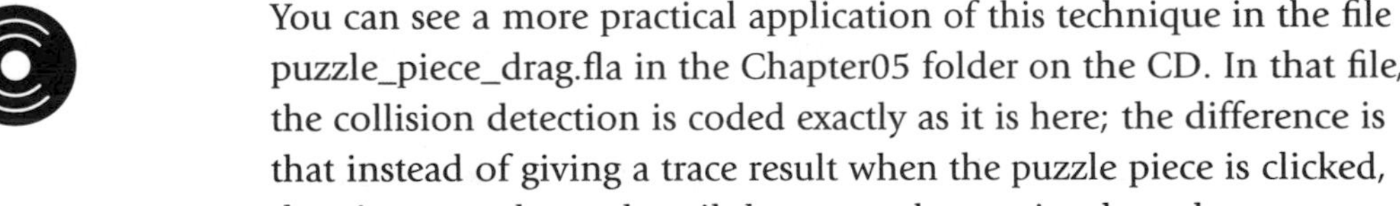

You can see a more practical application of this technique in the file puzzle_piece_drag.fla in the Chapter05 folder on the CD. In that file, the collision detection is coded exactly as it is here; the difference is that instead of giving a trace result when the puzzle piece is clicked, the piece gets dragged until the mouse button is released.

Detection Using Math

As you just saw, using the `hitTest()` method is pretty painless. I've already hinted that creating collision-detection scripts based on math is more difficult than that. So this is probably an appropriate time to tell you what makes this type of collision detection so much better than attempting to use `hitTest()` for all your collision-detection needs. Let's start by listing the limitations of `hitTest()`.

Object-shape restrictions. As you saw earlier in this chapter, the `hitTest()` method only works with the bounding box of a movie clip or a point and the shape within that movie clip. How would you detect collisions between two pool balls or between a ball and an angled line? With `hitTest()`, the collision detection for those situations would not be accurate because it doesn't handle collision detection between the shapes within two movie clips. Using math, we can create collision-detection scripts for many shapes.

Inhibited code-graphics independence. This concept can be tough to grasp. In all the examples given so far in this book, we have updated the position of a movie clip on the screen by grabbing its current position, adding to it, and then changing the position of that movie clip. It is better practice to keep track of where objects on the screen should be *in memory*. For instance, you could have a variable that stores the *x* position of the ball. When it is time to update the position of the ball with the *x* velocity, you would add to the variable that stores the *x* position and then set the position of the clip on the screen from that variable. This is useful because we can detect a collision before setting the position of the movie clip on the Stage. With `hitTest()`, the object must be physically moved on the screen, and then the collision detection is based on the overlap of two graphical elements. We will be using code-graphics independence throughout the rest of the chapter.

Frame-rate dependence. This limitation is related to the one above. Imagine a game of *Pong*: There is a paddle that's 10 units wide on the left side of the screen. The ball, also 10 units wide, is moving toward the paddle with an *x* speed of -30 units per frame. It is possible for the ball to be on the right side of the paddle on one frame and to appear on the other side of the paddle on the next frame (see Figure 5.10). With `hitTest()`, no collision would have been detected because the two clips must overlap during a frame (or *within* a frame, for those of you more comfortable thinking of frames in terms of physical space rather than time duration). It is not smart enough to know that the ball went through the paddle. Using math, we can tell if a collision took place in between frames.

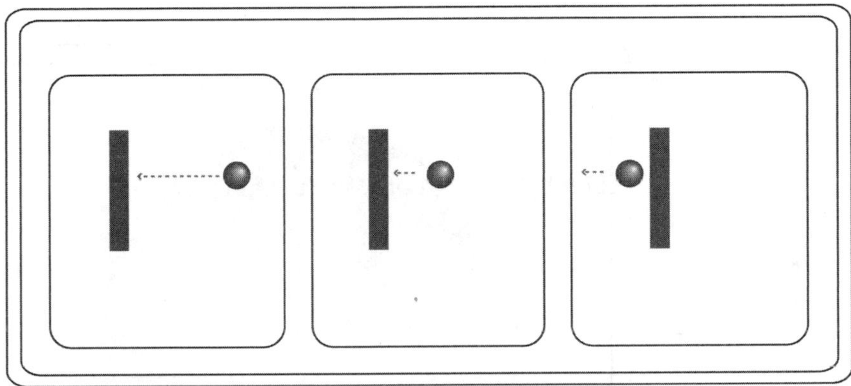

FIGURE 5.10
Collision was not detected because of the "snapshot" nature of frames.

To recap, using math for collision detection will enable you to:

- Write scripts that can handle detecting collisions between irregular shapes.
- Write frame-independent collision-detection scripts.
- Handle all the collision detection and movement in memory rather than basing it on the placement of the graphics.

What follows is a description, with examples, of how to think about and script collision detection between various types of shapes. For some of these we extend the detection script so that it works independently of the frames, and for some we do not.

For some types of collision detection, frame independence doesn't give us any advantages. One such type is line-line collisions; when two lines are intersecting, they are most likely not moving, which means we do not need to use frame-independent collision detection on them. But for some situations, such as circle-line or circle-circle collisions, frame-independent collision detection is a must, especially for fast-paced games such as pool or pinball.

Point-Circle Collision Detection

We begin the examples of mathematical collision detection with one of the simpler types. A good example of where we might use point-circle collision detection is a dart game. The dart's tip is the point, and the target is made up of a series of concentric circles (see Figure 5.11).

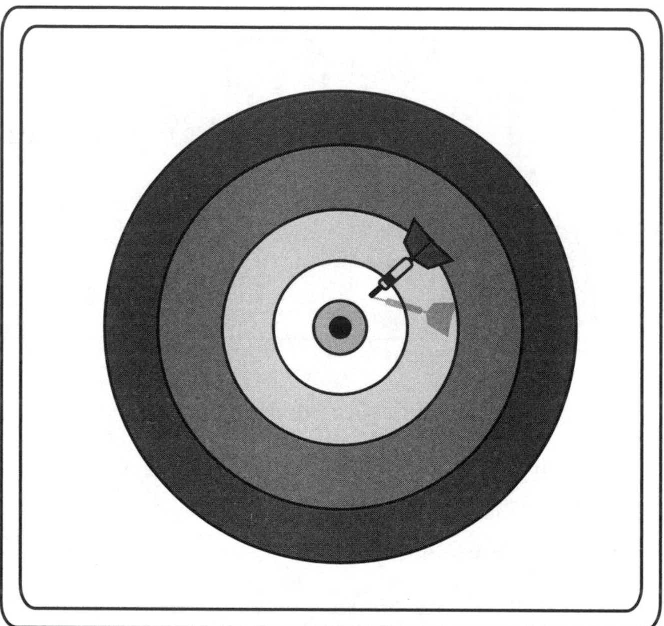

FIGURE 5.11
Dart and target.

So how do we determine if a point and a circle are colliding? Imagine that you have two movie clips: a circle and a dot (the point). Assume the registration point of the circle movie clip is at the actual center of the circle. Because the point and the circle are movie clips, you can easily find the positions of both. Also, using the distance equation developed in Chapter 3, "Game Math" (and listed below in ActionScript), we know we can find the distance between the point and the circle. With this information, we can write the one condition that determines if a collision is taking place (see Figure 5.12):

If the distance between the point and the center of the circle is less than the radius of the circle, then the point is colliding with the circle.

Note that the radius of a circle is one-half its diameter.

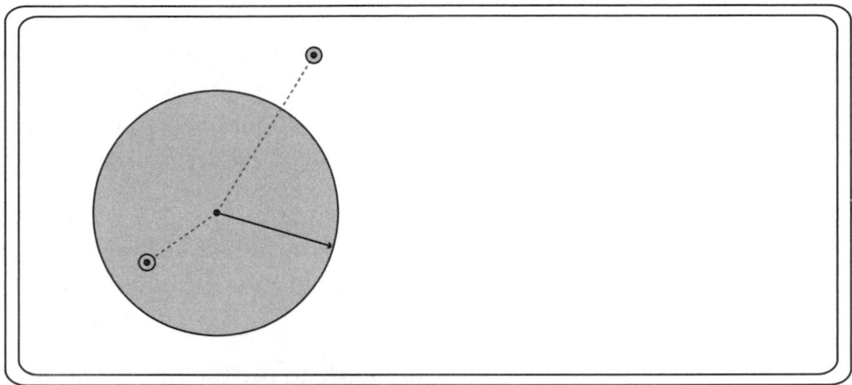

FIGURE 5.12
Calculating point-circle collision.

To see this in action, open point_circle.fla from the Chapter05 folder on the CD. In this file there are three movie clips—two points and one circle. One of the points is outside the circle and has an instance name of `point_clip1`, and one of them is inside the circle with an instance name of `point_clip2`. The circle has an instance name of `circle_clip1`. The ActionScript in this file was built to determine if a point is colliding with a circle. Here are the first 13 lines.

```
//Define point 1
var point1:Object = {};
point1.x = point_clip1._x;
point1.y = point_clip1._y;
//Define point 2
var point2:Object = {};
point2.x = point_clip2._x;
point2.y = point_clip2._y;
//Define circle 1
var circle1:Object = {};
circle1.x = circle_clip1._x;
circle1.y = circle_clip1._y;
circle1.radius = circle_clip1._width/2;
```

What is being done with the ActionScript here is very important and is similar to what is going to be used for most games and examples given in this book. We create an object for each movie clip. An object (of type `Object`), when first created, is nothing more than an empty storage device. This can be likened to a file cabinet. When you first build (or buy) a file cabinet, it is empty. You then use it to store information about certain things, like your car or house. Unlike a file cabinet, an

`Object` object is not a visual or tactile thing—it is data stored in memory. Storing information in this fashion is a good practice because it removes the data from the interface. This separation enables you to add or remove movie clips from the Stage without losing the data stored in the object. Later you can reassociate the object with another movie clip.

In future scripts within the book, these objects will contain many other properties corresponding to attributes of the shape that it represents. For example, in the case of a pool ball, the object would contain the ball's color.

Some programmers choose to use the movie clip itself as the object to store this information. Even though it is not a recommended practice, in some cases it is acceptable, but in others—for instance, where a movie clip may not always be on the Stage—it is not a good idea. Imagine a game in which an enemy character is coming after you. This enemy may leave the screen for more ammo and then come back in 30 seconds or so. In this case it is probably a good idea to remove the movie clip from the Stage (for performance reasons) but retain the object that stores the enemy's characteristics so that we don't have to start "rebuilding" the enemy from scratch.

In line 2 of the ActionScript above, we create a new object, called `point1`, that we intend to use as a storage container for information about the point_clip1 movie clip. The action `var point1:Object = {}` is shorthand for creating a new empty object and giving it a name. (The long-winded way is `point1 = new Object()`, so you can see why we like the shorthand.) In lines 3 and 4 we simply create variables on the object to represent the position of the `point_clip1` movie clip. Lines 5–8 create an object for `point_clip2` and store information about it in the same way as the `point1` object does. Next, an object is created to store the information about the `circle_clip1` movie clip. It stores the *x* and *y* positions of the movie clip as well as its radius.

The rest of the ActionScript defines the collision-detection function and uses it to test for collisions.

```
//Build collision detection function
function pointToCircleDetection(point, circle) {
      var xDiff:Number = circle.x-point.x;
      var yDiff:Number = circle.y-point.y;
```

```
5          var distance:Number =
           ➥Math.sqrt(xDiff*xDiff+yDiff*yDiff);
6          if (distance<=circle.radius) {
7               trace("Collision detected!!");
8          } else {
9               trace("No collision detected.");
10         }
11    }
12    //Check for a collision between point1 and circle1
13    pointToCircleDetection(point1, circle1);
14    //Check for a collision between point2 and circle2
15    pointToCircleDetection(point2, circle1);
```

First we define a function named `pointToCircleDetection` that accepts two parameters: `point` and `circle`. Both `point` and `circle` are objects passed in when the function is called. To detect a collision, as we spelled out earlier, we have to compare the distance between the point and the circle with the radius of the circle. To make this comparison, we must determine the distance using the Pythagorean theorem (the method shown back in Chapter 3). Lines 3–5 show this. In line 6 we compare the distance with the radius of the circle, and if the distance is less than or equal to the radius, we execute a trace action to inform us that a collision has been detected. If this condition is not met, then a trace action is executed to inform us that no collision has occurred. In lines 13 and 15 we call the detection function while passing in objects whose collision we would like to check. For instance, in line 13 we pass in `point1` and `circle1`. The script will then check for a collision between `point1` and `circle1`. When you generate an SWF movie, you should see two traces in your Output window. The first collision detection detected a collision, and the second did not.

Circle-Circle Collision Detection

In this section, we discuss the logic and scripts needed to determine if two circles are colliding. We will cover this for both frame-dependent and frame-independent situations.

By *frame dependence,* we mean that in every frame we check for a collision, based on where the objects are now (this is like taking snapshots in time). With *frame independence,* in every frame we check to see if a collision has happened at some point between the last frame and the current frame. The frame-dependent collision detection for two circles is a simple extension of the point-circle collision-detection technique. The frame-independent collision detection for two circles involves a lot more logic and math.

Let's look at the easy one first.

Frame-Dependent Circle-Circle Detection

Here's our case of frame-dependent circle-circle collision detection:

If the distance between two circles is less than or equal to the sum of their radii, then a collision is occurring.

This principle is illustrated in Figure 5.13.

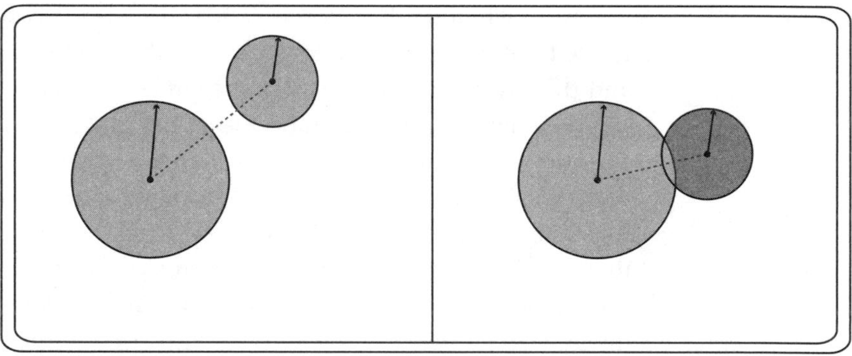

FIGURE 5.13 Frame-dependent circle-circle collision detection.

To see an example of this in ActionScript, open circle_circle1.fla from the Chapter05 folder on the CD. There are two movie clips on the Stage, circle_clip1 and circle_clip2. The ActionScript assigns *x* and *y* speeds to each circle and moves the circles around on the Stage. In every frame it checks to see if they are colliding.

As with the point-circle collision detection, we store information about each movie clip in an object. Here is the ActionScript that does this:

```
//Define object for the first circle
var circle1:Object = {};
circle1.clip = circle_clip1;
circle1.x = circle1.clip._x;
circle1.y = circle1.clip._y;
circle1.radius = circle1.clip._width/2;
```

```
7     circle1.xmov = 3;
8     circle1.ymov = 1;
9     //Define object for the second circle
10    var circle2:Object = {};
11    circle2.clip = circle_clip2;
12    circle2.x = circle2.clip._x;
13    circle2.y = circle2.clip._y;
14    circle2.radius = circle2.clip._width/2;
15    circle2.xmov = -1;
16    circle2.ymov = 0;
```

First, an object called `circle1` is created to store the information about `circle_clip1`. In line 3 you may notice something you haven't seen before. We are creating a reference to the movie clip with a name of clip in the object itself. Doing this enables us to point to the movie clip using this new reference. For instance, the action `circle1.clip._x = 100` would move the *x* position of `circle_clip1` to `100`. (We will use this technique of creating references to movie clips frequently throughout the book.) The next three lines create variables to store the circle's position and radius. In lines 7 and 8, we assign an *x* speed and a *y* speed to the circle. Lines 9–16 do for `circle_clip2` what the first eight lines of ActionScript did for `circle_clip1`.

Next in the ActionScript, we create a function called `moveCircles`. This function updates the positions of the circles based on their speeds.

```
1     function moveCircles() {
2           for (var i = 1; i<=2; ++i) {
3                 var circle:MovieClip = this["circle"+i];
4                 circle.x += circle.xmov;
5                 circle.y += circle.ymov;
6                 circle.clip._x = circle.x;
7                 circle.clip._y = circle.y;
8           }
9     }
```

In this function, a `for` loop loops through and moves each circle. This ActionScript is not unfamiliar (see balloon_pop_many.fla), although this is the first time we have used the movie-clip reference from an object. Remember that we are storing references to `circle_clip1` and `circle_clip2` as the clip variable on both the `circle1` and `circle2` objects, which is where we use them. In lines 6 and 7, you can see that the circles are moved by using the movie-clip reference clip that exists on each object.

The function that detects collisions between the circles is called `CircleToCircleDetection`. It is almost exactly the same as the collision-detection script used in the point-circle collision-detection script.

```
function CircleToCircleDetection(circle_a:Object,
➥circle_b:Object) {
     var xDiff:Number = circle_a.x-circle_b.x;
     var yDiff:Number = circle_a.y-circle_b.y;
     var distance:Number =
     ➥Math.sqrt(xDiff*xDiff+yDiff*yDiff);
     if (distance<=circle_a.radius+circle_b.radius) {
          trace("Collision detected!!");
     }
}
```

The `CircleToCircleDetection` function accepts two parameters, `circle_a` and `circle_b`. First the ActionScript finds the distance between those two movie clips. Then it reaches a conditional, which checks to see if the distance between the circles is less than or equal to the sum of their radii. If it is, then it executes a trace action.

Finally, it creates an `onEnterFrame` event that calls the `moveCircles` function and `CircleToCircleDetection` function in every frame (I'm just mentioning this to wrap up the script; you won't see this event in the code above). Generate an SWF to see it work.

Frame-Independent Circle-Circle Detection

OK, that was the easy one! Now it's time to talk about frame-independent circle-circle collision detection. The math in this gets a little tough, so before continuing, I would like to recap why it's important for you to slog through this. With all the collision-detection scripts created so far, Flash checks one time per frame to see if there is a collision right now. You can think of this as taking snapshots in time. I am sure you can imagine that if an object is moving fast enough, then in one frame it is on one side of an object, and in the next frame it is on the other side of the object. The collision-detection method we've been using wouldn't be able to detect that kind of collision because, as far as it is concerned, a collision never happened. But the collision-detection method I'm about to introduce can tell (no matter how fast the object is going) if there was a collision between the previous frame and the current frame. This script has direct application to games like pool, pinball, air hockey, miniature golf, or any game in which two balls (circles) can collide.

Let's discuss the logic needed for frame-independent collision detection. First, it is important to realize that we still can only check for a collision every frame—we can't check in between frames. What we will cover here is how to tell if a collision should have happened in between frames. In Chapter 4, we introduced the equations for position and velocity. In Chapter 3, we introduced how to get the distance between two points. If we know the *x* and *y* speeds of each circle (which we do), then we can write equations that specify the *x* and *y* positions of each circle. With these position equations, we can write an equation that determines the distance between the two circles. This leaves us with an equation for the distance between the two circles that is dependent on one variable—time (well, OK, for us it's really frames). If we wanted to, we could stick any time into this equation and find the distance that the circles would be apart at that time. Likewise, we could insert a distance and then solve for the time during which the two circles would be this distance apart. It is the latter example that we are interested in now. The same main condition must be met for the two circles to be colliding: The distance between the two circles must be less than or equal to the sum of their radii. So this is what we do:

1. Write equations for the *x* and *y* positions of both circles. These equations are based on the *x* and *y* speeds.
2. Use the equations for the *x* and *y* positions of both circles to write an equation for the distance between the two circles.
3. In the distance equation, use the sum of their radii for the distance and solve for the time (which is frames).
4. Do this for every frame. If the time is less than or equal to 1, then the collision happened between the last frame and the current frame.

Let's look at this in math form before touching the ActionScript.

1. For circle 1:

```
x1 = xl1+xmov1*t
y1 = yl1+ymov1*t
```

For circle 2:

```
x2 = xl2+xmov2*t
y2 = yl2+ymov2*t
```

The variables xl1, yl1, xl2, and yl2 represent the position of the circle at the end of the previous frame (because we have not yet updated this frame). The variable l stands for "last," as in "last frame." The variable t represents the time starting from the end of the previous frame.

2. The distance between the two circles:

   distance= $\sqrt{(x2-x1)^2+ (y2-y1)^2}$

3. Set the distance as the sum of the radii and solve for time:

   distance=radius1+radius2= $\sqrt{(x2-x1)^2+ (y2-y1)^2}$

   Solving for the time is very difficult. We must insert the equations for *x1*, *y1*, *x2*, and *y2*. We then square both sides of the equation (to get rid of the square root sign). What we are left with is a quadratic equation. Quadratic equations have two solutions, which means that when we solve for the time, we will get two answers. Conceptually we can see why in this case we will get two separate times. Imagine two circles moving toward each other. At one time they will be touching on an edge. As time goes on, they will move through each other, but just as they are about to separate, they will be touching exactly at one point again. The two times found by solving the quadratic equation give the two times that a collision can occur. When we have our two answers, we look at the lower of the two times and discard the other one.

   By defining these constants,

   $$R = radius1+radius2$$
   $$a = -2*xmov1*xmov2+xmov1^2+xmov2^2$$
   $$b = -2*xl1*xmov2-2*xl2*xmov1+2*xl1*xmov1+2*xl2*xmov2$$
   $$c = -2*xl1*xl2+xl1^2+xl2^2$$
   $$d = -2*ymov1*ymov2+ymov1^2+ymov2^2$$
   $$e = -2*yl1*ymov2-2*yl2*ymov1+2*yl1*ymov1+2*yl2*ymov2$$
   $$f = -2*yl1*yl2+yl1^2+yl2^2$$
   $$g = a+d$$
   $$h = b+e$$
   $$k = c+f-R^2$$

we can write the vastly simplified quadratic equation as

$$g*t^2+h*t+k = 0$$

Using the quadratic formula to solve for the time, we arrive at

$$t1=\frac{-h+\sqrt{h^2-4*g*k}}{2*g} \quad \text{and} \quad t2=\frac{-h-\sqrt{h^2-4*g*k}}{2*g}$$

4. This calculation is performed for every frame. If either of the times is less than or equal to 1, then a collision happened between the previous frame and the current frame. This works for any possible velocity; there is no limit.

If you are interested in seeing this math worked out more rigorously, check out circ_circ_frame_independent.pdf in the Chapter05 directory on the CD. It shows this worked out manually.

Solving Quadratic Equations

Any equation in which the variable has an exponent of 2 (and no other terms with a higher exponent) is a *quadratic equation*. For instance, $a\times t^2+b\times t+c = 0$ is a quadratic equation. All quadratic equations have two solutions; this means there are two values for the variable for which the equation is valid. The simplest example is $x^2 = 4$. This is a quadratic equation with the two solutions 2 and -2. There is a formula called the *quadratic formula* that is used to find the two solutions. Using $a*t^2+b*t+c = 0$ as an example, here are the solutions for t:

$$t=\frac{-b+\sqrt{b^2-4*a*c}}{2*a} \quad \text{and} \quad t=\frac{-b-\sqrt{b^2-4*a*c}}{2*a}$$

In the circle-circle example given in this section, the quadratic equation was manipulated until it could be written in standard quadratic-equation form. From there it is easy to solve.

Now let's look at an example of this in ActionScript. Open circle_circle2.fla from the Chapter05 folder on the CD. There are two movie clips on the Stage, ball1 and ball2. At its most fundamental level, the ActionScript used here performs all of the following tasks:

1. It defines an object for each movie clip to store information about that movie clip.

2. It defines a function that updates the position of the movie clips in memory (not on the Stage).
3. It defines a function that checks for collisions between any two balls (circles).
4. It defines a function that physically places the balls on the screen.
5. It creates an `onEnterFrame` event to call all these functions in every frame.

Here is the ActionScript that defines the objects:

```
1     var game:Object = {};
2     game.numBalls = 2;
3     for (var i = 1; i<=game.numBalls; ++i) {
4           var name:String = "ball"+i;
5           game[name] = {};
6           game[name].clip = _root[name];
7           game[name].xpos = game[name].clip._x;
8           game[name].ypos = game[name].clip._y;
9           game[name].radius = game[name].clip._width/2;
10          game[name].xmov = 0;
11          game[name].ymov = 0;
12    }
13    game.ball1.xmov = 1;
14    game.ball1.ymov = 2;
15    game.ball2.ymov = 1;
```

First we create an object called `game`. This object will store all the other objects we create. The only reason for having this *container* object, `game`, is to avoid polluting the Timeline with unneeded data. We can keep track of everything about the balls in the `game` object. In the second line, we set a variable on the `game` object that stores the number of balls we have chosen to use.

Next, we loop for each ball, create an object for it, and store information about that ball in its object. Notice that we are giving the balls no starting speeds. In lines 13–15 we assign starting velocities to the balls.

Then comes the following ActionScript:

```
function moveBalls() {
      for (var i = 1; i<=game.numBalls; ++i) {
            var ob:Object = game["ball"+i];
```

```
            ob.tempx = ob.xpos+ob.xmov;
            ob.tempy = ob.ypos+ob.ymov;
        }
    }
```

This function loops through the list of balls (in this case, just two) and updates their temporary positions in memory to their current positions plus their speed. We do not yet update the position of the actual movie clip on the Stage. I encourage you to get into this habit of creating a temporary position of the movie clip in memory because when we start dealing with collision reactions, we will update the temporary position of the movie clip (due to multiple collisions or forces) possibly several times before we actually place the movie clip on the Stage.

Let's analyze an example. Imagine that you are coding a game in which a ball bounces off a wall. This ball may be moving very fast. Now imagine that on one frame the ball is not colliding with the wall, and on the next frame you detect that half of the ball is colliding with the wall. When this happens, you do not want to update that ball's position on the Stage to show this. Rather, it is a good idea to update its position in memory to reflect where the ball *should* be and then render the ball on the screen. So, if it is detected that the ball is colliding with the wall (no matter how deep into the wall the ball is), then we should update the ball's position in memory so that the ball is just barely touching the wall. At the end of the frame, we render the ball on the screen, and it looks as if it is just barely touching the wall (which is what we want). In real life, a ball would not move past the wall boundary.

Next we create a function to render the balls onto the Stage.

```
    function renderBalls() {
        for (var i = 1; i<=game.numBalls; ++i) {
            var ob:Object = game["ball"+i];
            ob.xpos = ob.tempx;
            ob.ypos = ob.tempy;
            ob.clip._x = ob.xpos;
            ob.clip._y = ob.ypos;
        }
    }
```

This function simply sets the physical position of each movie clip using the value of the *x* and *y* position variables on the object, which are `xpos` and `ypos`.

Now (drum roll, please) we come to the function that handles the collision detection itself. It's a fairly large function, but it follows exactly what we discussed about the logic for determining the collisions.

```
function ballToBallDetection(b1, b2) {
	//set the speed variables
	var xmov1:Number = b1.xmov;
	var ymov1:Number = b1.ymov;
	var xmov2:Number = b2.xmov;
	var ymov2:Number = b2.ymov;
	//set the position variables
	var xl1:Number = b1.xpos;
	var yl1:Number = b1.ypos;
	var xl2:Number = b2.xpos;
	var yl2:Number = b2.ypos;
	//define the constants
	var R:Number = b1.radius+b2.radius;
	var a:Number = -
	➥2*xmov1*xmov2+xmov1*xmov1+xmov2*xmov2;
	var b:Number = -2*xl1*xmov2-
	➥2*xl2*xmov1+2*xl1*xmov1+2*xl2*xmov2;
	var c:Number = -2*xl1*xl2+xl1*xl1+xl2*xl2;
	var d:Number = -
	➥2*ymov1*ymov2+ymov1*ymov1+ymov2*ymov2;
	var e:Number = -2*yl1*ymov2-
	➥2*yl2*ymov1+2*yl1*ymov1+2*yl2*ymov2;
	var f:Number = -2*yl1*yl2+yl1*yl1+yl2*yl2;
	var g:Number = a+d;
	var h:Number = b+e;
	var k:Number = c+f-R*R;
	//solve the quadratic equation
	var sqRoot:Number = Math.sqrt(h*h-4*g*k);
	var t1:Number = (-h+sqRoot)/(2*g);
	var t2:Number = (-h-sqRoot)/(2*g);
	if (t1>0 && t1<=1) {
		var whatTime:Number = t1;
		var ballsCollided:Boolean = true;
	}
	if (t2>0 && t2<=1) {
		if (whatTime == null || t2<t1) {
```

```
33                      var whatTime:Number = t2;
34                      var ballsCollided:Boolean = true;
35                  }
36              }
37              if (ballsCollided) {
38                  //Collision has happened, so throw a trace
39                  trace("Ouch!!");
40              }
41      }
```

First we give the function a name, `ballToBallDetection`, and set two parameters, `b1` and `b2`. When this function is called, the two objects will be passed in and represented by `b1` and `b2`. In lines 2–11 we define the speed and position variables needed. Next, we define all the constants in terms of the speed and position variables. The variable names match what we discussed earlier in this section.

With lines 24–26 we solve the quadratic equation. In line 24 we set a variable called `sqRoot` whose value is equal to the square-root term in our solution to the quadratic equation (remember that there are two solutions, both of which contain the same square-root term). We set this as a variable so that it can be reused for both solutions (lines 25 and 26). At this point, we have two times at which the balls will collide. What follows in the ActionScript (lines 27–36) is logic to determine if the time was in the past, the present, or the future. If the time is in the past or the present, then it is less than or equal to 1, and a collision has occurred. If the time is in the future (greater than 1), no collision has occurred. If a collision has occurred, then we store the time at which this collision happened (using the `whatTime` variable). We will use this information in Chapter 6, "Collision Reactions." Also, when a collision is detected, a variable called `ballsCollided` is set to `true`. When `ballsCollided` is `true`, a final `if` statement executes a trace action to let you know that a collision was detected.

Generate an SWF to see this work.

With this collision-detection script, you can determine when in the future a collision may happen. When you solve the quadratic equation for `time1` and `time2`, it tells you any time in the future when the balls will intersect, even if it is a million frames into the future.

Looking more than one frame into the future is something I have not yet found a need for, but should a use come for it, we'll know how to do it!

Line-Line Collision Detection

In this section, we will discuss the equations for lines and line segments and how to tell when lines are intersecting. I have never encountered a situation in which I needed a collision-detection script for two moving lines, so we will just cover detection for two stationary lines.

It may not be immediately obvious to you how—or where—this type of collision detection might come in handy. As an active member of many Flash user boards on the Internet, I frequently see the question of how to tell if two lines are intersecting (see Figure 5.14). The most important application of this that we will see is in circle-line collision detection. One step in the process of detecting the collision of a circle and a line is to test to see if two lines are intersecting.

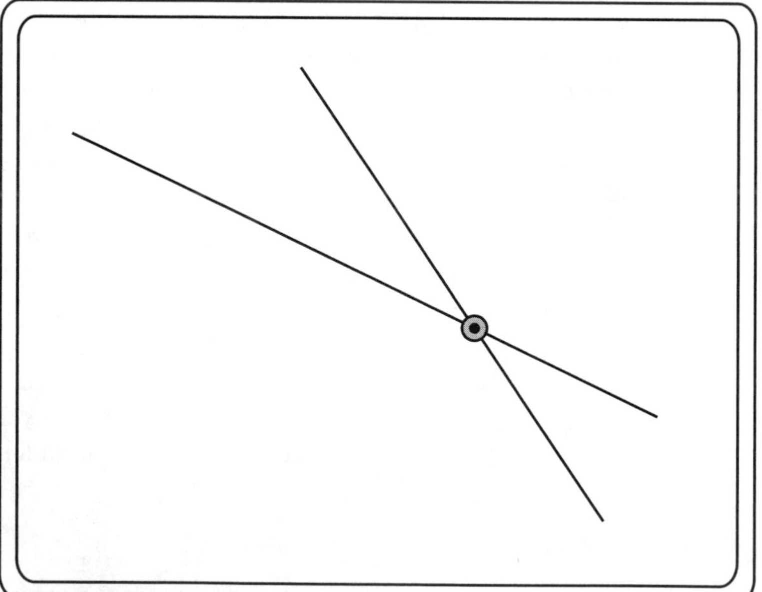

FIGURE 5.14 Two lines intersecting.

The Equation of a Line

Time once again to think back to your high school math class. You may remember this equation:

```
y = m*x+b
```

where m is the slope of the line, and b is the y intercept (the spot where the line intersects the y-axis). This is the equation for a straight line. The slope, m, is defined as the rise over the run of the line (see Figure 5.15). For instance, if the line is at a 45° angle, then the rise of the line equals the run, so the slope is 1. If you have a line that is closer to horizontal, then its rise is less than its run, and therefore the slope is small—far less than 1. If the line is exactly horizontal, then the rise is 0, and therefore the slope is also 0.

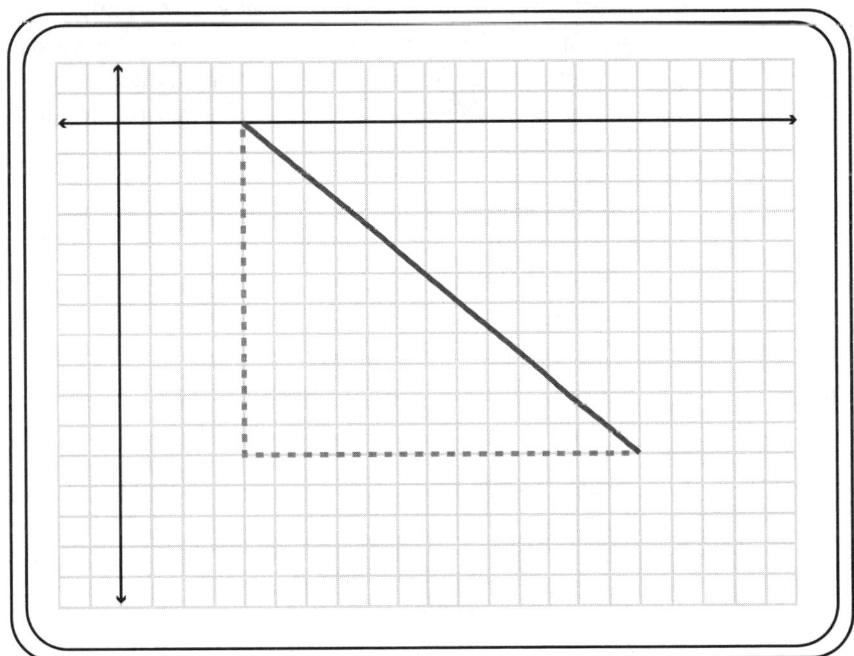

FIGURE 5.15
Graphical representation of slope.

If you know the slope and *y* intercept of a line, then you can draw that line. Open draw_line.fla in the Chapter05 directory on the CD. You'll notice that there are no movie clips in this file. The ActionScript it contains builds an object that represents the properties of a line (its slope and *y* intercept) and then draws the line using two functions. Here are the first few lines of ActionScript in this file, which are used to build the object.

```
root.createEmptyMovieClip("clip", 1);
clip.lineStyle(0, 0x000000, 100);
var line1:Object = {};
```

```
4       line1.m = 1;
5       line1.b = 100;
```

In the first line, we simply create an empty movie clip on the Stage. The line that will be drawn using this ActionScript will be drawn in this movie clip.

It is a good programming practice to create a movie clip to hold lines drawn with Flash's dynamic drawing tools. Why? Because this procedure makes cleanup easier—you can just remove the movie clip when needed. For instance, if you create a drawing application (in which dynamically creating lines is a common occurrence), then you will most likely want a "clear screen" function. It is much easier to remove one movie clip that contains all the drawn lines than to remove many individual lines. Also, if all the lines had been drawn on the main Timeline, then the cleanup would be all the more difficult.

In line 2, we specify a line style for the movie clip. Before anything can be drawn in the movie clip, we have to tell Flash how we want it to be drawn. This method tells the movie clip that we want the line to be a hairline (which is a thickness of 0), the color to be black (which has a hex value of 0x000000), and the alpha value to be 100.

Lines 3–5 create an object called `line1` that holds the variables `m` (for the slope of the line) and `b` (for the *y* intercept).

Next, we write two functions that work together to draw the line.

```
function findY(line:Object, x:Number) {
      var y:Number = line.m*x+line.b;
      return y;
}
function drawLine(line:Object) {
      //Choose an x
      var x:Number = 300;
      //Find the y
      var y:Number = findY(line, x);
      //Move the pen
      clip.moveTo(x, y);
      //Choose another x
```

```
13          x = 0;
14          //Find the y
15          y = findY(line, x);
16          //Draw line
17          clip.lineTo(x, y);
18      }
19      drawLine(line1);
```

The function `findY` was created to calculate the y position from the `line` object passed in and the x position (using the equation for the line $y = m \times x+b$). After that, starting on line 5, we use the `drawLine()` function. You need two points to draw a line, of course, and so this function chooses two x positions, finds the appropriate y positions from them, and draws a line between this pair of points. On line 11 you see the `moveTo()` method. This method is used to move the starting position of the Flash "pen" to the coordinates passed in. (The Flash pen, sometimes called the virtual pen, is a place that you cannot see, with the coordinates (0,0), where Flash will start drawing if you were to call the drawing methods.) The `moveTo()` method only moves the position of the pen—it draws no lines. There is a method called `lineTo()`, found in line 17, that handles drawing the line. It draws a line from the current pen position to the coordinates passed in. The final line is what calls the function. This function call passes in a `line1` object reference to the `drawLine()` function. The `drawLine()` function then uses this reference to access information on the object.

It is important to note that all lines are infinite in length, although in this case we are showing only a portion of the line in question. A portion of a line is called a *line segment.*

Intersecting Lines

All lines that are not parallel to each other intersect at some point, and any two lines that have the same slope are parallel. So, to tell if two lines intersect, you simply compare their slopes. If the slopes are not equal, then they *do* intersect somewhere in space (see Figure 5.16). In this section, we're going to learn how to find out at what coordinates any two lines intersect.

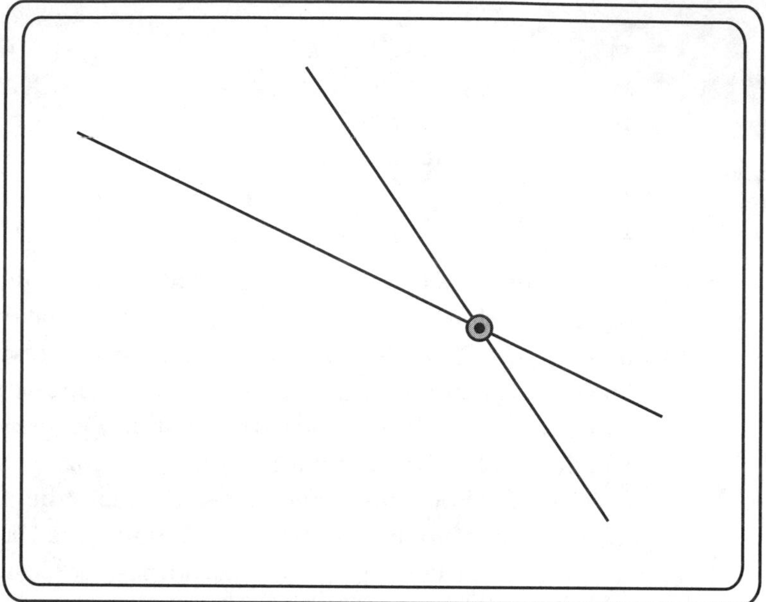

FIGURE 5.16
Slope 1 ≠ Slope 2; therefore they intersect at some point

First, let's look for the point of intersection. Say we have two lines whose equations are

```
y = m1*x+b1
```

and

```
y = m2*x+b2
```

At the point where these two lines intersect, the *y* value (in the equations above) is the same, and the *x* (in the equations above) is the same. With this knowledge, we set the two equations equal and write:

```
m1*x+b1 = m2*x+b2
```

and we solve for *x* to get:

```
x = (b2-b1)/(m1-m2)
```

This is the *x* position at which the lines intersect. To find the *y* position, simply stick this *x* value back into either of the two line equations (I've chosen the first):

```
y = m1*x+b1
```

Open lines_intersecting.fla from the Chapter05 folder on the CD to see this in action. This file uses the same functions as we did in the previous example. Also, because we are now dealing with two lines, we have created a second line object. There is an instance of a movie clip on the Stage called dot that, when calculated, will be moved to the point of intersection. Here is the function that calculates the intersection.

```
function findIntersection(line_a:Object, line_b:Object) {
        var x:Number = (line_b.b-line_a.b)/(line_a.m-
        ➥line_b.m);
        var y:Number = line_a.m*x+line_a.b;
        dot._x = x;
        dot._y = y;
}
```

This function accepts two parameters, line_a and line_b, which are references to line objects. It then uses the equation we derived above to find the *x* position of the intersection. When this *x* position is found, it is plugged into the equation for the line represented by the line_a object to find the *y* position. Then the dot movie clip is placed on the Stage using these two values. When you test the movie, you will see that the dot appears over the intersection of the two lines.

Determining If Two Line Segments Are Intersecting

This is an easy extension of what we have already accomplished in this section. The technique we just introduced enables us to determine if two lines are intersecting. To determine if two line segments intersect, we find the coordinates of the intersection between these lines as if they were not segments and then check to see if this point falls within the boundaries of each segment (see Figure 5.17). It may not be obvious when something like this would be useful. Without thinking very hard, I can only come up with one common use, but it's a big one. It occurs when detecting a frame-independent collision between a circle and a line. This is covered in detail in the next section.

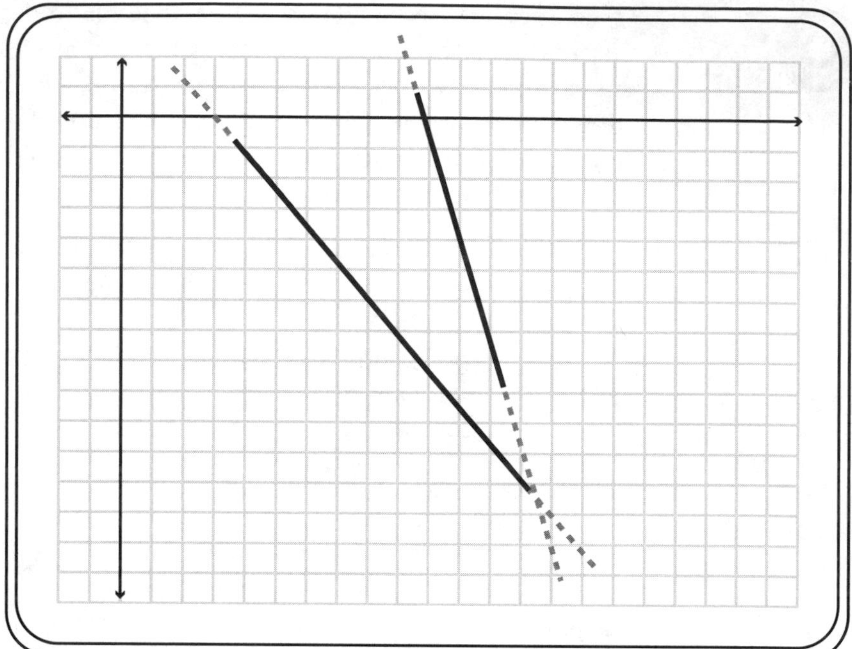

FIGURE 5.17
Lines intersect, but the segments do not; therefore there is no collision.

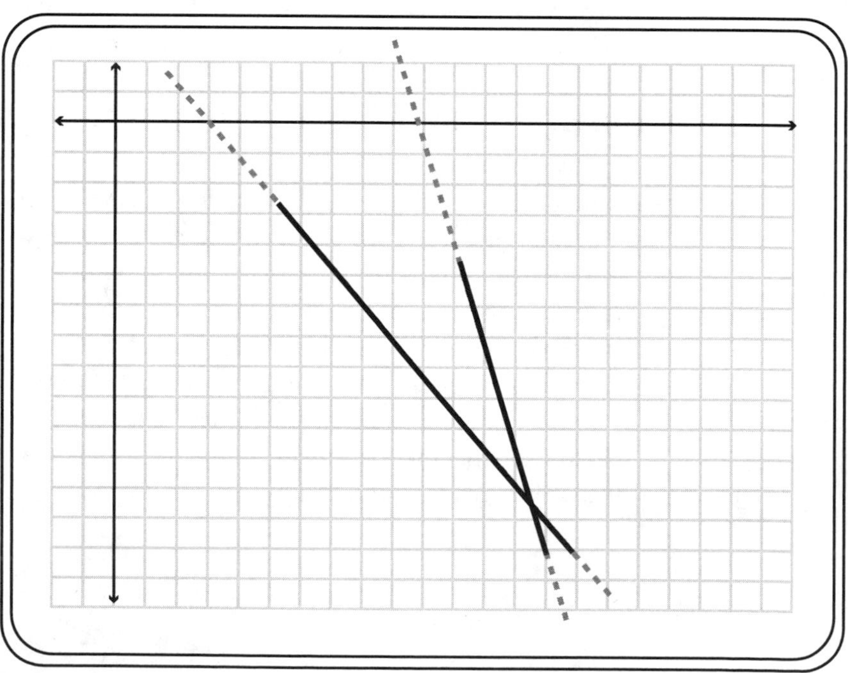

Lines intersect, and so do the segments; therefore a collision is occurring.

Open line_segments_intersecting.fla in the Chapter05 directory. After defining the objects that represent the lines in this file, we add two variables, `x1` and `x2`, that are the boundaries of the line segment. I modified the `drawLine()` function from the same function in the previous example file to take the `x1` and `x2` boundaries of each line and to find the `y1` and `y2` boundaries from them. Here is the modified `drawLine()` function.

```
1    function drawLine(line:Object) {
2         //Choose an x
3         var x:Number = line.x1;
4         //Find the y
5         var y:Number = findY(line, x);
6         line.y1 = y;
7         //Move the pen
8         clip.moveTo(x, y);
9         //Choose another x
10        x = line.x2;
11        //Find the y
12        y = findY(line, x);
13        line.y2 = y;
14        //Draw line
15        clip.lineTo(x, y);
16   }
```

In this function we move the pen to one boundary and then draw a line to the other boundary. The result is a visual representation of the line segment. After this function is called, the line object contains the *x* and *y* coordinates for both of the line-segment boundaries. Before this function is called, the line object only contains the `x1` and `x2` line boundaries. The `y1` and `y2` boundaries are calculated in this function, on lines 5 and 12, and then stored on the line object in lines 6 and 13.

The `findIntersection()` function also has a major addition for our current purposes—it now checks the point of intersection to see if it is within the segment boundaries on both lines. Here is the function:

```
function findIntersection(line_a:Object, line_b:Object) {
     var x:Number = (line_b.b-line_a.b)/(line_a.m-
     ➥line_b.m);
```

```
3           var y:Number = line_a.m*x+line_a.b;
4           dot._x = x;
5           dot._y = y;
6            ((x>=line_a.x1 && x<=line_a.x2) || (x<=line_a.x1
            ➥&& x>=line_a.x2) || (y>=line_a.y1 &&
            ➥y<=line_a.y2) || (y<=line_a.y1 && y>=line_a.y2)) {
7               var segment_a:Boolean = true;
8           }
9           if ((x>=line_b.x1 && x<=line_b.x2) || (x<=line_b.x1
            ➥&& x>=line_b.x2) || (y>=line_b.y1 &&
            ➥y<=line_b.y2) || (y<=line_b.y1 && y>=line_b.y2)) {
10              var segment_b:Boolean = true;
11          }
12          if (segment_a && segment_b) {
13              trace("The lines are intersecting!!");
14          }
15      }
```

The first five lines of this function are identical to the `findIntersection()` function in the previous example. What follows in the remainder of the function are conditional statements that check to see if the intersection point is within the boundaries of the segments. Lines 6–8 check to see if the point is between the *x* boundaries or between the *y* boundaries of `line_a`. If it is, then the point lies on the segment. Lines 9–11 do the same thing as 6–8, but for `line_b`. If the point lies within the boundaries of both segments, then a trace action is executed, letting you know that an intersection has been encountered.

You might have expected to see a section on point-line collision detection before circle-line collision detection. I didn't include that technique for two reasons. First, in my experience, point-line collision detection is not very useful. Second, unless you are doing frame-independent collision detections, it's almost impossible that a point-line collision will ever be detected.

If you are really interested in point-line collisions, pay special attention to the final scripts developed in the next section. Using them, you'll be able to set the radius of a circle to 0 and thereby detect point-line collisions (a circle of radius 0 is a point).

Circle-Line Collision Detection

In this section, we discuss frame-independent circle-line collision detection. This operation has direct application to any game that involves a ball bouncing off (or rolling down) a banked wall or hill—games like pinball and miniature golf.

We begin by discussing the logic needed to detect a collision between a circle and a line. We are assuming that the line is stationary and the circle is moving. We are also assuming that a collision is not yet taking place when detection begins (so if the ball is colliding with the line when the script starts, then the script will fail). In the previous section, we developed a way to determine where two lines intersect. We will use that here as well. A ball in motion builds an imaginary line as it moves (its trajectory). We determine where this line of trajectory and the main line intersect. When this is found, we use trigonometry to figure out the precise spot at which the circle collides with the line. Then we find the point of collision on the line (where the circle touches the line). Finally, we look at the current position of the circle and figure out how long it will take for the circle to reach the collision point. If this result is less than or equal to one frame, then a collision has occurred.

To recap, this is the process of frame-independent circle-line collision detection more concisely:

1. Determine the intersection point between the path of the circle and the line.
2. Use trigonometry to find the coordinates of the circle when it initially collides with the line.
3. Find the coordinates of the point of collision on the line itself.
4. Calculate the number of frames it takes for the circle to move from its current position to this collision position. If this number is less than or equal to 1, then a collision has occurred.

You have already seen how to accomplish steps 1 and 4 in the sections above. So before dissecting an example FLA file, let's look at how to accomplish steps 2 and 3.

The results of step 1 show us where the path of the circle intersects the line (see Figure 5.18). This intersection point is where the center of the circle would touch the line if it were to make it this far along the path. (After we add collision reactions in the next chapter, the circle will not make it this far; it will have reacted and rebounded when its edge touched the line.) As you can see, this is not the point at which a collision first occurs. If you were to take the circle and slide it backward along its path until only one point intersected with the line, then you would have found the collision point. We can find this point using trigonometry. A right triangle is formed by the radius of the circle, the segment of the circle's path between the line-line intersection and the collision point, and the piece of the line that is between these two intersections.

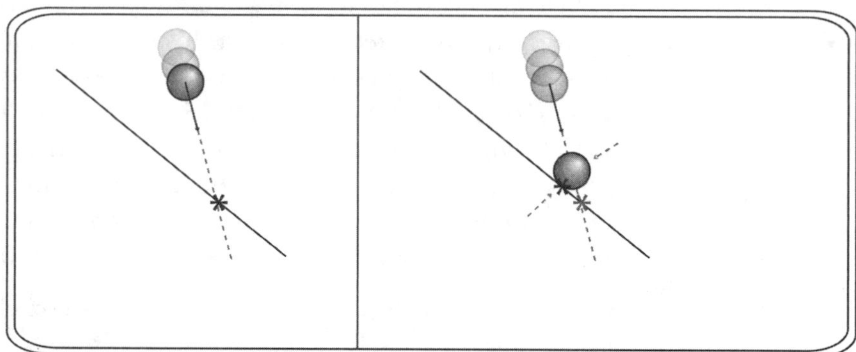

FIGURE 5.18
Path of ball intersecting with line compared with ball colliding with line.

The angle gamma in Figure 5.19 is the difference between the angle of the path of the ball and the angle of the line. Our goal in this step is to find the position of the circle when it first touches the line. Remember, we're going to find this position by using some trigonometry. Be sure to look at the image above to help you understand the relationships between the values we're using. The length of the path segment, *r*, is equivalent to *radius/sin(gamma)*. We find this relationship by inspecting the right triangle and using the projection information discussed in Chapter 3. This relationship tells us the length of that line segment. With that information, we can use trigonometry again to find the position of the circle. The *x* position of the circle at first collision is the *x* position of the line intersection of the path and line minus *r×cos(theta)*. And the *y* position of the circle at the first collision is the *y* position of the line intersection of the path and the line minus *r×sin(theta)*. (Theta is the angle that the path of the ball makes with the *x*-axis.)

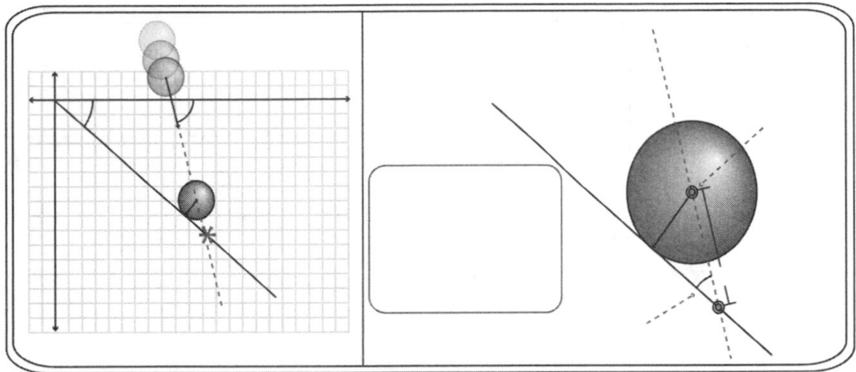

FIGURE 5.19
The measurements referred to in the text.

In step 3, we are looking for the actual point where the circle touches the line—the point of contact. In the previous step we found the point where the circle is when it touches the line, but not actually the point on the circle that touches the line. To find this point, we must imagine a line drawn from the center of the circle through the point of contact. This is a line perpendicular to the line with which we are colliding. We then find the intersection between these two lines. This point is what we are looking for. We can compare this point with the boundaries of the line segment to determine if the collision happened.

There is only one thing we have not discussed in how to create the perpendicular line—the equation for that line. We know the equation for the main line (it is stored in the line object), and we know that this new line is perpendicular to the main line. A line perpendicular to another line has a slope that is the negative inverse of it. So if the main line has a slope of 3, then all lines perpendicular to it have a slope of -1/3 (see Figure 3.20).

Wow—there are a lot of steps to this, but the result is something cool: frame-independent collision detection! Let's look at an example. Open circle_line.fla from the Chapter05 folder on the CD. There are two movie clips on the Stage. One of them has an instance name of `ball1` and will be the movie clip that represents a circle. The other movie clip does not have (or need) an instance name. It is there so that we can use `attachMovie()` to create new instances of it. It will contain a line that will be drawn using ActionScript. There is a lot of ActionScript in this file, more than 100 lines. We are going to focus on describing the ActionScript in the `getFrame()` function. But first, here is an overview of all the ActionScript for this example of circle-line collision detection.

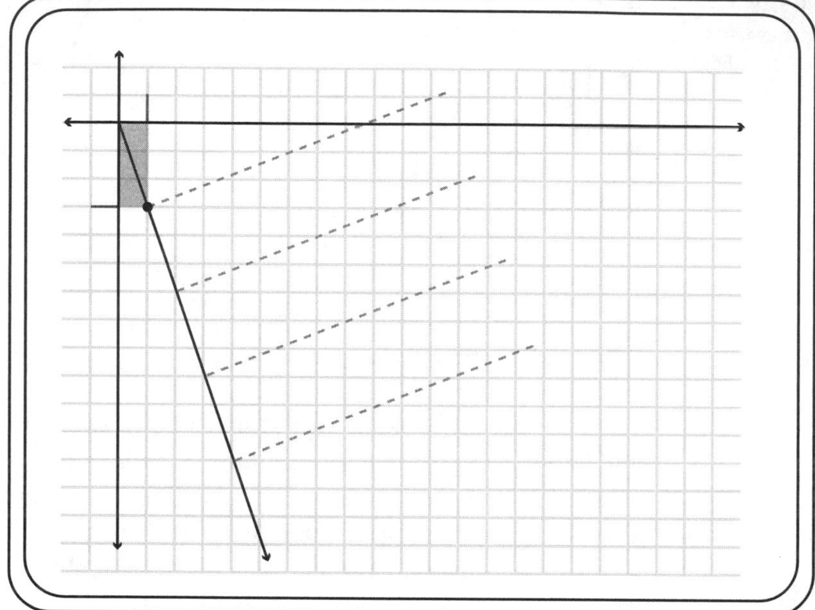

FIGURE 5.20
All lines perpendicular to a line with a slope of 3 have a slope of -1/3.

- An object called `ball` is created to hold information about `ball1`.
- A function is created to make it easy to create lines on the Stage. An object is created for each line to store information about that line.
- A function called `getTempPositions()` is created. This function is not yet necessary for what we're going to do with this file. However, when you later add gravity and collision reactions, this function will be more useful. Its duty is to create a temporary position in memory of all moving objects. It was built to handle updating positions due to gravitational, wind, or other external forces.
- A function called `render()` takes the temporary position of each moving object and sets that as the real position. It then physically places the movie clips on the screen. In this file we only have one moving object, so the function is quite simple and short.
- A function called `getFrames()` handles the collision detection.
- A function called `bankCollisionDetect()` was created to loop through all the lines on the screen and call the `getFrames()` function for each line.
- An `onEnterFrame` event calls `getTempPositions()`, `bankCollisionDetect()`, and `render()` in every frame.

Now let's look at the getFrame() function. This function does several things:

1. Finds the intersection between the path of the ball and the line.
2. Finds the position where the ball should be for initial contact.
3. Determines the point of contact and compares that with the boundaries of the line segment.
4. Calculates the number of frames it will take for the ball to reach the collision point.

Steps 3 and 4 are not dependent on each other, and in this function they swap places. Here is the ActionScript for step 1.

```
1     function getFrames(tempLine:Object, point:Object) {
2           //Step 1
3           var slope2:Number = point.ymov/point.xmov;
4           if (slope2 == Number.POSITIVE_INFINITY) {
5                 slope2 = 1000000;
6           } else if (slope2 == Number.NEGATIVE_INFINITY) {
7                 slope2 = -1000000;
8           }
9           //The y intercept of the ball trajectory
10          var b2:Number = point.y-slope2*point.x;
11          //intersection point
12          var x:Number = (b2-tempLine.b)/(tempLine.slope-
            ➥slope2);
13          var y:Number = tempLine.slope*x+tempLine.b;
```

In this step, we search for the intersection between the path of the ball and the line. The slope of the path of the ball is its *rise* over its *run*. Notice lines 4–8. If the ball has no speed in the *x* direction (xmov=0), then the slope is either infinity or -infinity. But because our calculations break down at infinity and -infinity (and nowhere else), we add some simple conditional logic that sets the slope to either 1,000,000 or —1,000,000 if infinity or —infinity, respectively, was detected. (We use 1,000,000 because it is a high enough number that our collision detection will be accurate, but not high enough to make the calculations fail.) Lines 9–13 should look familiar by now—they are what determines the intersection between the two lines.

Now we move on to the ActionScript for step 2.

```
1   //Step 2
2   //The angle that the ball is moving
3   var theta:Number = Math.atan2(point.ymov,
    ➥point.xmov);
4   //The difference between the angle of the line and
    ➥of the ball trajectory
5   var gamma:Number = theta-tempLine.angle;
6   //modify x and y
7   var sinGamma:Number = Math.sin(gamma);
8   var r:Number = point.radius/sinGamma;
9   //The ball's position at point of contact
10  var x:Number = x-r*Math.cos(theta);
11  var y:Number = y-r*Math.sin(theta);
```

In this step, we want to find out where the ball should be (its *x* and *y* positions) when it first collides with the line. We do this by using the trigonometry described earlier. The variable names are the same as described before and match the figure. Lines 10 and 11 give us what we're looking for.

We perform step 4 next, before step 3. Here is the ActionScript for this step.

```
//Step 4
//Now find how long it will take to get to the
➥point of contact
var dis:Number = Math.sqrt((x-point.x)*(x-
➥point.x)+(y-point.y)*(y-point.y));
var vel:Number =
➥Math.sqrt(point.xmov*point.xmov+point.ymov*point.
➥ymov);
var frames:Number = dis/vel;
```

This step is refreshingly short. Here we calculate the number of frames it will take the ball to get from its current position to the point at which it is colliding with the line. Thinking back to the chapter on basic physics, we remember that *distance = velocity×frames*. If we solve this equation for frames, we get *frames = distance/velocity*. So if we find the distance between the current position and the collision point, and the velocity along that line, then we can find the number of frames it takes to get there! In line 2, we employ the Pythagorean theorem yet again to obtain the distance. In line 3, we use that same theorem one more time, to find the velocity along the path. Finally, in line 4, we get the number of frames by taking the ratio of distance and velocity.

To see a more detailed representation of how the time (frames) can be found, see line_ball_time_calculation.pdf in the Chapter05 directory.

In step 4, we check the physical point of contact to see if it is within the boundaries of the line segment.

```
1    //Step 3
2    //now check to see if point of contact is on the
     ➥line segment
3    var slope2a:Number = -1/tempLine.slope;
4    var b2a:Number = y-slope2a*x;
5    //point of contact
6    var xa:Number = (tempLine.b-b2a)/(slope2a-
     ➥tempLine.slope);
7    var ya:Number = slope2a*xa+b2a;
8    if ((xa>tempLine.x1 && xa<tempLine.x2) ||
     ➥(xa<tempLine.x1 && xa>tempLine.x2) ||
     ➥((ya>tempLine.y1 && ya<tempLine.y2) ||
     ➥(ya<tempLine.y1 && ya>tempLine.y2))) {
9         //within segment boundaries
10   } else {
11        //not within segment boundaries
12        //set frame1 high
13        var frames:Number = 1000;
14   }
15   return frames;
```

To find the coordinates of the point of contact, we imagine a line drawn through the center of the circle and the point of contact. The goal is to find the slope and y intercept of this line (which means we know everything about it) and then, with that information, to see where this line intersects with the main line. This intersection is the point of contact. We know the slope of the main line, and we know that all lines perpendicular to it have a slope that is the negative inverse of its own. Line 3 shows how we find the slope of the imaginary line. Remembering that the equation for a line is y =m×x+b and remembering that we have the coordinates for one point on that line (the center of the circle), we can plug in the x, y, and m (slope) values to find b (the y intercept). Line 4 shows this. Now we have all the information we need about both lines, so we can find the intersection between them. Lines 6 and 7 obtain the coordinates of the line intersection using the technique we have used a few times now. This code block ends with a conditional statement that compares this point (the intersection) with the boundaries of the line segment. If the point falls within the boundaries, then nothing happens. If this point (which is the intersection between the two lines) does not fall within the segment boundaries, then a collision did not happen and so `frames` is set to 1000 (something high). If the frames variable value is less than or equal to 1 and the point of contact was within the boundaries of the line segment, then the collision is valid. The last line of code returns the `frames` variable as the result of the function. The function that called the `getFrames()` function, `bankCollisionDetect()`, has the frames returned to it and can then check to see if the frames are less than or equal to 1.

We will see this again in the next chapter, Chapter 6. You are on your way to creating a game with advanced techniques!

Point-Rectangle Collision Detection

After what you have seen in this chapter so far, what remains is very simple to understand and apply. (We will not be including frame-independent collision-detection scripts in this or the next section.)

Because this is not frame-independent collision detection, point-rectangle collision detection is like taking snapshots in time. And if the point is going fast enough, it can move through the rectangle without a collision being detected.

The logic for detecting a collision between a point and a rectangle is simple. The position of the point is compared with the position of each wall of the rectangle (see Figure 5.21). If the point's *x* position is greater than the *x* position of the left wall and less than the *x* position of the rectangle's right wall, and the point's *y* position is greater than the *y* position of the top wall (remember that the *y*-axis is inverted in Flash) and less than the *y* position of the bottom wall, then a collision is occurring.

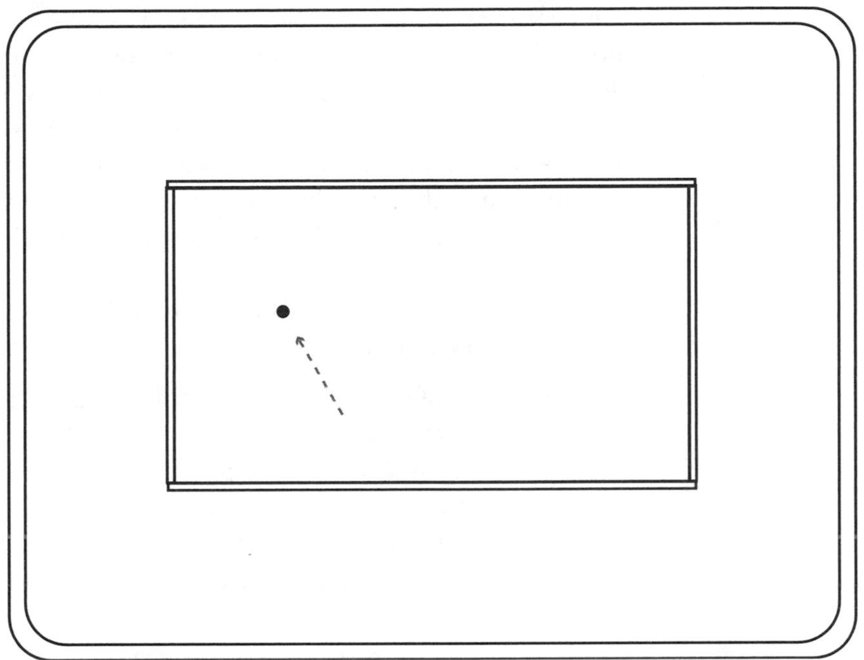

FIGURE 5.21
The x and y positions of the point are compared to those of the walls.

Open point_rectangle.fla to see an example. There are two movie clips on the Stage, point_clip1 and rectangle_clip1. The ActionScript creates an object to store the information for the point and for the rectangle. Then, in every frame, the point is moved, and a check is performed to detect collisions. Here is the ActionScript used to create the objects.

```
//Create an object to store information about point_clip1
var point1:Object = {};
point1.clip = point_clip1;
point1.x = point1.clip._x;
point1.y = point1.clip._y;
point1.xmov = 3;
point1.ymov = 1;
//Create an object to store information about
➥rectangle_clip1
var rectangle1:Object = {};
rectangle1.clip = rectangle_clip1;
rectangle1.x = rectangle1.clip._x;
rectangle1.y = rectangle1.clip._y;
rectangle1.width = rectangle1.clip._width;
rectangle1.height = rectangle1.clip._height;
```

You have seen this many times by now. We create an object for each movie clip on the Stage to store information about that movie clip. Notice that, for the rectangle, we are storing its position (its registration point is at the upper-left corner) as well as its width and height. Next in the ActionScript are two functions, one for creating a temporary position of the point in memory and the other to position the movie clip on the Stage. We will not list these functions here because they are identical to what we have seen several times already. Here is `pointRectangleDetection()`, the function that detects collisions between the point and the rectangle.

```
1     function pointRectangleDetection(point:Object,
      ➥rectangle:Object) {
2          //position of the point
3          var x:Number = point.x;
4          var y:Number = point.y;
5          //left and right walls
6          var x1:Number = rectangle.x;
7          var x2:Number = x1+rectangle.width;
8          //top and bottom walls
9          var y1:Number = rectangle.y;
10         var y2:Number = y1+rectangle.height;
11         //check to see if the point is within all of the
           ➥walls
12         if (x>x1 && x<x2 && y>y1 && y<y2) {
13              trace("Collision Detected!!");
14         }
15    }
```

This function accepts two parameters, `point` and `rectangle`, which are references to two objects. First, two variables are created that represent the position of the point. Then in lines 6–10, the *x* and *y* positions of the walls are assigned to variables. Finally, in line 12, a conditional is started that checks to see if the *x* position of the point is greater than the left wall but less than the right wall, and that the *y* position of the point is greater than the top wall and less than the bottom wall. If this condition is met, then a collision is occurring, and a trace action is executed.

Finally (although this is not shown above), an `onEnterFrame` event calls `getTempPositions()`, `pointRectangleDetection()`, and `render()` in every frame.

Rectangle-Rectangle Collision Detection

Like point-rectangle collision detection, collision detection between two rectangles is easy to perform. Rectangle_a is colliding with rectangle_b if all of the following are true:

1. The *x* position of the right wall of rectangle_a is greater than the *x* position of the left wall of rectangle_b.
2. The *x* position of the left wall of rectangle_a is less than the *x* position of the right wall of rectangle_b.
3. The *y* position of the bottom wall of rectangle_a is greater than the *y* position of the top wall of rectangle_b.
4. The *y* position of the top wall of rectangle_a is less than the *y* position of the bottom wall of rectangle_b.

Figure 5.22 illustrates these principles visually.

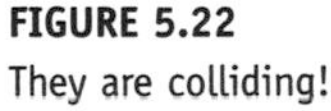

FIGURE 5.22
They are colliding!

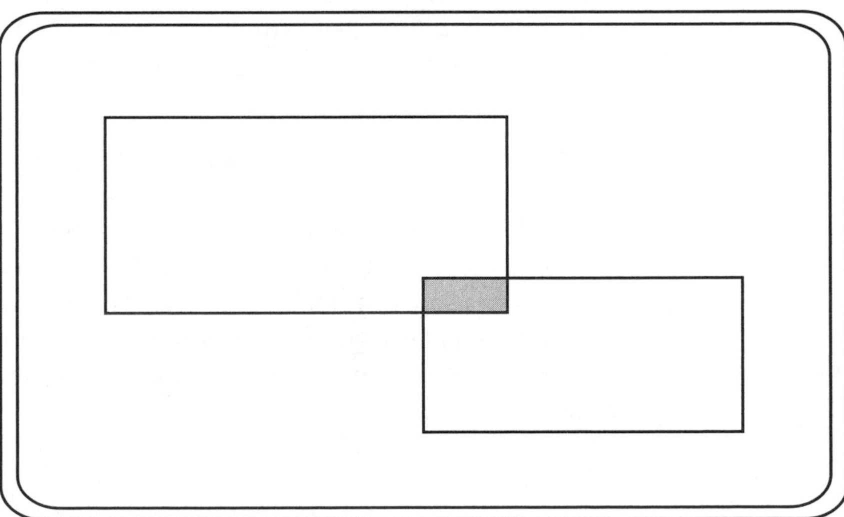

To see an example, open rectangle_rectangle.fla from the Chapter05 directory on the CD. The ActionScript in this file is very similar to the previous example, so we will only discuss the function that handles collision detection, `RectangleRectangleDetection()`. Here is the ActionScript:

```
1     function RectangleRectangleDetection(rectangle_a:Object,
      ➥rectangle_b:Object) {
2            //left and right walls
3            var x_a1:Number = rectangle_a.x;
4            var x_a2:Number = x_a1+rectangle_a.width;
5            //top and bottom walls
6            var y_a1:Number = rectangle_a.y;
7            var y_a2:Number = y_a1+rectangle_a.height;
8            //left and right walls
9            var x_b1:Number = rectangle_b.x;
10           var x_b2:Number = x_b1+rectangle_b.width;
11           //top and bottom walls
12           var y_b1:Number = rectangle_b.y;
13           var y_b2:Number = y_b1+rectangle_b.height;
14           //check to see if the point is within all of the
             ➥walls
15           if ((x_a2>x_b1 && x_a1<x_b2) && (y_a2>y_b1 &&
             ➥y_a1<y_b2)) {
16                 trace("Collision Detected!!");
17           }
18    }
```

This function accepts two parameters, `rectangle_a` and `rectangle_b`, which are references to objects. In lines 2–14, we set variables to store the positions of the left, right, top, and bottom walls of both rectangles. Then, in line 15, an `if` statement uses the logic we mentioned above to determine if a collision is taking place. It compares the positions of the walls in `rectangle_a` with the positions of the walls in `rectangle_b`. If the condition is met, then the rectangles are colliding and a trace action is executed.

Collision Detection with Advanced Shapes

In this chapter, we have developed frame-independent collision-detection logic and scripts for circle-line collisions (or point-line collisions, if you set the radius to 0). This is much more powerful than you might realize. With this knowledge, you can create simple or complicated shapes without any extra-fancy math. For instance, think of an octagon. Ordinarily you might not know how to detect a collision between a circle and an octagon. Well, why not put eight lines together and run a detection script for each of those lines? Suddenly, circle-octagon collision detection is a very easy thing! The shape in question doesn't have to be regular, either; you can create a star shape, a triangle, or even the shape of a house; the detection works because each line is treated separately (see Figure 5.23).

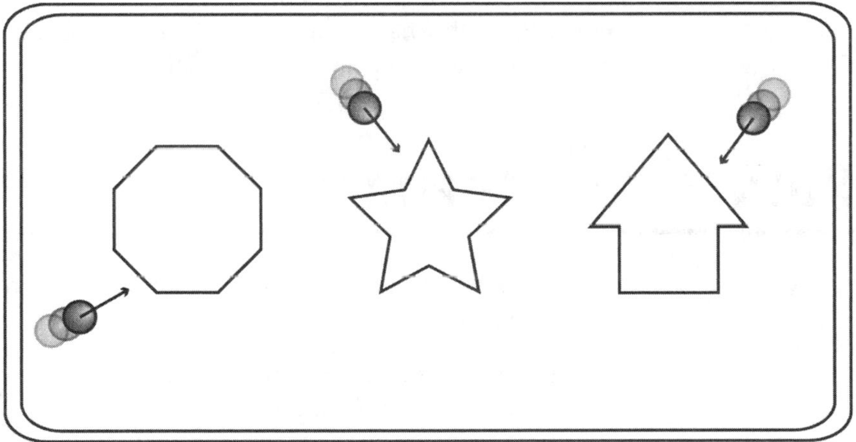

FIGURE 5.23
Many shapes can be created with line segments. Collision detection is performed on each line segment separately.

There is one problem you may encounter: multiple collisions at once. Imagine a rectangle shape and a ball colliding with the corner. It is likely that your script will detect two separate collisions. This is fine if you just want to know if a collision took place, but if you want to use a collision *reaction* (covered in the next chapter), then which line should the circle react to? The answer is simple: Keep track of the `frames` variable for each collision. The lowest one is the collision that occurred first. You can then make the circle react to the appropriate collision.

If you are interested in developing your own collision-detection scripts for shapes not covered here (for instance, point-ellipse collisions), follow this simple formula:

1. List the conditions that must be met for a collision to take place.
2. Figure out how to determine if each condition is met.

You may have to pick up a book on geometry or trigonometry if you are looking for the equations that define more complicated objects such as ellipses or toroids (doughnut shapes). See Appendix A, "Developer Resources," for book suggestions.

Collision detection is a fundamental requirement for most games, however simple they may be. With what you've learned in this chapter, you can detect collisions between almost any two objects. Combine all this knowledge with what you'll gain in the next chapter, and you will soon be creating advanced games like pinball and billiards!

Points to Remember

- A collision occurs when two separate shapes share one or more points in space.
- In Flash, you can use two main types of programmatic collision detection: `hitTest()` and math.
- Using math is considered the superior method of collision detection because in addition to confirming detections in the present, you may also be able to use it to determine the future time and location of a collision.
- Limitations of `hitTest()` include its limited capabilities with complex shapes, its close relationship to specific graphics or movie clips, and its dependence on frame rates.

- Code-graphics independence is a liberating method of working with movie clips. It uses objects to store information about each movie clip. Storing information in an object—separate from its actual interface element—is a good practice because it enables you to add or remove movie clips from the Stage without losing the data.
- You can use the Linkage feature to enable ActionScript to create an unlimited number of new instances of any kind of symbol (not just movie clips) in the Flash file's Library.
- Loops are an immeasurably helpful tool to use with ActionScript, especially when your work involves performing identical tasks on a number of elements such as movie clips.
- Using math for collision detection also enables you to work with irregular shapes, write frame-independent collision-detection scripts, and handle all of the code in memory, rather than basing it on the placement of the graphics.
- The frame-independent collision-detection logic (and scripts) that you've learned here can be applied to the creation of any other simple or complicated shapes by breaking them down into lines.

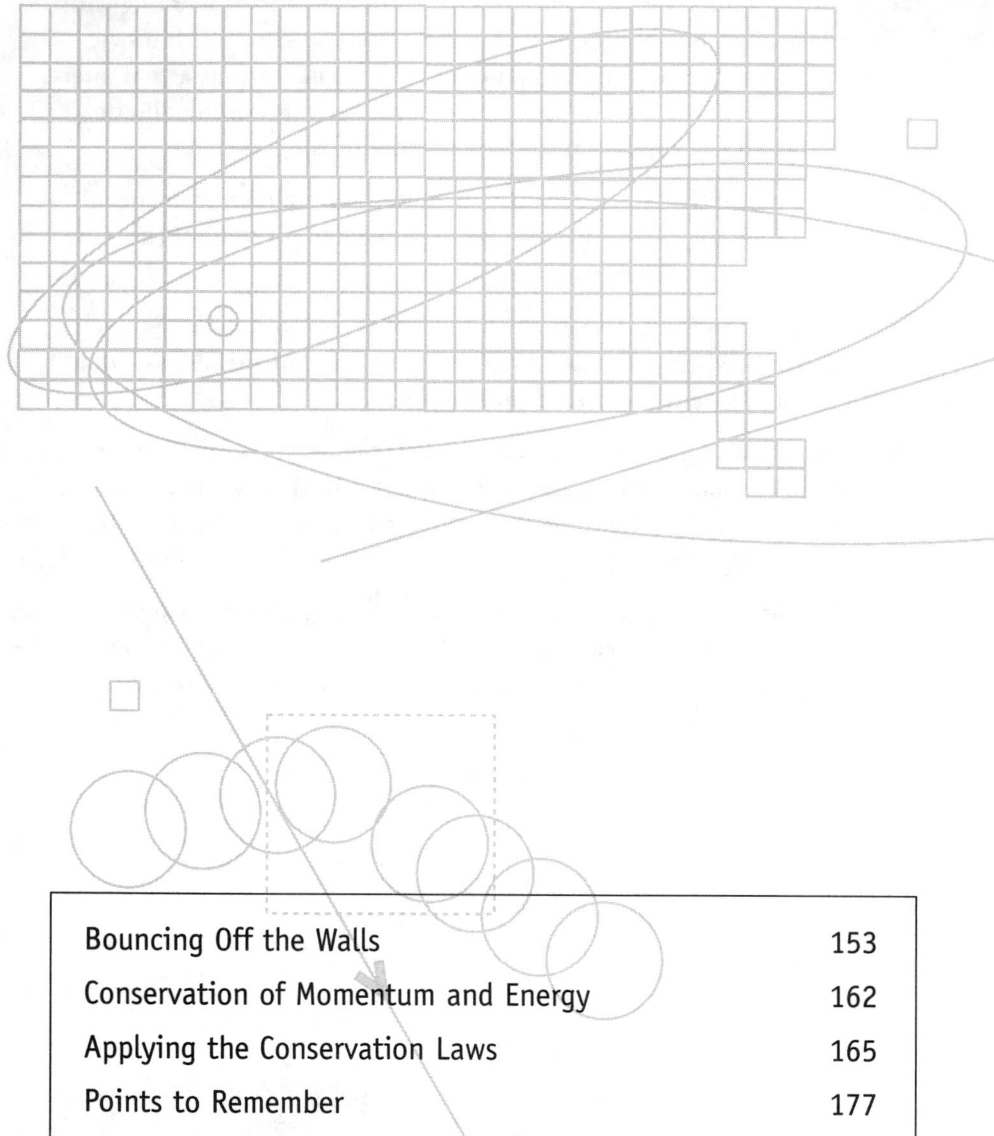

Bouncing Off the Walls 153

Conservation of Momentum and Energy 162

Applying the Conservation Laws 165

Points to Remember 177

CHAPTER 6

COLLISION REACTIONS

IN THIS CHAPTER, THINGS REALLY START TO COME TOGETHER. YOU WILL BE applying many ideas you learned from previous chapters. In Chapter 4, "Basic Physics," you learned the concepts and equations needed to move movie clips around the screen. With the added concepts of gravity and friction, you were able to add even more realism to a programmed system. In Chapter 5, "Collision Detection," you learned how to detect collisions between many types of objects—some moving, some not. The logical next step is to learn the physics and equations involved in making objects (movie clips) react to a collision in a physically realistic way. In this chapter, we will look at several useful examples of collision reactions (see Figure 6.1). For a few of them, we'll also learn about (and apply) the laws of conservation of momentum and energy. By the end of this chapter, you will be able to program billiard-ball collisions, a box or a ball bouncing off a floor or wall, and even a ball bouncing off an angled line! Suddenly games like pinball, pool, and air hockey won't seem quite as mysterious.

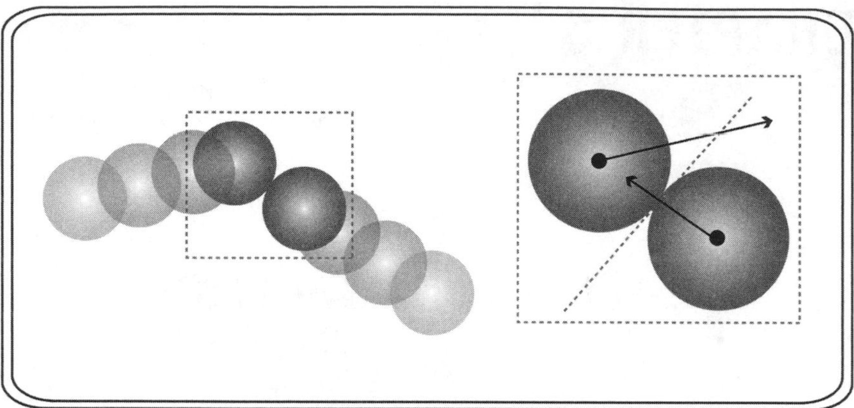

FIGURE 6.1
Collision reactions.

I've divided the collision types we'll cover in this chapter into four loosely connected categories:

- **Object-wall collision reactions**—This type of reaction occurs when an object like a circle or a rectangle collides with a wall or a floor.
- **Circle-line collision reactions**—This type of reaction occurs when a circle collides with an angled line (for example, in pinball physics).
- **Rectangle-rectangle collision reactions**—This type of reaction occurs when two rectangular objects collide straight on (no rotation).
- **Circle-circle collision reactions**—This type of reaction occurs when two circles (for example, billiard balls) collide at any angle.

We are sticking to these collision reactions for several reasons. The main reason is that most other collision detections do not need a physical reaction. For instance, a point collision with a balloon will most likely result in an animation of a balloon popping, not a programmed reaction. The intersection between two lines is usually used to determine something bigger, like the collision between a ball and a line, so we do not attempt to program any reaction for two lines intersecting.

Another reason that we're only covering a few types of collision detection and reactions is that it's often a good idea to assume that simpler shapes are being used. If your game involves throwing a baseball at a watermelon, then instead of developing specified circle-ellipse collision-detection techniques, it would be faster to assume that the watermelon is a circle (or even a rectangle). The collision detection will be good enough, and the script will run faster than if you were detecting a more complicated shape. This corner-cutting technique is used in almost every major computer game on the market. For instance, in *Tomb Raider*, the main character is assumed to be a cylinder, rather than a person with complicated proportions. (Betcha didn't know that, did you?) This geometric approximation makes the collision detection much easier.

Bouncing Off the Walls

A wall is any object that cannot move as a result of a collision but that can be collided with. For instance, if you throw a tennis ball at a wall, the wall does not move, but it certainly gets hit! By this definition, even the paddles in a simple game of Pong are considered walls (see Figure 6.2). In that case, they are walls that can move, but their movement is not the result of a collision. In this section, we'll look at collisions with walls and collisions with lines of any angle, which are often used as walls. (Later in this chapter, we'll work with the less stationary objects.)

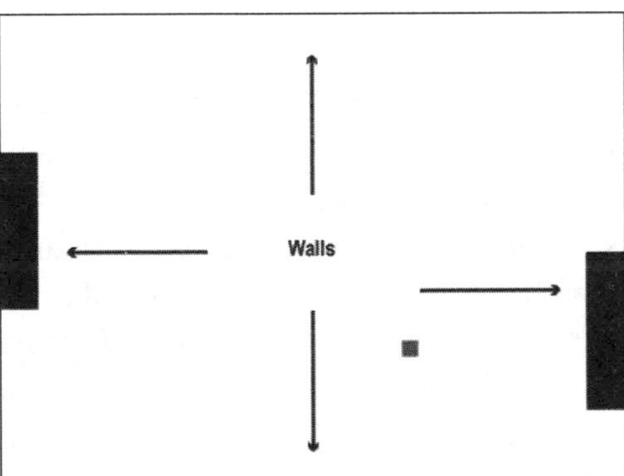

FIGURE 6.2
Walls.

Object-Wall Reactions

An object-wall collision (affectionately called *ball-wall*) is the easiest type of collision for which to program a reaction. Think of the tennis ball example again. When the tennis ball bounces off the wall, it rebounds at the same speed at which it struck the wall. (Because this is an elastic collision—more on that later—there's no energy lost in the collision, and therefore no loss in speed.) This is good news for us because it means that when we detect a collision with a wall, we can just reverse the object's speed. Note that we would only reverse the speed component that is perpendicular to the wall, as shown in Figure 6.3.

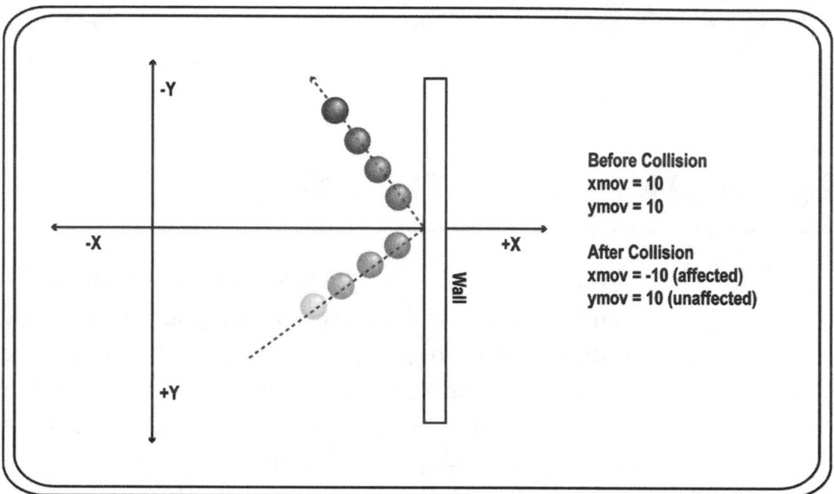

FIGURE 6.3
Speed before and after collision.

Let's look at a practical example of this. Open pong1.fla in the Chapter06 directory. This is an unfinished version of a very simple game, *Pong*. In Pong, a ball moves across the screen, and it is up to you to keep it from leaving the screen on your side (the left). There are two paddles on the screen that move vertically. One paddle is on the left boundary of the game area, and the other is on the right boundary of the game area. The left paddle is controlled by the user (that's you), and the right paddle is controlled by the computer using a simple AI script (discussed in Chapter 11, "Artificial Intelligence"). There is an instance of a ball movie clip on the Stage (within the board movie clip); it's a square shape, but it's still called a ball. The registration point for this movie clip is its top-left boundary. Collision detection occurs between the ball and the paddles and between the ball and the top and bottom of the game area. If the ball collides with a paddle, then its *x* speed is reversed. If the ball collides with the top or bottom of the game area, then its *y* speed is reversed.

We are not going to discuss most of the ActionScript in this file. Rather, we are going to focus on the areas where collision reactions are used. If you have read through the previous chapters on collision detection and physics, then you are familiar with just about all the ActionScript in this file. Two things may be new to you though:

- The game.gameAI() method (which will be discussed in Chapter 11).
- The manner in which the methods were created. All the methods were created on the game object itself, rather than in the Timeline. This is not a necessity, but it brings us a little bit closer to coding in an object-oriented way.

A function that belongs to an object is called a *method*. This is just a terminology shift; there is really no substantive difference between the two. Like many people whose first programming language is ActionScript, I often use the terminology incorrectly. I sometimes say "method" when I mean "function," or the other way around. Wasn't it Shakespeare who said, "That which we call a function by any other name would still process data?"

In this particular file, collision reaction is implemented in every place where a collision-detection script sits. We check for collisions in the methods game.checkForWalls() and game.checkPaddleCollisions(). Here is the ActionScript for the game.checkForWalls() method:

```
1     game.checkForWalls = function() {
2           if (this.ball.tempy<0) {
3                 //hit top wall
4                 this.ball.tempy = 0;
5                 this.ball.ymov *= -1;
6           } else if
            ➥(this.ball.tempy+this.ball.radius>this.height) {
7                 //this bottom wall
8                 this.ball.tempy = this.height-
                  ➥this.ball.radius;
9                 this.ball.ymov *= -1;
10          }
11    };
```

If you remember from the previous chapters, we usually create a temporary position in memory describing where an object will be, tempx and tempy. We use this temporary position to check for collisions. The upper boundary of the game board is 0; the lower boundary is game.height. In line 2 of this ActionScript, we check to see if ball.tempy is less than 0. If it is, then a collision is occurring with the top wall, and the if statement is entered. Line 4 sets ball.tempy = 0, which positions the ball right up against the top wall. This is a necessary step. Due to the frame-based nature of Flash MX, ball.tempy could be substantially less than 0, and if we did not set it right up against the boundary and only reversed the speed when a collision occurred instead, then it would look as if the ball went into the wall rather than bouncing off of it. In line 5, we finally perform the very simple collision reaction: We reverse the *y* speed of the ball.

The `else if` piece of the conditional statement, in line 6, checks to see if the *y* position of the ball's bottom edge is greater than the *y* position of the game's lower boundary. (The bottommost part of the ball is its *y* position plus its height.) You may recall that the value for the *y* position of the game's bottom boundary was set earlier in the frame as `game.height`. Because the `checkForWalls()` method belongs to the game object, we can access this property by using `this.height`, which we do in line 6. If this condition is satisfied, then we know the ball is colliding with the bottom wall, and we enter this piece of the `if` statement (lines 7–9). In line 8, we set the position of the ball so that it sits right up against the bottom wall. We do this for the same reason as we did it for the top wall—so the ball doesn't look as if it has gone through the wall. In line 9, we reverse the ball's *y* speed; this is our collision reaction.

Now let's look at the `game.checkPaddleCollisions()` method:

```
game.checkPaddleCollisions = function() {
      if (this.ball.tempx
      ➥<this.leftPaddle.x+this.leftPaddle.width &&
      ➥this.ball.tempx+this.ball.radius
      ➥?>this.leftPaddle.x ?&&
      ➥this.ball.tempy+this.ball.radius
      ➥?>this.leftPaddle.y && this.ball.tempy
      ➥<this.leftPaddle.y+this.leftPaddle.height) {
            //left paddle collision detection
            this.ball.tempx = this.leftPaddle.x
            ➥+this.leftPaddle.width;
            this.ball.xmov *= -1;
      }
      if (this.ball.tempx
      ➥<this.rightPaddle.x+this.rightPaddle.width &&
      ➥this.ball.tempx+this.ball.radius
      ➥>this.rightPaddle.x &&
      ➥this.ball.tempy+this.ball.radius
      ➥>this.rightPaddle.y && this.ball.tempy
      ➥<this.rightPaddle.y+this.rightPaddle.height) {
```

```
8                   //right paddle collision detection
9                   this.ball.tempx = this.rightPaddle.x -
                    ➥this.ball.radius;
10                  this.ball.xmov *= -1;
11          }
12      };
```

In this ActionScript, the `if` statements look complicated, but the concept here is one that you have already used in Chapter 5, when we talked about rectangle-rectangle collision detection. Each checks for a collision between two rectangles—the ball and a paddle. We saw how to perform rectangle-rectangle collision detections in the previous chapter. Here, we check for the following conditions:

- The left side of the ball has a smaller *x* than the right side of the paddle.
- The right side of the ball has a greater *x* than the left side of the paddle.
- The top side of the ball has a smaller *y* than the bottom side of the paddle.
- The bottom side of the ball has a greater *y* than the top side of the paddle.

If all four of these conditions are met, then a collision has occurred between the ball and the paddle. This check is done in exactly the same way in lines 2 and 7: once for the left paddle and once for the right paddle. If the condition in line 2 is met, then the ball is colliding with the paddle, and lines 4 and 5 are executed. Line 5 positions the ball so that it is just barely touching the paddle on the right side. Line 5 reverses the ball's *x* speed. Likewise, if the condition in line 7 is met, then the ball is placed so that it is just barely touching the paddle on the right, and its speed is reversed.

Keep in mind that we are not using frame-independent collision detection here. This means that if you were to take this young game and try to make it into a full-grown game in which the ball gets steadily faster, then you might encounter the typical "snapshot" collision-detection problems. Thus, if the ball is moving fast enough, it may move straight through a paddle. You can, if you choose, use the ball-line collision-detection scripts developed in the previous chapter for each wall of the paddles. This would give you frame-independent *Pong*.

Now let's look at another example: a ball falling under gravity and bouncing off a floor. Open ball_floor.fla in the Chapter06 directory. On the Stage, you see the movie-clip instances `ball_clip` and `floor_clip`. The ActionScript in this file creates an object called `ball` to store information about `ball_clip`, sets a temporary position for the ball, checks for a collision with the floor, and renders the ball. If the script detects a collision between the ball and the floor, then the ball is set to be touching the floor, and its speed is reversed. There is one added feature involved in this process that has not yet been introduced: *decay*. In this example, a variable called `decay` is set with a value of `.6`. Here is the ActionScript for the collision-detection function.

```
function ballFloorDetection() {
      if (ball.tempy+ball.radius>floorY) {
            ball.tempy = floorY-ball.radius;
            ball.ymov *= -1*decay;
      }
}
```

If a collision is happening, then the ball's speed is reversed and multiplied by the variable `decay`. Decay is a way to have the ball bounce less high on each successive bounce; it lowers the magnitude of the speed by a percentage each time a collision happens. All decay values are between 0 and 1. For instance, in this file we are using a `decay` of `.6` (set at the top of the frame, not shown here). That means each successive bounce will rebound with only 60 percent of the speed with which it collided in the first place.

The possible values for decay are all positive numbers (including zero), but the realistic range is between 0 and 1. If decay is set to 0, then the ball will stick to the ground. If decay is set to 1, then the ball will bounce to the same height forever. If the decay is set to a value greater than 1, the ball will bounce higher on each successive bounce (which is no longer a decay). When you generate an SWF from this file, you'll see that the ball will bounce a few times and then stop. This mimics the behavior of a regular old basketball. The goal of this chapter is to show you how to program realistic reactions. Adding a decay factor is one easy way to add realism to your floor or wall collision reactions.

Circle-Line Reactions

Circle-line, or ball-line, reactions occur when a ball collides with a line at any angle (such as the angled walls in a game of pinball). Three steps are required to find the resultant *x* and *y* velocities of a ball after a collision with a line:

1. Project the *x* and *y* velocities onto the line of action (for example, the line, or the bank, if you're still thinking pinball) (see Figure 6.4).

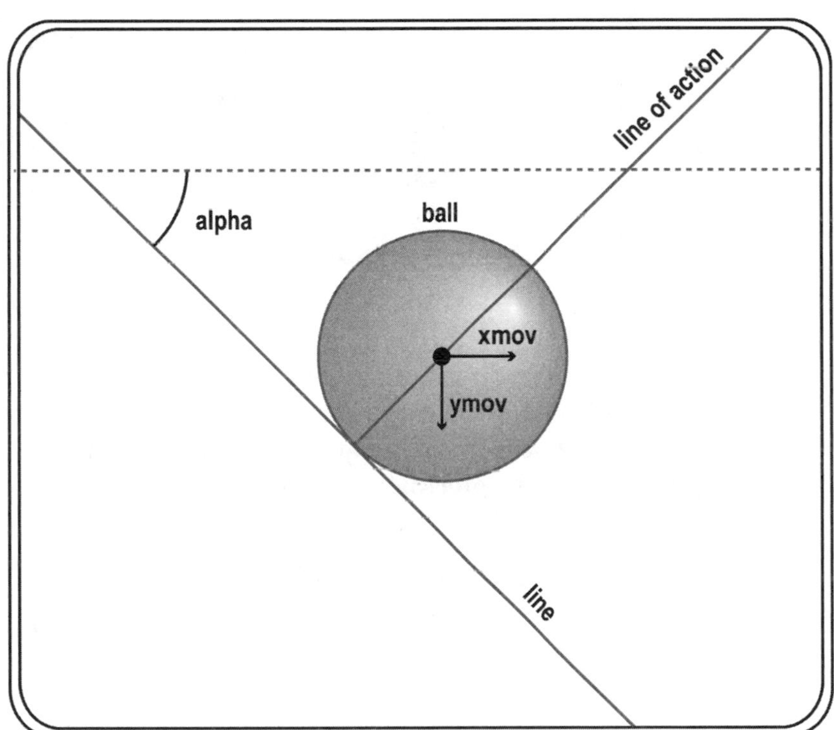

FIGURE 6.4
The x and y velocities projected onto the line of action.

When two objects collide, the momentum affected is the component that lies along the *line of action*—the imaginary line that runs perpendicular to the tangent line that goes through the point of collision.

2. Reverse the velocity that lies along the line of action. This is done because the only piece of the velocity affected by the collision is the one that lies along the line of action. The velocity that lies along the "real" line (the one that the ball collides with) is unaffected by the collision.

3. Project the velocities that are along the line and the line of action back onto the *x* and *y* axes. This gives us the final result we were looking for: the *x* and *y* velocities after the collision.

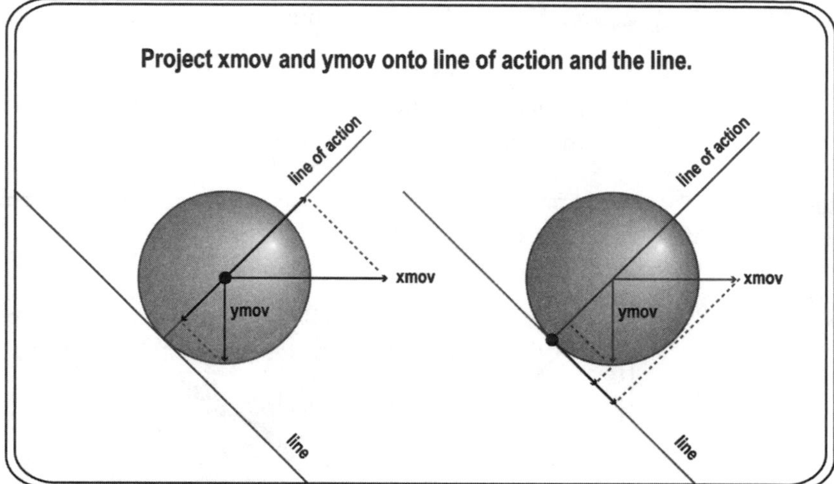

FIGURE 6.5
Xmov and Ymov projected onto the line of action and the line.

Now that you've seen the quick overview of how to find those velocities, we'll go through it step by step. Let's call the *x* velocity of the ball *vxi* (*v* for "velocity," *x* for "*x* direction," *i* for "initial") and the *y* velocity of the ball *vyi*. The projection of *vxi* and *vyi* onto the line of action is *vyip* (*p* stands for "prime"):

```
vyip = vyi*cos(alpha)-vxi*sin(alpha)
```

The projection of *vxi* and *vyi* onto the line itself is *vxip*.

```
vxip = vxi*cos(alpha)+vyi*sin(alpha)
```

Now that step 1 is complete, we move on to step 2 and reverse *vyip* (remember that *f* stands for "final").

```
vyfp = -vyip
vxfp = vxip
```

Notice that the final velocity along the line *(vxfp)* is unchanged. Now we move on to step 3 to project *vyfp* and *vxfp* back to the *x* and *y* axes to arrive at the final velocities, *vxf* and *vyf*.

```
vxf = vxfp*cos(alpha)-vyfp*sin(alpha)
vyf = vyfp*cos(alpha)+vxfp*sin(alpha)
```

These two values, *vxf* and *vyf*, are the *x* and *y* velocities of the ball at the moment after the collision. Using this in ActionScript is not difficult. Let's take a look at an example. Open the file ball_line.fla in the Chapter06 directory. The ActionScript in this file is very similar to that in the ball_line.fla file you saw in Chapter 5. The main addition to the ActionScript in this file is the function `ballLineReaction()`. Here is that function:

```
function ballLineReaction(tempLine:Object, point:Object,
➥x:Number, y:Number) :void{
      var lineDecay:Number = tempLine.lineDecay;
      var alpha:Number = tempLine.angle;
      var cosAlpha:Number = Math.cos(alpha);
      var sinAlpha:Number = Math.sin(alpha);
      //get the x and y velocities of the ball
      var vyi:Number = point.ymov;
      var vxi:Number = point.xmov;
      //project the x and y velocities onto the line of
      ➥action
      var vyip:Number = vyi*cosAlpha-vxi*sinAlpha;
      //project the x and y velocities onto the line
      var vxip:Number = vxi*cosAlpha+vyi*sinAlpha;
      //reverse the velocity along the line of action
      var vyfp:Number = -vyip*lineDecay;
      var vxfp:Number = vxip;
      //translate back to Flash's x and y axes
      var vyf:Number = vyfp*cosAlpha+vxfp*sinAlpha;
      var vxf:Number = vxfp*cosAlpha-vyfp*sinAlpha;
      //set the velocities of the ball based from the
      ➥results
      point.xmov = vxf;
      point.ymov = vyf;
      point.tempx = point.x+point.xmov;
      point.tempy = point.y+point.ymov;
}
```

This function is called from the `getFrames()` function when a collision has been detected. A reference to the line object is passed in as `tempLine`, and a reference to the object that represents the ball is passed in as `point`. The *x* and *y* positions of the ball at the point of contact are also passed into this function. Line 2 sets a variable called `lineDecay`. This is a value between 0 and 1 that reduces the rebound velocity. (The concept of decay was introduced earlier in this chapter; if decay has a value of 1, then no decay occurs.) Next, we set variables to store the cosine and sine of the line angle (lines 4 and 5). We store these values because they are needed more than once throughout the ActionScript, and as you've already seen, it is quicker for Flash to reuse the variables than to calculate the sine and cosine repeatedly. To match variable names with what we worked out in this section, we set two variables, `vyi` and `vxi`, from the *y* and *x* velocities of the ball (lines 7 and 8). In line 10, we project `vyi` and `vxi` onto the line of action, and in line 12, we project `vxi` and `vyi` onto the line. We then reverse the velocity along the line of action, `vyip`, and multiply it by `lineDecay`. The act of reversing this velocity is the reaction to the collision. Next, in lines 17 and 18, we project back onto the *x* and *y* axes. In lines 20 and 21, we update `xmov` and `ymov` on the `ball` object with the new velocities. Finally, we update `tempx` and `tempy` on the ball object (lines 22 and 23).

Generate an SWF from this file to see it in action. You will note that three lines are created. The ball falls under gravity onto a line and bounces around a bit. Eventually, the ball comes to a rest in a small dip (see Figure 6.6).

FIGURE 6.6
The ball will eventually rest in the dip.

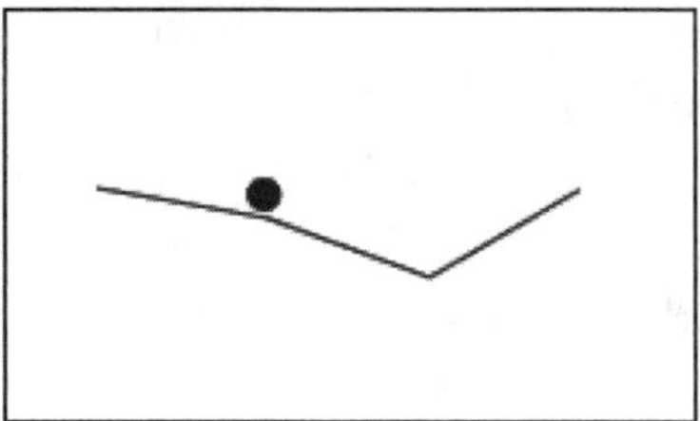

CONSERVATION OF MOMENTUM AND ENERGY

In this section, we're going to discuss two physical laws that give us some mathematical relationships that help determine the resultant velocities of two collided objects. But before discussing the *laws* of conservation of momentum and conservation of energy, we of course need to introduce the *concepts* of momentum and energy.

Review: What Are Momentum and Energy?

Momentum is a quantity associated with all objects and characterized by an object's mass and velocity. Momentum is a vector whose direction is given by the velocity. Mathematically, this is momentum:

```
momentum = mass*velocity
```

Usually the variable for momentum is the letter *p*. Here is an example of how you would use ActionScript to calculate the momentum of something moving in the *x* direction:

```
p = mass*xmov
```

Momentum is not too difficult to conceptualize. Imagine a 100-pound man and a 200-pound man running at the same velocity. Common sense tells you that the 200-pound man has more momentum. But now you can prove that with this equation: The 200-pound man has twice the momentum.

Energy is a little bit more difficult to explain, even though we are all familiar with it in various everyday forms. It is the measure of a system's capability to do work. Energy is classified into two main categories: *kinetic energy* and *potential energy*. Kinetic energy (which is all we will use in this chapter and indeed the whole book) is the energy associated with the movement of an object. Potential energy is the energy stored in an object that can be converted to kinetic energy. This includes the energy stored in an object raised off the ground (gravitational potential energy), electrical energy, nuclear energy, and chemical energy.

Kinetic energy is dependent on an object's mass and speed. Mathematically, here is the kinetic energy of an object:

kinetic energy = (?)*mass*speed^2

Kinetic energy is usually represented by *E*, *KE*, or *T* (don't ask me why). We will use *KE* or *ke* to represent kinetic energy. Here is an example of how this equation would be written in ActionScript:

```
ke = (?)*mass*speed*speed
```

The Conservation Laws

Now that we've introduced momentum and energy, it is time to spell out the simple laws of conservation of momentum and conservation of energy. Basically, these laws, or rules, state that the quantities of momentum or of energy will not actually change in the course of a collision. (In other words, in this case the word *conserve* simply means "doesn't change.") Let's start with momentum. The momentum of an object (or system) is conserved if the total force on it is 0. As an example, consider two billiard balls moving toward each other. Ball1 has the momentum *p1_initial*, and ball2 has the momentum *p2_initial*. If we sum these two momentums, then we get the total momentum before the collision, *P_initial*. After the balls collide and rebound, each has a new momentum—*p1_final* and *p2_final*. If we sum these two momentums, we get *P_final*. According to the conservation law for momentum, the total momentum after the collision is the same as the total momentum before the collision (if there is no net external force acting on the system, such as wind). If this condition is met, then *P_initial* = *P_final* (see Figure 6.7).

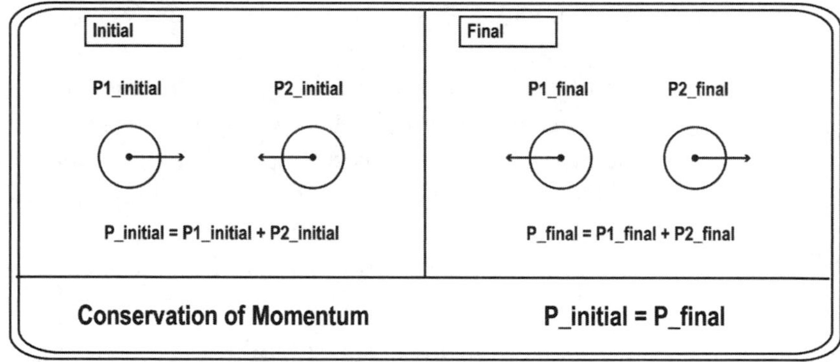

FIGURE 6.7
The total momentum after the collision is the same as the total momentum before the collision.

It is important to note that we are talking about *elastic* collisions here. In elastic collisions, both kinetic energy and momentum are conserved. We aren't going to get into inelastic collisions, in which only momentum is conserved (for example, rain sticking to a ball in the air, hence changing the mass of the object).

The billiard-ball example given previously describes the most common and likely use you'll have for applying this conservation law: the collision and rebound of two objects. This law applies to other types of events as well, events involving individual objects dividing into pieces (for example, a stage separating from its base rocket ship, or a plate breaking). We aren't going to cover those here because they are not commonly used in Flash games.

Like momentum, energy is conserved when the final energy is equal to the initial energy. A more complicated definition for the energy-conservation law exists, but it includes some concepts that take a lot of explanation. It should be assumed that in all the cases we deal with in this book, the total energy at the instant before a collision is the same as the energy at the instant after the collision. Let's use the same billiard-ball example to spell this out. The sum of the kinetic energy of each ball before the collision—*ke1_initial* and *ke2_initial*—is *KE_initial*. The sum of the kinetic energy of each ball after the collision—*ke1_final* and *ke2_final*—is *KE_final*. The law of the conservation of energy tells us that the final kinetic energy is the same as the initial energy, so *KE_initial* = *KE_final*.

Applying the Conservation Laws

In this section, we'll apply these two conservation laws to help us find the motion of objects after a collision.

The derivation of the equations here is also shown worked out on paper in collision_reaction.pdf in the Chapter06 directory on the CD-ROM.

You may be wondering why we have introduced these conservation laws. The reason is that we're going to apply them to help us find the motion of objects after a collision—we are looking for structures and relationships that will enable us to determine the new velocities of objects after they collide. In this section, we'll derive the equations that can tell us the new velocities of two collided objects. We will then apply these equations in two cases: two rectangles colliding and two billiard balls colliding.

Let's assume that two objects, object1 and object2, are moving toward each other. Object1 is of mass *m1* and velocity *v1i*, and object2 is of mass *m2* and velocity *v2i*. The two objects collide elastically. We want to learn the new velocities of each object after the collision.

In these equations, *i* signifies "initial" and *f* signifies "final."

Before the collision

Momentum of the objects:

```
p1i = m1*v1i
p2i = m2*v2i
Pi = p1i+p2i
```

Kinetic energy of the objects:

```
ke1i = (1/2)*m1*v1i²
ke2i = (1/2)*m2*v2i²
KEi = ke1i+ke2i
```

After the collision

```
p1f = m1*v1f
p2f = m2*v2f
Pf = p1f+p2f
```

Kinetic energy of the objects:

```
ke1f = (1/2)*m1*v1f²
ke2f = (1/2)*m2*v2f²
KEf = ke1f+ke2f
```

Apply the law of the conservation of momentum

```
Pi = Pf = P
m1*v1i+m2*v2i = m1*v1f+m2*v2f
KEi = Kef
(1/2)*m1*v1i²+(1/2)*m2*v2i² = (1/2)*m1*v1f²+(1/2)*m2*v2f²
```

Rearranging and combining these two equations, we get the following:

```
v1i-v2i = v2f-v1f
V = v1i-v2i
```

So,

```
v1f = v2f-V
```

Using this equation with the equation for *P*, we get the final results:

```
v2f = (P+V*m1)/(m1+m2)
v1f = v2f-v1i+v2i
```

If you are interested in seeing more of the in-between steps in the preceding derivation, you can check out collision_reaction.pdf in the

Chapter06 directory. To use this information, all we need to do is calculate the values for *P* and *V* and then use the last two equations. In the next section, we'll look at an example of how we might use this in Flash.

Rectangle-Rectangle Reactions

Open rectangle_rectangle.fla in the Chapter06 directory. You may notice that this is the same file we used in Chapter 5—with a few modifications and additions. During the object definitions at the beginning of the ActionScript, we add `rectangle1.mass = 1` and `rectangle2.mass = 1`. In conservation-of-momentum situations (for example, collisions), the mass of any one specific object is not important. What is important is the *relative* masses—how the masses compare. Here, as you can see, both objects have a mass of 1. If we set the mass of both objects to 1,000,000, the result would be the same. If the mass of `rectangle1` is 5 and the mass of `rectangle2` is 1, then `rectangle1` is five times as massive as `rectangle2`. This would produce the same results as if `rectangle1` had a mass of 50 and `rectangle2` had a mass of 10 (in both cases, the mass ratio is 5 to 1).

Another change to this file is that instead of executing a trace action when a collision is detected, we execute a function called `reaction()`. This function calculates the new velocities of the objects after they have collided.

```
function reaction(a:Object, b:Object) :void{
        var m1:Number = a.mass;
        var m2:Number = b.mass;
        var v1i:Number = a.xmov;
        var v2i:Number = b.xmov;
        var V:Number = v1i-v2i;
        var P:Number = m1*v1i+m2*v2i;
        //the new x speed of b
        var v2f:Number = (P+m1*V)/(m1+m2);
        //the new x speed of a
        var v1f:Number = v2f-v1i+v2i;
        //take the new speeds and put them in the objects
        a.xmov = v1f;
        b.xmov = v2f;
        //update the tempx positions with the new speeds
```

```
16        a.tempx = a.x+a.xmov;
17        b.tempx = b.x+b.xmov;
18    }
19    function getTempPositions():void {
20        rectangle1.tempx = rectangle1.x+rectangle1.xmov;
21        rectangle1.tempy = rectangle1.y+rectangle1.ymov;
22        rectangle2.tempx = rectangle2.x+rectangle2.xmov;
23        rectangle2.tempy = rectangle2.y+rectangle2.ymov;
24    }
```

The parameters `a` and `b` are references to the rectangle objects. They are passed into this function when it is called. Lines 2 and 3 set the mass variables. Lines 4 and 5 set the initial speed variables. The next two lines set the quantities `V` and `P`. Lines 9 and 11 solve for the new speed of each object. We then take these new speeds and update the `xmov` variable in each of the objects (lines 13 and 14). Because we are updating the `xmov` variables, we also need to update the `tempx` variables (lines 16 and 17).

Generate an SWF to test this file. You will see that when the two objects collide, they rebound realistically. You can change the mass values of each of the rectangles to convince yourself that the physical realism holds up.

To see an example of this in Flash (not in a game) with multiple rectangles of different masses, check out railroad.fla in the Chapter06 directory (see Figure 6.8). This file was created with Flash 5, so don't be surprised if the ActionScript looks a little different from what you would expect with Flash MX 2004.

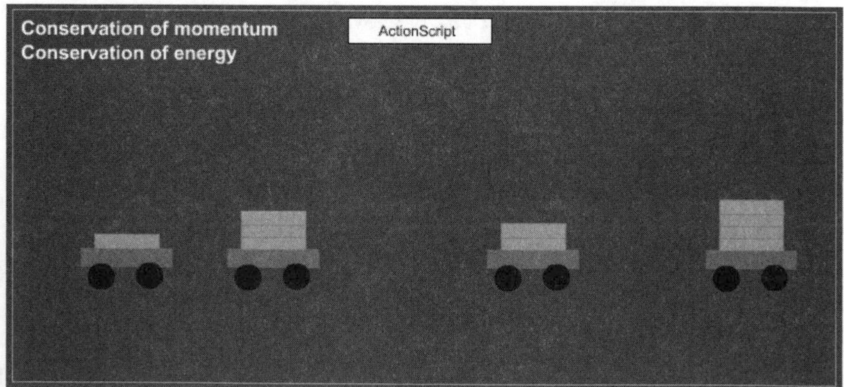

FIGURE 6.8
The railroad example.

Circle-Circle (Billiard-Ball) Reactions

The steps involved in showing the realistic reaction from colliding billiard balls are more complicated than those for a reaction of two rectangles. The conservation equations we developed do not change at all; the trick is to figure out what is conserved. Remember, when two objects collide, the momentum affected is the component that lies along the line of action. For instance, in the rectangle collision discussed previously, the line of action is the imaginary line between the two centers of the rectangles, which is along the *x*-axis. Therefore, the momentum affected lies along the *x*-axis. If these two rectangles were also moving in the *y* direction, then their *y* velocities would be unaffected when colliding. When two balls are colliding, their line of action is drawn between the two centers (see Figure 6.9). The amount of momentum that lies along this line is what is affected in the collision, so we must use trigonometry to find the velocity of each ball that lies along this line. Finding the amount of one vector that lies along another line is called *projection,* and it was covered extensively in Chapter 3, "Game Math." Here we project the *x* and *y* velocities of each ball onto the line of action. The velocity components that lie along the line of action are what are affected by the collision. We can then use the conservation equations to find the new velocities. With the new velocities, we can project backward to get the new velocities along the *x* and *y* axes (see Figure 6.9).

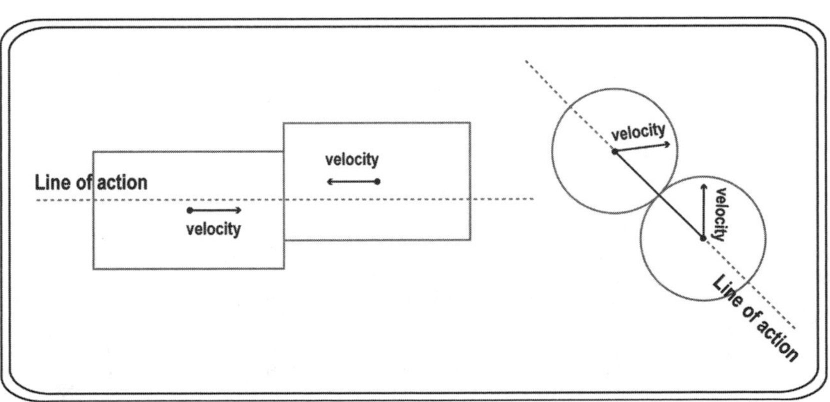

FIGURE 6.9
Colliding rectangles versus colliding billiard balls.

If this sounds confusing, that's only because it *is* confusing! If you just want to use the result, then skip ahead a few pages to where we dissect the FLA file. If you are interested in understanding how we arrive at the ActionScript, then stay right here. (And if you want to see this worked out on paper, then open up billiard_ball_reactions.pdf from the CD.)

We have two billiard balls, ball1 of *x* velocity *xvel1* and *y* velocity *yvel1*, and ball2 of *x* velocity *xvel2* and *y* velocity *yvel2*. Our goal is to project the *x* and *y* velocities onto the line of action. We can then apply the conservation equations to these velocities (see Figure 6.10).

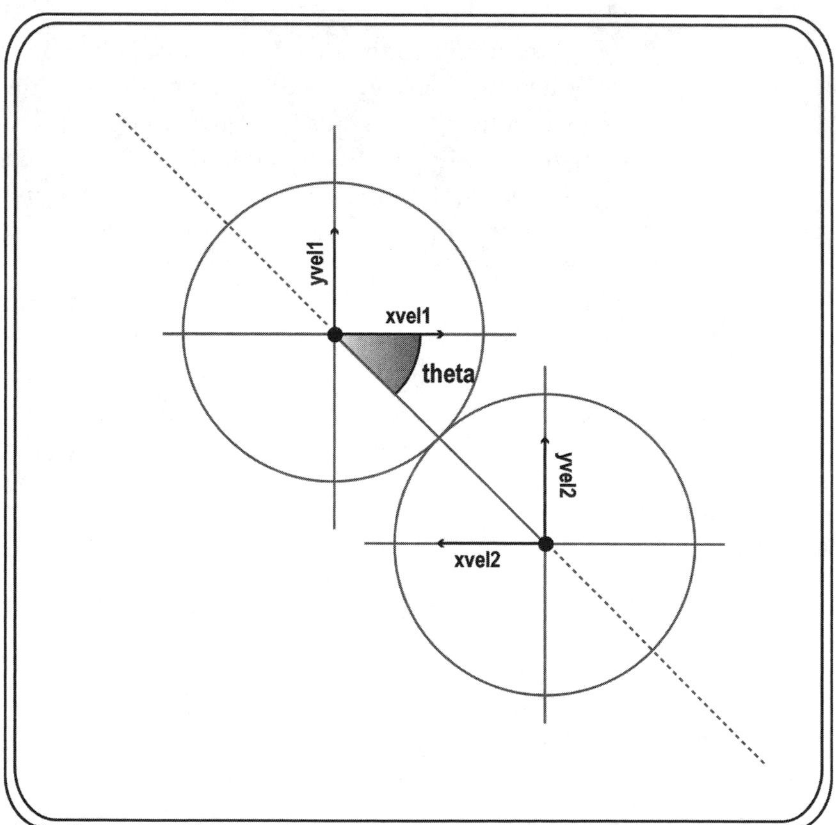

FIGURE 6.10
Our goal is to project the *x* and *y* velocities onto the line of action.

The velocity along the line of action from the projection of ball1's *x* and *y* velocities we call *xvel1prime*, and it is calculated as follows:

```
xvel1prime = xvel1*cos(theta)+yvel1*sin(theta)
```

This equation is made up of the projection of the *x* and *y* velocities of ball1 using the angle theta, which is the angle that the line of collision makes with the *x*-axis. The component of the velocity of ball1 that is perpendicular to the line of action (which is unaffected by the collision) is:

```
yvel1prime = yvel1*cos(theta)-xvel1*sin(theta)
```

You'll see that this equation is also a combination of the projection of the *x* and *y* velocities of ball1. The component of the ball2 velocity that lies along the line of action we call *xvel2prime:*

```
xvel2prime = xvel2*cos(theta)+yvel2*sin(theta)
```

The component of the velocity of ball2 that is perpendicular to the line of action (which is unaffected by the collision) is:

```
yvel2prime = yvel2*cos(theta)-xvel2*sin(theta)
```

Using the conservation equations developed earlier in this section, we use the mass of each ball, along with *xvel1prime* and *xvel2prime* (see Figure 6.11), to find the new "rebounded" velocities of each ball along the line of action. They are *v1f* and *v2f* (as before, *f* indicates "final").

FIGURE 6.11
xvel1prime and xvel2prime.

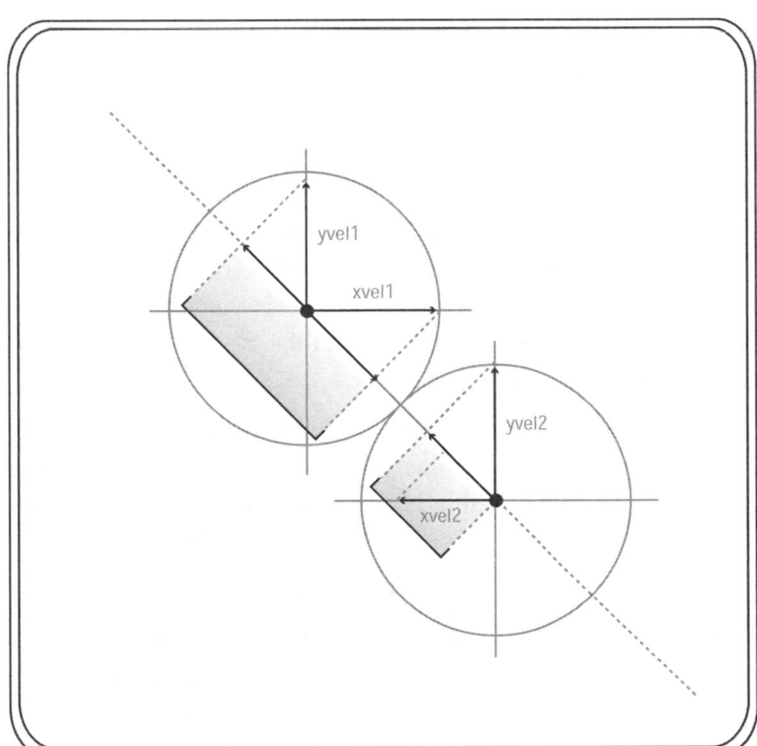

Using *v1f* and *v2f* and *yvel1prime* and *yvel2prime,* we can find the new velocities along Flash's *x* and *y* axes. This requires us to project back out from the line of action to the axes using the angle theta. Here are the new velocities of each ball:

```
xvel1 = v1f*cos(theta)-yvel1prime*sin(theta)
yvel1 = yvel1prime*cos(theta)+v1f*sin(theta)
xvel2 = v2f*cos(theta)-yvel2prime*sin(theta)
yvel2 = yvel2prime*cos(theta)+v2f*sin(theta)
```

And here's a boiled-down recap of the process we've just completed:

1. Project the *x* and *y* velocities of each ball onto the line of action. This is necessary because at the time of collision, the only velocities (momentums) affected are those that lie along the line of action.
2. Apply the conservation equations to these projected velocities to find the new velocities after the collision.
3. Using the new velocities along the line of action and the velocities perpendicular to the line of action, project everything back onto Flash's *x* and *y* axes. This will provide the final new velocities after a collision has occurred.

Now let's see this in ActionScript. Open billiard_ball.fla in the Chapter06 directory. The ActionScript in this file is almost identical to that of circle_circle2.fla in Chapter 5. The differences in the ActionScript are as follows:

1. We add a `mass` variable to the ball objects during the object definitions at the beginning of the ActionScript. For the `ball1` object, we set the `mass` to `1` with the action `game.ball1.mass = 1`, and for the `ball2` object, we set the `mass` to `1` with the similar statement `game.ball2.mass = 1`.
2. In the `ballToBallDetection()` function, we no longer execute a `trace` action when a collision is detected. Instead, we call a function called `ball2BallReaction()`. When it's called, we pass the `ball2BallReaction()` function the following information:

   ```
   b1, b2, xl1, xl2, yl1, yl2, whatTime
   ```

   If you remember, `b1` and `b2` are references to the ball objects, `xl1` and `yl1` are the starting positions of `ball1`, `xl2` and `yl2` are the starting positions of ball2, and whatTime is the number of frames since the last frame that it takes for the collision to occur (this number is between 0 and 1).

3. We add a function called ball2BallReaction(). This function calculates what the new velocities of each ball should be after the collision.

Here is the ball2BallReaction() function:

```
function ball2BallReaction(b1:Object, b2:Object,
➥x1:Number, x2:Number, y1:Number, y2:Number,
➥time:Number):void {
     //get the masses
     var mass1:Number = b1.mass;
     var mass2:Number = b2.mass;
     // —-set initial velocity variables
     var xVel1:Number = b1.xmov;
     var xVel2:Number = b2.xmov;
     var yVel1:Number = b1.ymov;
     var yVel2:Number = b2.ymov;
     var run:Number = (x1-x2);
     var rise:Number = (y1-y2);
     var Theta:Number = Math.atan2(rise, run);
     var cosTheta:Number = Math.cos(Theta);
     var sinTheta:Number = Math.sin(Theta);
     //Find the velocities along the line of action
     var xVel1prime:Number =
     ➥xVel1*cosTheta+yVel1*sinTheta;
     var xVel2prime:Number =
     ➥xVel2*cosTheta+yVel2*sinTheta;
     //Find the velocities perpendicular to the line of
     ➥action
     var yVel1prime:Number = yVel1*cosTheta-
     ➥xVel1*sinTheta;
     var yVel2prime:Number = yVel2*cosTheta-
     ➥xVel2*sinTheta;
     // Conservation Equations
     var P:Number = (mass1*xVel1prime+mass2*xVel2prime);
     var V:Number = (xVel1prime-xVel2prime);
     var v2f:Number = (P+mass1*V)/(mass1+mass2);
```

```
25          var v1f:Number = v2f-xVel1prime+xVel2prime;
26          var xVel1prime:Number = v1f;
27          var xVel2prime:Number = v2f;
28          //Project back to Flash's x and y axes
29          var xVel1:Number = xVel1prime*cosTheta-
            ➥yVel1prime*sinTheta;
30          var xVel2:Number = xVel2prime*cosTheta-
            ➥yVel2prime*sinTheta;
31          var yVel1:Number =
            ➥yVel1prime*cosTheta+xVel1prime*sinTheta;
32          var yVel2:Number =
            ➥yVel2prime*cosTheta+xVel2prime*sinTheta;
33          //change old pos
34          b1.tempx = b1.xpos+bl.xmov*time;
35          b1.tempy = b1.ypos+b1.ymov*time;
36          b2.tempx = b2.xpos+b2.xmov*time;
37          b2.tempy = b2.ypos+b2.ymov*time;
38          b1.xmov = xVel1;
39          b2.xmov = xVel2;
40          b1.ymov = yVel1;
41          b2.ymov = yVel2;
42      }
```

Lines 2–9 in this ActionScript handle initializing all the variables we need from the ball objects. References to the two colliding ball objects are passed into this function as `b1` and `b2`. The variables being initialized are the *x* and *y* velocities of each ball and their masses. We need to know the angle of the line of action, so we calculate it in lines 10–12; in lines 10 and 11, we calculate the `rise` and `run` of the line of action, and then in line 12, we calculate the angle using atan2. Because we will be using the sine and cosine of theta several times, in lines 13 and 14, we set variables to hold those values so that they don't need to be calculated repeatedly. In lines 16 and 17, the velocity of each ball is projected onto the line of action. These are the velocities affected during the collision. Next, we calculate the velocities perpendicular to the line of action. They are only included to help us project back onto the Flash axes. In lines 21–27, the conservation equations are applied. The results of this (lines 26 and 27) are the new velocities along the line of action after the collision. Now that we have the new velocity along the line of action, we can translate back to Flash's *x* and *y* axes. We do this in lines 29–32. These are the new velocities of each ball, and they need to be stored on each ball. But first we set the temporary position of the ball to be exactly where the balls should have been when they first collided (lines 34–37). Now we change the velocity on the ball objects in lines 38–41.

Generate an SWF to test this file. You will see that when the two balls (see Figure 6.12) collide, they react in a realistic way. Close the SWF and change the mass of one of the balls to something bigger, like 10 or 20. Then test the file again, and you will see that the conservation equations are working properly. You have just learned the hardest part of making a game of pool!

FIGURE 6.12
The two balls.

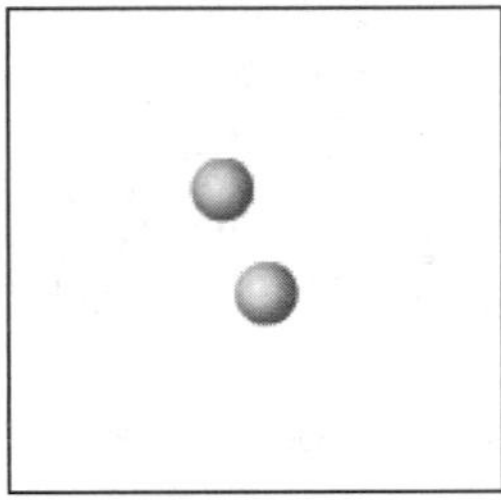

If you would like to look at another implementation of this, see realGravity.fla in the Chapter06 directory. This file was created with Flash 5 quite some time ago, so the ActionScript may look slightly different from what is presented here (but it still works perfectly well, of course). The file has collision detection and reactions of four massive spheres (see Figure 6.13). Each sphere attracts all the other spheres gravitationally. The result is four spheres slowly moving toward one another. When they collide, they bounce off each other.

FIGURE 6.13
Four spheres.

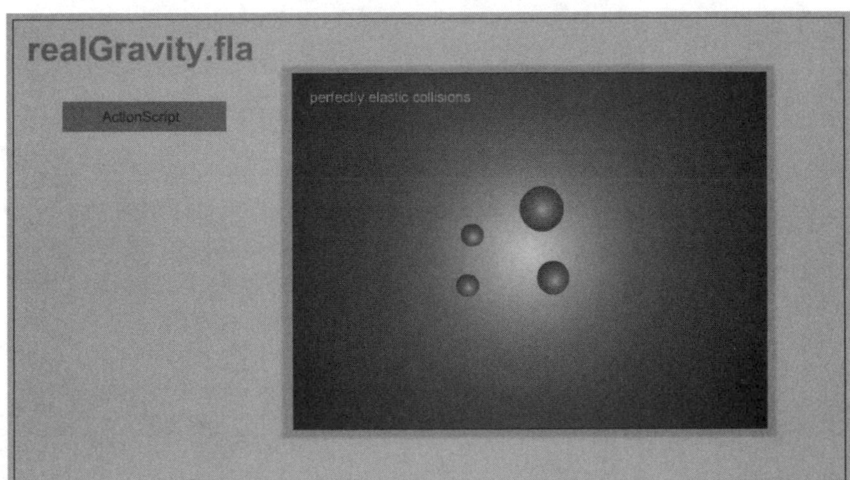

Ever-Evolving ActionScript

I have written and rewritten collision detection and collision reaction scripts many times, and the more experienced I become as a programmer, the more ways I see to program these events better. Everything that I have shown you so far has worked very well for me. However, I will inevitably encounter a situation—maybe even before finishing this book—where one of the collision detection or reaction techniques that I have written does not do what it should. It may work well in most situations, but then one particular case crops up that I didn't take into account, and where my script won't work.

What I am saying is that these scripts are a great starting place, and for the games used in this book, they work very well. However, as Flash grows as a programming platform, and as the demand for complicated or original games gets larger, we will be forced to further refine these techniques—techniques with which we currently have no problems. We may even have to scrap them for newer and better ways. If these issues rof Flash growth and development interest you, then you should try to keep up by reading related topics on Flash resource sites. In addition, future revisions of this book will undoubtedly contain additions to these scripts, and some may even be completely rewritten.

In this chapter, we covered the major types of collision reactions, including rectangle-rectangle reactions, billiard-ball reactions, and ball-line reactions. With this knowledge, you will be able to add a new level of realism to your games. You will see the collision reactions you learned in this chapter applied to at least two of the games, *9-ball* and *Pinball*, in Part III, "The Games," of this book.

Points to Remember

- In designing an object, it is often better to use a shape that is simpler than, though similar to, the particular final shape you had in mind. This will allow for easier, faster collision detection, which might be worth the trade-off of a specific complex shape.
- Creating methods on the `game` object itself, rather than in the Timeline, is a good programming practice that helps keep the process flexible and not tied to graphics on the screen.
- `Decay` enables you to control the slowdown of an object by lowering the magnitude of its speed by a percentage each time a collision with a wall or floor occurs. This enables a bouncing ball in Flash to act more like a ball would in real life; it eventually stops bouncing.
- Momentum is a vector which is stated mathematically as *momentum* = *mass*×*velocity*. The momentum of an object (or system) is conserved if the total external force on it is 0.
- Energy is the measure of a system's capability to do work. Kinetic energy is associated with the movement of an object. Potential energy is stored in an object and can be converted to kinetic energy (a ball sitting on the roof of a house has potential energy that is converted to kinetic energy when it falls). Energy is conserved when the final energy in a collision is equal to the initial energy.
- The quantities of momentum or of energy do not change in the course of a collision in a closed system (that is, one with no net external forces). Think of hitting a cue ball dead-on into another ball and seeing the cue ball sit perfectly still while the other moves away.
- Elastic collisions are those in which *both* kinetic energy and momentum are conserved.
- When two objects collide, the momentum that is affected is the component that lies along the line of action.

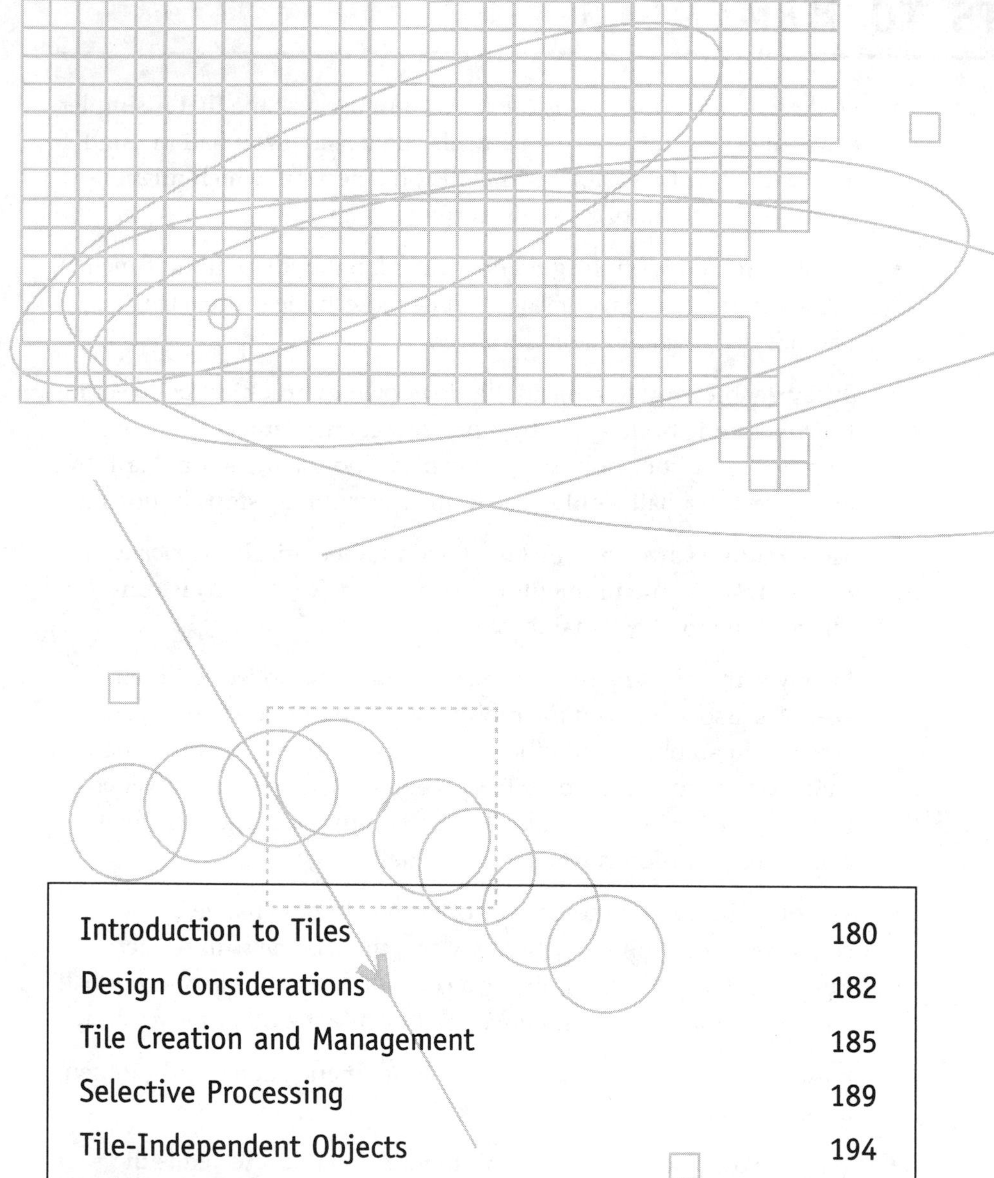

Introduction to Tiles 180
Design Considerations 182
Tile Creation and Management 185
Selective Processing 189
Tile-Independent Objects 194
Adding a Character to the World 197
Defining Worlds with XML 203
Points to Remember 208

CHAPTER 7

TILE-BASED WORLDS

YOU HAVE PROBABLY NOTICED THAT MANY GAMES THAT USE A TOP-DOWN OR three-dimensional view tend to have a large map (an area that defines the world of the game). It would be a tremendous amount of work for a graphic artist to create every scene in the game without being able to reuse any visual assets. Luckily for the graphic artists (and, as we will see, for the programmers as well), the concept of *tile-based worlds* can make game creation much easier. In a tile-based world, we can reuse all graphical assets and also assemble worlds with code.

From *Diablo* to *Pac-Man*, tile-based worlds (TBWs) are used to make game creation more efficient and to lighten CPU load. In this chapter, you will learn about these and other advantages of using a TBW. We will close by looking at a simple example of how the tile-based world of a game like *Pac-Man* can be created. This is a must-read chapter for anyone who is serious about becoming a game programmer.

Introduction to Tiles

A *tile*—also known as a *cell*—is a rectangular (usually square) area of a map. A tile can be any size, but it is often set up to be approximately the size of the character you are using, or at least the size of the part of the character that touches the ground, such as feet or wheels. The map is composed completely of tiles. You probably won't be surprised to hear that in Macromedia Flash, a tile is a movie clip. For example, imagine a top-down view of a ten-by-ten grid of square tiles in Flash. Each tile can have as many frames as you want. Frame 1 might contain a patch of grass. If the entire ten-by-ten grid were showing frame 1, then the world would look like a big patch of grass because you wouldn't see a difference between one tile and the next. You might have other frames in this tile—for instance, one for a bush or a rock. In this way, you can create your game environment by "tiling" the tile movie clips (just like you would tile your kitchen) and then setting each tile to a specific frame. Perhaps frame 2 is of a patch of grass, frame 5 is a sidewalk, and frame 6 is water. Using these three frames, you can create a TBW that looks like a grassy park with a pond and a walkway meandering through it. Of course you also can add many more types of tiles to produce more complicated designs. By creating a grid like this—using tiles that have multiple frames—you are creating a TBW!

In the Chapter07 directory on the CD, you'll find a game called *Shark Attack!* (shark_attack.swf) that we at Electrotank created for a client. This game is a very good example of a TBW (see Figure 7.1). Use the arrow keys to move the character around in this isometric world.

This simple technique is very powerful. You can create a whole city using tiles for grass, road, sidewalks, bushes, walls, and so on. This enables you to reuse your graphical assets efficiently and conveniently. In the case of puzzle games that use TBWs, such as *Pac-Man* and Minesweeper, the complexity of the tiles is low. They usually just have a few different items that they need to show, such as a dot to be collected or a maze wall. These games profit from the use of TBWs mostly because TBWs reduce the amount of processing that occurs by using a simple math trick. This trick is explained in the next section.

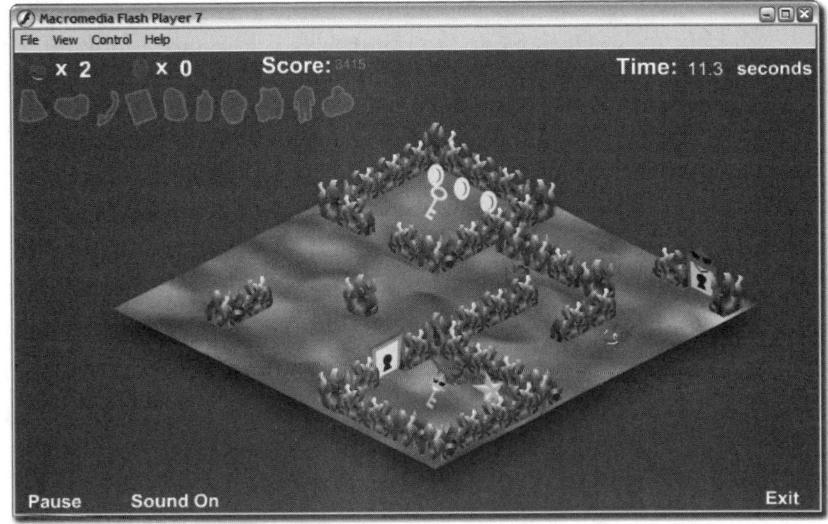

FIGURE 7.1
In *Shark Attack!*, the fish needs to avoid the shark, overcome obstacles, get the key, and unlock the door.

One of the most convenient programmatic benefits of using TBWs is their capability to easily store information about certain areas of the map. To take advantage of this, I use a two-dimensional array in which each element represents a tile in the world. An object is stored in each element, and then information about the tile that it represents is stored in this object. For instance, if a tile represents a rock, then information might be stored in the object to say a rock exists in this spot and that the character cannot move through it. If the tile were sand, then information might be stored to specify that the character should be slowed to half its regular speed when passing through this cell. In a game like *Pac-Man*, in which there might be a 15-by-15 grid, a two-dimensional array would hold objects that represent each tile. That's 225 (15 times 15) objects. Each object would contain information saying if it was a wall, if it was empty, or if it contained a dot to be collected. This information is stored (in this case, the two-dimensional array) in a *data structure*. A common alternative to the two-dimensional array data structure is to store and name the objects logically. In the *Pac-Man* example, the 225 objects would be created and given logical names, each based on the cell it represented. So, for instance, the name of the object representing the cell in the third column and eleventh row would look something like cell3_11. This is the way we store data in the example game we're working with in this chapter.

Another very useful feature of TBWs is their capability to store the information needed to build the world in an external file or database. Using a standardized protocol like XML, you can easily store such information. This is great news because it means you can create a game and load in an unlimited number of levels!

Sounds good right? In Chapter 9, "Level Editors," we've included everything you need to know to fully understand and create your own level editors.

Now, let's dig deeper into creating tile-based games. We'll start with some design considerations and then move into the nuts and bolts.

Design Considerations

As with any style of game, special considerations are necessary to create a smooth, professional game. Tile-based games are no exception. Even though most of this chapter deals with design-independent issues, having your design plans in mind throughout the process will be helpful during development and result in a cleaner, more professional game.

The View

We'll get into rendering the view later in this chapter, but we'll need to have a plan for the view we want to use before we even get started. This is important not only for the obvious reasons that it affects the tile art itself, but it also affects the game play. The view must be such that the action can be clearly seen by the player. If your game involves a character jumping over objects, then a direct top-down view wouldn't be that effective. This type of game would be better displayed at an angle that showed some height. If we angle down a little, we can more clearly convey obstacle heights and the player relationship.

As you can see in Figure 7.2, the angled or isometric view clearly shows the height of the obstacle.

FIGURE 7.2
The height of the obstacle is clear.

Seamless Tiles

When creating a tile-based world, it is important to design your tiles to fit together nicely. One major advantage of tile-based game development is the way you can use a few tiles to build a very large world. Because these few tiles will be used in multiple places, they must be carefully designed to give the player the illusion that each one is meant to be exactly where it is. There are a few tricks and rules to follow to ensure your tiles fit together.

Most tiles will need to fit anywhere in your map; because of this, it is good practice to have generic edges. In other words, the tiles you are creating will be more versatile if the edges are designed to match the edges of your other tiles (see Figure 7.3). If we were making a snow-boarding game with rock obstacles, the tiles with the rocks will need edges that match up perfectly with the snow tiles. Otherwise, you'll see an ugly edge.

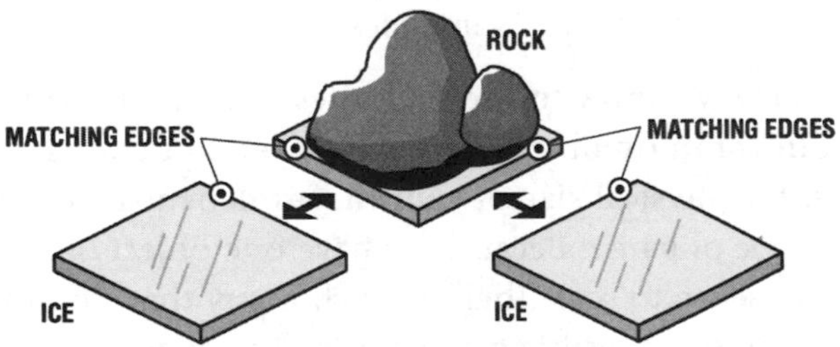

FIGURE 7.3
The edges of the tiles match.

However, not every feature in your game will fit into a single tile. You might have some features that span multiple tiles. No problem. These situations just call for a few more tiles.

Figure 7.4 shows how we would slice up a larger obstacle into tiles. Notice how we design them so that we can reuse the parts to make variations on the obstacle.

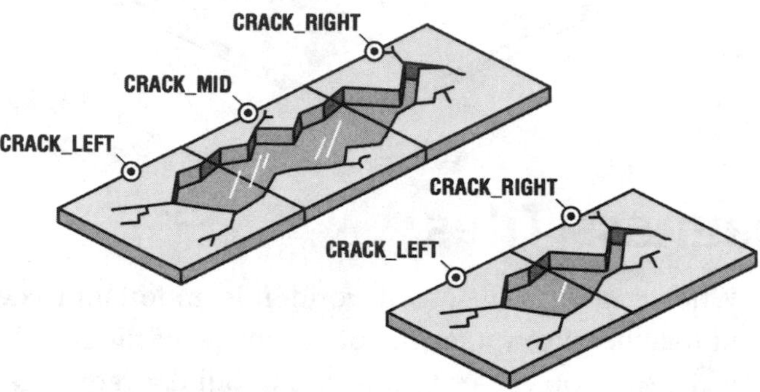

FIGURE 7.4
Breaking up a larger obstacle into tiles.

You could even repeat the middle section of this ice break to create a longer crack in the ice.

Scale

Just how big should your tiles be? Well, consider this. Due to the nature of a tile-based game, all your tiles will be the same size and usually represent the floor of the game world. Because of this, it is generally best to design your tiles to be about the same relative size as the base of any objects or obstacles you plan to use in the game. This includes the player, which is probably the most important element to which you want to relate the scale of your game tiles.

Ok, now we know to keep our tiles roughly the same size as the base of our common objects and the player, but that is merely a relational rule; the physical size of your tile art depends a lot on the style, size, and type of game. Because we have one object or feature per tile, it makes sense to scale them in such a way that we can fit enough of them onto the visible game area so that game play is maximized. If our game has us racing through the world jumping and avoiding obstacles, we will want to make sure the player can see far enough ahead to see what's coming.

TILE CREATION AND MANAGEMENT

In Chapter 8, "The Isometric Worldview," we'll continue our discussion about TBWs as we explore their role in isometric-view games.

Most TBWs in Flash are going to be in either top-down view or 3D isometric view, like *Shark Attack!* The way you store and manipulate the tile data is exactly the same for both of those views, but the way you display the tiles on the screen is not. In this chapter, we look at how to create the tiles in the top-down view and how to store information about those tiles. In the last part of this section, we'll introduce a very powerful but simple math trick that can greatly reduce the processing needed to use a TBW.

Creating the Grid and Storing Information

To build the grid of tiles on the screen, you must use *nested loops*—loops within loops. If you wanted to build just one straight line of ten tiles, you would only need to use one loop. In each iteration of that loop (remember that in this example there would be ten iterations per outer loop), you would use `attachMovie()` to create an instance of a movie clip, and then you would place it in the correct spot on the Stage. Because a grid has several of these types of lines right under each other, we loop the loop to create the entire grid. Remember that we have one loop to create a row of tiles, so then we run this loop one time for each row we want to add.

Think of the inner loop as a day and the outer loop as a week. The inner loop loops through 24 hours in a day, but it does this from start to finish for each day (the outer loop). So over the course of one week, there would be 7×24 iterations.

We have an outer loop set to loop, say, ten times. For each loop, there is an inner loop that adds the movie clip tiles to the row. Here is sample ActionScript that handles just adding one line of ten movie clips to the Stage.

```
for (var i:Number=0; i<10; ++i) {
        //code to add and place the movie clip
}
```

That would add one horizontal line of ten movie clips. To make this a grid, we need to start this loop one time for each row that we want to add. So we add an outer loop.

```
for (var j:Number=0; j<10; ++j) {
        for (var i:Number=0; i<10; ++i) {
                //code to add and place the movie clip
        }
}
```

What happens is this:

1. The outer loop starts at `j=0` (which is the first row). While `j=0`, the inner loop runs from `i=0` to `i=9`, placing movie clips. The first row is now complete.
2. The outer loop moves to `j=1` (which is the second row). While `j=1`, the inner loop runs from `i=0` to `i=9`, placing movie clips. Row 1 is now complete.
3. And so on, eight more times.

Open grid.fla in the Chapter07 directory on the CD-ROM to see an example. You will see two movie clips on the Stage. One of them has an instance name of `grid`, and the other has no instance name but has a Library name of `tile`. This movie clip also has a linkage identifier of `tile` so that we can create instances of it on the Stage using ActionScript. In addition, the tile clip has eight frames, each with a different tile. The grid movie clip was placed there so that we can attach the movie clips to it. Building the grid in a movie clip is cleaner than attaching dozens of movie clips to the main Timeline. This is the first in a string of example files we'll look at in this chapter, each one building on the previous. By the end of the chapter, you'll have a very simple *Pac-Man*–like start to a game. The ActionScript in this file does three things:

- Creates an object called `game` that we use to store information about the grid.
- Creates a function called `buildGrid()` that builds the grid on the Stage and builds the data structure that we use to store information about each tile.
- Executes the `buildGrid()` function.

Here is the ActionScript used to create the `game` object.

```
1     var game:Object = new Object();
2     game.columns = 10;
3     game.rows = 10;
4     game.spacing = 30;
5     game.depth = 1000;
6     game.path =  this.grid;
7     game.numberOfTypes = 8;
```

Line 1 creates the `game` object, and all the following lines add information to that object. Lines 2 and 3 define the dimensions of the grid; line 4 defines the spacing (the number of units between the registration points of the tiles). The next line sets a variable to the object called `depth`. This value will be incremented and used to assign a depth to each newly-created movie clip. As we have seen in the previous chapters, we are starting to make it a habit to store references to movie clips in an object. That makes our code more object-oriented. So in line 6, you can see that a reference to the `grid` movie clip is created. Whenever we want to do anything with the grid, we don't have to type *"grid"*—we type *game.path*. The reference `game.path` will be interpreted as "grid" because that is the reference we pointed it to in line 6 of this code. If at some point during the game-design process we had to change the name or location of the `grid` movie clip, then all we would have to do to update the code would be to change the `game.path` reference to point to the new grid location. If we did not use this `game.path` reference, then changing the name or path to `grid` would be a large undertaking because we'd have to update a lot of code. The final line of ActionScript sets a variable called `numberOfTypes` on the `game` object. This variable stores the number of tile types that exist in this game definition. Because we have eight frames in the tile clip, each a different tile, then we give `numberOfTypes` a value of `8`.

Next, a function called buildGrid() is defined.

```
1     function buildGrid() {
2          for (var j:Number=0; j<game.rows; ++j) {
3                    for (var i:Number =0; i<game.columns;
                     ➥++i) {
4                    var name:String = "cell"+i+"_"+j;
5                    var x:Number = i*game.spacing;
6                    var y:Number = j*game.spacing;
7                    var type:Number = 1;
8                    game.path.attachMovie("cell", name,
                     ➥++game.depth);
9                    game.path[name]._x = x;
10                   game.path[name]._y = y;
11                   game[name] = {x:i, y:j, name:name,
                     ➥type:type, clip:game.path[name]};
12              }
13         }
14    }
```

This function uses nested loops, as described earlier in this section. The outer loop loops through the number of rows. In each iteration of the outer loop, the inner loop loops through for each column. Each tile (which we call a *cell* here) is named uniquely by using the row and column of the cell as part of that cell's name. For instance, if the cell belongs to column 8 and row 6, the name would be cell8_6. In lines 5 and 6, the intended position of the new movie clip is calculated, and then a variable called `type` is created with a value of `1`. This refers to the frame that the tile will display. In this example, we start each tile on frame 1. Next, the movie clip is created and positioned. In line 11, we do something really important—we create an object to store information about the cell that was just created, such as its type, its name, and a reference to the movie clip it represents.

The final line of ActionScript in this file (not shown) is `buildGrid()`. It calls the function that we just dissected to create the grid. The grid is shown in Figure 7.5.

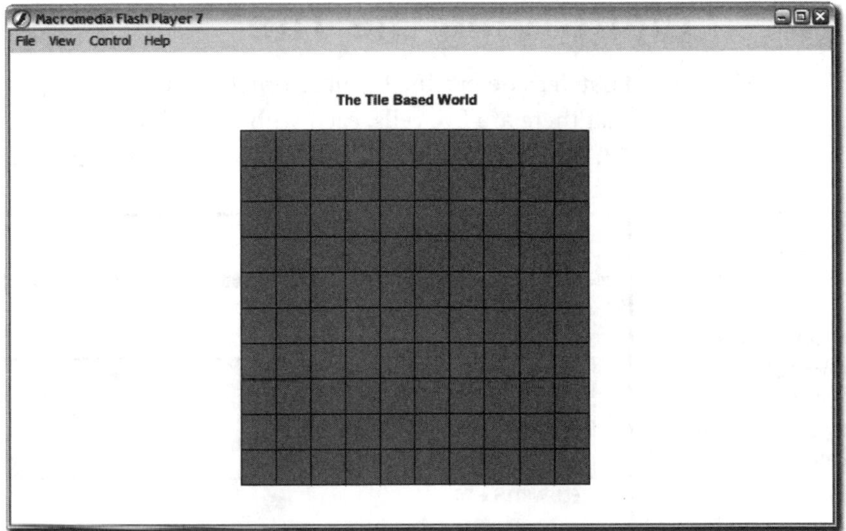

FIGURE 7.5
The grid.

SELECTIVE PROCESSING

Now it's time to introduce the trick I mentioned: a simple but powerful maneuver that lightens the processor load in TBWs tremendously. Imagine this: If the game of *Pac-Man* were written in Flash, how would you detect if the *Pac-Man* character was colliding with a dot to be collected (or eaten, or whatever it is that *Pac-Man* does with it)? First of all, in *Pac-Man*, everything moves fairly slowly, and precision isn't important, so `hitTest()` would not be a bad choice. Many early game programmers (including myself at one time) have guessed that you'd need to loop through the entire board, constantly performing `hitTest()`, to see if *Pac-Man* has collided with any dots. That is not a very efficient process. Luckily, a trick exists that enables us to discover easily which cell *Pac-Man* is in, and therefore we only need to check for a collision in that cell. And of course, one collision detection is a lot less CPU-intensive than 100 collision detections. Let's see how to determine which cell *Pac-Man* is in.

Identifying the Tile

First, let's determine his horizontal location. In Figure 7.6, you can see that there are five cells, each with a width of 20. *Pac-Man*'s *x* position is 53. Which cell is he in? The following code helps us find out:

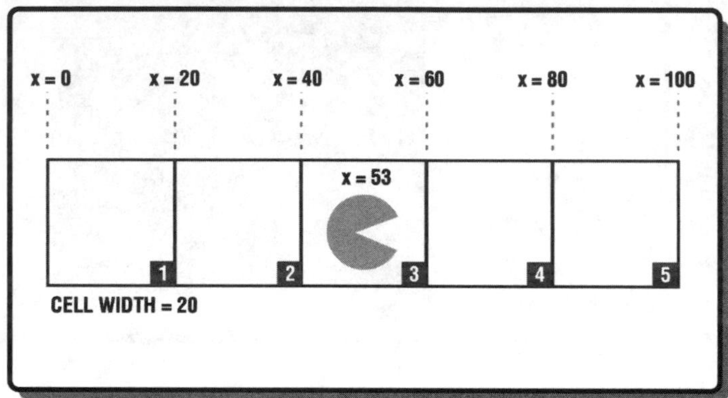

FIGURE 7.6
Five cells, each with a width of 20.

PAC-MAN® ©1980 Namco Ltd., All Rights Reserved. Courtesy of Namco Holding Corp.

```
1      var spacing:Number = 20;
2      var x:Number = 53;
3      var cell_column:Number = Math.floor(x/spacing);
```

In line 1, we set a variable called spacing. That is the width of each cell. Line 2 creates a variable called x that stores the position of *Pac-Man*. In line 3, we employ the simple math trick by dividing the position by the spacing. We then round that number down to the nearest integer. With this trick, we can easily find which cell *Pac-Man* is in! This works in the same way for the vertical position (see Figure 7.7).

Like the horizontal example, this one also contains five cells, each with a width of 20. The *y* position of *Pac-Man* is 30. Here is how you find the number of the cell he's in:

```
1      var spacing:Number = 20;
2      var y:Number = 30;
3      var cell_row:Number = Math.floor(y/spacing);
```

By putting both of these together, we can locate *Pac-Man*'s position in the grid. We find the row and the column he's in, and that specifies the cell in the grid (see Figure 7.8).

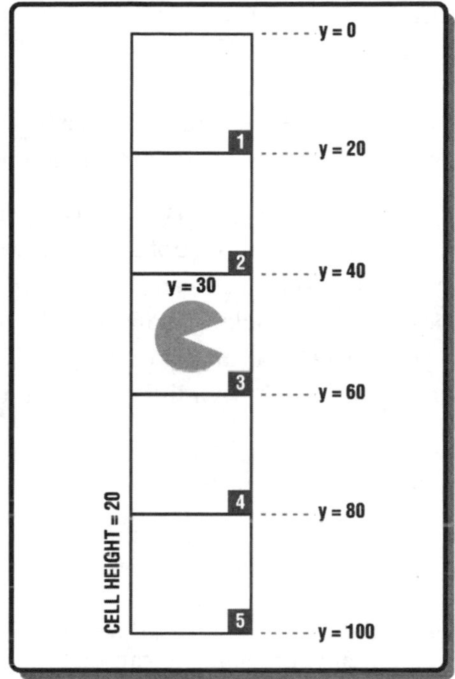

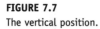

FIGURE 7.7
The vertical position.

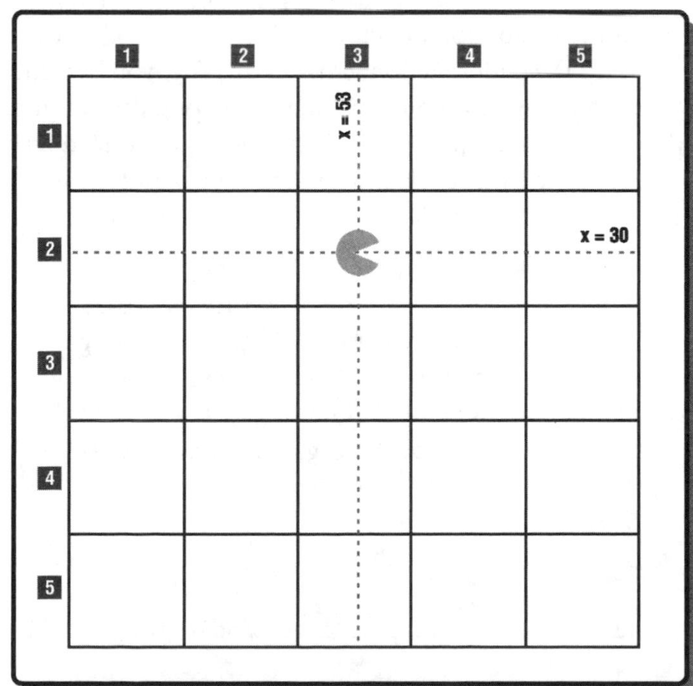

FIGURE 7.8
Locating *Pac-Man's* position in the grid.

```
var spacing:Number = 20;
var x:Number = 53;
var y:Number = 30;
var cell_column:Number = Math.floor(x/spacing);
var cell_row:Number = Math.floor(y/spacing);
```

Now that we know which cell *Pac-Man* is in, we can perform a `hitTest()` between the *Pac-Man* movie clip and a dot in that tile. Perhaps you can now understand why this is such a powerful trick. If you are making a game in which the character is walking around, and a few tiles contain water, then when your character is in one of those cells, you can make him swim, drown, or just slow down a little bit. What typically happens is the following:

1. You detect which cell the character is in.
2. You look up the object that represents that cell.
3. You look at the type of cell that your character is in. If it is a cell of fire, for example, then your character might get hurt. If it is a cell with a secret key, then your character can pick it up and gain points.

Now let's look at a simple example of this trick. Open grid_click.fla in the Chapter07 directory. This file is a modified version of grid.fla. With the added ActionScript in this file, you can click a cell and its type changes. If you click one cell enough times, it arrives back at its original cell type. I've used the trick I just introduced to determine which cell was clicked when the mouse button was pressed. Here is the added ActionScript:

```
function gameClicked(mx, my) {
      var x:Number = Math.floor(mx/game.spacing);
      var y:Number = Math.floor(my/game.spacing);
      var cell:String = "cell"+x+"_"+y;
      var ob:Object = game[cell];
      if (ob.type<game.numberOfTypes) {
            ++ob.type;
      } else {
            ob.type = 1;
      }
      ob.clip.tile.gotoAndStop(ob.type);
}
```

```
13    var changeGrid:Object = new Object();
14    changeGrid.onMouseDown = function(){
15          var mx:Number = _xmouse;
16          var my:Number = _ymouse;
17          if (game.path.hitTest(mx, my)) {
18                gameClicked(game.path._xmouse,
                  ➥game.path._ymouse);
19          }
20    };
21    Mouse.addListener (changeGrid);
```

Look at lines 13–21 first. Here we add our "changeGrid" listener to the Mouse object, which lets us trap the onMouseDown event and process the click coordinates. If these coordinates are over the grid movie clip (referenced by game.path), we call the gameClicked() function, passing the coordinates of the mouse into gameClicked(). In lines 2 and 3, we use the trick described in this section to determine the cell that was clicked. In the following line, we construct the name of the object that contains information about this cell, and then in line 5, we create a reference to that object called ob. Lines 6–10 check to see if ob.type is less than 8, and if it is, we increment it; otherwise we set it back to 1. Finally, on line 11, we change the frame where the movie clip is to match that of the tile type.

Create an SWF from this file and test it out. Click the cells to change the cell types. Types 2–8 are walls. You can easily create unique configurations of the board.

Getting the Position Within the Tile

Sometimes it is important to know exactly where you are within a particular tile. In other words, sometimes you need to convert your world position to a position local to the tile you are on. This is also fairly easy to accomplish using the modulo operator (%). This quickly gives you the leftover distance from the origin of the tile.

```
var spacing:Number = 20;
var x:Number = 53;
var y:Number = 30;
var localPos_x:Number = x % spacing;
var localPos_y:Number = y % spacing;
```

This is especially useful when dealing with independent objects or when altering a tile by adding things like blast marks and so on. Situations may also arise where you need to deal with certain areas of a tile differently than others.

Tile-Independent Objects

Tile-based games aren't all tiles; you also have the player and any objects that move. These elements interact with other independent objects as well as the tiles and aren't based on your tile grid. No sense managing objects that aren't there. If a player shoots a bullet, for example, create the bullet when it is fired, let it manage itself for the span of its life, and finally let it destroy itself at the end of its life cycle. In this section, we'll discuss creating, managing, and destroying tile-independent game elements and how they may alter the game environment.

Creating Objects

When developing a game, efficiency is extremely important and can have a major impact on the performance and manageability of the game engine. With tile-based games, this is more vital than ever because of the vast worlds that you need to manage. When dealing with both tile-based objects and tile-independent objects, you don't want any unnecessary overhead. One effective way to reduce the overhead with tile-independent objects that have limited life spans is to create them only when needed.

If our game had a cannon and we wanted to fire a cannon ball into our world, we'd want to create the ball at the moment it is first visible and has the potential to affect the game and then bestow the object with logic to manage itself.

The code for creating a new projectile object, in this case a cannonball, works like this.

```
//THE POSITION WHERE THE NEW PROJECTILE IS TO BE CREATED
var pos_x:Number = 32;
var pos_y:Number = 18;
var pos_z:Number = 6;
//AND THE VELOCITY OF THE PROJECTILE
```

```
var velocity_x:Number = 6;
var velocity_y:Number = 8;
var velocity_z:Number = 3;
//CREATE THE OBJECT
attachMovie("cannon_ball_Clip", "cannon_ball", 10);
//PASS THE NEW OBJECT SOME VALUES TO BEGIN WITH
cannon_ball.pos_x = pos_x;
cannon_ball.pos_y = pos_y;
cannon_ball.pos_z = pos_z;
cannon_ball.velocity_x = velocity_x;
cannon_ball.velocity_y = velocity_y;
cannon_ball.velocity_z = velocity_z;
```

Managing Objects

After the object has been created, it must be managed. Each object will behave differently, and we wouldn't want to manage every moving object with one giant loop. The most efficient way is to let the objects manage themselves. Most of the functionality will be defined in the `onEnterFrame` loop.

Let's examine the `onEnterframe` function for our cannonball projectile that we have created.

```
//DEFINE ACTIONS THAT HAPPEN EVERY FRAME WHILE OBJECT EXISTS
cannon_ball.onEnterframe = function(){
        //CALCULATE NEW POSITION BASED ON VELOCITY
        pos_x += velocity_x ;
        pos_y += velocity_y;
        pos_z += velocity_z;
        //ADJUST VELOCITY AND FALL FOR GRAVITY
        velocity_x *= .9;
        velocity_y *= .9;
        velocity_z -= 1;
        //CHECK FOR COLLISION WITH GROUND
        if (pos_z <= ground_height){
              //HIT GROUND
              pos_z= ground_height;
              //DO ACTIONS ACCORING TO GAME THEME
        }
}
```

Destroying Objects

After an object has done what it came to do, remove it from the game completely. There is no need to keep it around and certainly no need to have it using up valuable processing power after its usefulness is gone. Destroying a movie clip is fairly simple. In your movie clip's `onEnterFrame` loop, simply check if the object is still part of the game, and if it's not, just have it remove itself with a single line of code.

```
this.removeMovieClip();
```

That's it. Really! After this code has executed, the clip will cease to exist. The clip will be removed from the Stage, and any `onEnterFrame` code will stop executing.

Placing your loops within an `onEnterFrame` function results in much more manageable and predictable code than using the `setInterval` function. `setInterval` is very useful for evoking actions at prescribed times in the future, but for consistent, frame-based actions, `onEnterframe` is the better choice.

Altering the World

Bombs, bullets, and so on may change the world—they might destroy a bridge, for example. Here we'll explain how to change tile attributes based on object impact.

Let's say our cannonball misses its mark and lands on a featureless tile of grass. "That's gonna leave a mark!" as the saying goes. The blast needs to be created at the tile level, within the tile clip that was hit. Making this change on the tile level may not make much difference if your game uses a top-down view, but if your game uses an isometric view, creating the blast within the tile helps you keep the depths under control.

Altering the world in this way is pretty simple, but you will need to use both of our selective processing tricks from the previous section. First, we need to determine which tile the cannonball lands on, and then we must determine the local position within that tile.

```
var spacing:Number = 20;
var x:Number = 153;
var y:Number = 130;
```

```
//FIND THE AFFECTED TILE
var cell_column:Number = Math.ceil(x/spacing);
var cell_row:Number = Math.ceil(y/spacing);
var var cell:String = "cell"+ cell_column +"_"+ cell_row;
var ob:Object = game[cell];
//FIND OUR LOCAL POSITION
var localPos_x:Number = x % spacing;
var localPos_y:Number = y % spacing;
//ATTACH OUT BLAST CLIP
ob.attachMovie("blast_mark", "blast_mark", 10, {_x:
➥localPos_x, _y: localPos_y});
```

ADDING A CHARACTER TO THE WORLD

In this section, we're going to add a character to the simple world we have just created. Our character is nothing more than a ball. The goal is to be able to move the ball around the grid using the arrow keys. If a cell has a type of greater than 1, it is a wall, and we will not let the ball enter this cell.

A character can be anything from a ball to a human. In most games, a character is something the game player can relate to, usually some living being. In the example given in the next section, the character is a ball.

When an arrow key is pressed, we look ahead to see where the edge of the ball would be if we were to move it there. If the edge is in an acceptable cell (`type = 1`), then we move the ball there; if not, then we disregard the key press. More specifically, if the right arrow key is pressed, then we look at the ball's current position plus the ball's speed plus the ball's radius to find a number that represents the location of the right edge of the ball if it were to be moved one quantity (or unit) of speed to the right. We then check to see in which cell that far-right point is. If it is in a cell of `type = 1`, then we move the ball there (see Figure 7.9).

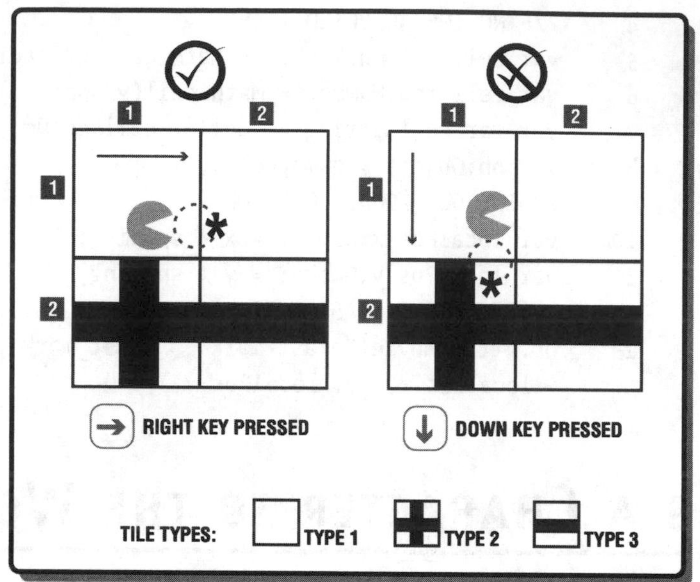

FIGURE 7.9
Looking ahead: Where is he going to go?

PAC-MAN® ©1980 Namco Ltd., All Rights Reserved. Courtesy of Namco Holding Corp.

To see this in action, open character_in_grid.fla in the Chapter07 directory. You will see a new movie clip inside the grid movie clip. It is the character and has an instance name of `ball`. The ActionScript has three additions:

- A function called `initializeBall()` that creates an object to hold the information about the character (which is a ball). This function also creates a few new variables on the `game` object.
- A function called `moveBall()` that moves the ball to a new position if that new position is valid.
- An `onEnterFrame` event that checks for key presses in every frame. If one of the arrow keys is pressed, then the `moveBall()` function is called.

Here is the `initializeBall()` function:

```
function initializeBall() {
      game.speed = 3;
      game.path.ball.swapDepths(10000);
      game.ball = {startx:1, starty:1,
      ➥clip:game.path.ball};
```

```
5           var x:Number = (game.ball.startx-
            ➥1)*game.spacing+game.spacing/2;
6           var y:Number = (game.ball.starty-
            ➥1)*game.spacing+game.spacing/2;
7           game.ball.clip._x = x;
8           game.ball.clip._y = y;
9           game.ball.x = x;
10          game.ball.y = y;
11          game.ball.radius = game.ball.clip._width/2;
12      }
```

The purpose of this function is to initialize all objects and variables needed to hold information about the ball. Line 2 sets a variable called speed to the game object. This represents the speed at which the ball can move. If a key press is detected on any frame, then the ball will be moved that amount. The next line moves the ball movie clip to a high depth. This is done so that we can see it over the tiles that were attached to the Stage. If we do not send the ball to a higher depth than the tiles, then it will be hidden behind the tiles. In line 4, an object called ball is defined on the game object. This object is used to store information about the ball, such as the starting position of the ball and a reference to the movie clip that represents it. You'll notice that we set the variables startx and starty both to 1. This is because we are going to start the ball in the first tile. The next two lines use the startx and starty position to calculate the place on the Stage where the ball needs to be placed. We add game.spacing/2 to both positions so that the ball will be centered in the tile rather than on its registration point. In lines 9–11, we store the *x* and *y* positions of the ball and its radius on the ball object.

Next, let's look at the onEnterFrame event. We'll save the moveBall() function for last.

```
_root.onEnterFrame = function() {
      if (Key.isDown(Key.RIGHT)){ moveBall("right");}
      if (Key.isDown(Key.LEFT)){ moveBall("left");}
      if (Key.isDown(Key.UP)){ moveBall("up");}
      if (Key.isDown(Key.DOWN)){ moveBall("down");}
};
```

This function checks to see if any of the four arrow keys are pressed during each frame. Each arrow key has its own `if` statement that moves the ball by calling the `moveBall()` function and passing the desired move direction as a string.

Now let's look at the `moveBall()` function. It is not complicated, but it is fairly long because we repeat the same sorts of actions for each arrow key (four times).

```
function moveBall(dir) {
ob = game.ball;
if (dir == "right") {
      var tempx:Number = ob.x+ob.radius+game.speed;
      var tempy:Number = ob.y;
      var cellx:Number = Math.floor(tempx/game.spacing);
      var celly:Number = Math. floor
      ➥(tempy/game.spacing);
      var tempCell:Object = game["cell"+cellx+"_"+celly];
      if (tempCell.type != 1) {
            return;
      } else {
            ob.x += game.speed;
            ob.clip._x = ob.x;
      }
} else if (dir == "left") {
      var tempx:Number = ob.x-ob.radius-game.speed;
      var tempy:Number = ob.y;
      var cellx:Number = Math. floor
      ➥(tempx/game.spacing);
      var celly:Number = Math. floor
      ➥(tempy/game.spacing);
      var tempCell = game["cell"+cellx+"_"+celly];
      if (tempCell.type != 1) {
            return;
      } else {
            ob.x -= game.speed;
            ob.clip._x = ob.x;
      }
} else if (dir == "up") {
      var tempx:Number = ob.x;
```

```
29          var tempy:Number = ob.y-ob.radius-game.speed;
30          var cellx:Number = Math. floor
            ➥(tempx/game.spacing);
31          var celly:Number = Math. floor
            ➥(tempy/game.spacing);
32          var tempCell = game["cell"+cellx+"_"+celly];
33          if (tempCell.type != 1) {
34               return;
35          } else {
36               ob.y -= game.speed;
37               ob.clip._y = ob.y;
38          }
39     } else if (dir == "down") {
40          var tempx:Number = ob.x;
41          var tempy:Number = ob.y+ob.radius+game.speed;
42          var cellx:Number = Math. floor
            ➥(tempx/game.spacing);
43          var celly:Number = Math. floor
            ➥(tempy/game.spacing);
44          var tempCell = game["cell"+cellx+"_"+celly];
45          if (tempCell.type != 1) {
46               return;
47          } else {
48               ob.y += game.speed;
49               ob.clip._y = ob.y;
50          }
51     }
52 }
```

This function accepts a parameter called `dir`, which represents the string that is passed in, telling the function which key was pressed. In line 2 of the function, we set a reference to the `game.ball` object called `ob`. Setting a temporary reference is not absolutely necessary, but it does make the typing a little shorter and can help during editing and debugging. Next, we have an `if` statement that checks to see if `dir` is "right," "left," "up," or "down." Very similar actions are repeated for each of the four pieces of this conditional statement. First let's look at lines 3–14, the "right" conditional. The first action in this chunk of code, line 4, sets a variable called `tempx` that represents the ball's right edge. Because the user is trying to move the ball to the right, we check to see if the ball's right edge would still be in a valid cell if we moved it in that direction. To do this, we use our math trick to determine the cell using the variables `tempx` and `tempy`. We then check the object that represents the cell the ball would be over. If the type variable on that object is `1`, then it is a valid move. If it is not valid (line 9), then we `return` out of the function (line 10). If it is a valid type, then we update the ball's position (lines 11–14).

The next three parts of this big conditional statement do the same thing as the first part, except for the way they calculate the ball's edge and update the ball's position. The edge of the ball we are interested in depends on the direction of movement. If the down key was pressed, then we are interested in the lowest edge of the ball. If the left key was pressed, then we are interested in the leftmost edge of the ball. Finally—all together now—if the up key was pressed, then we are interested in the topmost edge of the ball.

Generate an SWF from this file, as in Figure 7.10. You can then use your arrow keys to move the ball around. Click the grid to add some walls. Move the ball around and notice how it will not enter a cell that has a wall. Notice that all walls are treated in the same way; it doesn't matter what the wall looks like or how much of the cell the wall occupies. Using creatively drawn walls or smaller cell sizes, this is not as apparent.

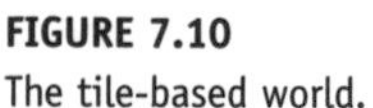
FIGURE 7.10
The tile-based world.

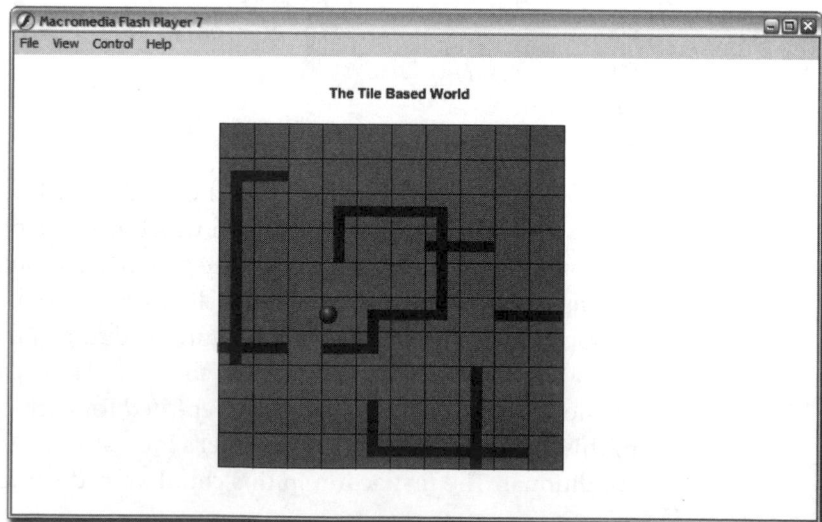

One other thing to note is that this is just one way to treat cells in a TBW. More advanced games have real collision detection within a cell. In that case, the ball could enter a cell that has a wall, but then collision detection checks would kick in to make sure the ball did not move through the wall itself.

Defining Worlds with XML

One of the best features of TBWs is the ease with which you can store the data that represents a world. For instance, for a game of *Pac-Man* (without the ghosts), you can easily create a text document to store the type of each cell. This text document is usually XML-formatted. At a later date, this information can be loaded into your game, and the world can be built. In this section, we'll look at a simple example of how to do this. (We're going to assume that you have some knowledge of XML and how to work with extracting data from `XML` objects in Flash.)

Figure 7.11 show the XML structure we will use to store the world data.

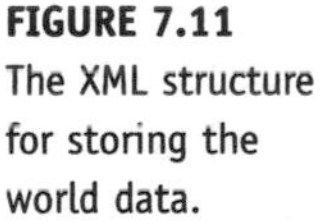

FIGURE 7.11
The XML structure for storing the world data.

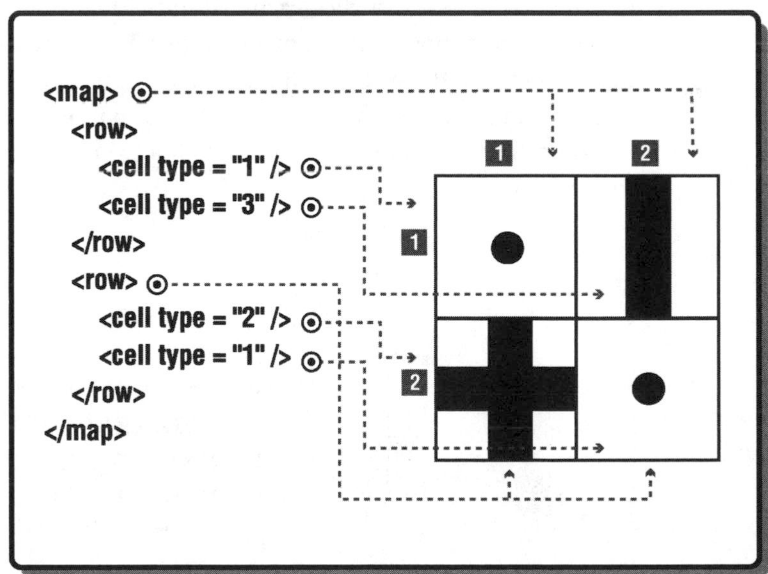

The XML listed in the figure only describes a two-by-two grid. We're going to create an XML file that describes a ten-by-ten grid, so there will be ten <row> nodes and ten <cell> nodes in each <row> node. In the XML in Figure 7.11, the first <row> node represents the first row of cells in a grid. The two <cell> nodes in the <row> node represent the two cells in that row in a grid. The type attribute in the <cell> node represents the frame that that cell should show.

Open game.fla from the CD. Take a look at the tile movie clip in the Library. It has a simple new addition—a movie clip with an instance name of dot on frame 1. As the ball moves over the dots, they disappear, much as they do in *Pac-Man*. There are three frame labels in this movie: Start, Create Game, and Play Game. The Start frame gives you two choices, Create Game or Play Game. If you click the Create Game button, then you are taken to the Create Game frame. On this frame, you can configure a level and then click to have the XML for this level generated. If you choose Play Game, you are taken to the Play Game frame. On this frame, the data for the level is loaded from an XML file, and the level is created. You can then move the ball around on this level, collecting dots.

Let's look at the Create Game label first. This is a very simple level editor. On this frame, you can click each cell individually to change its type. After you are happy with the configuration of the board, you can click the Generate XML button, and an XML document representing this map will be generated and shown in the Output window. The Generate XML button calls a function called generateXML(). Here is the ActionScript in this function:

```
function generateXML() {
    var xml:String = "<map>";
    for (var j:Number = 0; j<game.rows; ++j) {
        xml += "<row>";
        for (var i:Number = 0; i<game.columns; ++i) {
            var name:String = "cell"+i+"_"+j;
            var type:Number = game[name].type;
            var temp:String = "<cell
            ➥type=\""+type+"\" />";
            xml += temp;
        }
        xml += "</row>";
    }
```

```
        xml += "</map>";
        trace(xml);
}
```

This function creates an XML document like the one shown earlier in this section, except that it has ten `<row>` nodes and ten `<cell>` nodes per `<row>` node. First, a local variable called `xml` is defined with "`<map>`" as its value. Then we loop through the entire board. At the beginning of every outer loop, we append "`<row>`" to the `xml` variable. For each iteration of the inner loop, we create a `<cell>` node with a "`type`" attribute that stores the value of the current cell's type. This node is then appended to the `xml` variable. At the end of each outer loop, we append "`</row>`" to the `xml` variable, closing the current `<row>` node. After all the loops, we close the root node by appending "`</map>`" to the `xml` variable. Finally, we `trace` the `xml` variable so that its contents are shown in the Output window.

Generate an SWF file from this and test the XML generation. After you have created a level you're happy with, copy the contents from the Output window and save it to a file called game.xml in your current working directory. Now, how will this file of yours be used? You're about to find out. We're now going to discuss the Play Game frame; that's where this file will be loaded, and your level will be created from it.

Close the SWF file and look at the FLA file again. Move to the Play Game frame. This frame loads the game.xml file, interprets it, and builds the level. After the level is built, the character can move around the level collecting dots. There are a few ActionScript additions to this frame that you have not yet seen. There is a simple collision-detection function that checks for ball-dot collisions, and there is the code that loads and interprets the XML. Here is the code that loads the XML and defines the event handler for the `onLoad` event:

```
1    var boardXML:XML = new XML();
2    boardXML.onLoad = buildGrid;
3    boardXML.load("game.xml");
```

An XML document must be loaded into an `XML` object, so first we're going to create an `XML` object called `boardXML`. Also, so that we will know when the file is finished loading, in line 2, we set an event handler for the `onLoad` event for the `boardXML` `XML` object. When the file is finished loading, the function buildGrid() is called. In line 3, we load a file into the XML object, passing in the path to the file.

The buildGrid() function is changed substantially from the one you've gotten used to seeing in our previous examples. Here it interprets the XML and builds the level from it.

```
1    function buildGrid() {
2         var board:XMLNode  = new XML();
3         board = boardXML.firstChild;
4         var tempArray:Array = new Array();
5         tempArray = board.childNodes;
6         for (var j:Number = 0; j<game.rows; ++j) {
7              var tempArray2:Array = new Array();
8              tempArray2 = tempArray[j].childNodes;
9              for (var i:Number = 0; i<game.columns; ++i) {
10                  var name:String = "cell"+i+"_"+j;
11                  var x:Number = i*game.spacing;
12                  var y:Number = j*game.spacing;
13                  var type:Number = tempArray2[i-
                    ➥1].attributes.type;
14                  game.path.attachMovie("cell", name,
                    ➥++game.depth);
15                  game.path[name]._x = x;
16                  game.path[name]._y = y;
17                  game[name] = {x:i, y:j, name:name,
                    ➥type:type, clip:game.path[name],
                    ➥dot:game.path[name].tile.dot};
18                  game[name].clip.tile.gotoAndStop(type);
19             }
20        }
21        initializeBall();
22   }
```

Lines 2 and 3 create a new XML object to hold the first node of our boardXML object. The next two lines create an array of the child nodes of the <map> node. That means that every element in this array contains a <row> node. Lines 7 and 8 create an array that contains the child nodes of the jth <row> node from the tempArray array. The child nodes of a <row> node are the <cell> nodes. In line 13, we set a local variable called `type` that stores the number extracted from the `type` node of the ith `<cell>` node in the `tempArray2` array.

There is one more addition to the ActionScript on this frame—the `detectDot()` function. A reference to a cell movie clip is passed into this function, and a `hitTest()` is performed between `ball` and `dot`. If the `hitTest()` method returns a value of `true`, then a collision occurred, and `dot` has its visibility set to `false`.

```
function detectDot(tempCell) {
        if (game.ball.clip.hitTest(tempCell.dot)) {
                tempCell.dot._visible = false;
        }
}
```

This function is called from the `moveBall()` function. You may remember that in the `moveBall()` function, there are four chunks of code, one for each arrow key. If the place where you attempt to move the ball is valid, then the `detectDot()` function is called.

Generate an SWF from this file. When you click the Play Game button, you'll notice that your XML file has been loaded and interpreted. You can now move the ball around the map and collect dots (see Figure 7.12)! This is a very simple example of a TBW with an editor.

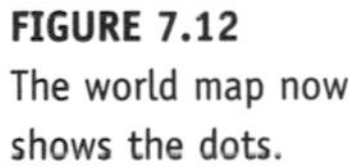

FIGURE 7.12
The world map now shows the dots.

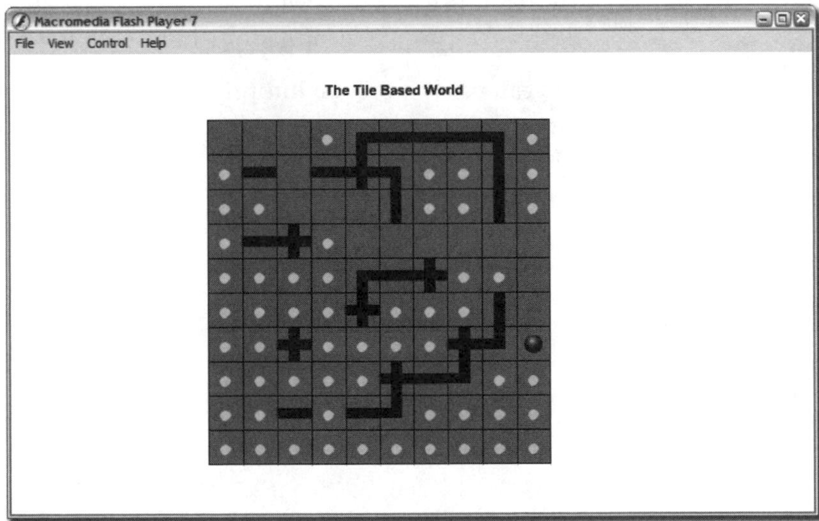

We've just presented a very simple method of using a level editor for tile-based games. In Chapter 9, we will go into more detail about level creation tools.

Points to Remember

- Tiles (also called cells) enable the reuse of most of the visual assets you create for a game and can be the building blocks for the appearance of many games.
- Tiles help you assemble an entire game world using code.
- Using a simple math trick only possible with TBWs, you can greatly reduce the processing power needed to run your game.
- A trick to pinpoint the location of a character enables you to perform collision detection only between the character and the objects in that cell, which reduces the code intensity because you are not checking for collisions with every object on the screen, only the ones in that cell.
- A tile is a movie clip.
- The data structure used with tile-based worlds (one object for each tile) makes storing information about each tile very easy.
- You can easily store the information needed to build a TBW in an external file or database. This information, which usually represents a level in a game, can be loaded in later, and the world or level is constructed from it.
- Nested loops are used to build a grid of tiles for your game.

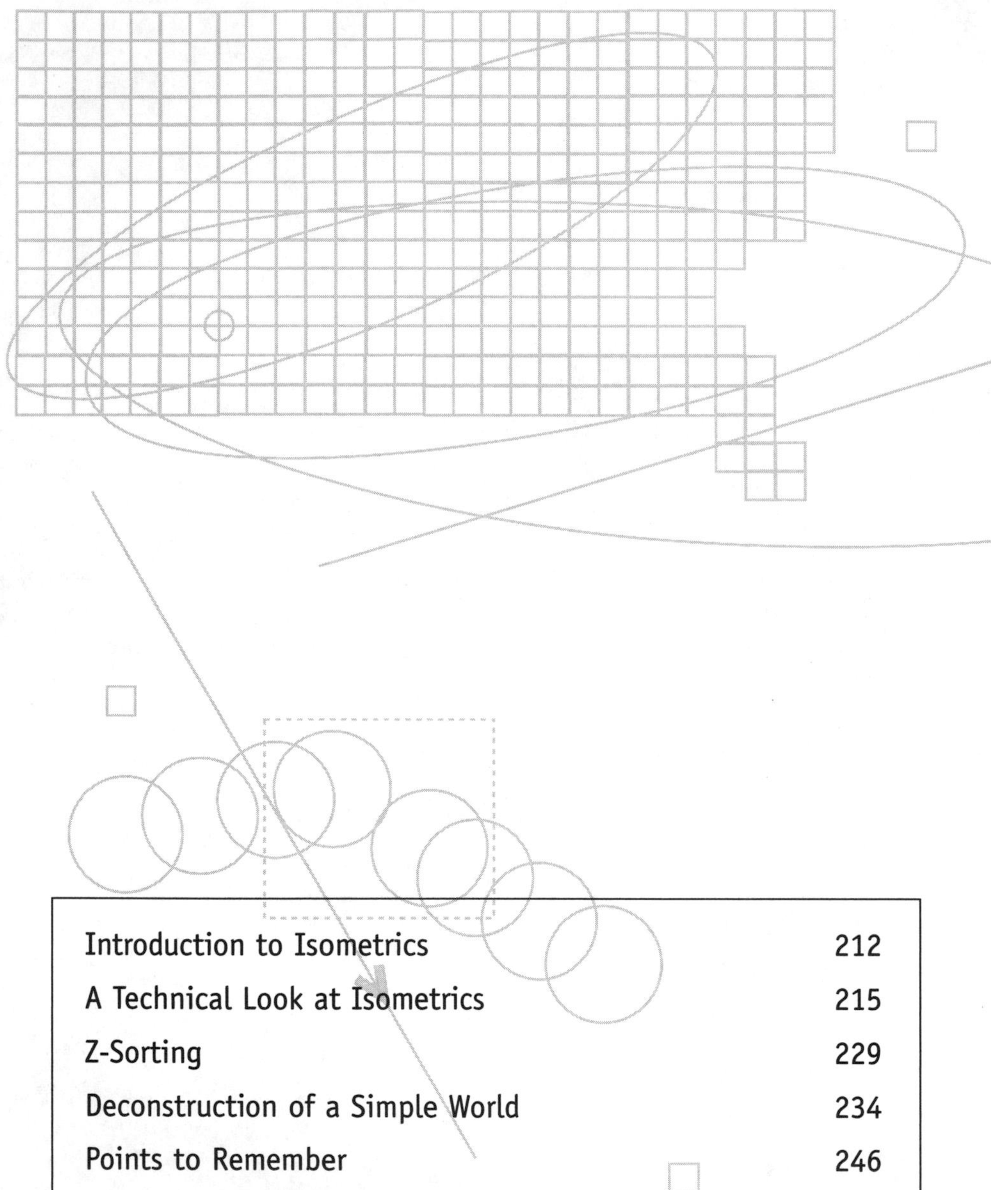

Introduction to Isometrics	212
A Technical Look at Isometrics	215
Z-Sorting	229
Deconstruction of a Simple World	234
Points to Remember	246

CHAPTER 8

THE ISOMETRIC WORLDVIEW

AN *ISOMETRIC* VIEW IS A SPECIFIC THREE-DIMENSIONAL (3D) VIEW. IN 3D, as you have undoubtedly seen in some non-Flash games, the camera (the viewpoint of your computer screen) can move anywhere and rotate anywhere. A specific position of this camera gives an isometric view. This view is popular in many games, including *Diablo II*, and has been shown to be very effective when used properly in Flash. In this chapter, we will discuss why this view is popular and how to treat it mathematically. We'll also provide real examples of how to use it. To get the most out of this chapter, you should have read (or be familiar with the concepts learned in) Chapter 7, "Tile-Based Worlds."

Introduction to Isometrics

Sometimes explaining and understanding a concept is easier with comparisons. With this in mind, we will briefly discuss 3D in games in general and then specifically talk about isometrics.

It is rare today to find professionally created games for sale that are not 3D. Even games that are typically only two-dimensional, such as card games, often have some sort of 3D element. As mentioned in Chapter 1, "First Steps," 3D can be applied to a game in many ways. Games like *Unreal Tournament* (see Figure 8.1) use a real 3D engine. A 3D engine can rotate objects and display them correctly onscreen, changing the camera's viewpoint at any time, and uses very detailed z-sorting. *Z-sorting* is the concept and act of placing one object on top of another to give the appearance of the first object being in front of the second. (In Flash, the objects we'll work with will be movie clips.) The sequence in which we arrange the objects is called the *stacking order*. Each object in the stack is at a specific depth—assigned by a relative numeric value, also known as a z-index. Z-sorting can be applied to several different types of situations, including a 3D world (as in this chapter) or the open windows of your operating system.

FIGURE 8.1
Unreal Tournament (Courtesy of Epic Games, Inc.).

For instance, your keyboard is in front of your monitor, so it has a higher z-sorting number—the closer to the game player, the higher the number. One of the most powerful things about advanced 3D engines, such as the one written for a game like *Unreal Tournament,* is that they can map bitmaps to shapes. For instance, the bitmap of a human face can be mapped onto the shape of a head, which is a polygon. When this shape rotates in the 3D world, it appears to be a human head. With this type of 3D engine, all shapes are rendered (created) onscreen mathematically. There are usually some premade bitmaps, like the human face mentioned previously, but for the most part, all the objects are created and moved on the fly. This type of engine is very processor-intensive, and because of the real-time creation of objects, it can limit the game's level of detail.

Early on in the online game world, developers discovered that a 3D world was great for many types of games but that changing camera views wasn't always important. With this in mind, some games were developed with only one camera view—an isometric view (the angles of which will be discussed in the next section).

At this point, before we talk more about the isometric view, it is important to note the concept of perspective. Imagine that you are standing on a long, straight road. As you look down this road, its two sides appear to converge far off in the distance. As we all know, the sides of the road do not actually converge in the distance. If you were to travel to the end of the road, you would see that it is just as wide at the end as it is at the beginning. This visual illusion is called perspective. Without perspective, the road would appear to stay the same width, and in fact it would probably be impossible to get a feeling for how long the road is. Perspective helps to give us an idea of an object's dimensions (see Figure 8.2).

FIGURE 8.2
Examples with perspective and no perspective.

Games that use an isometric view do not use perspective (see Figure 8.3). Why is this so important? Imagine creating a first-person-view 3D game in Flash. As a car drives past your character, the perspective of the car constantly changes. New parts of the car are revealed as the car moves by, and eventually it vanishes. As the character with the first-person view walks down the street, the perspective of every object on the screen constantly changes. To create a game like that, you need a true 3D engine. Yes, very limited versions of this can be created in Flash (with highly advanced tricks), but for the most part, it should not be considered a realistic possibility—not as of this writing, anyway. With an isometric view, there is no perspective. This means we can create many different angles of objects and then place those objects on the screen. For instance, with an isometric view, you can create a tree and place it anywhere in the world without having to worry about its size or perspective because those attributes never change (see Figure 8.4). This is good news for first-time, as well as seasoned, Flash developers because it means we can create 3D games without a 3D engine.

FIGURE 8.3
The well-known game *Diablo II* is a good example of a game with an isometric view.

FIGURE 8.4
A road in an isometric world never converges. But the amazing thing is, it looks great!

There is some controversy over what constitutes a 3D engine. In this chapter, I give you equations and functions to handle placing and moving objects in a 3D world and then map that onto a 2D screen. To some people, this is a 3D engine; to others (usually hard-core programmers), a 3D engine has to be able to handle real-time graphics rendering as well.

Let's recap the main points introduced here:

- An isometric view is a specific camera angle in a 3D world (mathematical specifics are in the next section).
- In an isometric world, you don't use perspective. The result is that you can create reusable objects instead of having to render them in real time.
- An isometric view is much less processor-intensive than other 3D views, which makes it more workable in Flash.

Next we will discuss the math, geometry, and trigonometry used to create this view and display it on a 2D screen (that is, projecting from a 3D to a 2D plane).

I don't mean to discourage anyone reading this chapter from attempting a more "real" 3D approach in games. With Flash's drawing API and with cool tricks (which you can find on the web or develop yourself), you can accomplish some amazing things.

A Technical Look at Isometrics

In this section, we'll take a different look at isometrics. We'll discuss everything you need to know to place objects in an isometric world and to map them back to the computer screen.

The Orientation of the Isometric World

Before moving forward, we need to look at the Flash coordinate system in a new way. Up to this point in the book, we have been seeing the coordinate system as two-dimensional; that is, having an *x*-axis and a *y*-axis. Flash does not have a *z*-axis, but if it did, the positive end would extend out past the back of the computer screen (see Figure 8.5).

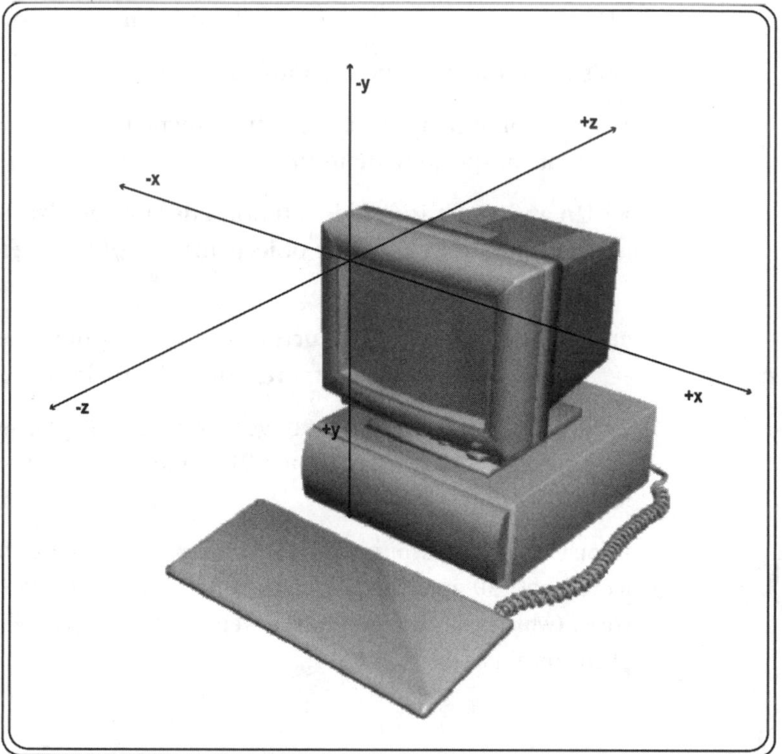

FIGURE 8.5
The *z*-axis.

The isometric world we will be dealing with can be conceptualized (and then treated mathematically) as a second 3D coordinate system sitting inside this Flash coordinate system. Let's call this second system "the isometric system" and the first "the Flash system." The Flash system is stationary; it cannot move because it is bound to your computer monitor. The isometric system is only isometric when it is oriented in a specific way within the Flash system. Please note that the isometric system does not change when its orientation changes. The only thing that makes it isometric is how it is seen from the Flash system (see Figure 8.6).

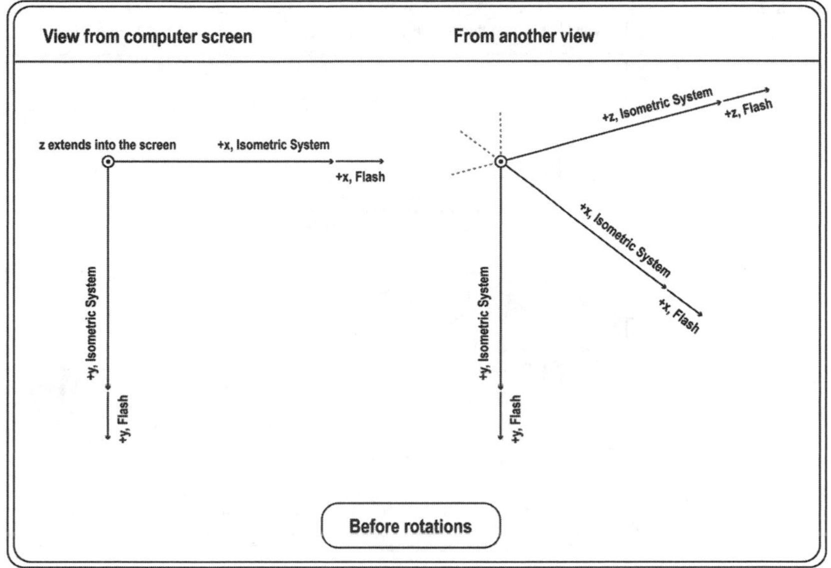

FIGURE 8.6
Before it is rotated, the new coordinate system is aligned with Flash's coordinate system.

Now let's assume that the isometric system is completely aligned with the Flash system. In this case, there is no difference between the Flash system and the isometric system; in fact, it is not yet isometric. What has to happen to this second system to make it appear isometric, as seen from the Flash system?

- It must be rotated 30° around its *x*-axis.

  The *x*-axis is treated like an axle, so it stays still while the coordinate system rotates. Before the rotation, all three axes lie along all three of Flash's axes. After the rotation, the isometric system's *x*-axis still lies along Flash's *x*-axis, but the other axes are no longer aligned (see Figure 8.7).

- It must then be rotated 45° around its own *y*-axis.

  During this rotation, the *y*-axis is treated like an axle, so it stays stationary while the rest of the isometric system is rotated around it (see Figure 8.8). When this rotation has been completed, all three isometric axes are in different positions from their starting places, and the system appears to be isometric, as seen from the Flash system (see Figure 8.9).

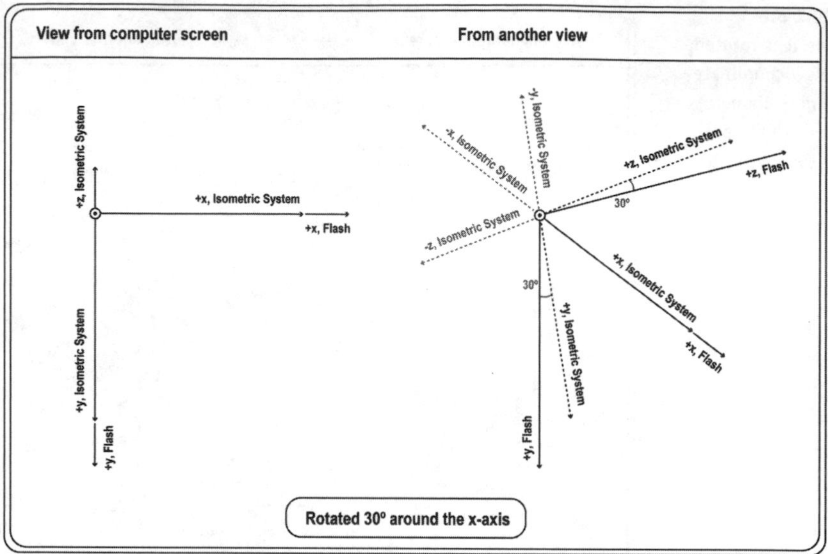

FIGURE 8.7
Rotated 30° around the *x*-axis.

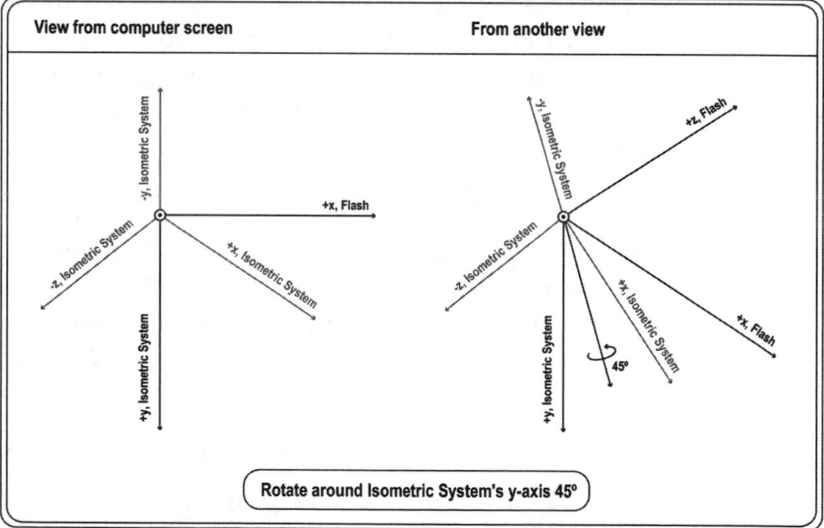

FIGURE 8.8
Rotated around isometric system's *y*-axis 45°.

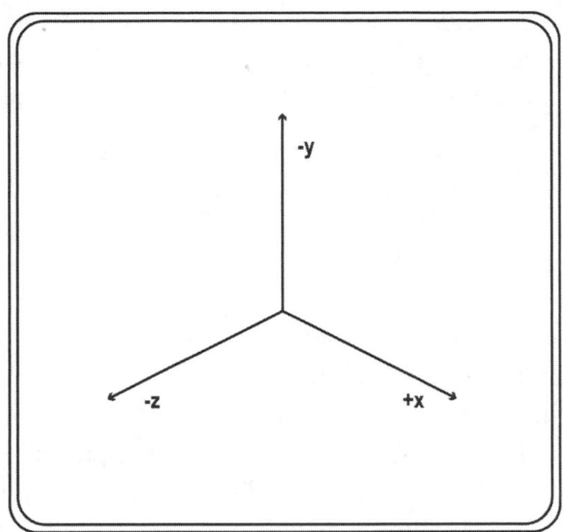

FIGURE 8.9
Final product: the isometric view as seen from the Flash coordinate system (your monitor).

Take a look at the demo.swf file in the Chapter08 directory on the CD-ROM. This file was created to help you visualize how these two rotations take place. It shows a straight-on orientation in the Flash system (before it is isometric) and then rotates the cube in two steps. When it is finished animating, the cube is seen in an isometric view (see Figure 8.10).

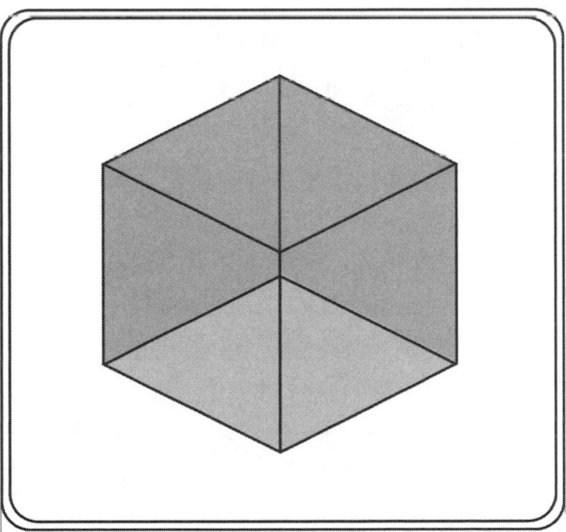

FIGURE 8.10
Cube in an isometric world.

Why is this view called isometric? If you look at the cube in Figure 8.10, you will notice that only three faces are exposed. The area of each face is the same. The prefix iso means "the same," and metric signifies "measurement."

Placing an Object in the Isometric World

Before continuing, I want to mention some restrictions we will be observing. First, look at the image in Figure 8.11.

Throughout this book, we have been advocating using code to describe visual elements—their position, speed, and other properties—and to store this information (as opposed to storing information in the movie clips themselves). If the position of something needs to be updated on the Stage, then we do so at the end of the frame after all needed calculations are done. We take the position that we have calculated in memory and then assign that value to the _x and _y properties of the movie clip. This technique will be used in this chapter as well—we will discuss the position coordinates in the isometric system and in the Flash system and how to move between them.

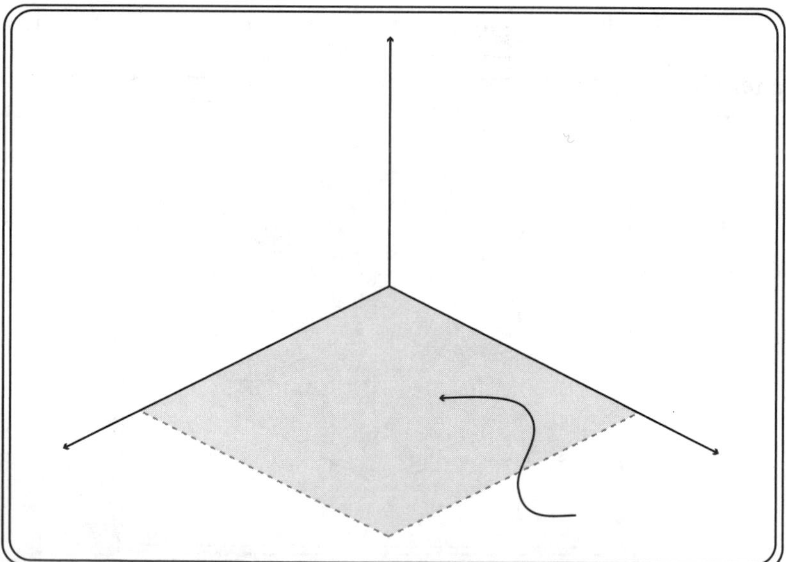

FIGURE 8.11
The x, y, z quadrant.

We are going to restrict where we place objects to the quadrant of the isometric world formed by the *x* and *z* axes. Specifically, if we extend this quadrant upward in the *y* direction, we form an *octant* (a quadrant infinite in size, extended in an orthogonal, or perpendicular, direction). This octant is shown in the Figure 8.12.

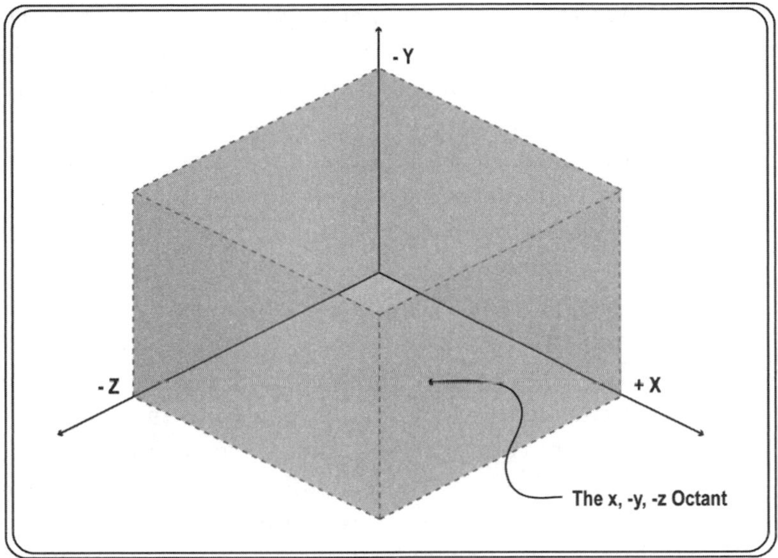

FIGURE 8.12
The x, y, z octant.

The reason we restrict object placement to this octant has to do with z-sorting. (As a reminder, z-sorting refers to changing the depth of movie clips to make them appear to be at the correct distance from the screen.) For instance, as a character walks around a tree, you want the character to appear behind the tree at some points but in front of it at others. Finding a good way to handle z-sorting has plagued Flash developers for a long time. With this octant restriction, we can use a technique I developed for z-sorting that makes it lightning-fast. We'll talk about this in the next section. To recap, we restrict object placement to this octant so that we can use a specific and fast z-sorting technique. If someone comes up with something better, please let me know!

When working with 3D worlds, the coding architecture we've been using throughout this book (mentioned in the first paragraph of this section) is no longer just good practice; it's a necessity. We will now store three coordinates that represent each visual element—*x*, *y*, and *z*—in an object. These are the coordinates of anything in the isometric world. For instance, a character could have the coordinates (100, 10, –50) in the isometric world. To display this character on the screen, we must determine the *x* and *y* positions of the movie clip on the screen that make the character look like it is sitting at those isometric coordinates. The next logical step is to find this linkage between the isometric system and the Flash system.

We know that the isometric system is related to the Flash system by the two rotations (30° and 45°) discussed in the previous section. Using our knowledge of trigonometry, we can map (project) any point from the isometric system into the Flash system. This is done in two steps, one for each rotation. To map from the isometric system to the Flash system, we start with the points in the isometric system and then apply the two rotations to the coordinates. This actually maps the coordinates from the isometric system to an in-between system (after the first rotation) and then from the in-between system into the Flash system. During the first rotation, the *y*-coordinate is unchanged (because the *y*-axis is the fixed axis around which the system rotates); during the second rotation, the *x*-coordinate remains unchanged. Here is the math to back it up. We start with the coordinates of a point *(xpp, ypp, zpp)*. The *pp* is a mathematical convention; when an *x*-coordinate is changed to a new system, it is usually called *xp* (or *x'*). This is read as "*x* prime." When it is changed two times (as we do in this case), it is called *xpp* (or *x''*). This is read as "*x* double prime." So we start out with *(xpp, ypp, zpp)*, and after the first rotation, we'll have *(xp, yp, zp)*. After the second rotation, we'll have *(x, y, z)*. Let's begin.

We start in the isometric system with points *(xpp, ypp, zpp)*. To map this to the Flash system, we must move through two angles. We treat them one at a time. First, we map the coordinates to the intermediate system by rotating them around the *y*-axis 45° to arrive at three new coordinates *(xp, yp, zp)*:

```
xp = xpp*cos(45) + zpp*sin(alpha)
yp = ypp
zp = zpp*cos(45) - xpp*sin(alpha)
```

Notice that *yp* is equivalent to *ypp*. This is because the system was rotated around the *y*-axis, so the *y*-coordinate was not changed. Next, we rotate the coordinates *(xp, yp, zp)* around the *x*-axis 30° to arrive in the Flash coordinate system *(x, y, z)*:

```
x = xp
y = yp*cos(30) - zp*sin(30)
z = zp*cos(30) + yp*sin(30)
```

We now have the coordinates of where *(xpp, ypp, zpp)* should appear in the Flash system. You may have noticed that while we end up with *(x, y, z)*, we still don't really have a *z*-axis in Flash. As mentioned earlier, we can think of a *z*-axis that moves into the computer screen. This conceptualization helps when trying to do things such as mapping from 3D to Flash's system. Movie clips have `_x` and `_y` properties but no `_z` property, so when this math is changed into ActionScript, we can forget about the final *z*-coordinate. If we were not using an isometric view, we would most likely want to have real-time perspective changes. In that case, you would want this *z*-coordinate to hang around because you would use it to calculate perspective. In our isometric case, though, we don't need it.

Let's see a working example of how to position an object, given its coordinates in the isometric system. Open position.fla in the Chapter08 directory (see Figure 8.13). There are two layers in this file: Assets and Actions. The Assets layer contains all the movie clips and buttons. At the top left of the Stage, you see three dynamic text fields. They are there to show you the current coordinates of the ball in the isometric system. On the right side of the Stage, two text fields show you the *x*- and *y*-coordinates of the ball in Flash's system. In the middle, there is a movie clip with an instance name of `floor`. `floor` contains a graphic of a square floor in an isometric world. Also contained in that movie clip are a movie clip with an instance name of `ball` and a movie clip with an instance name of `shadow`. The shadow clip will move around with the ball to help give you a better idea of where the ball is. As the ball changes *y* positions, the shadow does not; this helps the player visualize the object's location.

(A visual cue—or clue—in a 3D world would be that the ball changed size according to its location; a correlative cue in the isometric world is the location of the object's shadow to help you understand the behavior of the object itself.) On the bottom-right side of the Stage are two buttons with which you can control the ball's *y* position in the isometric world.

Use your four arrow keys to move the ball around. You can change the ball's *y* position by using the buttons on the bottom-right side of the screen. Notice that your ball will not move through the floor—we imposed the octant restriction.

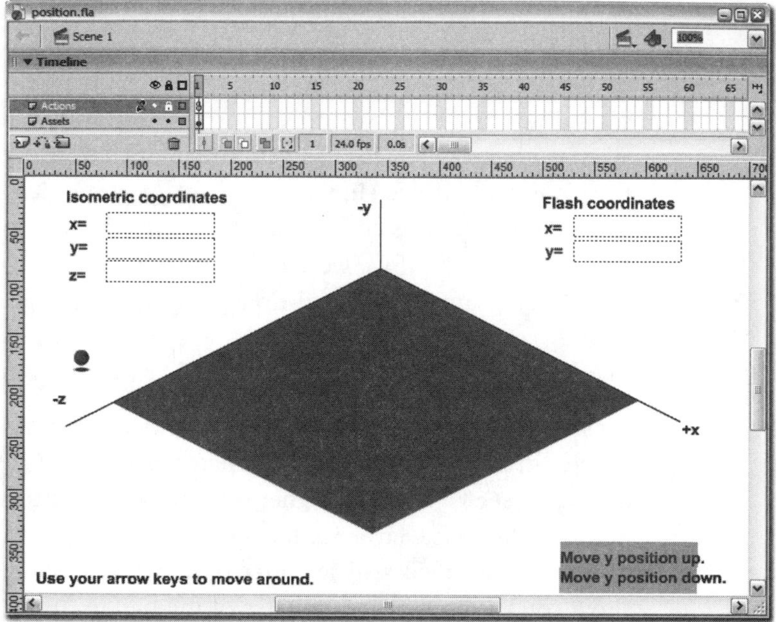

FIGURE 8.13
Open position.fla.

Now let's look at the ActionScript involved. I have created a class called `Isometric`, which is contained in a file in the directory called Isometric.as. This class contains three very helpful methods for working with isometrics. We will talk about two of these methods (`mapToScreen()` and `mapToIsoWorld()`) very soon, and we will save the third (`calculateDepth()`) for the next section.

The ActionScript in the Actions layer makes use of what was defined in the `Isometric` class and handles things such as capturing key events and placing the ball and shadow on the screen.

Let's look at the actions in the `Isometric` class. First, we see this:

```
function Isometric(x:Number, z:Number) {
     maxx = x;
     maxz = z;
     theta = 30;
     alpha = 45;
     theta *= Math.PI/180;
     alpha *= Math.PI/180;
     sinTheta = Math.sin(theta);
     cosTheta = Math.cos(theta);
```

```
10          sinAlpha = Math.sin(alpha);
11          cosAlpha = Math.cos(alpha);
12          leeway = 5;
13      }
```

This is the constructor method of the class. It is called to create a new instance of it. There are two parameters, x and z. We will discuss these in the next section because they apply only to the calculateDepth() method. In lines 4 and 5, we set the angles that are needed for the world to be isometric—30° and 45°. In the next several lines, we calculate the sine and cosine of these angles and store the values. (This way, we will not have to calculate them every time we need them.) In line 12, we set the value of leeway to 5. This is used to determine the number of valid depths per tile. With a leeway of 5, we can have up to 5 objects on a tile, all with unique depths.

Next is the mapToScreen() method:

```
1       function mapToScreen(xpp:Number, ypp:Number, zpp:Number):
        ➥Array {
2           var yp:Number = ypp;
3           var xp:Number = xpp*cosAlpha+zpp*sinAlpha;
4           var zp:Number = zpp*cosAlpha-xpp*sinAlpha;
5           var x:Number = xp;
6           var y:Number = yp*cosTheta-zp*sinTheta;
7           return [x, y];
8       }
```

This method takes the coordinates of a point in the isometric system and maps its *x*- and *y*-coordinates in the Flash system using the same math steps that we covered earlier in this section.

In line 7, we return the values *x* and *y* (which are the positions as they appear in the Flash system) as an array.

The final method of the class that we will discuss in this section does something we have not yet discussed:

```
function mapToIsoWorld(screenX:Number, screenY:Number):
➥Array {
    var z:Number = (screenX/cosAlpha-screenY/
    ➥(sinAlpha*sinTheta))*(1/(cosAlpha/sinAlpha+sinAlpha/
    ➥cosAlpha));
```

```
        var x:Number = (1/cosAlpha)*(screenX-z*sinAlpha);
        return [x, z];
    }
```

This function maps the coordinates *(x, y)* from the Flash system into the isometric system. Because we have only the *x*- and *y*-coordinates from the Flash system, we cannot map that to an *(x, y, z)* position in the isometric system; we can only map it to two coordinates. This method is useful when we want to capture the user's mouse position and then find out where that would be in the isometric world.

If you have ever played Electrotank's *Mini Golf* game, then you have seen this used; as you move the mouse around the character, the character rotates to follow. When you click, the character hits the ball. To calculate the angle the mouse made with the character, we map the mouse coordinates to the isometric world. The angle as it appears on the screen is not the angle that is truly in the isometric world.

We're not going to use this method in this section, but we will show a direct application of it in the final section in this chapter. I am not going to show the math involved in deriving these equations, as it got pretty hairy, but I will tell you that I used the equations in the `mapToScreen()` method and worked backward.

Select the frame in the Actions layer and open the Actions panel. Let's look at the first three lines of the ActionScript:

```
1   var iso = new Isometric();
2   var ball:Object = {x:0, y:0, z:0, clip:floor.ball,
    ➥shadowClip:floor.shadow};
3   var speed:Number = 5;
```

In line 1, we create an instance of the `Isometric` class. In the next line, we create an object called `ball`, which will be used to store all the information about the ball movie clip that we will be moving around in the isometric world. We initialize this object at position (0, 0, 0) and give it references to the ball movie clip and the shadow movie clip. In line 3, we set the speed. This simply specifies how much to move the ball every time an arrow key is pressed.

Next, we create a function called `captureKeys()`:

```
function captureKeys() {
     if (Key.isDown(Key.RIGHT)) {
          ball.x += speed;
     } else if (Key.isDown(Key.LEFT)) {
          ball.x -= speed;
     }
     if (Key.isDown(Key.UP)) {
          ball.z += speed;
     } else if (Key.isDown(Key.DOWN)) {
          ball.z -= speed;
     }
}
```

When this function is called, it checks to see which arrow keys are currently pressed down. If any are, then it changes the ball's position in either the *x* or *z* direction in the isometric system by the amount of `speed`.

Here is the function that is called to place the ball and shadow on the screen:

```
1    function placeBall() {
2         var temp:Array = iso.mapToScreen(ball.x, ball.y,
          ➥ball.z);
3         ball.clip._x = temp[0];
4         ball.clip._y = temp[1];
5         temp = iso.mapToScreen(ball.x, 0, ball.z);
6         ball.shadowClip._x = temp[0];
7         ball.shadowClip._y = temp[1];
8    }
```

In line 2, we call the `mapToScreen()` method of the `Isometric` class, passing in the ball's coordinates. The result is stored as an array called `temp`. We then use the values of this array to position the ball on the screen (lines 3 and 4). In line 5, we do almost the same thing as we did in line 2, except that we pass in `0` as the value of the *y* position. We then use this array to place the shadow movie clip on the screen. We passed in the value of `0` for the *y* position because the shadow should always be on the ground, which has a *y* position of `0`. However, the *x* and *z* positions of the shadow should always be the same as the ball's. This adds a very simple and helpful effect to an object that's moving around in a 3D environment. You can see how useful something like this is in Electrotank's *Mini Golf*. It is especially evident when the ball flies off a ramp—you can see the shadow move down the ramp as the ball goes through the air.

Now we come to a function called changeY(). As you can guess, this function changes the ball's *y* position. It is called when either of the two buttons at the bottom-right side of the screen is clicked.

```
function changeY(num) {
      ball.y += num;
      if (ball.y>0) {
            ball.y = 0;
      }
}
```

When this function is called, the ball's *y* position is increased by the amount of the parameter passed in. If the *y* position is ever below the floor, then we set it equal to the floor. This is so the ball cannot go through the floor.

Check out the bonus file position_with_ gravity.fla in the Chapter08 folder on the CD-ROM. It's similar to position.fla; the main difference is that this one has gravity so that the ball can bounce around in the isometric world.

Finally, we arrive at the onEnterFrame event:

```
_root.onEnterFrame = function() {
      captureKeys();
      placeBall();
      ignoreMe();
};
```

This event calls captureKeys() and placeBall() in every frame. Ignore the ignoreMe() function—it is there only to help display the coordinates on the screen for you to see when testing the file.

That's everything! You are now on your way to building an isometric world. It's best to make your isometric world a tile-based world. You will see an example of this in the final section of this chapter.

Z-Sorting

We've come across the concept of z-sorting a few times already in this chapter, and now we can finally discuss it in detail. Once again, z-sorting is the term used to describe the creation of the stacking order of movie clips. If two movie clips are overlapping, of course they can't both be on top. The one on top is said to have a *higher depth*. You are probably familiar with the concept of depth in Flash, but let's review a little bit and go over a few things you may not know about depths in Flash.

Each timeline in a Flash movie can have up to 16,384 depths, and each depth can hold only one movie clip. When you manually place movie clips in a timeline, they are assigned a depth starting at –16,383. Each additional movie clip manually placed in the timeline has a depth higher than the previous one, with numbers moving closer to 0. When you use ActionScript to create instances of movie clips, you assign them a depth. It is recommended by Macromedia (and is common practice) to assign positive depths to movie clips created with ActionScript. Depth 1 does not have to be filled before depth 2. This means that you can, for instance, use `attachMovie()` and assign the new movie clip a depth of 2,000,000.

Don't Go Too Deep!

Be careful how high a depth (see Figure 8.14) you use; if it is too high, then you can no longer easily remove the movie clip using `removeMovieClip()`. The highest depth to which you can assign a movie clip without losing the capability to use `removeMovieClip()` is 1,048,575. The depth 1,048,576 is too high. However, if your movie clip is above 1,048,575, you can use `swapDepths()` to bring that movie clip back down below this critical number and then use `removeMovieClip()`.

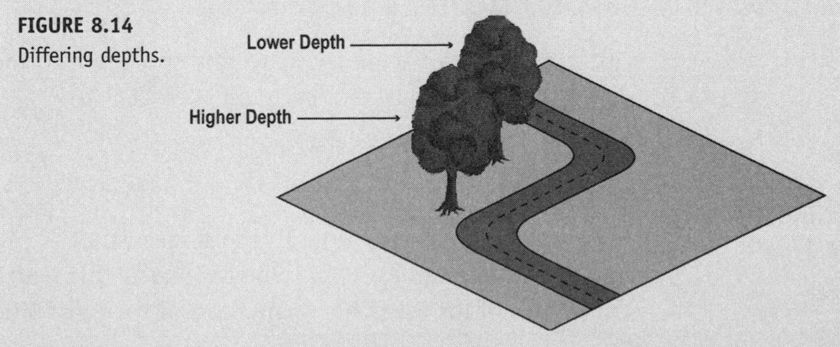

FIGURE 8.14
Differing depths.

The goal of z-sorting in our isometric world is to assign each movie clip to a unique specific depth so that the objects in the world appear to be stacked correctly. With z-sorting, we can make it so that a character can walk around an object such as a tree. The tree's depth remains constant while the character's depth changes as it moves.

Isometric worlds in Flash are usually also tile-based worlds. All the files presented in this chapter from now on use tiles to create the world. In addition to all the advantages of tile-based worlds that were introduced in Chapter 7, we can add z-sorting. Z-sorting in a tile-based world is much easier to handle than it is in a non-tile-based world. We assign a depth to each tile, with a gap of something like 5 between depths. Thus, one tile could have a depth of 100, and the next tile could have a depth of 105. Then, as the character moves onto the first tile, we give it a depth of 101, and when the character moves onto the next tile, we give it a depth of 106. Next, we'll discuss how to assign the depth to each tile.

As you know, to create a grid of tiles, you must use nested loops. One way to assign depth is to base it on where you are in the loop, but that's a limited technique that we won't use here. Instead, we use an equation that gives us a unique depth for each cell. This equation works for any *y* position, so if you decide to create a complicated isometric world in which there are multiple levels (such as the inside of a two-story house), then this equation still works perfectly, giving you the correct depths to use.

First we establish a boundary of the largest *x* tile number we expect to use. If it is a 10-by-10 tile-based world, then this boundary is 10. In the following mathematical exercise, we use the letters *a* and *b* to represent the maximum number of tiles that can be found in the *x* and *z* directions.

```
a = 10
b = 10
```

Then, assuming we are trying to find the depth of the tile specified by *(x, y, z)*, we can write the following:

```
var floor:Number = a*(b - 1) + x
var depth:Number = a*(z - 1) + x + floor*y
```

For these equations to give a valid final result (depth), *x*, *y*, and *z* must all be positive values. Thus, when we write this with ActionScript, we make use of the `Math.abs()` method of the `Math` object in Flash to ensure that the values are positive. Because we are assigning values based on the tiles themselves, we can use integers for *x* and *z*. For instance, the cell 3_5 would have an *x* of 3 and a *z* of 5. Because we are only dealing with one level (flat ground), the value of *y* remains 0. (See Figure 8.15).

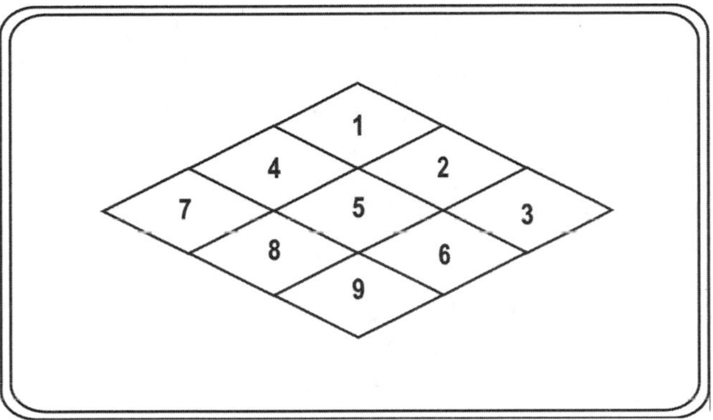

FIGURE 8.15
Each file contains its depth.

To see this in action, open depth.fla from the Chapter08 folder on the CD-ROM. In this file is a 10-by-10 grid of tiles created in the isometric world. When each tile is created, we assign a depth to it using the `calculateDepth()` method. There are two layers in the main timeline: Actions and Assets. The Assets layer contains one movie clip called `floor`. This movie clip contains the tile movie clip and the ball movie clip. The Actions layer contains a lot of ActionScript needed to create the tiles, change some of the tiles to display objects, and move the ball movie clip.

This file uses the `Isometric` class. We did not discuss the `calculateDepth()` method yet, so let's look at it now:

```
function calculateDepth(x:Number, y:Number,
➥z:Number):Number {
    var x:Number = Math.abs(x)*leeway;
    var y:Number = Math.abs(y);
    var z:Number = Math.abs(z)*leeway;
    var a:Number = maxx;
    var b:Number = maxz;
    var floor:Number = a*(b-1)+x;
    var depth:Number = a*(z-1)+x+floor*y;
    return depth;
}
```

This method contains the math equations we discussed earlier, translated into ActionScript. We multiply the value `leeway` by both `x` and `z` when they are passed in. This enables us to separate the depth of each tile by at least the value of `leeway` (5). Thus, one tile could have a depth of 250, and the next one would have a depth of 255. If leeway had a value of 1, then each depth would be 1 more than the previous. Notice the use of `Math.abs()` in lines 2–4. This ensures that the values of `x`, `y`, and `z` are positive. In lines 7 and 8, we calculate the depth and then return it in line 9.

Now let's look at the function that creates the tiles, `buildFloor()`:

```
1     function buildFloor(path) {
2          path.tile._visible = false;
3          world.tiles = [];
4          var y:Number = 0;
5          for (var j = 1; j<=10; ++j) {
6               for (var i = 1; i<=10; ++i) {
7                    if (j == 1) {
8                         world.tiles[i] = [];
9                    }
10                   var depth:Number = iso.calculateDepth(i,
                     ➥y, j);
11                   var name:String = "cell"+i+"_"+j;
12                   path.attachMovie("tile", name, depth);
13                   var clip:MovieClip = path[name];
14                   world.tiles[i][j] = {x:i, y:y, z:j,
                     ➥depth:depth, clip:clip};
15                   var x:Number = (i-1)*world.cellWidth;
16                   var z:Number = -(j-1)*world.cellWidth;
17                   temp = iso.mapToScreen(x, y, z);
18                   clip._x = temp[0];
19                   clip._y = temp[1];
20              }
21         }
22    }
```

An object in the timeline called `world` (which we'll see in the "Deconstruction of a Simple World" section later on) was created to store information about this isometric world. In line 3, we create an array on the `world` object called `tiles`. This is a two-dimensional array, and each element of the array is an object that represents a tile. In line 4, we set the variable y equal to 0. This is the level on which the tiles will be created. Look at line 10. This is where we find the depth of the current tile that is being added to the screen. We do this by passing in the *x* tile number, the *z* tile number, and the *y* level (0). In line 12, we add the tile using `attachMovie()` and assign it a depth from the variable we created in line 10 called `depth`.

Next, let's take a look at the function used to place the ball on the screen:

```
1    function placeBall() {
2         ball.x = ball.x;
3         ball.y = ball.y;
4         ball.z = ball.z;
5         var temp:Array = iso.mapToScreen(ball.x, ball.y,
          ➥ball.z);
6         ball.clip._x = temp[0];
7         ball.clip._y = temp[1];
8         var cellx:Number =
          ➥Math.ceil(ball.x/world.cellWidth);
9         var cellz:Number =
          ➥Math.ceil(Math.abs(ball.z)/world.cellWidth);
10        var depth:Number = iso.calculateDepth(cellx, 0,
          ➥cellz);
11        depth = depth+1;
12        ball.clip.swapDepths(depth);
13   }
```

Take a look at lines 8–12. In lines 8 and 9, we find the tile that the ball is currently on top of by using the trick learned in the "Precision Detection" section of Chapter 7 (a method for determining where the character is located so that we need to perform collision detection only in that cell). We then determine the tile's depth in line 10 by invoking the `calculateDepth()` method of the `Isometric` class. Next, in line 11, we increase the value of the `depth` by `1`. This is so that the ball appears on top of the current tile. (If we didn't do this, we'd be setting the depth of the ball to the same depth as the tile, which would destroy the instance of that tile.) Finally, in line 12 we set the ball's depth using `swapDepths()`.

That isn't all the ActionScript in this file. We don't explain all the ActionScript because you have seen the techniques used in the rest of this file before. In the next section, we will discuss some more of the ActionScript, as well as add some more to this file.

Generate an SWF from this file to see z-sorting in action. Two plants appears on the screen, along with a grassy tile-based ground and a sidewalk. The ball appears at the edge of the floor (see Figure 8.16). You can then use the arrow keys to move the ball around. Watch the ball move around the plants and the blocks sticking up through the floor; it appears in front of or behind the plant and the blocks as appropriate. You may notice that nothing is stopping you from moving the ball directly onto a cell that has an object, so the z-sorting can look a little bit odd if you move through an object. In the next section, we add a character who can walk around in this world. We also add some collision detection to make sure the character doesn't move onto a tile that contains an object.

FIGURE 8.16
Z-sorting in action.

Deconstruction of a Simple World

You have now seen the geometry and trigonometry needed to understand the isometric system's orientation with respect to the Flash system and how to handle z-sorting in an isometric world. With these concepts under your belt, it's an appropriate time to start thinking about more fun stuff, such as the isometric world itself. In this section, we deconstruct a file that contains a character and see how the character interacts with its surroundings.

Open iso_world.swf from the Chapter08 directory on the CD-ROM. You'll quickly see that this file looks almost the same as the depth.fla file we used in the previous section. The only cosmetic difference is that instead of moving a ball, you'll be moving a character (see Figure 8.17). In this movie, you can click anywhere on the tiles, and the character will start walking toward the point where you clicked. You'll see that a tile can be either grassy or concrete and can contain either no objects or a plant or block. The character cannot walk through an object and will stop walking when the next step would cause a collision.

FIGURE 8.17
Moving a character.

Now open iso_world.fla in the same directory. Here you'll see that not only does the file look similar, but the majority of the ActionScript is the same, too. Before talking about the ActionScript, let's take a look at the character movie clip itself. Open the Library and double-click the character Library item (see Figure 8.18).

Notice that there are 16 frame labels in this timeline. The artist who created this character created eight different angles of it. For each of the eight angles, there is a standing pose and a walking animation (called a *walk cycle*). The standing pose for the first angle is in the frame labeled stand1, and the corresponding walk cycle is in walk1. In the SWF, when you click somewhere on the tiles, the angle your mouse makes with the character (in the isometric world, not in the Flash system) is calculated. From this angle, the script determines which of the eight character angles to display. We then move to the walk cycle for that angle. When the character stops walking, we move to the stand frame for that angle.

Now double-click the tiles Library item. This is the movie clip that is attached to the screen several times to create the floor. There are two movie clips within this timeline, called innerTile and objects. The innerTile movie clip contains two frame labels, Grass and Concrete.

The objects movie clip contains two frame labels, Block and Plant. The Plant label has an isometric view of a plant, and the Block label has an isometric view of a thick tile that protrudes from the floor. With this simple setup, we can easily create many types of tiles. For instance, we can show a plant but change the floor of that tile to show concrete instead of grass. This simple architecture is very flexible.

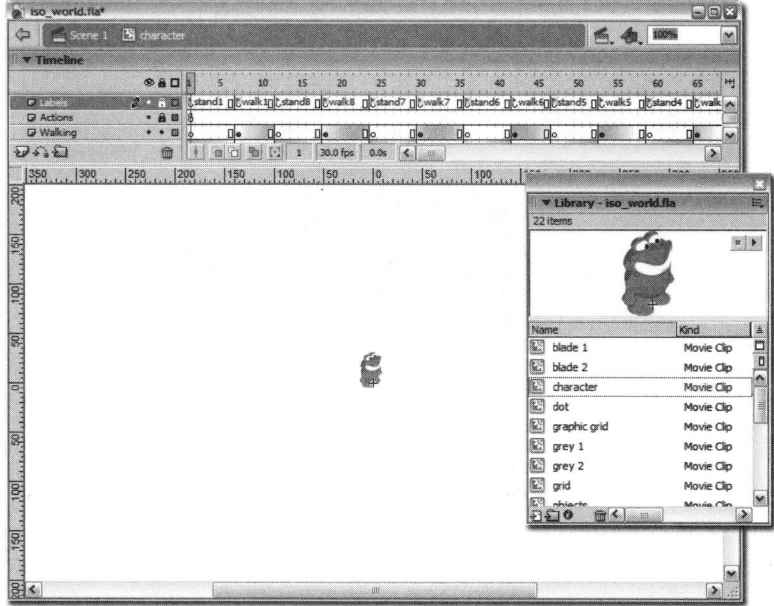

FIGURE 8.18
The character movie clip.

Now move back to the main timeline. Select the frame in the Actions layer and open the Actions panel. We are going to go through the majority of the ActionScript in this frame, much of which was not discussed in the previous section.

First, let's look at the `buildWorld()` function. This function is called to initialize the world itself. It creates the objects needed to store information about the world and calls functions to do things such as creating the tiles and initializing the character.

```
function buildWorld(maxx, maxz) {
    world = new Object();
    world.maxx = maxx;
    world.maxz = maxz;
    world.cellWidth = 29;
    world.width = maxx*world.cellWidth;
```

```
7        world.length = -maxz*world.cellWidth;
8        world.path = this.floor;
9        var path = world.path;
10       buildFloor(path);
11       buildCharacter(path);
12   }
```

In line 2, we create an object called `world` that is used to store information about the world. It stores the array that represents the tiles (created with the `buildFloor()` function), properties of the world dimensions (`maxx` and `maxz`), and the object that represents the character. This object will be discussed soon, when we cover the `buildCharacter()` function. Also stored on this object is the tile's width in the isometric world.

How Wide Is Your Tile?

You might wonder how you can find out the width of a square tile in an isometric world. Easy—you just use the Properties inspector to find the tile's width in the Flash system, and then divide this number by the square root of 2 (approximately 1.414). The result is the width of this tile in the isometric world. Alternatively, if you are the one creating the tile, then you can do this trick:

1. Draw a square in Flash (say, 100 by 100).
2. Rotate the square by 45°.
3. Scale down this square's height by 50 percent.

What you are left with (see Figure 8.19) is precisely what that square looks like in an isometric world. You also know what its width is in the Flash world because you created it (100, in this case).

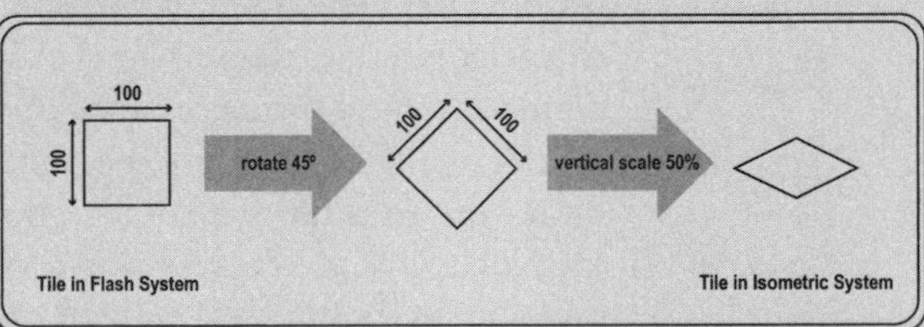

FIGURE 8.19
A tile in the Flash system and a tile in the isometric system.

Now let's look at the buildCharacter() function (which is called in line 11 of the ActionScript previously):

```
1     function buildCharacter(path) {
2          world.char = new Object();
3          world.char.tempx = 10;
4          world.char.tempy = 0;
5          world.char.tempz = -10;
6          world.char.speed = 4;
7          world.char.feeler = 10;
8          world.char.width = 10;
9          world.char.xmov = 0;
10         world.char.zmov = 0;
11         world.char.ymov = 0;
12         world.char.moving = false;
13         world.char.clip = path.character;
14         positionCharacter();
15    }
```

This function initializes the object that represents the character. This object is called char and is on the world object. In lines 3–5, we set the temporary position of the character to give it a starting place. Through the course of the other functions that are called, this temporary position becomes the character's current position (that is, tempx, tempy, and tempz become x, y, z). In line 6, we create a variable called speed. When you click a tile, the character attempts to walk there, and the speed at which the character walks is determined by the value of the speed variable.

Next, we set an oddly-named variable called feeler. This one requires a little explanation. In our previous file examples (and in this file as well), the object being moved around is represented by one point. We all know that a character in real life is three-dimensional and hence characterized by more than one point. If we use just one point to determine where the character is going, then when the character is on the edge of a tile bordering an object such as a block, some of the character is already on the block's tile. This is because the point that represents the character is still on the previous tile, but some of the graphic elements are overlapping the block. This presents a visual problem, but no actual programming problem. Everything still works, but it may not look as good as you would like. There is more than one way to handle, or eliminate, this visual issue. The most proper way is to treat the character as if it were a cylinder or a cube (as we mentioned in Chapter 6, "Collision Reactions"). We're going to take an even simpler approach—we'll use something called *feelers*. Imagine an insect walking around. Before the majority of the insect's body moves onto a new surface, its feelers first inspect that surface. In our case, we extend the feelers a distance of 10 pixels along the direction in which the character is walking. If the feelers find an object in a cell not yet (but almost) reached, the character stops moving. This works amazingly well in this file. The feelers are nothing you can see; they are just code. You will see this technique used in the `detectObjects()` and `worldClicked()` functions.

In line 12, we set a variable called `moving`. This always has a value of `true` or `false`. If `true`, then the character is moving.

In line 14, the function `positionCharacter()` is called. This function handles placing the character on the screen. It is called here but will also be called during every frame in an `onEnterFrame` event:

```
1    function positionCharacter() {
2         world.char.x = world.char.tempx;
3         world.char.y = world.char.tempy;
4         world.char.z = world.char.tempz;
5         var temp:Array = iso.mapToScreen(world.char.x,
          ➥world.char.y, ?world.char.z);
6         world.char.clip._x = temp[0];
7         world.char.clip._y = temp[1];
8    }
```

In lines 2–4, we set the character's *x*, *y*, and *z* positions based on its current temporary positions in memory. We then use this placement to determine the character's *x* and *y* placement on the screen using the `mapToScreen()` method of the `Isometric` class. Finally, we place the character on the screen.

The next logical step would be to discuss the function used to move the character from one point to another. However, during this movement collision detection occurs, using the feelers to see if the character is about to enter a tile that contains an object. So before we talk about how to move the character, let's talk about the functions that create the objects on the screen and change the types of tiles that are displayed.

```
function makeObject(x, z, object) {
     world.tiles[x][z].isObject = true;
```

```
        world.tiles[x][z].clip.objects.gotoAndStop(object);
    }
    function changeGroundTile(x, z, object) {
        world.tiles[x][z].clip.innerTile.gotoAndStop(object);
    }
    function changeManyGroundTiles(x, xnum, z, znum, object) {
        for (var i = 0; i<xnum; ++i) {
            for (var j = 0; j<znum; ++j) {
                world.tiles[x+i][z+j].clip.innerTile.
                ➥gotoAndStop (object);
            }
        }
    }
```

These three functions are fairly self-explanatory. The first one, `makeObject()`, adds an object (either a plant or a block) to a tile. It then sets the property `isObject` to `true` in the `tiles` array. We use the `isObject` property with the feelers when detecting a collision (more on this later). The next function, `changeGroundTile()`, simply changes the type of tile displayed. You can change a tile from grass to concrete or the other way around. The function `changeManyGroundTiles()` does the same thing as `changeGroundTile()`, except that it applies to many tiles at once. You specify the starting *x* and *z* positions and then how far to extend in each direction.

Now that we've discussed collision-detection, we can move on to the "next logical step" I mentioned previously—moving the character itself. When you click the mouse button, the well-named `worldClicked()` function is called. This function maps your mouse pointer's *x* and *y* positions onto the *x, -z* plane in the isometric world. It then takes these values and compares them with the world's boundaries. If the mouse was clicked within the world's boundaries and the character was not already moving, then many things happen. Let's look at those things.

```
function worldClicked(xm, ym) {
    var temp = iso.mapToIsoWorld(xm, ym);
    var xm:Number = temp[0];
    var zm:Number = temp[1];
    if (!world.char.moving && xm>=0 && xm<=world.width
    ➥&& zm>=world.length && zm<=0) {
        var x:Number = world.char.x;
        var z:Number = world.char.z;
```

```
8               world.char.startx = x;
9               world.char.startz = z;
10              world.char.endx = xm;
11              world.char.endz = zm;
12              var angleSpan:Number = 360/8;
13              var angle:Number = Math.atan2(zm-z, xm-x);
14              var realAngle:Number = angle*180/Math.PI;
15              realAngle += angleSpan/2;
16              if (realAngle<0) {
17                  realAngle += 360;
18              }
19              var frame:Number =
                ➥Math.ceil(realAngle/angleSpan);
20              world.char.clip.gotoAndStop("walk"+frame);
21              world.char.frame = frame;
22              world.char.moving = true;
23              var cosAngle:Number = Math.cos(angle);
24              var sinAngle:Number = Math.sin(angle);
25              world.char.xmov = world.char.speed*cosAngle;
26              world.char.zmov = world.char.speed*sinAngle;
27              world.char.feelerx = world.char.feeler*cosAngle;
28              world.char.feelerz = world.char.feeler*sinAngle;
29          }
30      }
```

The condition in line 5 checks to see if the clicked area is within the boundaries of the world and if the character is not already moving. If the condition is satisfied, then it is OK to prepare the character for movement. What does this preparation involve? For the character to be able to move, we must determine the angle at which to move, the angled frame (1 of 8) of the character to display, and the speed in each direction for the character to walk. In lines 8 and 9, we store the character's starting position. (This starting position is used later to determine if the character has reached the destination.) In the next two lines, we store the character's end position. Then, in line 12, we create a variable called `angleSpan` that stores the amount of degrees for each of the eight possible angles that the character can show. We will then use this value (along with the angle made with the mouse and the character found in line 14) to determine which of the eight frames to display in line 19. When using `Math.atan2()` to determine an angle, we'll sometimes get negative angles. Negative angles are perfectly valid, but I prefer to work with positive angles. Because angles are cyclic (that is, 350 is the same as –10), we can just add 360 to any negative angle to get its positive representation. This switch is performed in line 16. As mentioned previously, line 19 calculates which character frame number to display in the character movie clip. We apply this in line 20 and store the value in line 21. We then set the property `moving` to `true` on the `char` object. Next we store the values of the sine and cosine of the angle because they are used more than once (lines 23 and 24). We then use trigonometry to calculate the speed at which to move the character (lines 25 and 26), in the same way as we have done many times throughout this book. Finally, we set the `feelerx` and `feelerz` values. These are the values we will add to the temporary positions when checking for collisions.

Next we have the `moveCharacter()` function. This function is called in every frame.

```
function moveCharacter() {
     if (world.char.moving) {
          world.char.tempx = world.char.x+world.char.xmov;
          world.char.tempz = world.char.z+world.char.zmov;
          world.char.tempy = world.char.y+world.char.ymov;
          var sx:Number = world.char.startx;
          var sz:Number = world.char.startz;
          var ex:Number = world.char.endx;
          var ez:Number = world.char.endz;
          var tempx:Number = world.char.tempx;
          var tempz:Number = world.char.tempz;
          if ((ex-sx)/Math.abs(ex-sx) != (ex-tempx)
          ➥/Math.abs(ex-tempx) || (ez-sz)/Math.abs
          ➥(ez-sz) != (ez-➥tempz)/Math.abs(ez-tempz)) {
               world.char.moving = false;
               world.char.xmov = 0;
               world.char.zmov = 0;
               world.char.tempx = ex;
               world.char.tempz = ez;
               world.char.clip.gotoAndStop
               ➥("stand"+world.char.frame);
          }
     }
}
```

The first task of this function is to check if the character is moving. If so (that is, `moving` has the value `true`), then we move on. Lines 3–5 set the temporary position of the character based on its current position and its speed in each direction. We then create references to its starting and ending positions so that the already-long `if` statement in line 12 looks a little more reasonable. The condition we are looking for in line 12 is pretty simple, even though it looks complicated. We are trying to determine if the character has reached its destination. If it has, then the sign (+ or –) of the difference between A) its current position and the destination and B) the starting position and the destination will be different (in either the *x* or *z* direction).

Let's take an example of the character moving only in the *x* direction. The starting position is 10, and the end position is 100. The sign of the difference between the ending position and the starting position is + (positive). You find this by dividing the difference by the absolute value of the difference:

```
(endx-startx)/Math.abs(endx-startx)
```

We compare this value with the value of the sign of the difference between the end position and the current position. So if the current position is `30`, then `(100-30)/Math.abs(100-30)` is positive. Because this is the same as the sign from the starting and ending positions, the character has not yet reached the destination (whew!).

At some point, the character's current position will be greater than the destination—say, `105`. The value of `(100-105)/Math.abs(100-105)` is negative. Because this value no longer matches the positive value found with the starting and ending positions, we know the character has reached the destination. We perform this check for both the *x* and *z* directions. When one of these two conditions is met, the character needs to stop walking.

In line 13, we set the `moving` property to `false` and then the velocities to `0`. In lines 16 and 17, we set the character's temporary position to be the destination. Then, in line 18, we change the frame the character is displaying to the standing frame.

The last function we need to look at is `detectObjects()`. This function is called in every frame to determine if the character is about to step on a frame that contains an object (like a plant or a block).

```
1   function detectObjects() {
2        //Extend a little in the direction of motion
3        var x:Number = world.char.tempx+world.char.feelerx;
4        var z:Number = Math.abs
         ➥(world.char.tempz+world.char.feelerz);
5        var x_tile:Number = Math.ceil(x/world.cellWidth);
6        var z_tile:Number = Math.ceil(z/world.cellWidth);
7        if (world.tiles[x_tile][z_tile].isObject != true) {
8             x = world.char.tempx;
9             z = Math.abs(world.char.tempz);
10            x_tile = Math.ceil(x/world.cellWidth);
11            z_tile = Math.ceil(z/world.cellWidth);
12            var depth:Number =
              ➥world.tiles[x_tile][z_tile].depth+1;
13            world.char.clip.swapDepths(depth);
14       } else {
15            world.char.tempx = world.char.x;
16            world.char.tempz = world.char.z;
17            world.char.xmov = 0;
18            world.char.ymov = 0;
19            world.char.moving = false;
20            var frame:Number = world.char.frame;
21            world.char.clip.gotoAndStop("stand"+frame);
22       }
23  }
```

In lines 3–6, we add the `feelerx` and `feelerz` values to the temporary *x* and *z* values to determine which tile the feeler is touching. Then, in line 7, a conditional statement checks if there is an object in the tile that feelers are in. If there is, then we skip to the `else` leg of the ActionScript, which stops the character from walking, using the same code we used in the `moveCharacter()` function. If there is no object in that tile, then we enter the first leg of the `if` statement. We determine the depth of the tile that the character is currently on, and then add 1 to that depth. We then move the character to that depth using `swapDepths()`.

We now have discussed all the functions used in this file. Let's look at when these functions are called. Here are the last 17 lines of ActionScript in this frame:

```
1    var maxx:Number = 10;
2    var maxz:Number = 10;
3    var iso:Isometric = new Isometric (maxx, maxz);
4    buildWorld(maxx, maxz);
5    _root.onEnterFrame = function() {
6         moveCharacter();
7         detectObjects();
8         positionCharacter();
9    };
10   makeObject(2, 8, "plant");
11   makeObject(5, 4, "plant");
12   makeObject(6, 9, "block");
13   makeObject(5, 9, "block");
14   makeObject(5, 8, "block");
15   changeManyGroundTiles(2, 5, 3, 1, "concrete");
16   changeManyGroundTiles(6, 1, 3, 5, "concrete");
17   changeManyGroundTiles(6, 5, 8, 1, "concrete");
```

In lines 1 and 2, we set the number of tiles that are to be used in the world in both the *x* and *z* directions. We then create an instance of the `Isometric` class, passing in these *x* and *z* boundaries. They are used by the `Isometric` class instance when calculating depth. Next, in line 4, we call the `buildWorld()` function, passing in the *x* and *z* boundaries. The `buildWorld()` function stores this information on the `world` object and in turn calls the `buildFloor()` function, which uses these values. Next we set up an `onEnterFrame` event. This calls the functions `moveCharacter()`, `detectObjects()`, and `positionCharacter()` in every frame. The final eight lines of ActionScript place the objects on the screen and create the concrete tiles.

Generate an SWF from this file. Click different tiles around the world. Notice how the depth of the character changes as the character moves around a plant or a block (see Figure 8.20).

With this basic introduction to isometric worlds, you should be able to start making some very interesting and fun environments that can be used for games or chats.

FIGURE 8.20
The depth of the character changes.

Points to Remember

- An isometric world is the easiest type of 3D world to create in Flash.
- No perspective change occurs in an isometric world.
- One of the best features of an isometric world is that you can reuse graphical assets at any place in the world as-is because no perspective change occurs.
- An isometric system is created by rotating a system that is currently aligned with the Flash system by 30° around the *x*-axis and then by 45° around the new *y*-axis.
- Because of the useful (and fast) depth-calculation equation we use, we are able to restrict positioning to the *x, –y, –z* octant.
- Making an isometric system using tiles (that is, a tile-based world) is the most efficient and best way to create an isometric world. It makes collision detection and z-sorting much easier.

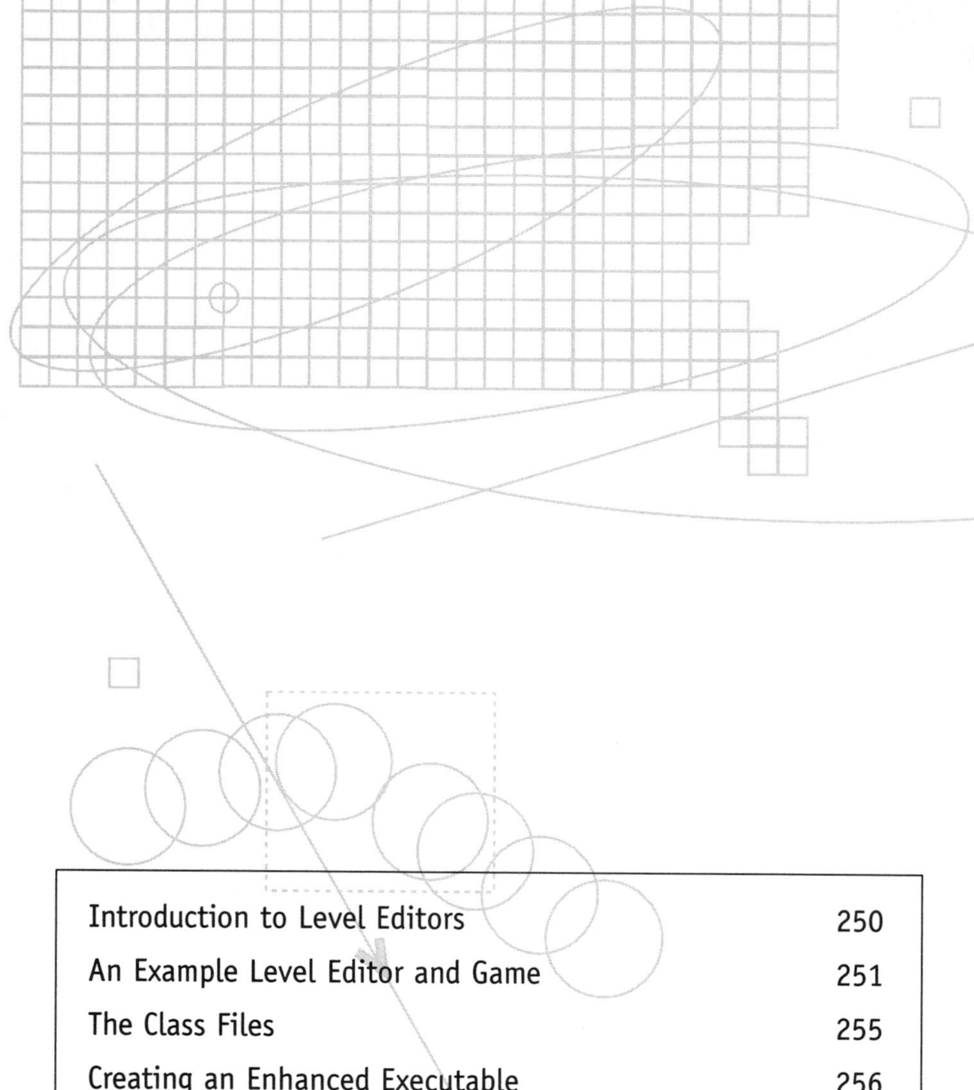

Introduction to Level Editors 250

An Example Level Editor and Game 251

The Class Files 255

Creating an Enhanced Executable 256

Points to Remember 261

CHAPTER 9

LEVEL EDITORS

AS YOU HAVE UNDOUBTEDLY LEARNED FOR YOURSELF, PROGRAMMING THE logic that governs the rules of a game can be a beast. Many new game programmers also learn something else: Defining the layout for a level in a game can be just as much of a beast. Having a game level built in memory based on hard-coded ActionScript can be cumbersome. Without a graphical user interface with which to build game levels, you may end up pulling your hair out.

In this chapter, we discuss the concept of level editors, which are a way to ease the job of level creation.

INTRODUCTION TO LEVEL EDITORS

A level editor is an application that provides a game designer with an easy way to create and edit levels for a game. Level editors are not needed for every game. Games such as *Poker*, *Tetris*, *Memory Match*, and *Pool* have levels that are always initially the same. A level editor is most useful for character- or vehicle-based games. This includes games like *Zelda*, platform games, driving games, and so on.

The most fundamental concept of the way a level editor works with a game is very simple. The game is programmed to load in data externally, usually from an XML file or from a database (which could also be loaded as XML), and the level editor is what creates this XML in the first place. For the sake of this chapter, we will only discuss saving a level as an XML file, which is just a text file that contains XML-formatted content.

So, with a level editor, you can create a level and save it as an XML file. Then, when the game is launched, it loads the XML file (such as Level1.xml), extracts and interprets the data stored in the file, and displays the level (see Figure 9.1).

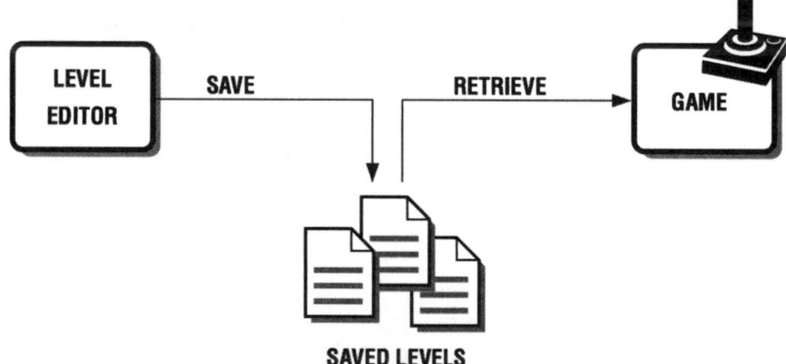

FIGURE 9.1
The editor saves to a file (or files); the game loads that file (or files).

Good level editors have an easy-to-use graphical user interface (GUI). The GUI lets you add items, enemies, walls, and other things to the level. You can easily save the level and then open the game to test the level. With a level editor, it is easy to experiment with different level layouts so that you can make the best level possible.

Next, you will be introduced to the level editor and game built for this chapter. We will then discuss how a Flash file can save information to a text file using a third-party tool. Finally, we will discuss some of the ActionScript used to accomplish this task.

AN EXAMPLE LEVEL EDITOR AND GAME

The game created for this chapter is just a partially finished game. It was taken far enough to illustrate the level editor/game combination. The graphics are not polished, and no sound has been added. We have already created three simple levels for the game (see Figure 9.2).

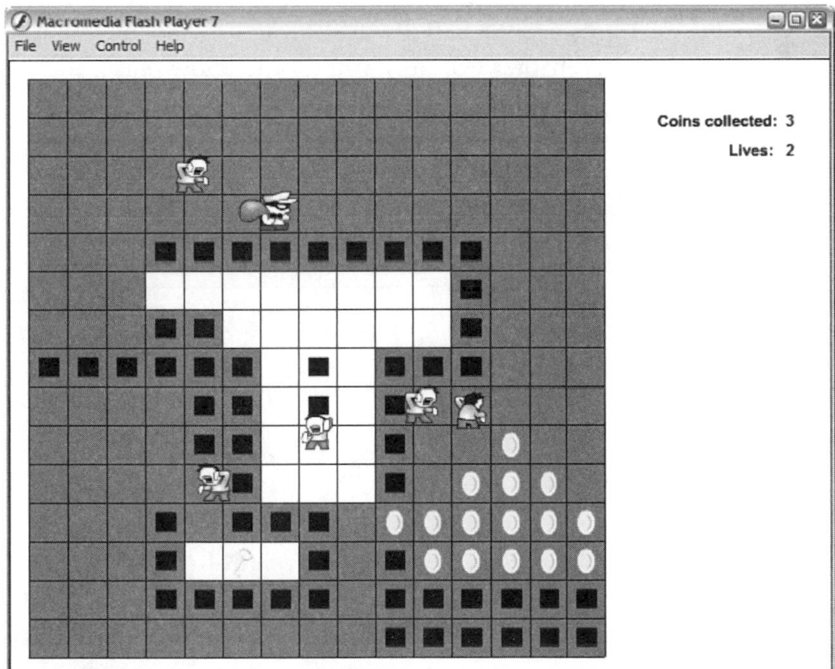

FIGURE 9.2
A level of the game.

The Game

Open game.swf in the Chapter09 directory of the CD-ROM. You will see that a level immediately appears. This is level 1, loaded from Levels/Level1.xml. You can control the thief character using the four arrow keys. If you collide with a zombie, then you die and have to start from the starting tile again. The goal in this overly-simple game is to collect the key on each level. Collecting coins is not mandatory.

There are three different terrains: water, sand, and grass. Aside from looking different, these three terrains are used in the same way. The hero (the thief) and the enemies (the zombies) can move over any terrain. If you were to extend the functionality of this game, then you might consider making the hero swim through the water.

When the hero collects the key, the next level is loaded.

The Editor

Now let's take a look at the editor. Open Editor.exe in the Chapter09 directory. We will discuss how this executable file was created later in this chapter. For now, you should know that it was made into an executable file because that enables the editor to save a level to a text file. An SWF file cannot do that.

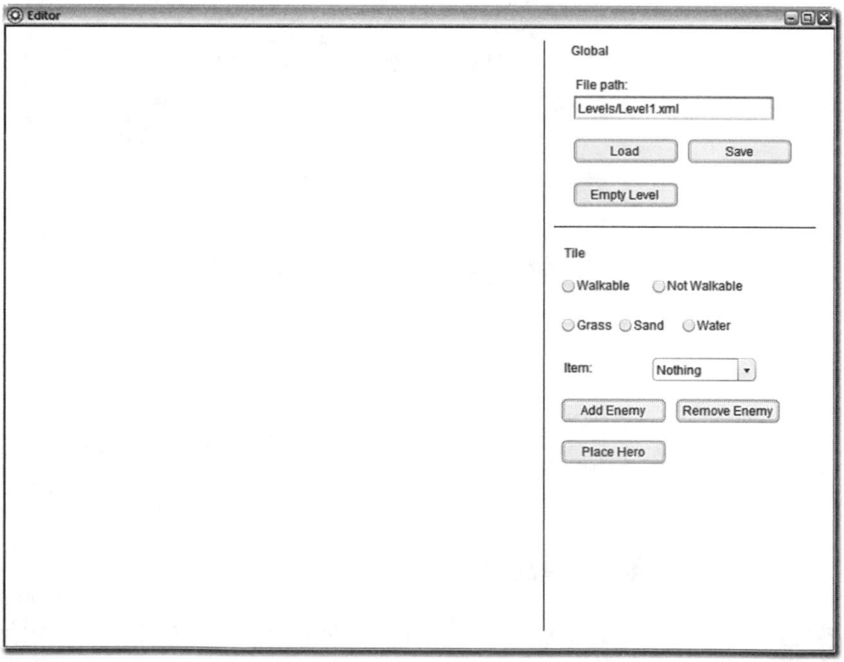

FIGURE 9.3
The Editor.

When opened, you will see several options on the right and a huge blank white area on the left. A level can be created or modified in the area on the left. The path to the level 1 file is already in the text field at the top right side of the screen. Under that text field, you see two buttons, Load and Save. Click the Load button.

After clicking the Load button, you will see the level loaded into the large area on the left (see Figure 9.4). One tile can be selected at a time by clicking on it. Click around on a few tiles to see this. You should also notice that when you click on a tile, the properties of that tile are displayed on the right.

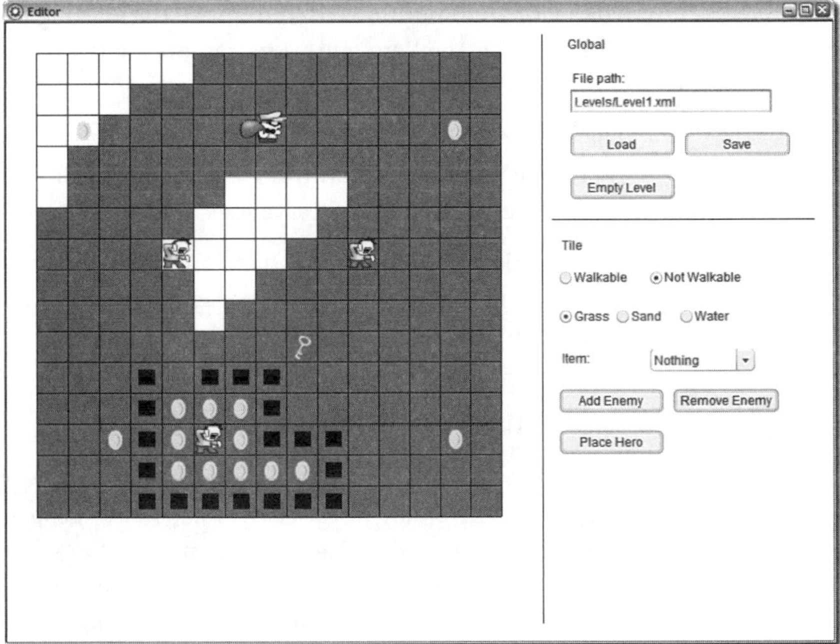

FIGURE 9.4
The Editor with a level loaded.

We mentioned that there are three types of terrain: water, sand, and grass. When a tile is selected, you will see its terrain displayed and the appropriate radio button selected. You can change its terrain by selecting another radio button.

There are three types of items that can exist on a tile: coin, key, or wall. When a tile is selected, you will see one of those three items or the word Nothing appear in the item combo box. In this editor, we only allow one item per tile. You can change the item on a tile by using the combo box.

There are two radio buttons labeled Walkable and Not Walkable. By default, a tile is Walkable, but you can change it to Not Walkable by selecting the Not Walkable radio button. If a tile is Not Walkable, then the hero and enemies cannot enter that tile. When a wall is added to a tile, it is automatically changed to Not Walkable.

You can add an enemy to a tile by selecting the Add Enemy button. You can remove an enemy from a tile by selecting the Remove Enemy button.

The Place Hero button is used to move the starting position of the hero to a new tile. The hero will be placed on the tile that is currently selected if the Place Hero button is selected.

The Empty Level button is simply used to start the level over fresh. To create a level, you can start from scratch using this button, or you can load a level, modify it, and save it as a new level.

Modify this level a little bit and then select the Save button. Open the Game.swf file again and notice your changes! That was easy—much easier than trying to write the XML file by hand.

Be on Your Best Behavior

Unless you are creating a level editor that will be distributed with a game, it is typically just used by a handful of people to create the levels for a game. With that in mind, it is important to realize that you might not want to spend endless hours refining the editor to be "idiot proof". For instance, you'll notice in this editor that you can add more than one key to a level, and you can add an enemy to the same tile as the hero or a wall. None of those things should be permitted. However, because just a few people will be using this editor to make levels, I can save the six hours of time it would take to add tons of validation and just trust that we'll be on good behavior while making levels.

The Class Files

Both the editor and the game use the same class files. Here are the classes that were created for this game/editor combo:

- **`Map`**—One instance of this class corresponds to one level. This class handles storing tiles, items, the hero, and enemies.
- **`Tile`**—For every tile in the map, we create an instance of this class. It knows its column and row, terrain, if it is walkable, and what items it is holding.
- **`Item`**—An item is a coin, key, or wall. An instance of this class is created for every item in the map. The tile that holds the item stores the instance of the class.
- **`Hero`**—Only one instance of this class is used. It knows its position and what column and row it is on. It is stored in the `Map` class instance.
- **`Enemy`**—An instance of this class is created for every enemy on the map. Each instance knows where it is on the map and at what speed it is moving.

The `Tile`, `Item`, `Hero`, and `Enemy` classes also store a reference to the movie clip that represents them.

There two important methods used that you should be aware of that all of these classes have: `toXML()` and `fromXML()`.

When a level has been created and is ready to be saved, we first extract the XML that represents the entire level by calling the `toXML()` method on the `Map` class instance. For instance, if we have been using an instance of the `Map` class called `myMap`, then the XML can be extracted and stored like this:

```
var myXML = myMap.toXML();
```

The `myMap` builds the XML representing itself and loops through the tiles that it is storing while calling the `toXML()` method on each tile. The `toXML()` method on each tile loops through the items that it is storing and calls the `toXML()` method on each item. The `Map` class instance also loops through the enemies, calling the `toXML()` method on them, and calls the `toXML()` method on the one `Hero` class instance.

The point here is that every class handles creating XML that represents itself. This makes creating XML that represents a level very easy. If we decide later that each enemy wants to use, say, an `Armor` class, then the `Enemy` class would call the `Armor` class's `toXML()` method, and the `Map` class would not need to be modified.

In the same way, every class has a `fromXML()` method. When a level is loaded, the XML that was just loaded is passed into the `fromXML()` method of the `Map` class instance—for instance:

```
myMap.fromXML(loadedXML);
```

The `fromXML()` method creates the `Hero`, `Enemy`, `Item`, and `Tile` instances and passes the XML representing each into their respective `fromXML()` methods. The `fromXML()` methods extract information from the XML passed in to configure themselves. For instance, an `Item` determines if it is a wall, key, or coin from the XML passed into it.

CREATING AN ENHANCED EXECUTABLE

At this time, no software exists that can be used to create enhanced standalone Flash movies for non-Windows operating systems.

There are several companies that make software used to extend the functionality of a Flash movie. Most of these software products take an SWF file and wrap it with an executable file that is programmed to accept commands. Flash can communicate with this executable via the `fscommand` function.

Here are a few companies that create such software:

- **MDM (Multidmedia Limited)**—Product name: Flash Studio Pro. `http://www.multidmedia.com.`
- **Northcode**—Project name: SWF Studio. `http://www.northcode.com.`
- **Rubberduck**—Product name: Screenweaver. `http://www.screenweaver.com.`

These three software products enable you to extend what can be done from Flash with hundreds of `fscommands`. Each takes an SWF file and wraps it in an executable file. They also give you the option to embed the Flash plug-in in the EXE or to use the plug-in that is already on a user's system.

Most of the functionality that you gain from these software products is in the `fscommands`, but here are a few options that are available through the software itself (to be applied to the executable file that you are creating):

- Disable right-click.
- Remove window borders.
- Make the window always run on top of all other windows.
- Assign a custom icon to the executable.
- Include additional files in the executable.

Here are a few things that can be accomplished with `fscommands` through the use of one of the third-party tools:

- Create or delete text files or directories.
- Download files from the Internet.
- FTP files from the Internet.
- Force the computer to display the Flash content in DirectX mode.
- Open a file browser pop-up window to enable a user to locate a file or location.
- Save a screenshot of the Flash content or a specific area within the Flash content.
- Set the desktop wallpaper on the user's computer.

Flash Studio Pro

Flash Studio Pro was used to create Editor.exe from Editor.swf.

Before you can use Flash Studio Pro, you must install it. Follow these steps to install Flash Studio Pro on a Windows machine.

1. Locate FlashStudioPro.exe on the CD-ROM. Double-click this file.

2. Follow the instructions given by the installer to install Flash Studio Pro.
3. After installation, launch Flash Studio Pro by double-clicking on the Flash Studio Pro desktop.

When launching Flash Studio Pro for the first time, you will see a "Flash Studio Pro tips" pop-up window. Close that window. Next, you will see a small window that has eight tabs (see Figure 9.5).

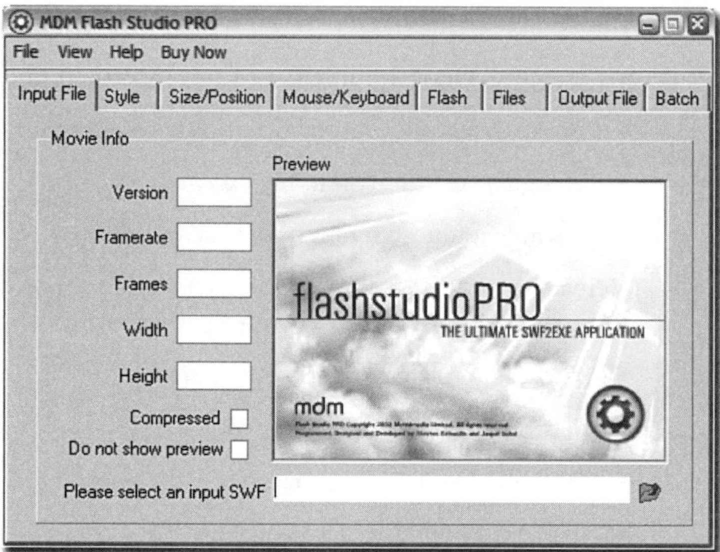

FIGURE 9.5
Flash Studio Pro.

Here is a brief overview of the purpose of each tab:

- **Input File**—Flash Studio Pro creates an executable file that holds at least one SWF file. On this tab, you specify the location on your hard drive of that SWF file.
- **Style**—On this tab, you can change visual properties of the file and the window in which it launches. This includes things like the window title, the window borders, and the icon used for the executable file.
- **Size/Position**—Here you can specify the size of the window and where on the screen it should position itself when launched.

- **Mouse/Keyboard**—On this tab, you can define how you want the window to respond to certain key presses and mouse interaction. You can set it up so that certain mouse interaction, such as a right-click, is ignored or is used to drag the window.
- **Flash**—This tab enables you to specify a few playback options for the Flash file, such as quality and background color.
- **Files**—Flash Studio Pro gives you the option to include files, such as extra SWF files or text files, in the final executable. You can specify which files to include on this tab.
- **Output File**—On this tab, you specify certain properties of the executable file, such as its name, output directory, its compression, and even an expiration date.
- **Batch**—You have the ability to specify multiple SWF files and have them converted to executable files. All SWF file names entered in this tab will be processed with the same options.

If you have not copied the directory for this chapter to your hard drive, then do that now. You cannot modify or create files on the CD itself.

In the directory, there is a file called Editor.fls. This is a Flash Studio Pro file. This file is used to store information like the path to the SWF that you want to make into an executable, the display properties, and the icon used for the executable file.

Open Editor.fls. You will get a warning window when you open Editor.fls because it will look for Editor.swf and will not find it because it is using an absolute path. Click "OK" on the window and then use the Input File tab to point to the correct location of Editor.swf.

Click on the Output File tab. You'll notice that the output file path is relative. It should already be pointing to your current directory. Click "GO" to generate a new executable file. It may take a minute to generate. After it is finished creating the file, you'll be asked if you would like to launch it. You can launch it by clicking "OK," or you can click "Cancel" to avoid launching it.

Every time you edit Editor.swf, you must re-create a new executable to incorporate it.

The ActionScript

Now let's look at the ActionScript that is used in conjunction with Flash Studio Pro to create a file to represent a level. This ActionScript can be found in Editor.fla, on the Actions layer at the Editor frame label.

```
1     function saveLevel() {
2           saveTo = ui_clip.filepath_txt.text;
3           saveContent = myMap.toXML();
4           fscommand("flashstudio.savetofile",
            ➥"saveTo,saveContent");
5           save_clip.gotoAndPlay(2);
6     }
```

Let's start with line 4, the `fscommand`. All Flash Studio Pro `fscommands` start with `flashstudio` as the first parameter. The value `flashstudio.savetofile` tells Flash Studio Pro that it should take the content of the next parameter and use that to create a text file. The second parameter is `"saveTo,saveContent"`. Even though that is just one string value, Flash Studio Pro parses it (using the comma) to arrive at two parameters, `saveTo` and `saveContent`. The first of those, `saveTo`, is evaluated to determine the location at which to save the file. The second, `saveContent`, is the string value that will be saved to the file itself.

Look at line 2. The variable `saveTo` is created to store the path at which the file should be created. Remember that there is a text field at the top right of this file. That text field is called `filepath_txt`, and it and all the other options below it are part of a movie clip called `ui_clip`. So, `ui_clip.filepath_txt.text` extracts the content of that text field and uses it to tell Flash Studio Pro where to create the file. If the file already exists, then it will be overwritten. If it does not exist, then it will be created.

In line 3, the variable `saveContent` is created. It is assigned the XML that represents the current level that is displayed. The reference `myMap` is the `Map` class instance that represents the level. The `toXML()` method on `myMap` is called to generate and return the XML representation of the level.

Line 5 simply tells a movie clip to play. That movie clip just displays "Saving..." for about one second to let the user know that something happened when the Save button was clicked.

Points to Remember

- A level editor is a much easier way to create or modify levels for a game than hard-coding information directly into the game or writing the XML by hand.
- A level editor saves information to a database or to text files. The game then loads that information from the database or text files.
- XML-formatted data is a convenient way to store the layout of a level.
- To have the Flash-made editor create a text file, a third-party tool must be used to create an executable.
- Flash Studio Pro is a recommended third-party tool for creating an executable from an SWF.

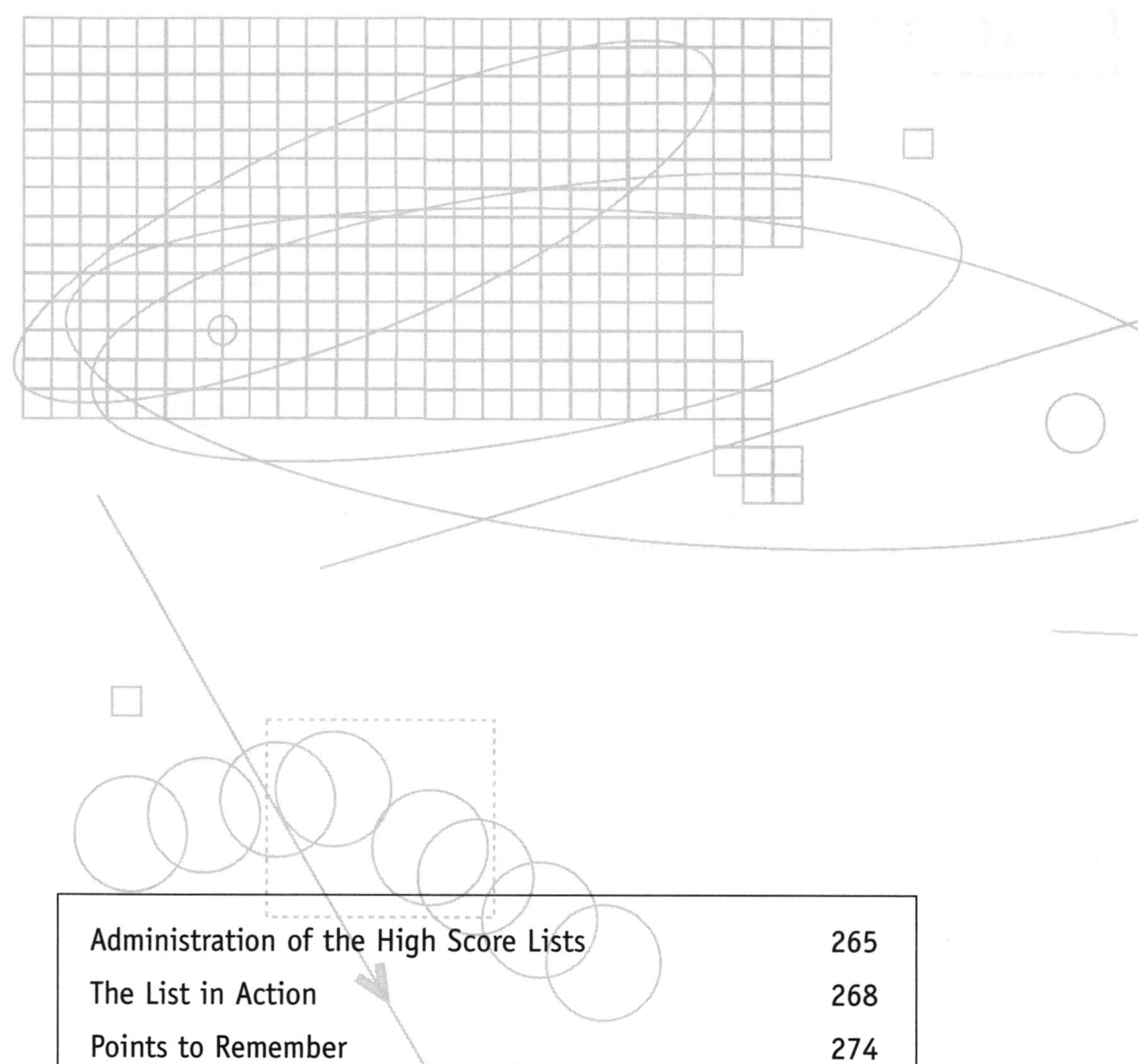

Administration of the High Score Lists 265

The List in Action 268

Points to Remember 274

CHAPTER 10

High Score List

A *HIGH SCORE LIST*—ALSO CALLED A *LEADER BOARD*—DISPLAYS A LIST OF the best scores for a game. The term "high score list" is somewhat of a misnomer because the list actually displays the best scores, which are not always the highest scores. A good example is golf, in which the lowest score is the best score.

In this chapter, you will learn how to add a high score list to a game, as well as how to configure and administer it. We provide you with all the files you need to get a high score list working in a game. However, you will need a Windows server to use it successfully. Your Flash game saves your score by contacting a server-side script and sending it information (which, in this case, it stores in the database). Our high score list uses ASP pages as the server-side scripts and a Microsoft Access database to store the information. And—in case I haven't made this point clear already—ASP pages typically need a Windows server to be interpreted correctly.

Note that you can also run ASP with an Apache server using ChiliASP. This enables you to use ASP pages on Linux or Unix.

Encryption

As you may know, I (Jobe) co-own a popular Flash game site called Electrotank. More than 2 million people play our games every month. When you run a site with that many people playing your games, you are bound to get some people who will try to figure out a way to cheat the high score list. Using some unethical tools, they can look at the ActionScript in the game and find the URL to which the game points when submitting a high score. From this information, they can easily create something that submits fake scores to the score list. The score list, of course, doesn't know the difference between the fake scores and the real scores. This leads to a really annoying problem: cheaters. If there is a way for people to cheat, they will eventually find it. This is not as rare as you may think. It occurs on many small sites as well. Because this problem isn't going away, you just need to take a few extra steps to make cheating more difficult.

With the files included for this book, we've increased the high score list security a little bit: We have enabled *encryption*. It is definitely not foolproof—in all likelihood this system will get hacked, too—but it will make the hackers' job much harder, so fewer people will attempt to hack it. When submitting a score, we encrypt everything in Flash before sending it to the server. When the server receives the information, it then decrypts it and uses it. Good encryption algorithms require a key to encrypt or decrypt. In the directory for this chapter on the CD-ROM, you will find a class called `Crypto` (Crypto.as). This class is used by the `HighScoreList` class discussed later in this chapter to encrypt a score before sending it to the server.

You may be thinking, "That sounds like pretty tight security; why can it still be hacked?" Well, we are storing both the encryption algorithm and the key in the game file. That is a security issue, but we can't do much about that. After you understand everything in this chapter, you can take these files and try to increase the security yourself. One thing you can do is load the key from a separate file, and maybe even load the encryption function through another SWF file. This is still not hack-proof, but every step you take is one more that a hacker will also have to go through. You want to make it not worth the hacker's while.

Administration of the High Score Lists

The name of the administration tool we use for the high score lists is UberScore Administrator. This tool gives you a lot of control over the lists. It enables you to perform the following administrative duties:

- Create an unlimited number of high score lists.
- Give each list a name and configure certain properties differently for each.
- Set one list to consider lower scores to be better and another list to have higher scores be better.
- Limit the number of scores displayed.
- Set a score list to accept only one score from a person, or to accept many. (If you set it to accept just one, then it will accept another only if it is better than that user's current score.)
- Delete a user.
- Edit the information about a high score list (sort order, number of scores, name of list).

In order for a person to be able to submit a score, that person must be a registered player. We will show you how to register (or create) a player later in this chapter.

Assuming that you have a Windows server up and properly running, take the entire hs directory that's in the Chapter10 directory on the CD and upload it to your Windows server. Remember the URL of this directory—we'll call it the "score URL."

Go to the score URL in your web browser. You should see a basic HTML page load displaying these two links: Administer Users and Administer Scoreboards (see Figure 10.1). Click the Administer Users link. At this point, you have not created any users, but you will see a couple of "test" users I created so that you can learn what the Administrator looks like with real data. When there are user names in the system, you will see letters at the top that are links that correspond to the first letters of those names. For instance, if the user "Frank" is in the system, then you will see the letter *F* at the top. You can click the *F* to view all the users whose names start with *F*. You can delete a user by clicking the Delete link next to the user's name. That's all you need to know about administering users.

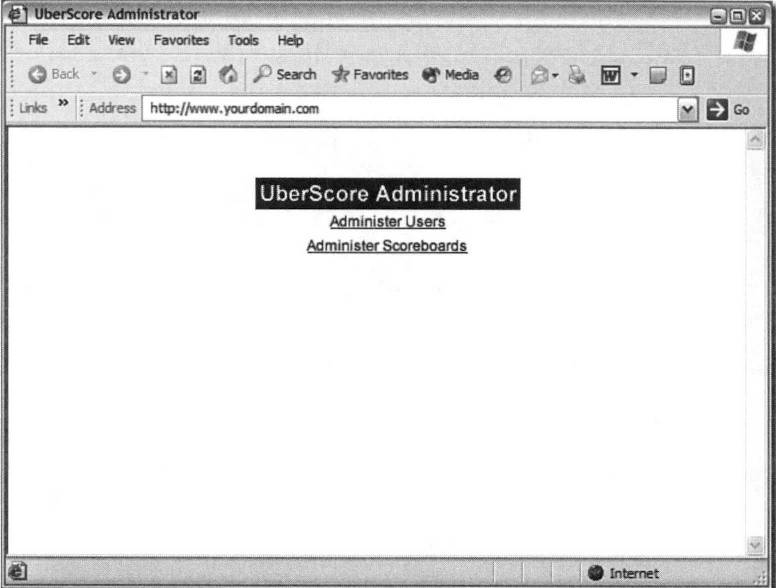

FIGURE 10.1
Basic HTML page load display.

Click the Back to UberScore Administrator link. From there, click Administer Scoreboards to enter the Board Administrator area. A scoreboard is the same thing as a high score list. You have not created any yet, so you probably won't see any in a list on this page. However, if one is left in the database from testing, feel free to delete it; in any case, you'll see in this area that you can edit, clear, or delete any existing scoreboard. You can create a new scoreboard by clicking the Create New Board link. You are presented with five configurable fields (see Figure 10.2):

- **Board Name.** I recommend using the name of your game here.
- **Return Count.** The number you insert here is the maximum number of scores that is returned in the high score list. A number between about 50 and 100 is typical.
- **Multiple Scores Per User.** This is a drop-down list that lets you choose Yes or No. If you choose Yes, then any person can have an unlimited number of scores in the list. If you choose No, then a person can have only one score at a time.

- **Only Insert If Better.** This field also lets you choose either Yes or No. If Yes, then a person's score will be inserted only if it is better than a score he or she already has in the list. This works in conjunction with the Multiple Scores Per User field. If a user has opted to have multiple scores, then of course it doesn't matter if the score is better or worse. If the user can have only one score, and Insert Only If Better is set to Yes, then the user's score can be replaced by a better score but not a worse score. If Insert Only If Better is set to No and Multiple Scores Per User is set to Yes, then every time the user gets a score, it will replace the current score, even if it is worse.
- **Sort Order.** The choices here are Ascending and Descending. If you choose Descending, that means a higher score is better, so the scores will be listed from highest to lowest. If you choose Ascending, then a lower score is better, and the scores will be sorted from lowest to highest.

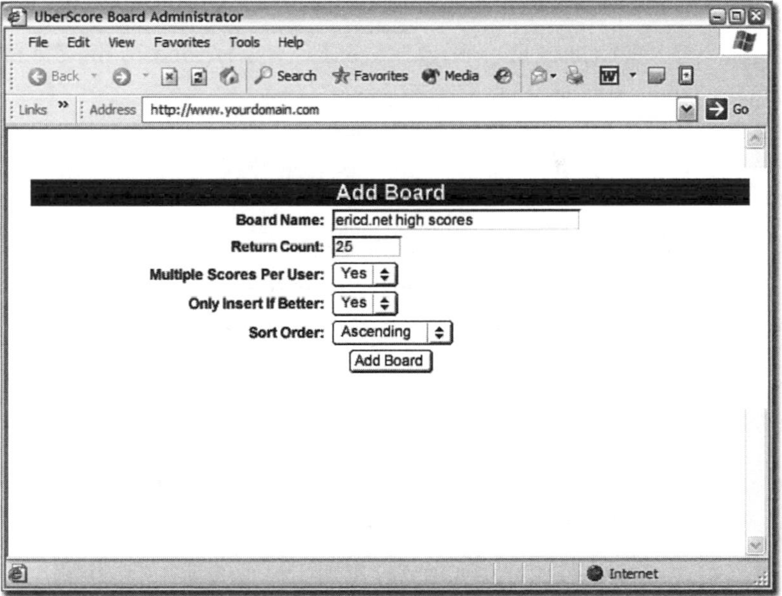

FIGURE 10.2
The five configurable fields.

As you have seen, with this administration tool, you can view or delete users as well as manage the scoreboards. What you cannot do with this tool is create (or register) users, log in, or submit scores. Those are done directly from the game, and we'll talk about them in the next section.

The List in Action

You now know how to create and manage scoreboards using the UberScore Administrator. Create a new scoreboard and then continue with this section. Remember the `BoardID` number because you'll need it below. In this section, you will learn how to use a High Score List movie clip that's in a source file on the CD. We are going to discuss only a few portions of the ActionScript provided, as the rest of it is fairly straightforward and not within the scope of this book.

Open highscore.fla in the Chapter10 directory on the CD. You will see one layer in the main Timeline: High Score Clip.

This layer contains only one movie clip with a library name of High score clip. This movie clip contains the capability to register a new user, log in an existing user, submit a user's score to the high score list, and load and display the scores for a high score board.

A class called `HighScoreList` was created to handle talking to the server-side scripts.

The User-Interface Frames

There are five labeled frames in the High Score List movie clip, corresponding to the five possible screens a user might see when attempting to submit a score.

Init. On this frame, the user is given a choice to log in or to view the high scores. If Login is selected, then the user is taken to the Login frame. If View Scores is selected, then the user is taken to the Scores frame, and the scores are loaded and displayed. This frame also contains most of the ActionScript that uses the `HighScoreList` class. It will be discussed below.

Login. On this frame, the user can log in by entering a user name and password and then clicking Submit. When Submit is clicked, the information is sent to the server, and the user is taken to the Message frame, where a status message is displayed. The server determines if the login information is valid and sends a response. If the information is invalid, then an error message is displayed on the Message frame. If the information is valid, the user's userID is extracted from the XML returned from the server and stored in the instance of the `HighScoreList` class. Also, as part of this example file, after logging in a random score is submitted to the server. This will be discussed below as well. After the score is submitted, the user is taken to the Scores frame.

In addition to the Submit button, there is another button labeled "Need to register?" on the Login frame. If clicked, then the user is taken to the Register frame. A user must be registered to be able to log in, and a user must log in before submitting a score.

Register. The user can register a new account on this frame. There are three fields on this frame: Username, Password, and Email. When the user clicks Submit, the information is sent to the server, and the user is taken to the Message frame. If the server sees the information as acceptable, then the user's information is added to the database. If the server does not accept the information, then an error message is displayed on the Message frame. After a user successfully registers, the user is automatically logged in, and a score is submitted. The user is then taken to the Scores frame.

Message. This frame was created to show the user a message. For instance, when registering (assuming the registration information is valid), the user will see "Registering...", then "Logging in...", then "Submitting score...", and then "Loading score list...." If an error happens to occur along the way, then the error message is displayed.

Scores. On this frame, you can see the high score list for a particular `BoardID`. The list is displayed in a List component.

The *HighScoreList* Class

The Init frame contains most of the ActionScript that links the `HighScoreList` class to the user interface. The `HighScoreList` class was created to talk to the UberScore server-side scripts. This class has methods such as `login`, `submitScore`, and `loadScores`, all of which handle creating special XML-formatted documents to send to the server. When a response is received, the class handles parsing it and making the results available.

Here are the exposed methods for the `HighScoreList` class:

- `login(username, password)`—The user's username and password are passed in when calling this method. This is used to log in a user.
- `register(username, password, email)`—The user's proposed username, password, and email are passed in when executing this method. It is used to register a new user.
- `submitScore(score)`—This submits a score for a user that has logged in. The score is passed into the method.
- `loadScores()`—When this method is executed, the score list for the associated `BoardID` is loaded.
- `setBoardID(BoardID)`—This method is how you associate a `BoardID` with the instance of the `HighScoreList` class. The `BoardID` is passed into the method.
- `setURL(url)`—With this method, you inform the `HighScoreList` class where the HS.asp script is located. For instance, `http://www.mydomain.com/scores/HS.asp`.
- `setNumbered(numbered)`—The loaded score list can be displayed with just usernames and scores, or it can be numbered as well. By default, the scores are not numbered. To display numbered scores, this method must be called and a Boolean value of `true` or `false` must be passed in. If `true`, then the scores will be numbered.
- `setEncryptionKey(theKey)`—When submitting a score to the server, the entire score XML packet is encrypted. The server can decrypt it if it knows the encryption key. An encryption key is a unique string that can be used to take an encrypted string and decrypt it. It is also used to encrypt a string. The HS.asp page has the key "ThisIsTheKey" hard-coded into it, so we will use that key here.

  You might be wondering how we capture the server response for the four methods that talk to the server: `login`, `register`, `loadScores`, and `submitScore`. The `HighScoreList` class has only one event, and it is fired when a response from the server is received, `onComplete`.

- `onComplete (transaction, response)`—This is an event that is fired when a response is received from the server. The parameter transaction is a string representing one of the four possible transactions: "Login," "Register," "SubmitScore," and "LoadScores." The response parameter is an object. The response object always has `success` as a property. If `success` is `true`, then the server did what it was asked to do. If `success` is `false`, then an error occurred, and the response object contains an error property storing the error message. The response object is also used to pass around extra information, such as the score list.

Note that if your SWF file is being hosted on a domain separate from the one that contains the HS.asp file, then you need to put policy files on both domains to give access to each. Policy files are simple XML files that tell the Flash Player which domains are allowed access. Please view the Flash help files for more information on this topic.

The Frame ActionScript

On the Init frame, you will see the ActionScript that is used to create a new instance of the `HighScoreList` class, configure it, and talk to it.

```
1   var hs:HighScoreList = new HighScoreList();
2   hs.setURL("http://www.mydomain.com/hs/HS.asp");
3   hs.setBoardID(4);
4   hs.setEncryptionKey("ThisIsTheKey");
5   hs.setNumbered(true);
```

First, a new instance of the `HighScoreList` class is created. It is given a reference name of `hs`. Next, the URL of the HS.asp server-side script is set. The class uses this URL to send and receive information. In line 3, we set the `BoardID` that corresponds to a high score board. You will need to change the number passed in here to that of the board that you created. In line 4, we set the encryption key (used for sending scores) to the same key that the server-side scripts use, ThisIsTheKey. Finally, in line 5, we configure the instance of the `HighScoreList` class to return the score list as a numbered list.

To use the `onComplete` event, we must assign it an event handler. That is also done on the Init frame.

```
hs.onComplete = function(transaction:String,
➥response:Object) {
     if (response.success == false) {
          showMessage(response.error);
     }
```

```
5           if (transaction == "Login") {
6               if (response.success) {
7                   showMessage("Submitting score...");
8                   submitScore(score);
9               }
10          } else if (transaction == "Register") {
11              if (response.success) {
12                  showMessage("Logging in...");
13                  hs.login(username, password);
14              }
15          } else if (transaction == "SubmitScore") {
16              if (response.success) {
17                  showMessage("Loading score list...");
18                  hs.loadScores();
19              }
20          } else if (transaction == "LoadScores") {
21              if (response.success) {
22                  scores = response.scores;
23                  gotoAndStop("Scores");
24              }
25          }
26      };
```

As you'll recall, the `onComplete` event is fired when a response is received from the server as a result of logging in, registering, submitting a score, or requesting the high score list. The first parameter contains a string representing the transaction that was just completed. The second parameter contains the `response` object.

In lines 2–4, we check to see if the transaction was successful. If it was not, then we show the error via the `showMessage` function defined on the Message frame. Then we proceed to an `if…else if` statement that handles each transaction that was just completed. The logic follows. If the user was successfully logged in, then the function submits the score. If the user was successfully registered, then the user is logged in. If the score was submitted successfully, then the score list is loaded. If the score list was loaded successfully, then the program proceeds to the Scores frame.

Notice that in line 22 we extract the scores from the `response` object and store them in an array called `scores`.

On the Scores frame, there is only one line of ActionScript:

```
scores_lb.dataProvider = scores;
```

This frame contains a `List` component with an instance name of `scores_lb`. As you know, you can populate a List component by assigning an array to its `dataProvider` property. The array must be an array of objects, and each object must have a `label` property. The `label` property is used by the `List` component to populate the text field associated with that item in the list (See Figure 10.3). For instance, if the top score in the list is 333 and belongs to Kelly, then the label would read "Kelly   333." If you configured the `HighScoreList` class instance to number the score list, then the first label would read "1. Kelly   333."

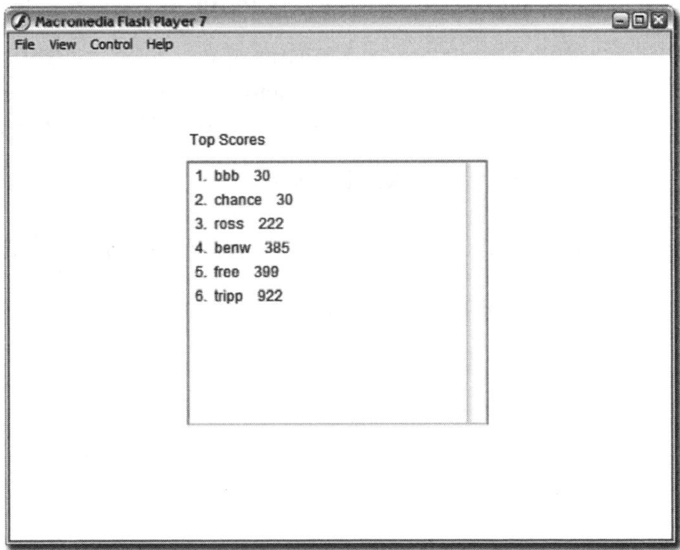

FIGURE 10.3
An example of a Top Scores list.

The rest of the ActionScript in this movie clip is straightforward. There are a few `Button` component instances and `TextInput` component instances.

You should be able to take this movie clip and modify it for use in a game. All you have to do is:

- Modify the URL to point to HS.asp.
- Create a new board for the game and use its `BoardID` with the `HighScoreList` class.
- Bring in the score value (to be submitted) from the game itself. Don't apply it randomly like in this example.
- Modify the look of the movie clip to fit your game.

Points to Remember

- You need a Windows server to run the server-side scripts.
- With UberScore Administrator, you have control over many attributes of a high score list, including the number of scores returned, the sort order, and whether a user can submit multiple scores.
- The encryption key in a server-side script must match the encryption key in the Flash High Score List movie clip. If the keys do not match, the server-side script will not correctly interpret the information.
- The user must be logged in to submit a score.

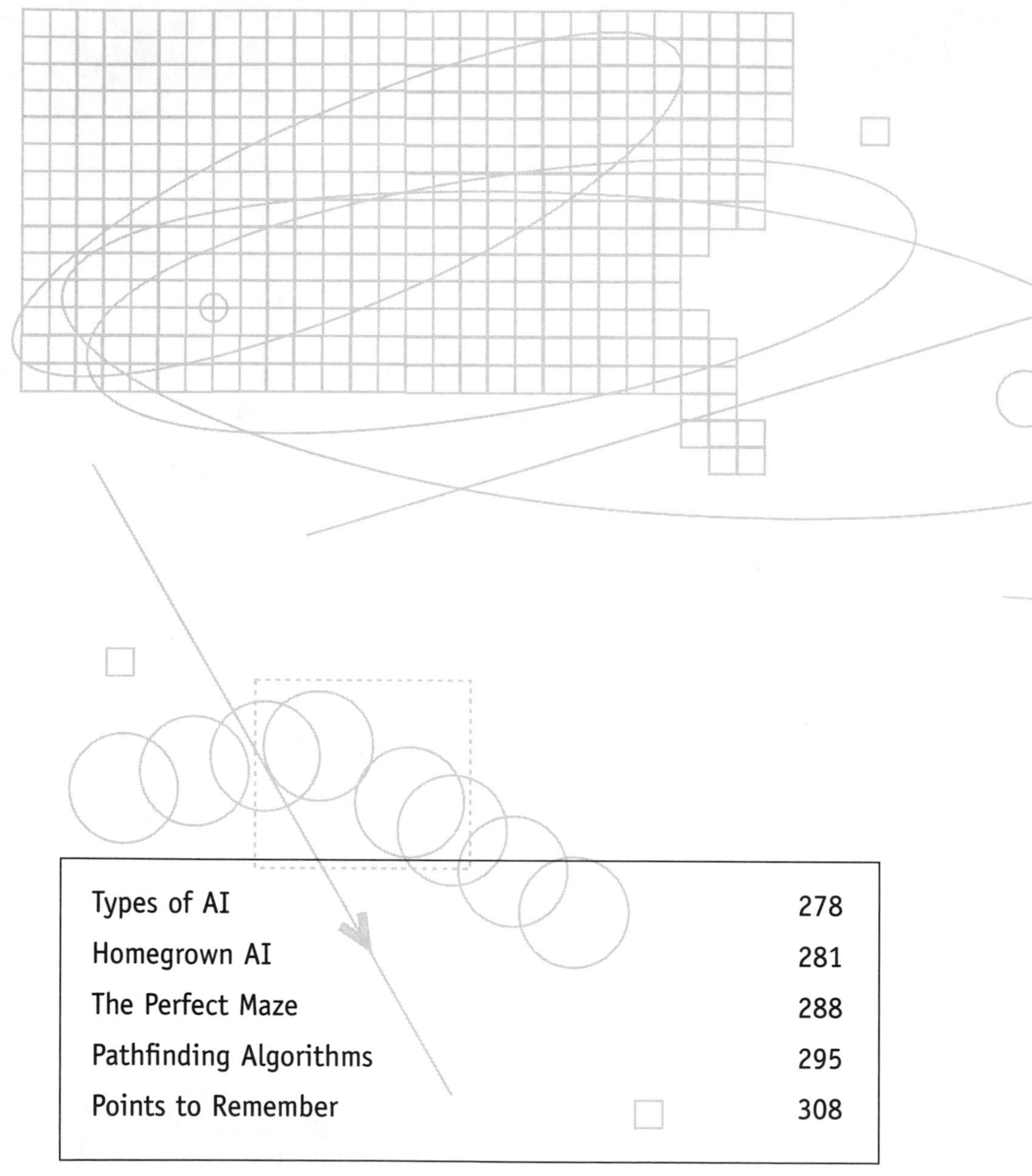

Types of AI 278
Homegrown AI 281
The Perfect Maze 288
Pathfinding Algorithms 295
Points to Remember 308

CHAPTER 11

ARTIFICIAL INTELLIGENCE

ARTIFICIAL INTELLIGENCE (AI) IS A MACHINE'S CAPABILITY TO PERFORM tasks that we think require intelligence. For example, if in real life a cop was trying to capture someone on foot, then he would try to take all possible shortcuts. The shortcuts would depend on where he was, where he wanted to go, and his own knowledge of the area involved. In a computer game, a character can be programmed with similar behavior; this is one possible application of AI.

The concept of AI has been around for a long time. Noted philosophers in the 1800s debated whether machines could think. The concept of AI was thrust a little more into the public eye in the 1980s with the upsurge of arcade games. But what really got people interested in this topic was the famed chess match that pitted IBM's *Deep Blue* against chess Grandmaster, Garry Kasparov, in 1997. Kasparov lost the six-game match, and (as they say) history was made. Since then, artificial intelligence has rooted itself even further into games much more complicated than chess. You have probably seen some pretty amazing AI used in real-time strategy games. Specifically, *Pikmin* for the Nintendo GameCube and *Command & Conquer: Generals* for the PC have very impressive AI.

Getting back to reality (meaning Flash, of course!), you probably know that as smart as you think this program is, Flash simply doesn't have the power to support an ActionScript-written, *Deep Blue*-level of intelligence. However, it can write a good-enough script to produce the kind of AI you'd need to make most of your games interesting and fun. Certainly there are some games in which no AI is needed, such as multiplayer checkers (because your opponent has a brain!), but for many games, even ones as simple as *Pong* or a basic platform game, AI of some sort is a requirement to keep the game player engaged. In this chapter, we introduce the topic of AI in Flash, mention the major flavors of AI in games, and give example implementations.

TYPES OF AI

You now probably have a pretty good idea of what AI is, so let's focus for awhile on what you can *do* with it. More specifically, we will talk about the role of AI in gaming. Here are some of the major uses of AI in games today.

Pathfinding. This is one of the biggest topics for game developers, especially those who are new to AI. *Pathfinding* is the act of finding a path between one point and another. In a game like *Diablo* (or in our example iso_world.fla file from the last chapter), you click to walk to a location. If an object is in your way, then you walk around it. In most advanced games of this sort, the entire path that you walk is calculated at the moment you click (rather than as you walk).

Pathfinding also works for your enemies. Using various pathfinding techniques, an evil critter can be programmed to scamper around objects toward you.

Although many types of pathfinding algorithms exist, the one that is considered by all authorities to be the best is A* (pronounced "A Star"). This algorithm will be covered in the last section of this chapter.

Level generation. Some games rely on random but intelligent level creation at runtime. For instance, if you play a certain game twice, the level architecture (walls and rooms) can be the same from one game to the next, but the enemies and secret items could be in new positions. Alternatively, the entire level could be completely new from one game to the next, as is the maze in this chapter. This type of level generation is driven by an AI. Sometimes the AI is a popular algorithm known to many developers; at other times, it may have been created from scratch for a particular game.

Enemy behavior. Using pathfinding, an enemy can know how to find you, but what does he do when he gets to you? He could hit you with a sword, he could change his mind and run away, or maybe he just wants to chat. In addition to the pathfinding AI, a separate AI controls enemy-behavior options. This can be one of the most complicated components to program in enormous games created for worldwide distribution (or so I've heard). However, an AI of this sort for an RPG in Flash could be much simpler, as the rest of the game would probably be much simpler (as compared with one from the big boys).

Neural networks. A *neural network* is an AI that can learn. It gives results based on internal numeric parameters that are adjusted in real time. The result is a machine that can behave differently in different situations. This concept has only recently begun to be used in games. Imagine some sort of strategy war game—you versus the AI, each armed with planes, tanks, ships, and soldiers. If you repeatedly use your planes to attack the enemy, then the AI will learn from this. It will think, "Hey, I need to take measures to prevent more plane attacks. I've got it! I'll send my tanks in to blow up his planes." This makes for a very "human" AI. A pattern is identified and deemed bad and then measures are taken to disrupt it. Neural networks are also largely used in e-learning applications. For example, an AI in a software application that teaches you touch-typing might be programmed to chastise you if you type naughty words, or to suggest you take a break when it detects that you are pounding on all the keys at once.

You Win Some, You Lose Some

It is very important to note that, to be used well in a game, an AI should offer a certain difficulty range. For instance, if you were playing against Deep Blue in a game of chess, you would be sure to lose. A game is only fun if you have a chance at victory. A game is also only fun if you know that there is a chance that you *won't* win—that way, if you do win, you have a sense of accomplishment. Thus, there should be a balance. Create AI that is perfect—as perfect as you can, anyway. You can always find ways to dumb it down or mix it up, but it's hard to introduce ways of making it smarter after you've written it. For instance, if you've created an AI that never loses a game of checkers, then you could do something as simple as making every other move of the computer be chosen randomly rather than intelligently. This would make the AI less effective but the game more fun. Exactly how much should you dumb down the AI? That can only be determined by testing the game with game players.

Turn-based games. An AI can be written to play turn-based games such as *Checkers* and *Chess*. Many different levels of AI exist for these types of games. The main two are ones that look at the board now and decide what the next best move is, and ones that form strategies, have a sense of history, and look ahead. You can find a lot of AI algorithms (not many in ActionScript) on the Internet for games like *Chess*, *Checkers*, *Connect Four*, and *Scrabble*.

Custom logic. Any of the types of AI I've already mentioned can make use of custom logic. I list this as a separate category to include the miscellaneous AI uses that don't belong in the other categories. You can use AI to control just about anything in a game, from behavior to colors to volume to repercussions to speed to difficulty. As a basic example, in the Chapter11 directory, you'll find a simple game of *Pong* with an AI. The opponent paddle is intelligent enough to follow the ball. You can also create an AI to determine when a certain event should happen in a game. For instance, if you think the user is performing too well in a car-racing game (and if you like being cruel to your game players), you might initialize a thunderstorm to make the game a little more difficult.

In the rest of this chapter, we'll look at custom AI, AI used to generate a random but perfect maze, and A* pathfinding.

HOMEGROWN AI

In this section, we'll talk about creating your own AI, as opposed to using AI algorithms found elsewhere. The information presented here does not even scratch the surface of learning how to create *any* AI—that's another subject for a much longer, more technical book. The information here covers a specific AI.

To introduce you to the kind of script we're going to discuss, open shark_attack.swf from the Chapter11 directory on the CD-ROM, which should look familiar from Chapter 7, "Tile-Based Worlds." *Shark Attack!* (see Figure 11.1) is an isometric tile-based-world game with some AI enemies that I created for a company called Simply Scuba. You are the red fish. The goal is to collect the key and go to the door. Collect coins and objects as you go for more points. Watch out for the sharks, though; they are the enemies. Double-click the SWF file to open it. Play a few levels (there are only four included) and notice the behavior of the sharks. They are controlled with a fairly simple but effective AI. In this section, you will learn how an AI very similar to this was created.

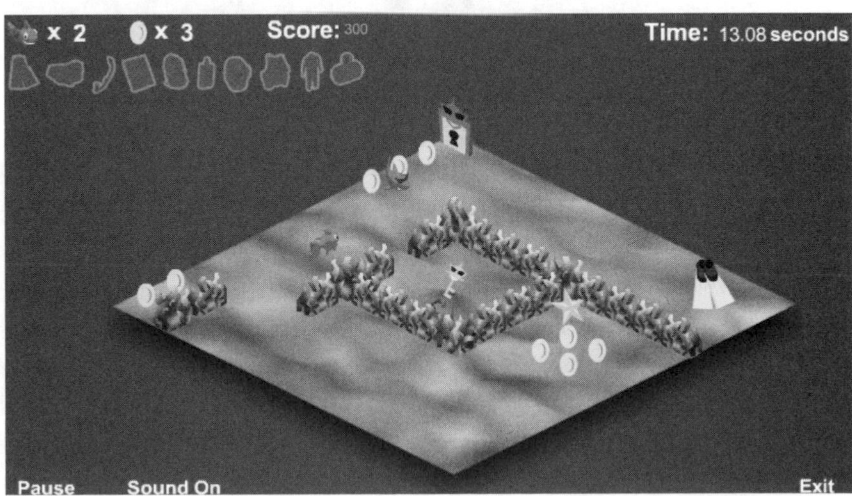

FIGURE 11.1
Shark Attack!

Rules for Controlling Characters

By this point in your odyssey through this book, you are ready to complete this game on your own!

Open run_away.fla in the Chapter09 directory of the CD-ROM. This file contains the enemy AI for an unfinished game called *Grave Robber* (see Figure 11.2). Here, we will look at how enemies (also called "baddies") behave. The baddies are zombies, and the good guy (well, as good as a thief can be) is human—he is controlled by you. You walk around trying to rob graves, and every time you do, the zombies try to "get" you. There are walls that you cannot pass through. In this file, there is no collision detection between the hero and the baddies because we are only illustrating behavior. Warning: This file (and in fact every example file we use in this chapter) uses tiles, so if you haven't yet familiarized yourself with tile-based worlds, then you might want to take the time to do so (see Chapter 7). We will only discuss the ActionScript used in the AI for this file, not the world creation or how we handle wall collisions.

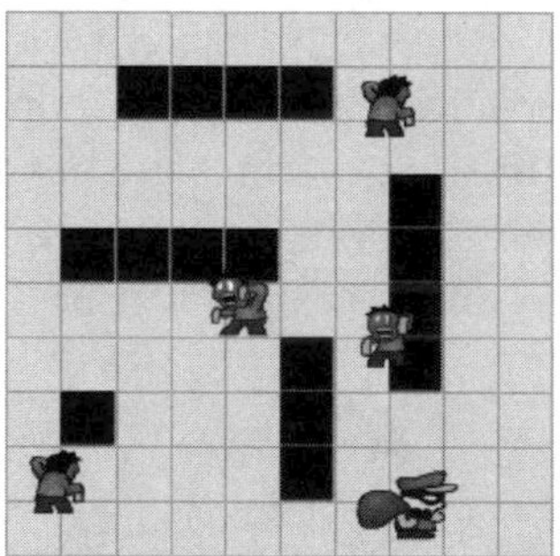

FIGURE 11.2
Grave Robber.

Use Test Movie to take a look at this world. Move around and try to notice the behavior of the enemy zombies. The AI used here is very similar to the AI used in the *Shark Attack!* game.

There is a script within the code that instantaneously changes the direction of the enemy's motion. To be concise, I'll call the running of this script an "update." Now let's look at the rules that the zombies follow in this update to produce their behavior: homing in on the thief.

- The characters' movement is restricted to horizontal only or vertical only at any given time.
- The update script checks the hero's location relative to the enemy's and stores the information as follows:

  Horizontal motion

    –1 if the hero is to the left of the enemy

    0 if the hero is in the same column

    1 if the hero is to the right of the enemy

  Vertical motion

    –1 if the hero is above

    0 if the hero is in the same row

    1 if the hero is below

- If the horizontal and vertical values are both 0, then the enemy is in the same tile as the hero, and the update does not change the path of motion.
- If either horizontal or vertical is 0, then the script changes the direction of motion to have the hero move along the other. For instance, if the horizontal value is –1 and the vertical value is 0, then the script knows that the hero is in the same row to the left, and it makes the enemy move left.
- If both the horizontal and vertical values are non-zero, then the script randomly chooses one of the two directions and makes the baddy move that way. For instance, if the vertical value is –1 and the horizontal value is 1, then the AI knows the hero is somewhere to the top right of the enemy. It then randomly chooses either vertical or horizontal and moves toward the hero in that direction.
- The update script contains a randomization condition (in the form of an `if` statement). At random times, the script chooses a completely random direction to move, no matter what the state of the board is. This is the AI's "dumb-down" feature. The frequency of this random "imperfection" makes the AI behave unpredictably.

Now we know the logic that is performed when the update script is executed. But *when* is it executed? Here are the conditions for which the update script can be executed:

- When the enemy bumps into a wall or any immovable object.
- When `maxtime` number of frames has passed since the last update. The value of `maxtime` is different for each enemy.

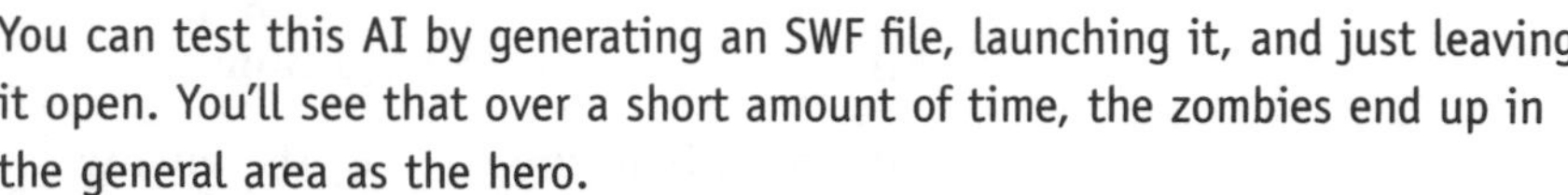

You can test this AI by generating an SWF file, launching it, and just leaving it open. You'll see that over a short amount of time, the zombies end up in the general area as the hero.

Drawbacks and Solutions

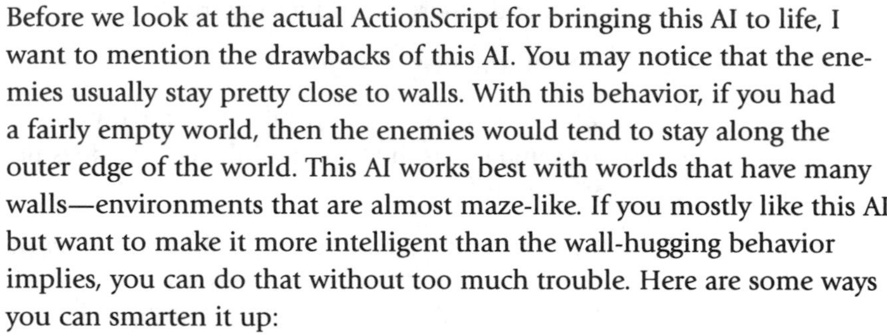

Before we look at the actual ActionScript for bringing this AI to life, I want to mention the drawbacks of this AI. You may notice that the enemies usually stay pretty close to walls. With this behavior, if you had a fairly empty world, then the enemies would tend to stay along the outer edge of the world. This AI works best with worlds that have many walls—environments that are almost maze-like. If you mostly like this AI but want to make it more intelligent than the wall-hugging behavior implies, you can do that without too much trouble. Here are some ways you can smarten it up:

- Program the update to make the character move toward the center of a tile to continue motion instead of hugging up against a wall. This is more of an aesthetic enhancement, but it also gives the appearance of greater intelligence.
- When a character collides with a wall, give higher priority to turning another direction rather than moving into the wall again. With the current AI, you can slam into the wall a few times before moving away. This is not all that noticeable because the collisions happen so fast, but it does happen.
- Add diagonal motion.

Enemy ActionScript

OK, now it's finally time to look at the ActionScript used in this AI. This function, `baddyAI()`, is called in every frame. It loops through an array of enemies and determines if it is time for an update. If it is, then it performs the update.

```
function baddyAI() {
    for (var i = 0; i<game.baddies.length; ++i) {
        var ob:Object = game.baddies[i];
        ++ob.time;
        var cell_x:Number =
        ➥Math.ceil(ob.x/game.cellWidth);
        var cell_y:Number =
        ➥Math.ceil(ob.y/game.cellWidth);
        var cell_over:Object =
        çgame.tiles[cell_x][cell_y];
        var cell_x_temp:Number =
        ➥Math.ceil(ob.tempx/game.cellWidth);
        var cell_y_temp:Number =
        ➥Math.ceil(ob.tempy/game.cellWidth);
        var cell_over_temp:Object =
        ➥game.tiles[cell_x_temp][cell_y_temp];
        if (!cell_over_temp.empty || ob.time ==
        ➥ob.maxtime) {
            ob.time = 0;
            ob.maxtime = 30+random(30);
            ob.tempx = ob.x;
            ob.tempy = ob.y;
            var tempDir = ob.dir;
            var xmov:Number = 0;
            var ymov:Number = 0;
            var speed:Number = Math.abs(ob.speed);
            var xsign:Number = (game.char.x-
            ➥ob.x)/Math.abs((game.char.x-ob.x));
            var ysign:Number = (game.char.y-
            ➥ob.y)/Math.abs((game.char.y-ob.y));
            if (random(10) == 0) {
                xsign = -1*xsign;
                ysign = -1*ysign;
            }
            if (xsign == ysign || xsign == -ysign) {
                var ran:Number = random(2);
                if (ran == 0) {
```

```
29                          xsign = 0;
30                      } else {
31                          ysign = 0;
32                      }
33                  }
34                  if (xsign != 0) {
35                      ymov = 0;
36                      xmov = xsign*speed;
37                      if (xmov>0) {
38                          var dir:String = "right";
39                      } else {
40                          var dir:String = "left";
41                      }
42                  } else if (ysign != 0) {
43                      xmov = 0;
44                      ymov = ysign*speed;
45                      if (ymov>0) {
46                          var dir:String = "down";
47                      } else {
48                          var dir:String = "up";
49                      }
50                  }
51                  ob.dir = dir;
52                  ob.clip.gotoAndStop(dir);
53                  ob.xmov = xmov;
54                  ob.ymov = ymov;
55              }
56          }
57      }
```

This is a pretty long function, but don't panic—there is a lot of reappearing information. That is mostly because of the several `if` statements and because everything we do for the *x* direction, we also do for the *y* direction. As with many of the files created in this book, here we have an object called `game` that stores information about the game. There is an array called `baddies` stored in game that contains one object for each enemy ("baddy") in the game. This function loops through the `baddies` array and checks out each baddy object to determine if it is time to run an update. Line 3 sets a temporary reference called `ob` to the current enemy that we are inspecting in the baddies array. In the next line, we increment the time property in ob. Remember that one of the conditions to determine if it is time for an update is if maxtime is the same as time. We will perform this check further down (line 11). In lines 5 and 6, we determine which cell the enemy is currently over, and in lines 8 and 9, we determine which cell the enemy would be over at the end of the frame. The cell that the enemy would be over at the end of the frame is given a temporary reference called cell_over_temp. In line 11, we check two conditions to determine if it is time for an update. First, if cell_over_temp is not empty (that is, if it contains an object), then we perform an update. Second, if the time variable is the same as the maxtime variable on the enemy object, then we also do an update.

Let's look at the update (starting in line 12). First we set time back to 0 so that the counter will start over. Next we semi-randomly set a new maxtime value. There is nothing special about the numbers chosen for this randomization. You can change them and get different behaviors for the enemies. If you are interested in repurposing this AI and want some control over its difficulty level, this is one line of code you might want to play around with. In the next two lines, we set the enemy's position to where it was at the beginning of the frame (lines 14 and 15). We then store the current direction of the enemy as tempDir. This is a string value that is "left", "right", "up", or "down". We then set the values of the *x* and *y* velocities to 0 so that we can reassign them from scratch (lines 17 and 18). In lines 20 and 21, we determine the sign for the *x* and *y* directions, specifying where the hero is with respect to this enemy. Remember, these can have values of –1, 0, or 1.

Are you interested in creating games along the lines of *Pac-Man*? The AI used here would probably work well for characters and figures like the ghosts in that game.

In lines 22–24, we insert the random dumbing-down process mentioned earlier in this section. This causes the script to reverse the direction of an enemy approximately one out of every ten times it runs.

In line 26, we determine whether the enemy is in the same row or column as the hero. If he is not, then we randomly choose either the *x* direction or the *y* direction to move in. We set the direction we do *not* want to move in to 0. So, when xsign is set to 0, we move toward the hero in the *y* direction. Next, in lines 34–39, we perform similar tasks for either the *x* or the *y* direction, depending on which is non-zero. For the direction that is non-zero, we set the speed in that direction and also set the temporary variable dir to store the string value of the direction of motion. This is then used in line 52 to display a certain frame in the enemy movie clip so that the zombie appears to be walking in the correct direction. In lines 53 and 54, we store the newly-established *x* and *y* velocities on the enemy object.

That's all of it! As far as AIs go, this one is elementary, but for simple games, it is good enough.

The Perfect Maze

You are probably very familiar with mazes—surprisingly fun puzzles that can keep you interested for a long time. In this section, we talk about the AI involved in creating random but perfect mazes. First, though, you should know what a perfect maze is, as opposed to an imperfect one. A perfect maze is one in which exactly one path exists between every two cells. In a perfect maze, you can choose any two cells, and a path always exists between the two—but only one. In a perfect maze, a looped path is not possible, and there are no closed-off areas (see Figure 11.3).

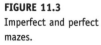

FIGURE 11.3
Imperfect and perfect mazes.

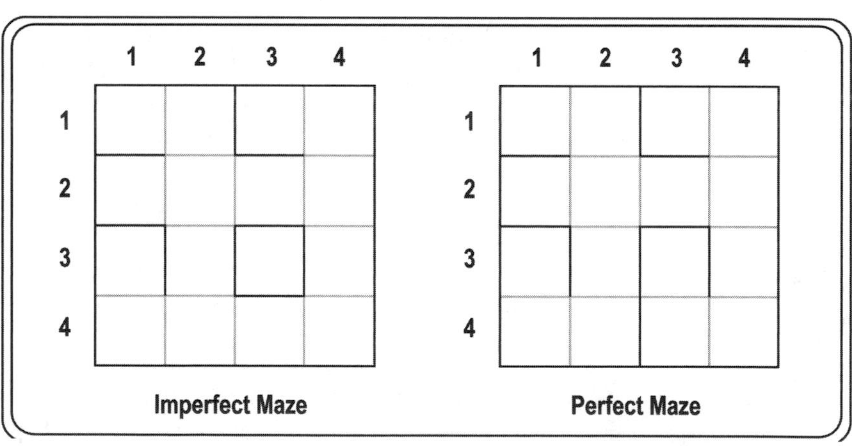

In Figure 11.3, you can see both perfect and imperfect mazes. The imperfect one has both a closed-off cell and multiple paths between some cells. The perfect maze has no closed-off areas, and only one path exists between any two cells. Figure 11.4 presents you with a larger, more interesting perfect maze.

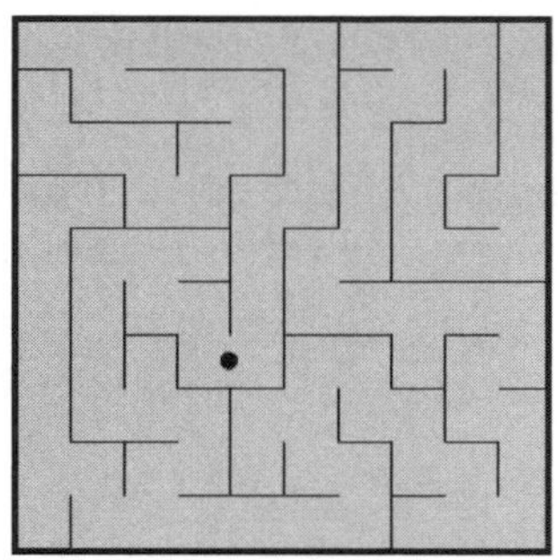

FIGURE 11.4
A larger perfect maze.

Rules for the Perfect Maze

This is a pretty simple application that makes use of two-dimensional arrays to store information about each tile. The maze is tile-based, and each tile has four walls. Now let's look at the rules for creating a perfect maze.

1. Choose how many rows and columns you want in the maze. You have rows×columns number of cells in this maze. All the walls of these cells are currently up. Create a variable called `cellsVisited` with a value of `0`.
2. Create an array called `visitedList`. When a cell is visited, it will be added to this array.
3. Choose a random starting cell. Make this the current cell. Increment `cellsVisited`.
4. If the value of `cellsVisited` is equal to the number of cells, your maze is finished. Otherwise, move on to step 5.
5. Create an array called `neighbors`. Look at each of the immediate neighbors of this cell. We will call them `"east"`, `"west"`, `"north"`, and `"south"`. Add any neighbor that has never been visited to the `neighbors` array. If any of the neighbors have at one time been visited, then they are not added to this array.
6. Randomly choose a neighbor from the `neighbors` array. If the `neighbors` array is empty (indicating that all the neighbors have been visited), then move on to step 9. Otherwise, continue to step 7.
7. Move to this randomly selected neighbor, knocking down the wall between the current cell and this neighbor cell.

8. Make this neighbor cell the current cell, and add it to the `visitedList` array. Return to step 5.
9. Move to the previous cell in the `visited` array, deleting the cell you are currently in from the `visitedList` array. Return to step 5.

The images in Figure 11.5 shows an example of how a 3×3 maze would be created.

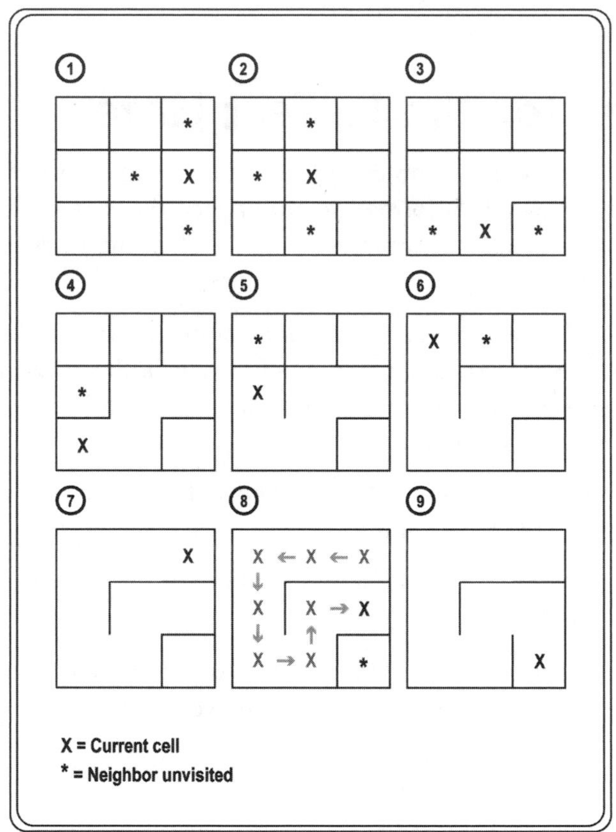

FIGURE 11.5
Maze creation.

Using ActionScript to Create the Perfect Maze

Now that you have a good understanding of the algorithm, let's take a look at how it can be written in ActionScript. If you truly understand this algorithm (which you can probably do without too much trouble), and if you have a firm grasp of ActionScript, you should be able to write the

ActionScript for this algorithm on your own. Just in case you don't want to try, though, we have done it for you.

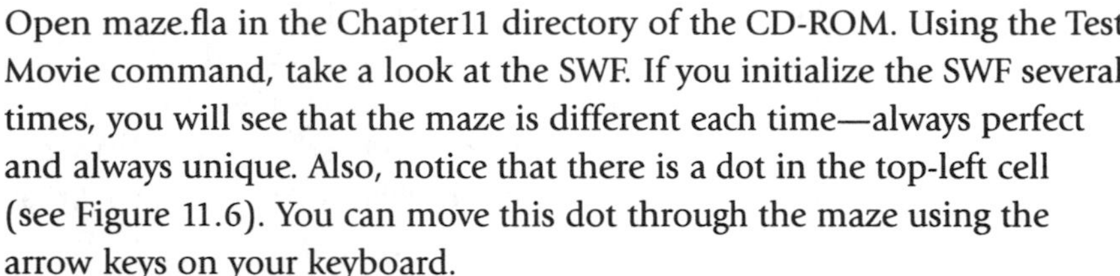

Open maze.fla in the Chapter11 directory of the CD-ROM. Using the Test Movie command, take a look at the SWF. If you initialize the SWF several times, you will see that the maze is different each time—always perfect and always unique. Also, notice that there is a dot in the top-left cell (see Figure 11.6). You can move this dot through the maze using the arrow keys on your keyboard.

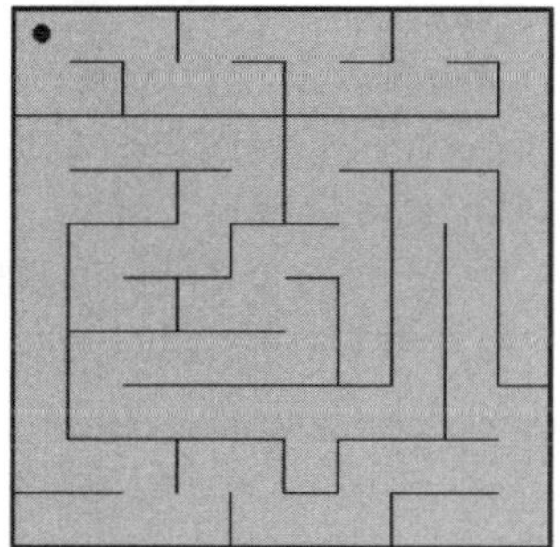

FIGURE 11.6
The dot in the top-left cell.

In maze.fla, there are three layers: Object Definition, Implementation, and Assets. The Object Definition layer contains the algorithm that creates the maze in memory. The Implementation layer contains the ActionScript needed to create a visual representation of the maze that we created in memory. The Assets layer contains the movie clips needed to display the maze.

We are most concerned with the ActionScript in the Object Definition layer because that contains the AI algorithm for maze creation. There are 75 lines of code in this frame, all for one long function.

```
var maze:Object = new Object();
maze.createMaze = function(horizontal, vertical) {
     this.rows = horizontal;
     this.columns = vertical;
     this.totalCells = this.rows*this.columns;
     this.startRow = random(this.rows)+1;
     this.startColumn = random(this.columns)+1;
     this.cellsVisited = 0;
     this.currentCell =
     ➥"cell"+this.startRow+"_"+this.startColumn;
```

```
this[this.currentCell] = {name:this.currentCell,
➥x:this.startRow, y:this.startColumn, exists:true};
this.visitList = [];
this.visitList.push(this[currentCell]);
while (this.cellsVisited<this.totalCells) {
    var cell:Object = this[this.currentCell];
    var neighbors:Array = new Array();
    if (cell.x-1>0) {
        //west cell
        var x:Number = cell.x-1;
        var y:Number = cell.y;
        var westCell:String = "cell"+x+"_"+y;
        if (!this[westCell].exists) {
            neighbors.push([westCell, "west",
            ➥"east", x, y]);
        }
    }
    if (cell.y-1>0) {
        //north cell
        var x:Number = cell.x;
        var y:Number = cell.y-1;
        var northCell:String = "cell"+x+"_"+y;
        if (!this[northCell].exists) {
            neighbors.push([northCell, "north",
            ➥"south", x, y]);
        }
    }
    if (cell.x+1<=this.rows) {
        //east cell
        var x:Number = cell.x+1;
        var y:Number = cell.y;
        var eastCell:String = "cell"+x+"_"+y;
        if (!this[eastCell].exists) {
            neighbors.push([eastCell, "east",
            ➥"west", x, y]);
        }
    }
    if (cell.y+1<=this.columns) {
        //south cell
```

```
                var x:Number = cell.x;
                var y:Number = cell.y+1;
                var southCell:String = "cell"+x+"_"+y;
                if (!this[southCell].exists) {
                    neighbors.push([southCell, "south",
                    ➥"north", x, y]);
                }
            }
            //randomly choose a neighbor
            if (neighbors.length>0) {
                var nextCell:Number =
                ➥random(neighbors.length);
                //knock down wall
                cell[neighbors[nextCell][1]] = true;
                //retrieve the name of the new cell
                var newName:String =
                ➥neighbors[nextCell][0];
                this[newName] = new Object();
                var newCell:Object = this[newName];
                newCell.exists = true;
                newCell.x = neighbors[nextCell][3];
                newCell.y = neighbors[nextCell][4];
                newCell.name = this.currentCell;
                //knock down the wall
                newCell[neighbors[nextCell][2]] = true;
                this.currentCell = newName;
                this.visitList.push(this.currentCell);
                ++this.cellsVisited;
            } else {
                //step back to the last cell
                this.currentCell = this.visitList.pop();
            }
        }
    };
```

We begin by creating an object called `maze`. Next, we add a method to this object called `createMaze()` that accepts two parameters that specify the number of columns and the number of rows to be calculated for the maze. They are stored as `columns` and `rows`. The total number of cells in this maze is calculated by multiplying rows by columns. This value is stored as totalCells. We then randomly select a cell to start from and store this as currentCell (lines 7–9). In line 10, we create an object that represents this starting cell and give it four properties: name, x, y, and exists. The exists property gives us an easy way to check if a cell has been visited. If exists is true, then the cell has been visited. Next, we create an array called visitedList and insert the object that represents the current cell into it. We have now given the AI a starting place. One cell exists; it is in the visited array. Now we can perform a while loop until the cellsVisited variable is equivalent to totalCells (line 13). When cellsVisited is equivalent to totalCells, the maze has been completed.

In line 14, we create a reference to the object that represents the current cell. Lines 15–51 perform step 5 from our list: The neighbors array is created. Then we check to the west, north, east, and south of the current cell for cells that have not yet been visited. If we find one, then we add it to the neighbors array. When it is added to the neighbors array, we store string names of the wall in each cell that would be knocked down if we chose to visit this cell. For instance, for the neighbor to the east, we store the string values "east" and "west". That means if we choose to visit this cell, then we will knock down the east wall in the current cell and the west wall in the neighbor cell. Visually, these are the same wall, but in code, each cell keeps track of its own walls.

In line 53, we start step 6. If the neighbors array is not empty, then we randomly choose a neighbor (line 54); otherwise, we step back in the visitedList array (lines 70–73). When a random neighbor is chosen, we perform steps 7 and 8 from our list, and we must also do the following:

1. Create an object for that neighbor cell.
2. Knock down the walls between the current cell and the neighbor cell.
3. Increment the cellsVisited variable.
4. Set the neighbor cell as the current cell.

This is all done in lines 54–69. As mentioned previously, if there were no elements in the neighbors array, then we move on to lines 70–73, where we step back to the previous cell.

I hope you'll agree that while this script was long, it wasn't all that complicated, right?

Visual Implementation of the Perfect Maze

We are not going to dissect the ActionScript found in the Implementation layer. However, I will briefly describe what it does. First, it calls the `maze.createMaze()` method. When that has finished, the `maze` object contains many other objects that are named in this fashion: `cell1_1`, `cell1_2`, `cell1_3`, and so on. This naming scheme is the same as in all the tile-based worlds you have seen or will see in this book. The ActionScript then performs a nested loop to add all the tiles to the Stage. During each iteration, the ActionScript looks up the corresponding cell object in the `maze` object and looks at its `east` and `south` properties. If `east` is not `true`, then the east wall is made visible. If `south` is not `true`, the south wall is made visible. The script only cares about the east and south walls of each cell because we can build the maze with only those pieces of information. The east wall of `cell1_1` is the same as the west wall of `cell2_1`, so we only need to display this wall one time. Likewise, the south wall of `cell1_1` is the same as the north wall of `cell1_2`.

The rest of the ActionScript in that frame handles the movie clip that the user moves through the maze.

PATHFINDING ALGORITHMS

As we've mentioned before, a pathfinding algorithm is one that finds any path between two points. Usually these two points are the centers of two different tiles in a tile-based world. (In fact, I can't think of an implementation of pathfinding that is not in a tile-based world.) To help get you started learning about pathfinding algorithms, here are a few of the most popular types. (Note: These algorithms perform the pathfinding all at once in memory and then give a complete path—usually in the form of an array—as the final result.)

- One that starts at the first tile and randomly walks from tile to tile (in memory) until the goal is reached.
- One that starts at both the starting tile and the goal tile and walks randomly until the paths intersect.

- One that moves in the direction of the goal from a particular starting point until it hits an obstacle. It then moves along the obstacle until it can get around it. This pathfinding trick—used by many real-life robots—is called *tracing*.

Each type of pathfinding algorithms has its strengths and weaknesses. Some are super-fast to compute but can yield very long or odd-looking paths. Some give nice-looking paths under certain conditions, such as in an environment with no concave obstacles like closets. As always, you have to weigh the pros and cons.

The best-known pathfinding algorithm is A*. Provided that you fulfill some conditions (that we will discuss in a while), A* is guaranteed to return the shortest possible path between two points. Like the other pathfinding algorithms, however, A* also has a drawback: It is slow. The A* algorithm is one of the most (if not *the* most) CPU-intensive pathfinding algorithms. Still, regardless of its speed, A* is used more than any other pathfinding algorithm in games. When you play games like *Diablo* and you click in an area on the screen, the character walks to that position. If there is an obstacle in the way, the character walks around the obstacle. In any game you play that has pathfinding capability like this, the game is probably using A*. In this section, we're going to introduce you to that algorithm and walk you through it.

In Figure 11.7, you can see a basic implementation of the A* pathfinding algorithm. What you see is a 20-by-20 grid. The white cells are empty cells. The black cells contain walls. The gray cell at the top left (point A) is the starting position of a character; the dark gray cell at the bottom right (point B) is the ending position of that character. The light gray path that connects the two is the path created by the A* pathfinding algorithm.

Every Flavor A*

Video games are a multibillion-dollar industry. As you can imagine, a lot of money has been spent trying to find better and faster pathfinding algorithms. To that end, many variations of A* exist. These variations usually result from optimizations and modifications to the A* algorithm. In the final portion of this section, we mention one example file that uses a version of the A* algorithm that has been optimized for speed.

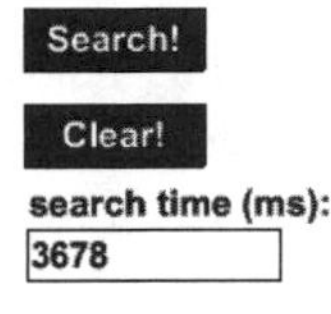

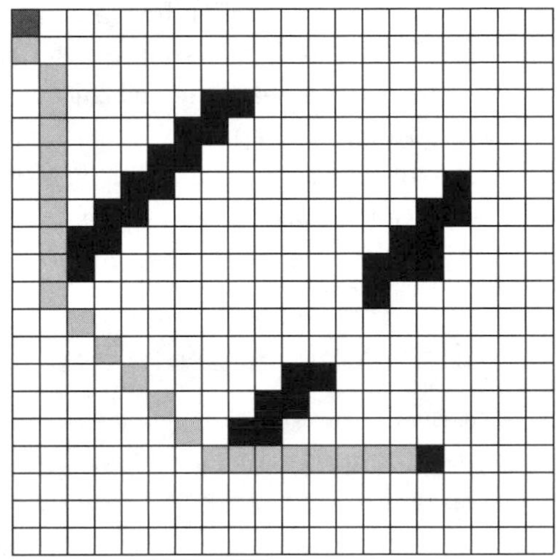

FIGURE 11.7
The A* pathfinding algorithm finds the way from point A to point B.

The A* Algorithm

Before we continue into that specific algorithm, however, you need to know a few more things about how we are going to proceed and the tools we'll use. I have written the A* algorithm in ActionScript and included two example files on the CD-ROM that use that ActionScript—but I will not be explaining the ActionScript to you line by line; instead, I'm going to tell you how to use what I have created. I will discuss in detail the algorithm itself using *pseudo-code* and then make some general references to the ActionScript. Pseudo-code is a representation of an algorithm in a code-like form (sort of like an outline of a chapter). It mentions what you should do in code without giving you a specific syntax. This means that pseudo-code is not language-specific; Java programmers, ActionScript programmers, C++ programmers—any kind of programmer—can read and understand it. One of the beauties of pseudo-code is that it tends to be pretty short. For instance, the pseudo-code used here is just over 30 lines, but the algorithm written in ActionScript is nearly 170. In pseudo-code, you might have a line that informs the reader to delete an element from an array, but in real code, you would have to loop through the array to find the element and then delete it, which would take several lines of code.

I learned the A* algorithm from pseudo-code found on gamasutra.com (see Appendix A, "Developer Resources," for pathfinding links). My pseudo-code of the A* algorithm bears a resemblance to the one that I found on Gamasutra (`www.gamasutra.com`), but it is not the same. If two people sit down and write plot summaries for *Star Wars: Episode II*, the summaries will probably both have the same content, but it will be described differently. The same thing applies here: They're two different descriptions of the same algorithm.

Branching Out with Pathfinding

Although primarily used for pathfinding, the A* algorithm is actually much more general than that. You can use it to find the solutions to many types of problems. My understanding of A* as applied to pathfinding is pretty solid, but my general understanding of A* regarding other applications is, well, nonexistent. If you are interested in using A* for tasks other than pathfinding, you can probably find any number of resource sites on the Internet to help you.

Basic A* Terminology and Functionality

As with many math-based concepts, the A* pathfinding algorithm uses a handful of terms you must be familiar with in order to proceed. These terms describe the states, actions, and results that go along with this process:

- A *node* is the representation of the current state of the system. In pathfinding, the current state is simply the tile that we are currently inspecting. So as far as we are concerned, a node is a tile.
- The act of *expanding* a node means that (in code) you visit each of the node's neighbors.
- A *heuristic*, in A*, is an educated guess based on a chosen unit of measurement that yields a number. (That is pretty vague, right? We will talk more about heuristics soon.)
- The *cost* is a numeric amount that we assign to the act of moving from one node to another.
- The *score* consists of the sum of the cost and heuristic of every node you visited along the path to the current node.

With these terms in place, let's see how they apply to the algorithm, and more generally, how A* works. As you now know, A* finds the shortest path between two points. But what measurement are we using? Time? Distance? Number of steps? While A* can be used to search according to pretty much any measurement, we choose to use distance. Other measurements might be time (to find the path that takes the shortest time to walk) or the number of tanks of gas used (to find the path that uses the smallest amount of gas in a car). We assign a value of 1 to the cost of moving between one tile and its vertical or horizontal neighbor (1 foot, 1 mile, 1 tile—it doesn't matter). The cost of moving between one tile and a neighboring diagonal tile is 1.41. The number 1.41 is the distance between the centers of two neighboring diagonal tiles.

The heuristic is the best guess of how far the center of the current tile (that you are inspecting during the search) is from the destination tile. You can make this guess fairly easily using simple logic. When visited, each node is assigned a score of f:

$$f = g + h$$

The value h is the heuristic—the best guess of the distance between that tile and the goal. The value g is the sum of the scores of every node visited along the path to the current node. This may be best understood with an analogy. Let's say you are planning a trip from New York to Paris. You are on a tight budget, so you want to find the path that will cost the least. You can think of New York, London, Lisbon, Brussels, Madrid, and Paris as nodes. In the course of your research, you calculate the cost from New York to London and store that, but you also calculate the costs of traveling from Lisbon to New York, London to Paris, and so on. In the end, if you apply other rules (not yet discussed) with A*, you find the best path (for the cost). Let's assume that this path turns out to be New York–Madrid–London–Paris. In New York (as in all nodes), $f = g + h$. Remember that g is the sum of all the fs of the previous nodes. Because New York is the starting node, there are no parents, so $g = 0$ in New York. For Madrid, $f = g + h$ as well (as in all nodes). In this case, g is not 0 because Madrid was visited from another node. The g value is consists of the f from New York, so g is the running total of cost up to the current node. If you were actually on this trip, then g would be the amount of money spent up to your current position.

At this point, it is appropriate to mention one of the most amazing features of A*—the way it handles terrain. Previously, I said that the cost of going from one tile to the next is either 1 or 1.41. That is true if all tiles are of equal size, but that statement does not always have to be true. Let's say some of the tiles are made up of water. Chances are, you probably don't want to send your character through the water unless it is absolutely necessary. Thus, you assign a cost of, let's say, 10 to any node transition (moving from one node to another) that involves water. This will not guarantee that the path does not go through the water, but it will give extreme preference to paths that don't. If the water is a stream going completely through the map and there is no bridge, then A* will certainly end up giving you a path through the water. However, if a bridge exists, and it is close enough, then A* will give you a path that includes the bridge. Alternatively, if your character is half man and half fish, then he may prefer water. In this case, you may give land a lower cost than water. With all this in mind, I should probably modify my initial statement that A* always finds the shortest path. Now that you know more, I can further specify that A* always finds the path with the lowest score. In many cases (such as those of maps in which there is no terrain change, like the implementations used later in this section), the path with the lowest score also happens to be the shortest path.

A* Spelled Out, Almost in English

Now let's look at the algorithm itself in pseudo-code.

```
AStar.Search
     create open array
     create closed array
     s.g = 0
     s.h = findHeuristic( s.x, s.y )
     s.f = s.g + s.h
     s.parent = null
     push s into open array
     set keepSearching to true
     while keepSearching
          pop node n from open
          if n is the goal node
               build path from start to finish
               set keepSearching to false
          for each neighbor m of n
```

```
16              newg = n.g + cost( n, newx, newy )
17              if m has not been visited
18                  m.g = n.f
19                  m.h = findHeuristic( newx, newy )
20                  m.f = m.g + m.h
21                  m.parent = n
22                  add it to the open array
23                  sort the open array
24              else
25                  if newg < m.g
26                      m.parent = n
27                      m.g = newg
28                      m.f = m.g + m.h
29                      sort the open array
30                      if m is in closed
31                          remove it from closed
32          push n into the closed array
33          if search time > max time
34              set keepSearching to false
35      return path
```

This algorithm makes use of two lists (which are arrays in Flash), `open` and `closed`. The `open` array contains the nodes that have at one time been visited. The `closed` array contains all nodes that have been expanded (that is, all its neighbors have been visited). We use the `open` array as a *priority queue*. We use the `open` array not only to store nodes, but also to store nodes in a certain order. We keep the array sorted from lowest score (*f*) to highest score. Every time we add a node to the `open` array or change the value of *g* in a node in the `open` array, we must re-sort the array so that the nodes are in order from lowest to highest score.

In lines 2 and 3, we create the empty `open` and `closed` arrays. In pathfinding, we need a starting place and a destination, so that comes next. `s` is an object that represents the starting node. We set `s.g` to 0 because the starting node has no parents, so the cost (*g*) to get to it is 0 (line 4). Next, we find the heuristic *h* for the start node. (Remember that the heuristic is the estimated cost from the current node to the goal.) We then store the value of *f*, which is the sum of `s.g` and `s.h`, on the starting node (line 6). Because `s` has no parents, we set `s.parent` to `null`. Next, we push the `s` node into the `open` array (line 8). The `s` node is now the first and only node in the open array.

In line 9, we set the variable `keepSearching` to `true`. While it remains `true`, we keep performing the A* search. When we have determined that we have found a path, that no path exists, or that we have been searching for too long, we will set `keepSearching` to `false`.

In line 11, we take a node from the priority queue. We then check if this node is the goal. If it is, we have reached the goal; we stop searching and build the path (lines 12–14). If it is not the goal, we expand the node. Expanding the node means that we visit each of the node's neighbors. In line 16, we find the *g* of the neighbor node, *m*, that we are currently looking at. We then check if this node has ever been visited. If it has not yet been visited, then we enter the portion of the algorithm in lines 18–23. We set the value of *g* on *m;* it is the *f* from its parent, *n*. Next we calculate and store the heuristic and *f* on *m*. Finally, we set the parent property to be that of the previous node, *n*. If this node has been visited before and now has a lower *g*, then we enter the portion of the algorithm in lines 25–31.

At this point, I want to mention something more about *g*. When a node is first visited, it is assigned a *g* based on the path taken to get to that node (as we have already discussed). However, it is possible, and likely, that that node will be visited again during the search through another possible path. If the *g* from this new path is lower than the *g* from the previously stored path, then we replace the old *g* with the new *g* (line 27). In line 26, we set the `parent` property of *m* to be the node that we are coming from. The `parent` property is what we use at the end of the search to construct the final path. We can move from the goal node all the way back to the starting position by following the `parent` properties. Next, we recalculate the *f* and then have to re-sort the open array. We re-sort the open array because we have just updated one of the nodes with a lower *f*, so this node may now take priority over another.

I have to be honest with you—I'm not quite sure what lines 30 and 31 are for! It was in the pseudo-code from which I learned the A* algorithm, and I have included it in my ActionScript implementation. However, it is a part of the algorithm that has never been visited during any of the example searches I have constructed (I put a `trace` action in that part of the code so that I would be informed if it was ever entered). Throughout my dozens and dozens of tests, I have never experienced a use for this. The algorithm, written in ActionScript, to the best of my knowledge works exactly as it should and always returns the path with the lowest score. However, I have kept that part of the algorithm around, even though it seems to be unnecessary, just in case I someday realize when it *would* be needed. If you are an A* whiz, then let me know your thoughts!

After all the neighbors of *n* are visited, we move on to line 32. In this line, we push *n* onto the `closed` array because it has been completely expanded. We then check the time to make sure that we haven't been searching for too long. If we have been searching too long, then we set `keepSearching` to `false`. Otherwise, we move on to the next node in the queue (line 11). If `keepSearching` is `false`, we stop searching and build the path.

You have now been formally introduced to A*! Don't feel bad if you are having trouble understanding the algorithm; it is not the easiest thing in the world to grasp. It took me several articles on the Internet before I felt like I fully understood basic A*.

Implementing A*

You have seen the A* algorithm and should have at least a basic understanding of how it works. I have written the A* algorithm in ActionScript as a class called `Astar`. Let's take a look at how it's used.

Open astar.fla in the Chapter 11/Astar directory on the CD-ROM. Generate an SWF from this FLA file to see what it does. You will see an isometric tile-based world with a character standing at a corner. The ground in this world is made of grass.

In the top right corner of the SWF file, you'll see several radio buttons. The top row of radio buttons is used to change the terrain of individual tiles in the world. The bottom row of radio buttons is used to add an object (like a plant or brick) to a tile.

You select a tile by clicking on it. There is a button in the bottom right of the SWF called "search." When clicked, a path will be determined from where the character is standing to the currently selected tile (see Figure 11.8).

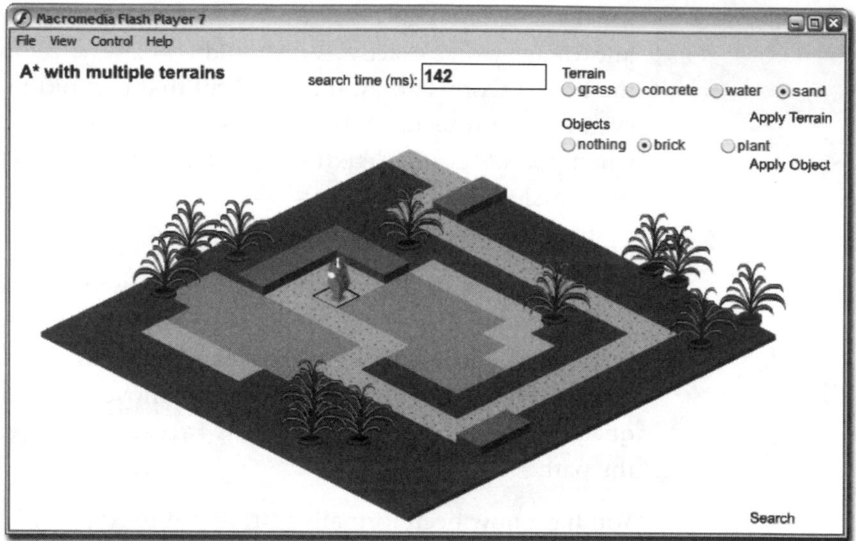

FIGURE 11.8
Astar.

The purpose of this file is to let you test how A* finds paths through various terrain. If you experiment with this file, you'll see that the character walks the path with the least cost. If you build a long row of water and want the character to walk to a tile on the other side of the water, then the character may walk around the water. If A* determines that it will cost too much to walk around the water, the character will be taken through the water.

This file uses four custom classes:

- `Map`—The `Map` class makes it easier to build a tile-based world. This class contains methods to enable you to get information about a tile, to add an object to a tile (like a plant, key, and so on), and to set the terrain for a tile.
- `Astar`—This class contains the A* search algorithm logic and is used to search for the lowest-cost path between two nodes. An instance of the `Map` class is passed into the `Astar` class when a search is performed. The `Astar` class inspects the tiles for terrain and returns the lowest-cost path as a result.
- `PQueue`—This class is a priority queue class. It sorts an array of nodes based on the cost. It also provides useful methods for adding and removing nodes from the queue.

- `Isometric`—The `Isometric` class is the one that was introduced in Isometric Worldview chapters.

Here are the `Map` class methods used in this file:

- `new Map(columns, rows)`—Creates a new instance of the `Map` class. When called, you pass in the number of columns and rows in the map's dimensions. The map created in this file is 15×15.
- `addTerrain(terrain_array)`—This method creates terrain in memory assigned to the map. Each element in the array is just a string.
- `setTransitionCost(terrain1, terrain2, cost, reversible)`— The cost associated with moving from one tile to another is dependant on the terrain of the initial tile and the terrain of the final tile. The first two parameters are strings representing a terrain type. The third is a number representing the cost of going from `terrain1` to `terrain2`. The fourth parameter is a Boolean value. If `reversible` is `true`, then the cost associated with moving from `terrain1` to `terrain2` is also associated to moving from `terrain2` to `terrain1`. If `false`, then the cost is not assigned to the reverse situation. For instance, moving from sand to quicksand might be easy, but moving from quicksand back to sand is very difficult, so the costs are different.
- `getTile(column, row)`—Returns a reference to the tile at `column` and `row`.
- `setStart(column, row)`—Sets the starting position for a path. It is used by the `Astar` class.
- `setGoal(column, row)`—Sets the ending position for a path. It is used by the `Astar` class.

Here are the `Astar` methods used in this file:

- `new Astar()`—Creates a new instance of the `Astar` class.
- `search(map)`—This method is used to find the lowest-cost path between two tiles. A reference to an instance of the `Map` class is passed in. The `setStart()` and `setGoal()` methods of that `Map` class instance must be called first so that the `Astar` class knows which two

tiles to use. This method returns an object as the result. This object has the follow properties:

- `path`—This is an array of the tiles included in the path from the starting tile to the destination tile.
- `setMaxSearchTime(milliseconds)`—By default, the `Astar` class will search for a path for 1700 milliseconds (1.7 seconds). If it does not find a path within that time, then it stops searching. You can change the maximum search time with this method.
- `pathFound`—This is a Boolean value. If `true`, then a path was found. If `false`, then a path was not found. A path might not be found if the destination is surrounded by tiles that you cannot walk through. Also, a path might not be found if the search time ever goes above the value of `maxSearchTime`, which is 1700 milliseconds by default.
- `searchTime`—This is the time in milliseconds that it took to find the path.

You do not interact directly with the `PQueue` class. The `Astar` class uses it internally for sorting the `open` list. The `Isometric` class was discussed in-depth in Chapter 8, "Isometric Worldview."

Tweaking the Numbers for Realism

The `Astar` class includes a property called `preventClipping`. If this value is `false`, then the search will truly return the shortest path. In this case, a character can walk across from one tile to another diagonally, and half of the character will appear on the two neighboring tiles as it moves from one tile to the next. If neighbors contain no obstacles, then this is what we would want to happen. However, if a neighbor contains an obstacle, then the character will appear to partially walk through the corner of that obstacle. Luckily there is a way around this unrealistic behavior. By default, the `preventClipping` property has a value of `true`. When `true`, the algorithm will not return a diagonal move from one tile to another if one of the neighbors contains an obstacle. This gives a path that is more realistic but is not necessarily the shortest. However, it is the shortest path that looks good (see Figure 11.9).

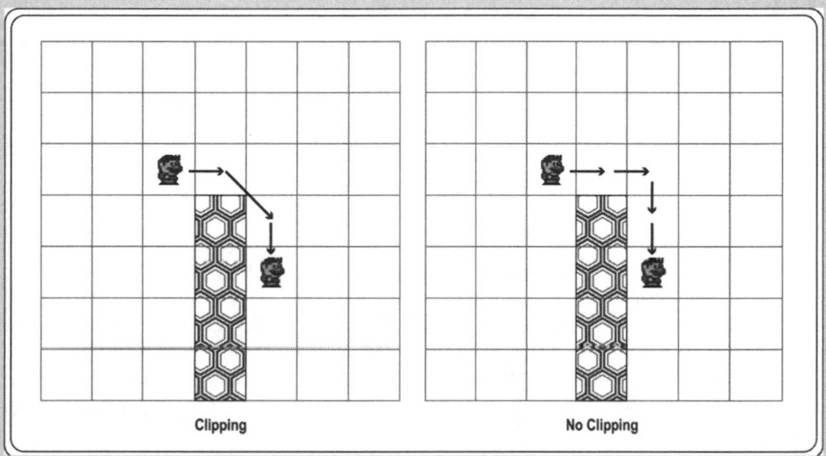

FIGURE 11.9
A representation of clipping versus no clipping.

In this A* implementation, I have modified the `cost()` function to return very large values for diagonal moves that would normally clip. The result is that with `preventClipping` set as `true`, the path moves more naturally around the object without any clipping. Diagonal moves are still made—just not when clipping would occur. If you prefer the pure A* path, then set `preventClipping` to `false`. To set the value of `preventClipping`, use the `setPreventClipping()` method and pass in the value `true` or `false`. The default value is `false`.

Not Fast Enough For You?

As you may have noticed in astar.fla, the speed at which the path is found is very slow. In iso_ai_astar.fla, the speed is *barely* acceptable. In that file, the search tends to take (at least on my computer) from 80 milliseconds (ms) to 400 ms. If you are interested in getting your hands on a blazingly fast (but less functional—no terrain support) implementation of A* in ActionScript, take a look in the astar_optimized folder. There you'll find some very fast A* files created by Casper Schuirink. What takes my A* 200 milliseconds, Casper's can do in 10 ms to 40 ms, and most typical searches are under 50 ms. As with all highly-optimized files, they also have their disadvantages. One major con, in this case, is that the files are not necessarily easy to port over to your own applications. Ease of use is sacrificed for speed, so be cautious.

Points to Remember

- Pathfinding is the act of finding a path between one point and another.
- Pathfinding and controlling enemy behaviors are the main areas in which you'll probably use AI.
- AI can be used to generate random maps.
- Using a special algorithm, you can generate a random perfect maze.
- A* (pronounced "A star") is the best pathfinding algorithm known. It is guaranteed to find the path of the lowest score, should any path exist, between two points.
- Although it's the best pathfinding algorithm, A* is also very CPU-intensive and slow.
- A* can handle multiple types of terrain and find the best path through these terrains to the goal.

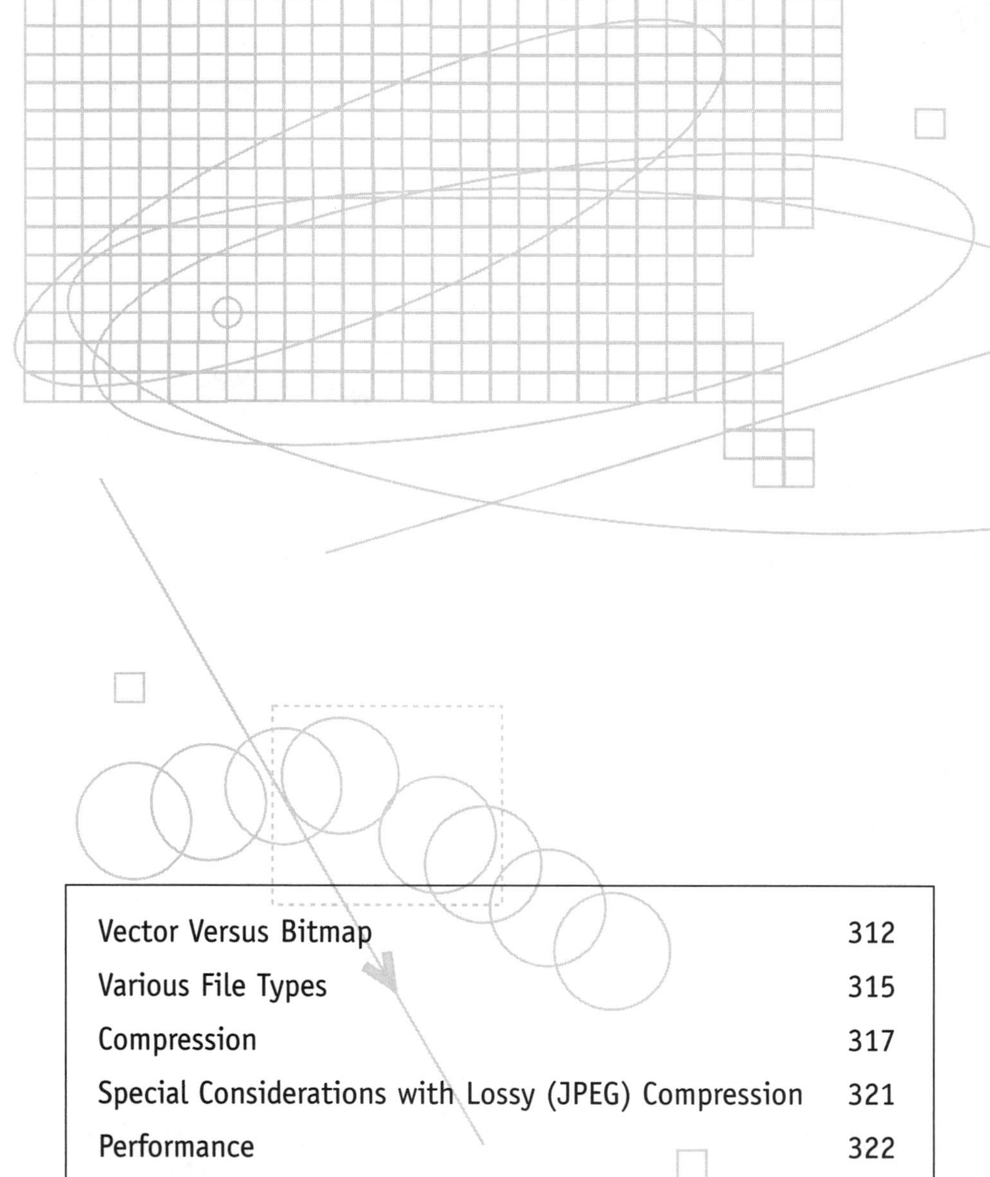

Vector Versus Bitmap	312
Various File Types	315
Compression	317
Special Considerations with Lossy (JPEG) Compression	321
Performance	322
Loading Graphics at Run-Time	326
Points to Remember	327

CHAPTER 12

Efficient Game Graphics

THEY SAY YOU NEVER GET A SECOND CHANCE TO MAKE A FIRST IMPRESSION. The same applies to your game. The way your game looks and feels to the user will have more impact on their impression of your game than any other aspects of it.

There are no hard and fast rules to graphics usage. In specific instances, one approach will perform or look better than another. It all depends on the game and what you want it to do. In this chapter, we'll discuss the different graphics types, file formats, and compression styles, along with performance tips and some tricks of the trade that will help you get the most of your graphics and make better games.

First things first though, let's explore some of the graphical options and issues that affect us as game developers.

Vector Versus Bitmap

There is a lot of discussion these days about which type of graphics is best to use in Flash games, vector or bitmap. The fact is that both graphics types have advantages and disadvantages. Depending on the particular situation, one type may be the clear choice over the other. For instance, if you are creating a game in a very simple cartoony style, then vector graphics would be the clear choice. On the other hand, if your game is in a slick, rendered 3D style, perhaps using graphics rendered from a 3D program, then bitmap graphics would be the obvious choice. In most cases, the best solution is to use them both together—bitmaps for some graphics and vector for others.

Using them together and leveraging their individual strengths, you can achieve the best balance of performance, download efficiency, and a smooth, professional appearance. The best approach to choosing the type of graphics to use in your game is to first understand how they work, how they are handled by the playback engine, and what kind of images they are best suited for.

Let's begin by exploring both vector and bitmap graphics types so we can better understand the ins and outs of each.

Vector Graphics

Vector-based graphics are images described mathematically by points and curves. Rather than storing the actual image pixel data, vector file types store a mathematical description of the image that can be rendered to the screen during run-time. Because of the way vector graphics are described, they are ideal for line work and graphical shapes.

Drawing tools such as Illustrator, Freehand, or Flash are commonly used to create vector-based graphics. Some common file types include Adobe Illustrator (.AI), CorelDRAW graphics (.CDR), Encapsulated Postscript (.EPS), and Shockwave Flash (.SWF).

Vector graphics are resolution-independent. Notice in Figure 12.1 how, even when we zoom into a small part of the vector image, the line quality is preserved.

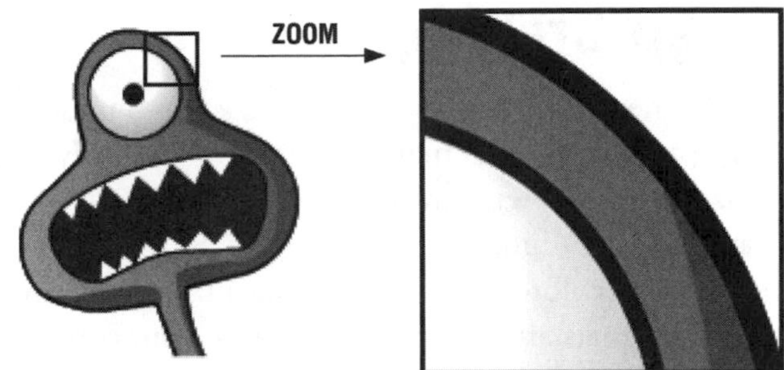

FIGURE 12.1
In a vector image, line quality is preserved at various zoom levels or sizes.

Advantages

The main advantages of vector-based graphics are file size and flexibility. Because the file is stored using a mathematical description rather than pixel data, the space required to save the file is usually much smaller than a bitmap file. I say "usually" because limits exist. Extremely complex images may require so many points and curves to describe the image that the amount of raw data needed can quickly exceed the amount of data a bitmap format would need.

Consider a simple, gradient-filled square at a screen size of 1"×1" (at 72dpi screen resolution). To describe this shape, a vector format would only need to save the *x* and *y* coordinates for the four corners and the fill color. A bitmap image of the same shape would have to save color data for each of the 5184 pixels.

Another major advantage is scale and position flexibility. Again, the mathematical description lends itself very well to scaling and stretching. Because the image is rendered at run-time, you can easily alter the scale of the image and still have clear, smooth lines and fills. If you are going to be changing the scale of your graphics during game play, vector-based images may be the way to go.

Disadvantages

On the flip side (yes, there is always a flip side), the same mathematical description that makes vector graphics so flexible and download-friendly can be detrimental to performance. Because the image is re-created and rendered during run-time, it requires additional processing power to draw. This may not be a big concern if your graphics are simple or if they are sitting still, but moving a complex vector graphic around will bring even the most powerful machines to a hitchy crawl.

Bitmap Graphics

The other main type of graphics file is the bitmap. You can think of this type of file as a pixel map. The image is basically a description of each pixel in the file with entries for color (Red, Green, and Blue), referred to as RGB, and Alpha (if applicable), RGBA. There are other file types that use a four color format (Cyan, Magenta, Yellow, and Black), but four color formats are for printing. Because your computer screen displays color in combinations of Red, Green, and Blue, RGB format is better suited for games, so we'll stick with that.

Bitmap files are created with such programs as Photoshop, Fireworks, Painter, and so on. Some of the most common web-based file types are Compuserve Graphics Interchange Format (.GIF), Joint Photographic Experts Group format (.JPEG), and Portable Network Graphics (.PNG).

These types of files are not resolution-independent. You'll notice that the graphic in Figure 12.2 looks identical to the vector graphic when displayed at 100 percent, but the pixels become noticeable if we zoom into a small part.

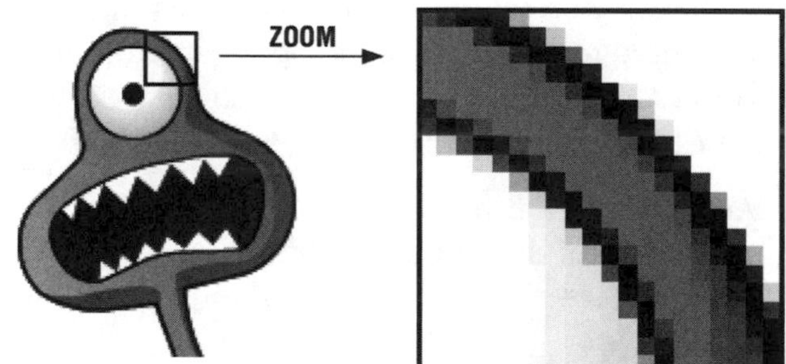

FIGURE 12.2
In a bitmap image, the line quality is not preserved when zoomed or sized.

Advantages

The major advantage to using bitmap files is performance. In most action games, I need to move graphics around very quickly, and the bitmap file format serves this purpose well. Bitmap graphics generally perform better than vector graphics because the bitmap graphic does not require the complex software rendering needed to reconstruct the image that vector graphics require. Because a bitmap's data is stored on a pixel basis, it's already in a format that is ready for the playback engine to draw. Also, bitmap rendering is largely a function of the graphics card.

This means that the bulk of the rendering process can be done by the hardware, which is far faster than software-rendered graphics such as line work or vector art that are handled by the CPU.

Bitmaps should, when possible, be placed on screen at even pixel positions for best performance. If an image is not placed on an even pixel or rotated on the Stage, it must be interpolated by the playback engine before drawing, which is very processor-intensive.

Bitmaps also offer the advantage of image complexity. Because the image is described with a pixel map, the complexity of the image itself does not affect performance. Photo-realism, complex shading, and tiny details are feasible with bitmaps.

Disadvantages

Bitmaps look and perform well at a 100 percent zoom level and when placed on even pixels. But if you need to deviate from this, you will see a significant drop off in both performance and image quality. It is not uncommon to want a graphic to zoom in or rotate; in these cases, a vector graphic may be the right choice.

Also, file sizes can quickly get out of hand when using large, complicated bitmaps. We'll discuss bitmap compression later in this chapter.

So, both vector and bitmap graphics are valuable tools in game development. You do not have to choose one over the other. Do not be afraid to use the both together in your games. Leveraging their individual strengths and understanding their weaknesses can help you push the envelope and make some killer games.

Various File Types

There are many file types for graphics, including GIF, JPEG, PNG, BMP, TIF, TGA, PICT, and so on. The list goes on and on, but when talking about Flash game graphics, there are really three big players: GIF, JPG, and PNG. Using the correct file type for your bitmaps is important because while you need your game to look great, you also need it to perform well. Understanding the graphics file options and using the appropriate types can help you get the most out of them.

Graphics Interchange Format (GIF). GIF is an indexed file type. This means that instead of the bitmap containing RGB information for the file, it contains an index lookup for a color pallet. The pallet can contain up to 256 color entries, including one for transparency. The GIF format was developed specifically for creating very small web graphics and is ideal for images with few colors and large areas of solid colors. The GIF format is considered "lossless" because the compression does not alter the file.

Joint Photographic Experts Group (JPEG). JPEG or JPG files are true-color (24-bit) files. These are ideal for saving web-based images such as photos or anything with smooth gradients or soft edges. JPEG is a lossy format and achieves file compression by interpolating image data. This is very effective at compressing full color images such as photos but doesn't handle crisp edges such as text or lines very well.

Portable Network Graphics (PNG). PNG files come in both flavors, PNG-8 and PNG-24. PNG-8 is an indexed file format and offers the same features as GIF files with the added benefit of semi-transparent alpha capabilities. PNG-24 is a true-color format like JPEG but does not use lossy compression. The main advantage to the 24-bit PNG file is that it offers the option for an 8-bit alpha channel (256 degrees of transparency). Both PNG formats are very effective for creating soft drop shadows or semi-transparent images for your games. The 8-bit, indexed version is preferred for graphics with large areas of flat colors, while the 24-bit, true-color version is preferred for images that are more photographic in style.

Don't worry about the lack of compression with 24-bit PNG files; Flash has the capability to use JPEG compression on these files, achieving good compression while maintaining your alpha channels.

Choose your bitmap file format and compression setting based on a balance of features, file size and image quality. Run-time performance is not impacted by your saved graphics types. All bitmaps are decompressed and converted to a true-color format before run-time rendering.

The characteristics of the various formats are summarized in Table 12.1.

TABLE 12.1 **Characteristics of Various Graphics File Formats**

Characteristics	GIF	PNG-8	JPG	PNG-24
Best For	Graphical images such as illustrations, icons, text, and so on.	Graphical images such as illustrations, icons, text, and so on where semi-transparent areas are needed.	Photographs or images with soft color transitions or gradients and transparencies	Photographs or images with soft color transitions or gradients.
Compression	Lossless. Image is compressed by removing duplicate pixel data. Reducing image colors can increase compression ratios.	Lossless. Image is compressed by removing duplicate pixel data. Reducing image colors can increase compression ratios.	Lossy. Image is compressed by removing image and color data, resulting in loss of image quality.	Lossless. Uses Flashed JPG compression.
Colors	Indexed. 8-Bits/256 colors or less.	Indexed. 8-Bits/256 colors or less.	24-Bit/ Millions of colors.	24-Bit/ Millions of colors.
Alpha	1-Bit/pixels can be either fully opaque or fully transparent.	256 levels of transparency per color pallet index.	No alpha support.	8-Bit/256 levels of transparency.

Compression

Using the Internet as a distribution network for your games means that you have to be concerned with file sizes. Even today, as more and more broadband users are surfing the web, a very significant portion of your audience still dials in with a modem. This means that the size of your files is a significant concern. Flash is an extremely efficient means by which you can deliver your games, but even with Flash's amazing capability to publish small files, it's mostly up to you to prepare your images cleverly so that Flash can do its job.

Compression Schemes

There are two main categories of image compression: lossless, such as GIF and PNG, and lossy, such as JPEG. Both are valuable methods with their own specialties. They compliment each other, and the usefulness of each depends on the specific graphic being compressed.

Lossless

Lossless compression does not omit original quality to save space. This style of compression removes duplicate pixel data and can recreate the pixels exactly as they were originally. This compression method works best with graphics that have large, solid areas of the same color or few colors overall. To get an idea of how lossless compression works, take a look at a single row of pixels in Figure 12.3. An uncompressed file would describe each pixel color, but with lossless compression, the pixel data can be abbreviated. This is the same style of compression used for data files, faxes, and so on.

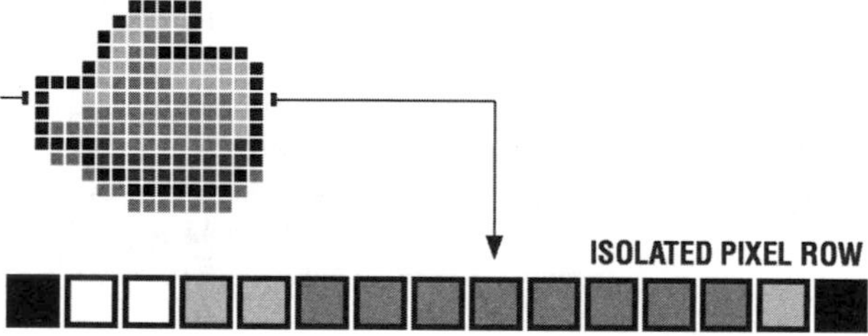

FIGURE 12.3
A single row of pixels can be abbreviated.

The following lists show you how the color data can be abbreviated:

Pixel Data before compression:

BLACK

WHITE

WHITE

LIGHT RED

LIGHT RED

DARK RED

DARK RED

DARK RED

DARK RED

DARK RED

DARK RED

DARK RED

DARK RED

LIGHT RED

BLACK

Pixel Data After compression:

BLACK

WHITE × 2

LIGHT RED × 2

DARK RED × 8

LIGHT RED

BLACK

Notice how much more efficient the compressed file is. Apply this procedure to an entire file, and you end up with considerable reduction in file size.

Generally, when talking about web graphics such as GIF and PNG-8, this type of compression is applied to indexed image files with colors reduced to anywhere from 2 to 256 colors. Indexed image files use a color table to store the color data and a lookup in that table for each pixel entry. This can save a lot of file space because only the index needs to be saved for each pixel rather than the RGB values, but it limits you to the number of colors available for your image. An indexed file's color table can contain anywhere from 2 to 256 color entries.

Lossy

Best used with photographic images, this compression scheme sacrifices image quality for file size. Hence the term "lossy," as you lose image quality. The amount of compression can be significant while maintaining high image quality, but using too much lossy compression will result in blurry and un-crisp images. Figure 12.4 shows JPEG compression on a sample graphic. Notice the drop in file size and quality as we increase compression. You can experiment with this on your own game images to achieve the best balance, depending on your needs.

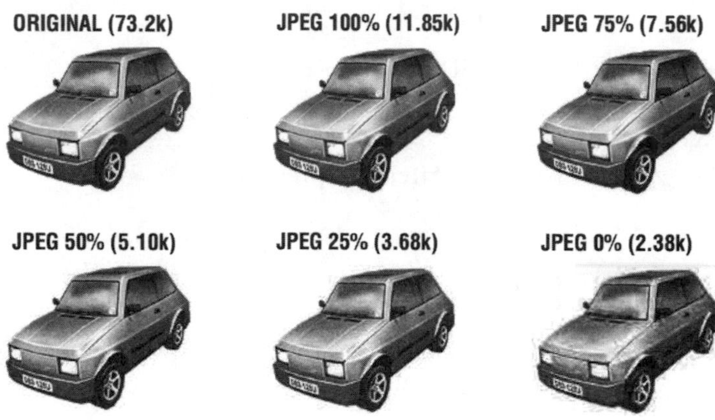

FIGURE 12.4
JPEG compression at various levels with resultant file sizes and image quality.

Only compress your images once. Trying to compress images that are already compressed (especially when lossy compression is used) will only result in lowering the quality. Always start with a high-quality image.

Using Flash's Compression Settings

Flash provides compression settings in the Bitmap Properties dialog box. The different graphics in your game will probably have different compression tolerances or needs. Rather than using the global image compression in the Publishing setting for your movie, for the best balance of compression and quality, treat each image individually, adjusting compression on a case-by-case basis through the Bitmap Properties dialog box. Let's have a look at the Bitmap Properties panel (see Figure 12.5).

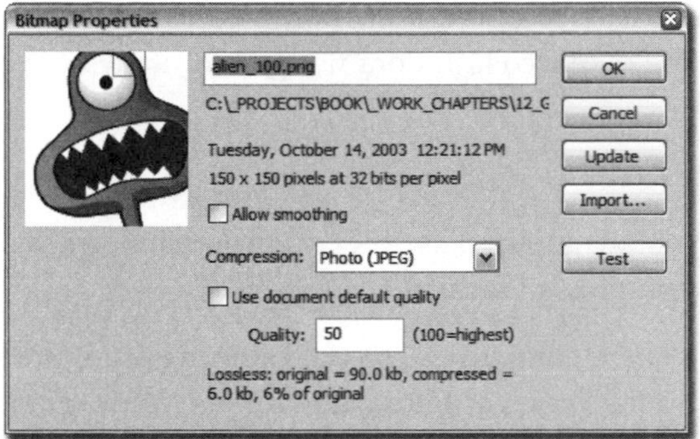

FIGURE 12.5
Bitmap Properties.

Special Considerations with Lossy (JPEG) Compression

If your graphics are to be compressed using JPEG compression, then it is recommended that you import your image files in the uncompressed PNG-24 format. By starting with the highest-quality image possible, you'll have the flexibility to experiment with compression settings in Flash. Also, using JPEG is a lossy compression method and it is never a good idea to double-compress your images. If you were to import an already-compressed JPEG file, Flash will compress it again when published, leaving you with an image that won't look nearly as good as it could.

When importing bitmaps suitable for JPEG compression, it is generally best to start with a high-quality, uncompressed file such as a 24bit PNG and adjust compression within Flash. This will give you the flexibility during testing to fine-tune compression on an image-by-images basis.

Special Considerations with Lossless (PNG, GIF) Compression

When working with files that you plan to use lossless compression with such as GIF or PNG, you may have more control over optimization in the program you are creating the image in, such as Photoshop,

ImageReady or Fireworks. This way, you can fine-tune the file before importing because Flash does not give you any options for optimizing these files.

Remember:

- If you are going to use JPEG compression, import the file in a 24-bit, uncompressed format.
- If you are going to use lossless compression, precompress the file in a program such as Photoshop, ImageReady, or Fireworks, then import the compressed file.

PERFORMANCE

Sometimes (more often than not), your game will need a graphic to move quickly and smoothly across the screen. This could be as simple as a custom cursor or as complicated as an entire background for a side-scrolling game. Achieving smooth movement can make or break a game. I have seen many shooter games, for example, that seem clunky and immature simply because the target cursor herks and jerks as you move the mouse to aim. This is one of the most common yet easiest performance issues to resolve. We'll explore this and some other performance techniques in this section.

Optimize Your Images

The first step in achieving maximum performance is efficient graphics. Rendering your game graphics to the screen is the most common cause of performance problems in any game where images are moving around. It is important when planning your game to consider the performance issues associated with your game design. Planning a game for performance in the beginning is a lot easier than trying to fix performance problems later in the process.

Although there are numerous ways to maximize performance, the main trick is to be sensible about your design. Smaller graphics render faster than large ones, and the more you move each frame, the longer the drawing process will take. If you are trying to achieve smooth motion at 30 frames per second, the frame will have to render in 1/30th of a second, or you will notice hitchy performance. With that in mind, try to keep too much from happening on the screen at once. A few smaller, well-placed images can give the same effect as one large image.

As we mentioned earlier in this chapter, the vector/bitmap question comes into play when discussing performance. Generally, bitmaps perform better because their data is in a format that doesn't require as much processing to be drawn to the screen. If you are planning a game with realistic 3D rendered graphics that cannot be accomplished with a vector file format, be sure to design the game so that these graphics can be displayed at 100 percent. On the other hand, if you need a graphic to zoom in and fly by the screen, this element should be designed as simply as possible so that the vector format can be used without creating a performance problem.

Simplify Vectors

Vector-based graphics can also be optimized for performance. The simple fact is that the more detail in your vector graphics, the more time the rendering process will require. So simplify. The most efficient way to have fast-rendering vector graphics is to start with efficient drawings. Using the drawing tools available in Flash is often the best approach to creating game-friendly vector graphics. However, this is not always possible. You may need more powerful drawing tools to create your images, or you may be provided with images from an artist you are working with in some other format such as AI or EPS. Either way, you'll want them to be as optimized as possible. Using Flash's Optimize Curves feature (see Figure 12.6), you can effectively simplify complex vector shapes, often without any noticeable effects.

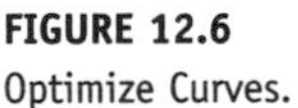

FIGURE 12.6
Optimize Curves.

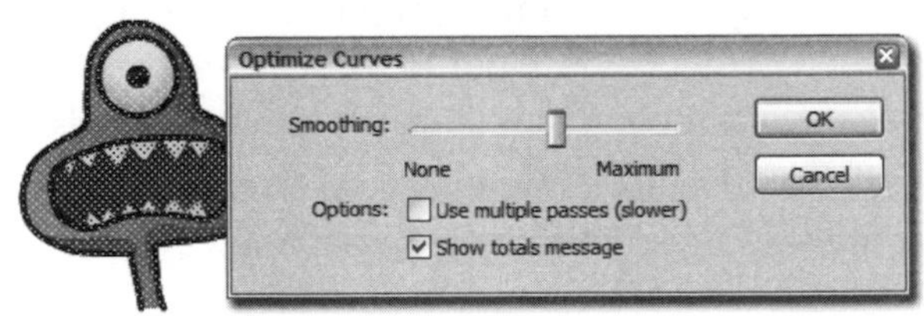

Alpha Channels

The alpha channel represents the transparency of your image. When Flash is rendering your graphics to the screen, anything that is not either completely opaque or completely transparent requires additional processing to render. This includes any soft edges or semi-transparent areas in your vector or bitmap graphics. Granted, if you don't have any soft or anti-aliased edges in your graphics, your game won't look as good and polished as it could, but keeping this potential performance drain in mind and using semi-transparent graphics wisely can save some performance for other game features.

Anti-Aliasing

Anti-aliasing is essentially the smoothing of the edges of your graphics or text. To fully understand anti-aliasing, let's begin with an understanding of aliasing. Aliasing is the effect where the edges of text, curves, and lines are displayed in terms of jagged horizontal and vertical segments that can look more like tiny steps than a smooth line. Anti-aliasing is the solution to this, whereby the edges are interpolated and visually smoothed by averaging the in-between pixels along the edges of the shape. Anti-aliasing is the default for Flash graphics but can be controlled individually for text objects. Small fonts may look sharper and more readable when not anti-aliased.

Bitmap Smoothing

Uncheck the smoothing option for better performance. Plan and prepare your bitmaps to not require any smoothing. Every little bit helps, and these little performance tricks add up.

Flash has the option to smooth bitmap images. This feature is found in the Bitmap Properties dialog box, along with the image compression settings (refer to Figure 12.5). For best performance, it is best to uncheck this feature. Smoothing your bitmaps enables Flash to interpolate the image for smooth rendering at any scale or position. This is useful in some cases where your image cannot be at the optimal 100 percent and at an even pixel position, but in most cases, if you have planned your game to avoid these potential performance hazards, enabling Flash to smooth your bitmaps can unnecessarily use valuable processor resources with unnoticeable results.

Optimize Your Code

Graphics performance can also be optimized through efficient coding. As I mentioned earlier, the main drag on performance in games is moving graphics around. If Flash has to interpolate a bitmap image file for rendering at an uneven pixel position, it will require significantly more processor recourses to accomplish the rendering task. Not only that, but it won't look nearly as good as the original.

One of the most common and noticeable instances of this is when a graphic is moved along with the mouse. In an aiming game, for example, where a gun or crosshair is moved with the cursor, it is desirable for the aiming graphic to move smoothly with the user's motion. Because the user can move the mouse very swiftly, the graphic must also move swiftly, or it will be painfully noticeable.

If using a bitmap graphic for the aimer, let's say a gun and crosshair, simply translating the position of the graphic to the mouse position will result in poor performance. This is because the mouse position in Flash is returned up to 8 decimal places; thus, a graphic placed at this location will not be at an even pixel position and must be interpolated in an extra rendering step before being drawn to the screen.

To work around this, simply convert the mouse position to an even pixel before translating the graphic.

```
_root.aimerClip._x = Math.floor(_root._xmouse);
_root.aimerClip._y = Math.floor(_root._ymouse);
```

The `Math.floor()` function executes much faster than rendering interpolation. Use this wherever you move your bitmaps, and you'll notice a significant performance boost.

It is also important to position your bitmaps at an even pixel position within your movie clips. When you create a new movie clip and drag and drop a bitmap from the Library, its initial position will likely need to be adjusted (see Figure 12.7). Depending on the usage of the graphic, you can line it up with the movie clip's registration point wherever you like, but adjusting a little one way or the other to achieve an even pixel position will help your performance a great deal.

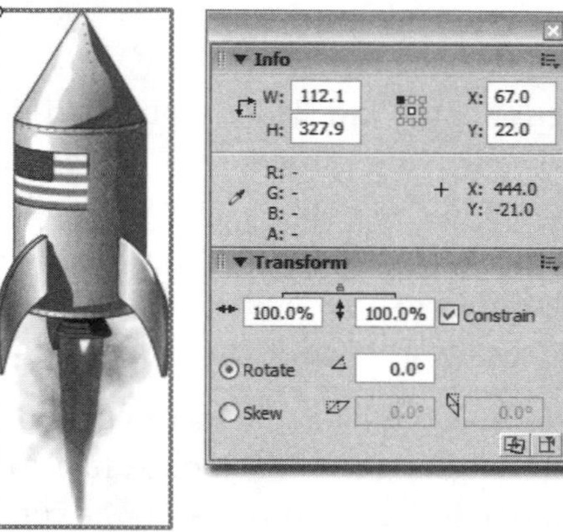

FIGURE 12.7
Adjusting position.

These optimizations may seem trivial, and you may not notice any difference with one graphic moving, but on slower machines or when your game animation gets intense, these optimizations will help to ensure stable performance.

LOADING GRAPHICS AT RUN-TIME

Rather than being locked into the images in your project's Library, it may be desirable to dynamically load graphical assets from a server during run-time. There are many advantages to doing this. For example, if your game has multiple levels, chocked full of stunning images, you may want to load graphics needed for later levels while the player is busy with level 1. This is a good way to increase the graphical impact of your games without making the player wait through an inconvenient initial load.

Another reason to use dynamic graphics is game flexibility. For game such as jigsaw puzzles or memory match games, you may want to pull graphics from the server as a means of easily updating the game without needing to recompile and upload your SWF. However, dynamically loading graphics doesn't always provide you with the options you have when using graphics from the Library. Flash only gives you the ability to load JPG or SWF files.

Let's take a quick look at how we dynamically load the graphics for this simple memory match game. The source file, memory_match.fla, is on the CD in the Chapter12 folder.

In this game, we've created a template movie clip named `card_template` and placed it on the Stage just off screen. This movie clip contains everything we need for the match game cards but the graphics. However, we have included two placeholder movie clips where the graphics will go. This is where we dynamically load the graphic files we have saved earlier.

The placeholder clips are called:

```
cardback_placeholder (Placeholder for the back of the card)
car_placeholder (Placeholder for the face of the card)
```

On frame 1, we include ActionScript that duplicates this movie clip for each card we need in the game and loads the appropriate external graphics file for each.

```
//IMPORT THE GRAPHICS
_root[cardname].card_placeholder.loadMovie(graphicname);
_root[cardname].cardback_placeholder.loadMovie(cardback);
```

This code is contained in a loop that duplicates the template card (`cardname`) and identifies graphic URLs for the variables `graphicname` and `cardback`. This is repeated for each card that we need.

Loading dynamic graphics is that simple and useful too. Experiment with the match game and create your own match games using these techniques.

POINTS TO REMEMBER

- Use both vector and bitmap graphics, depending on your specific graphic needs.
- Process your indexed GIFs and PNGs before importing into Flash for maximum control.
- When lossy JPEG compression is to be used, import uncompressed 24-bit files and use Flash to compress (compress only once).

- Use JPEG compression on 24-bit PNGs with alpha channels to get both good compression and various levels of transparencies for images that are photographic in nature.
- The PNG-8 format offers a good solution for images with few or large areas of similar colors where varying levels of transparencies are needed.
- Optimize your vector graphics too. You'll see better performance with less complicated shapes.
- Semi-transparent graphics and anti-aliased edges perform worse than solids. Use them wisely.
- Avoid unnecessary smoothing of your bitmaps.
- Place bitmaps at even pixel positions within your game, and keep them at 100 percent scale wherever possible.
- Dynamically loading graphical assets at run-time is a good way to add flexibility or to manage downloads.
- Every little bit helps. Optimize for performance and file size wherever possible, and it will add up.

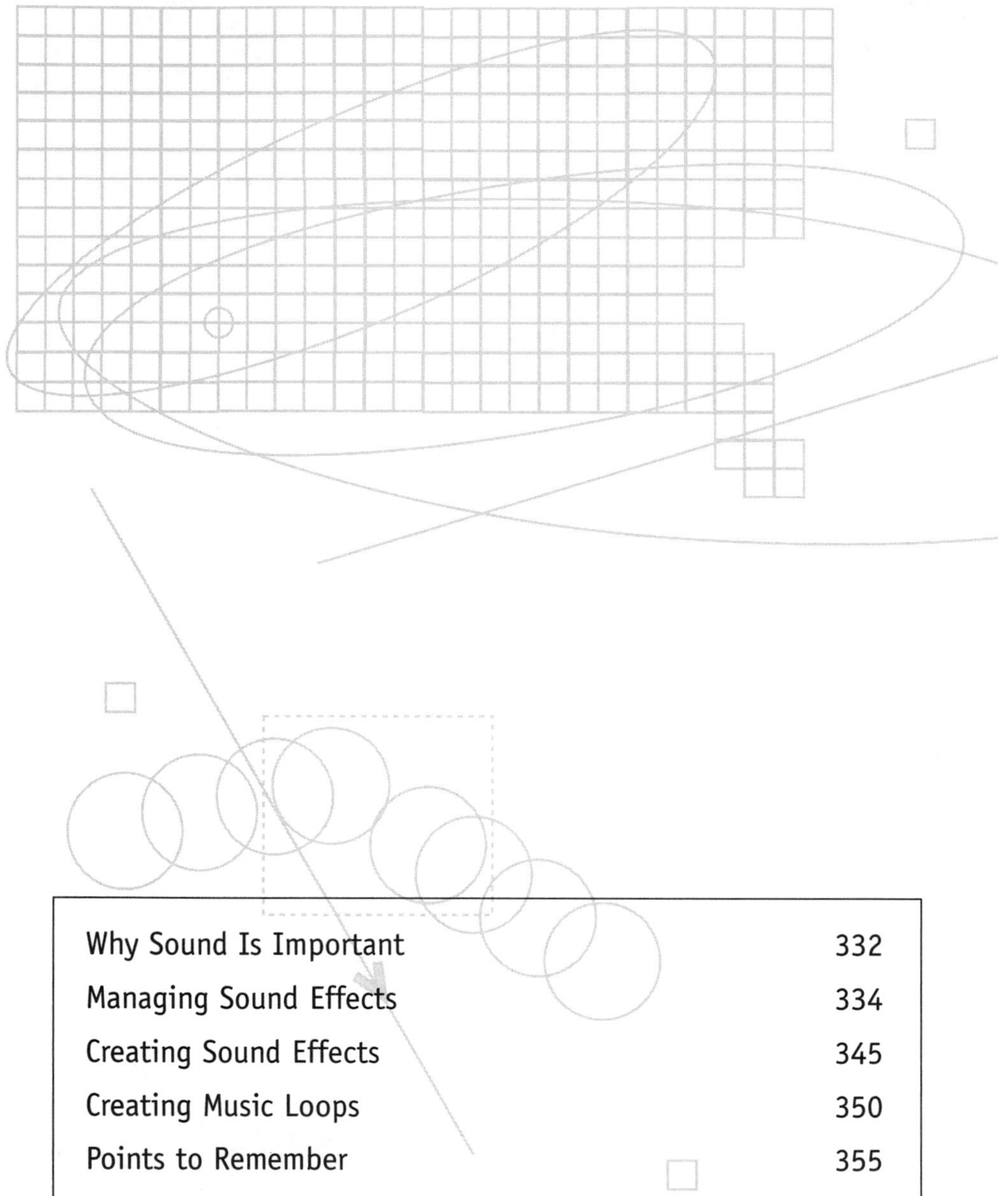

Why Sound Is Important 332
Managing Sound Effects 334
Creating Sound Effects 345
Creating Music Loops 350
Points to Remember 355

CHAPTER 13

THE SOUND OF GAMES

SOUND IS PROBABLY THE MOST NEGLECTED AREA OF FLASH GAME DESIGN. Between hatching a game idea, creating the graphical assets, programming, and debugging, it's not surprising that not much time is devoted to finding or making the perfect sounds. Sound effects and music add a lot to a game—much more than you may realize. Sounds can connect with a person on an emotional level and invoke fear, excitement, surprise, sadness, or playfulness. Used properly, sound effects and music can make a good game extraordinary. In this chapter, we discuss sound effects and music loops—how to make them and why sound should not be neglected in *your* games.

Why Sound Is Important

As you develop a game, there are three senses you can use to involve a game player: touch, sight, and sound. Until computers start emitting odors and flavors, those are all we have to work with. The visuals (sight) and the control (touch) of a game tend to get a lot of attention during game design and development. In this chapter, we focus our attention on the odd sense out, hearing. Sounds used in a game can be any of the following:

- **Songs**—Full-length musical compositions created or licensed for your game. Songs can play in the background during the game or be triggered to play after something happens (for example, winning the game).
- **Music loops**—Short pieces of music that play repeatedly. A music loop can range from about one second to several seconds in length, and they have a file size that is a fraction of that of a full song.
- **Sound effects**—Sounds triggered by the result of an action or synchronized with a visual event.
- **Voice**—Spoken-language clips recorded or licensed for your game. Voice can be used in animations before a game, throughout the game to show characters talking, or as a sound effect (for example, a person yelling "Ouch!" when struck by a sword).

Music and voice are not always necessary in your games, but sound effects definitely are. Here are the top three reasons why you should not neglect sound in your games:

- **Sounds can encourage the player to feel a certain way**—This is usually achieved through songs or music loops. For instance, in a murder mystery, eerie music would help most people get into the spirit of the game. If instead of eerie music, carnival music is playing, then the mood will be decidedly different. For a racing game, you would probably choose upbeat music—something that makes the players feel that they need to react quickly. Adding music is one major step in getting someone immersed in the game.

- **Sounds can evoke immediate emotional responses such as surprise, fear, and laughter**—To use the murder mystery example again, imagine you are sleuthing in a dark room, when suddenly a chandelier falls to the floor next to you. Unless you have your speakers turned off, this loud crash will probably startle you—a response intended by the game developer. Another, smaller-scale example of this is collecting coins in a typical side-scrolling adventure game like *Super Mario Brothers.* You may not jump for joy every time you collect a coin, but somehow that "ding" gives you a good feeling.
- **Sounds can convey information**—A sound can let you know that your character has just been hurt, or that a secret door has been opened, for example. Two of the most common uses of sound to convey information are to let you know that your character has just collected an item, and to give you an idea of how far away something is (depth).

Sometimes, if you play your cards right (so to speak), sounds can achieve two or more of these goals at the same time. For example, let's say you're playing a game in which you must solve a puzzle somewhere in a house. When you do, you get to open a locked door to another room, and a short, cheerful tune is played. The sound conveys the information, "Hey, you did something right!" as well as helps to elicit an emotional response of satisfaction or excitement.

After playing a good game, I rarely find myself thinking, "Wow, the sounds in this game are great!" This isn't because of bad sound; if the sounds are doing their job, then they will most likely not stand out. It's often the same in movies. In many scenes, frantic music enhances the suspense or action. You probably don't notice how much of an effect the sound has. If someone doesn't really notice the sound in your game, then the sound is most likely doing its job properly. More often than not, sounds that stand out are sounds that do not belong.

In the rest of this chapter, we will talk about how to use and create sound effects and loops and how to use ActionScript with sound files to create effects.

Managing Sound Effects

There are two ways to use sound effects in Flash. You can place a sound directly on a frame, or you can pull it from the Library with ActionScript using `attachSound()`. Using frames to hold your sounds is easy and predictable; the sound plays when that frame is reached. The advantage of using this technique is that you can control the volume and other sound properties in the authoring environment. With `attachSound()`, the sound can be started or stopped using ActionScript. Furthermore, you have control over the volume and panning of the sound in real-time. With sounds placed on a frame, however, you cannot change these properties (pan and volume) of the sound after they have been set in the authoring environment—the game player's actions are not going to affect the properties. In short, as always, there are advantages and trade-offs either way. In this section, we discuss both ways of using sound effects in your games through the use of several example files.

Sound Placed on Frames

It is important to use descriptive label names. For instance, if the sound file is named gunfire.wav, consider naming the label "gunfire." You may have three or four different gunfire sounds, and the capability to quickly identify one from another can save you a lot of time and confusion.

I've seen the source files for many Flash games over the last few years, and one thing I often find is that people put their sounds all over the place. It's ok to place your sounds within the specific movie clips that make them. This can actually be very helpful for action-based sounds that are timed to correspond to animations, but if you haphazardly place sounds in a hundred different clips, making any changes can be a disaster.

Using Flash's `Sound` object is a good way to keep your event-based sounds organized (we'll discuss that further later in this chapter), but if you want to use sounds that you can mix and edit in the Timeline and still call with code, a dedicated sounds movie clip can do the trick.

The technique is simple. We create a movie clip whose sole purpose is to hold sounds. There is one sound on each frame. Each frame has a frame label and an action that sends the playhead in that movie clip back to frame 1. We then create a function outside of this movie clip, which I usually call `playSound()`. This function accepts a parameter that should be the name of the sound or the label of the frame that needs to be played. It then tells the sound effects movie clip to play that specific frame. That's it!

On/Off Toggles

Now—because it's so easy, and because I want to introduce you to it before we jump into the example file—let's set up the toggle. As you can guess, a sound on/off toggle is a button that a game player can click to turn the game sound on and off. If you spend a lot of time finding the best sounds for your game, then you probably want people to hear them (and they probably want to, too). But the truth is (sssshhh!) that many players will play your game over the Internet when they are in the office, and they won't want anyone to hear that they aren't working. There are plenty of other situations in which a person might not want the sound to play. So all in all, it's a good idea to provide the game player a way to turn the sound on and off.

Let's look at an example. Open missiles.fla in the Chapter13 directory. This is a simple game (never completed). The triangle at the bottom of the screen is a ship. You can move the ship left and right with the left and right arrow keys, and you can make it fire a shot vertically by pressing the spacebar. The object is to shoot as many bubbles as possible. In this file, we only have two sounds—the sound of the ship firing and the sound of a bubble popping. To the left of the Stage you will see a movie clip called soundFX.

Double-click this movie clip to look inside. There are three layers in it. You can ignore the bottom layer, Text. It is only there so that we can find the movie clip on the Stage. Without the text inside this movie clip, we would have a hard time locating it. The top layer, Labels, contains two frame labels, shoot and pop. The layer in the middle, Actions, contains actions on three frames. On frame 1, there is just a `stop()` action, so the movie clip doesn't play until told to do so. The actions on the two labeled frames are the same: `this.gotoAndStop(1)`. When a sound plays, the playhead immediately moves back to frame 1 and waits for further instructions.

At the top of frame 1 on the main Timeline, you'll find the function `playSound()`:

```
function playSound(name) {
      if (soundOn) {
            soundFX.gotoAndPlay(name);
      }
}
```

This function accepts a parameter called name. This is also the label of the frame we want to play. An if statement in this function checks to see if the sound toggle is on or off. The Boolean variable soundOn = true is on frame 1, just before this function. That sets the sound toggle to "on." If that value ever becomes false, the function ends without advancing to the frame and playing the sound. In line 3 of this function, we tell the soundFX movie clip to go to a certain frame to play a sound. This is a very useful technique. We can now add as many sounds as we want to the soundFX movie clip and then play those sounds very easily.

Select the Ship movie clip at the bottom of the Stage, and if it's not already open, open the Actions panel. On line 19 of the ActionScript, you will see the action _root.playSound("shoot"). This action is executed when the script shoots a missile (that is, when the spacebar is pressed). Now select the instance of the Bubble movie clip and open the Actions panel. On line 12 of the ActionScript, you will see _root.playSound("pop"). This calls for the pop sound to be played when the bubble detects that it has been hit with a missile.

There is a button in the bottom-right of the screen called Toggle Sound. This button has been programmed to toggle the sound on and off. Remember that the sound is considered on if soundOn has a value of true, and off if soundOn has a value of false. Here is the ActionScript on this button:

```
1    on (press) {
2         soundOn =!soundOn;
3    }
```

The action in line 2 is executed when the Toggle Sound button is clicked. The action used here is a quick shortcut that is commonly used for toggling Boolean values. What you see to the right of the = sign is called a *ternary operator*. That means it's an operator with three operands, which are (in this case) soundOn, false, and true. This is a conditional statement. If the first operand has a value of true, then the entire statement takes the value of the second operand; otherwise, it takes the value of the third operand. This is equivalent to our having written an if statement like this:

```
on (press) {
     if (soundOn) {
          soundOn = false;
```

```
        } else {
            soundOn = true;
        }
    }
```

The one-line conditional statement syntax is used occasionally through the games programmed in the third section of this book. It's an easy way to toggle a value in one line of code instead of using the more intricate if/else statement.

Setting Volume for Frame-Based Sounds

Just because you are using frame-based sounds doesn't mean you don't have any control over how they are played. Using the Sound object with your soundFX movie clip can extend this method and give you specific control over basic attributes such as volume and pan. Let's look at a method for controlling volume this way.

First, set up the Sound object for your soundFX movie clip. To do this, create a new sound object for your soundFX movie instance. Also define variables for the desired minimum and maximum allowed volumes.

```
        root.sndObj = new Sound("soundFX");
        soundFX.max_volume = 100;
        soundFX.min_volume = 0;
```

Now, any sounds that play in that movie clip are governed by the `sndObj` that we set up. Let's make a couple buttons to turn the volume up or down. This example will increase the volume by 10. Use the `Math.min()` function to top it off at the max.

```
    on(release){
        var current_volume =_root.sndObj.getVolume();
        var new_volume = Math.min(_root. soundFX.max_volume,
        ➥current_volume+10);
        root.sndObj.setVolume(new_volume);
    }
```

Respectively, to decrease the volume by 10, the code would be pretty much the same, except that we subtract 10 rather than add it. This time, use the `Math.max()` function to limit the range to the minimum.

```
    on(release){
        var current_volume =_root.sndObj.getVolume();
```

```
        var new_volume = Math.max(_root.
        ➥soundFX.mix_volume, current_volume-10);
        root.sndObj.setVolume(new_volume);
}
```

That's it! You have just seen a very simple technique for adding sounds to games. In the next section, we'll show another technique for adding sounds to games that gives you a bit more control using ActionScript.

Sound Controlled with ActionScript

To control a sound with ActionScript, you pull it from the Library and attach it to a sound object using `attachSound()`. To pull a sound from the Library, you must give it a linkage identifier, just as you would do with a movie clip when it's to be used with the `attachMovie()` function (as we discussed in Chapter 5, "Collision Detection"). The advantage of using ActionScript to control sounds rather than placing them on a frame is that ActionScript gives you much more control. You can change the sound's volume or pan at any time. Also, you do not have to start playing a sound at its beginning—you can start it at any place. For instance, you can start a sound that is four seconds long at the third second, and as a result, you'll hear just the last second of the sound. In this section, we will look at three examples of controlling sounds with ActionScript.

Controlling Sound Based on Object Speed

For our first example, open ball.fla from the Chapter13 directory on the CD. In this file, you'll see a ball and four walls. The ball has been given an initial velocity, and it falls under gravity. The result is a ball that bounces off the walls, much as a basketball would, eventually stopping. This file uses a sound effect called bounce.wav, with a linkage identifier named bounce. The sound's volume depends on how hard the ball hits each wall. The *pan* of the sound—that is, the amount and volume that the sound plays in each speaker—depends on the ball's *x* position. You've already seen the ActionScript used to bounce the ball around in Chapter 4, "Basic Physics," Chapter 5, "Collision Detection," and Chapter 6, "Collision Reactions." What is new in this file is the function called `playSound()`, for which the ActionScript is shown here.

```
1     function playSound(x, speed) {
2           if (soundOn) {
3                 var ballX = x-left;
4                 var factor = ballX/(right-left);
5                 var pan = -100+factor*200;
6                 var maxSpeed = 15;
7                 var minSpeed = 1;
8                 speed = Math.abs(speed);
9                 var factor = speed/(maxSpeed-minSpeed);
10                if (speed<minSpeed) {
11                      var factor = 0;
12                }
13                var vol = factor*100;
14                if (vol>0) {
15                      bounce = new Sound();
16                      bounce.attachSound("bounce");
17                      bounce.setPan(pan);
18                      bounce.setVolume(vol);
19                      bounce.start();
20                }
21          }
22    }
```

This function is called whenever a collision is detected. The *x* position of the ball is passed into this function so that we can determine how much to pan the sound. The speed of the ball when it collided with the wall is also passed into this function so that we can determine the volume needed. The speed passed in is the speed affected by the collision. For example, when the ball hits the floor, we pass in the *y* speed (not shown) because the *x* speed is unaffected. In line 3, we set a variable called `ballX`. The *x* position passed into this function is the ball's *x* position on the main Stage. What we need to know in order to properly set the pan is the ball's *x* position with respect to the walls. The variable `ballX` stores the position of the ball with respect to the left wall. In line 4, we set a variable called `factor`. The concept illustrated here is a very useful one called *normalization*. The variable factor is a *normalized* number; that means it will always be between 0 and 1. We are looking for the ball's distance from the left wall in normalized terms. If `factor` is 1, then the ball is all the way over on the right wall; if it is 0, then the ball is on the left wall. If it is between 0 and 1, then the ball is somewhere in between the two walls. You find a normalized value by taking the value you want to normalize, in this case `ballX`, and dividing it by its maximum possible value, which in this case is the total distance between the left and right walls.

Next, we set a variable called `pan` to store the pan amount (line 5). A `pan` of –100 means that all of the sound comes out of the left speaker, and a `pan` of 100 means that the sound comes completely out of the right speaker, for a total possible difference of 200 between left pan and right pan. We can set the pan value by starting with –100 and adding to it the value of `factor*200`. If `factor` is 1, then `pan` is 100, so the sound will play from the right speaker. If `factor` is 0, then `pan` is –100, and the sound will play completely from the left speaker.

In lines 6–9, we determine another factor variable, this one for speed. We will use this normalized number to determine the volume settings. If `factor` is 1, then the volume is maximum; if `factor` is 0, the volume is minimum. We use the current speed and the maximum speed allowed to determine the `factor` variable. Finally, in lines 15–19, we create a sound object (line 15), attach the bounce sound to that object (line 16), set the pan of the sound (line 17), set the volume of the sound (line 18), and finally play the sound (line 19).

Generate an SWF from this file. You can see that the volume is dependent on the speed at which the ball collides with the wall. Also notice how the pan changes with the position of the ball.

Controlling Sound Based on Factors Other Than Speed

For the next example, open billiard_ball.fla in the Chapter13 directory. This file was taken directly from Chapter 6 and modified to play a sound when a collision occurs. In this section, I'm going to show how you can dynamically change the volume of the sound based on information other than speed. In the case of a ball bouncing off a wall, the volume is dependent on the speed of the ball. However, imagine two billiard balls moving very quickly in the same direction. If ball 1 is just a little bit faster than ball 2, then it may catch up and collide with ball 2. However, even though these two balls are moving very quickly, that doesn't mean the collision should be loud because they may just barely collide. Instead of using speed, we will look at the *change* in speed. The volume of the sound is completely based on the difference between the speed before the collision and the speed after the collision.

Here is the playSound() function:

```
1     function playSound(speedDiff) {
2           if (soundOn) {
3                 var maxSpeed = 5;
4                 var factor = speedDiff/maxSpeed;
5                 var volume = 100*factor;
6                 hit = new Sound();
7                 hit.attachSound("hit");
8                 hit.setVolume(volume);
9                 hit.start();
10          }
11    }
```

In line 3, we set a variable called maxSpeed with a value of 5. The value tells the script to play the sound at maximum volume when the speed difference hits that amount (and of course you can alter that value to suit yourself). Right now, if a speed difference of 5 occurs on a collision, then we will hear the volume at its maximum. Let's look at the two lines of code that call this function, inside the ball2BallReaction() function:

```
1     var speedDiff = Math.sqrt((b1.xmov-xVel1)*(b1.xmov-xVel1)
      ➥+(b1.ymov-yVel1)*(b1.ymov-yVel1));
2     playSound(speedDiff);
```

In line 1, we use the Pythagorean theorem (the distance equation) to find out the difference between the speed before the collision and the speed after the collision. This value is then passed into the playSound() function (line 2).

Generate an SWF to verify for yourself that this works properly. Go back to the FLA file and change some of the velocity variables; keep retesting to convince yourself that this method works well. You can use this dynamic volume technique with a game of pool or any other game where two moving objects collide at potentially varying speeds.

Volume Controlled Through Acceleration

Until now, we've been talking about simple speed. Now, in our third example, we'll add acceleration into the mix and outline a simple technique used for acceleration and deceleration in racing games. Imagine a car sitting at the starting line in a racing game. When it's time to start driving, you must accelerate, and an acceleration sound plays. What happens if, during the middle of the acceleration, you decide to decelerate? Well, you need to play a deceleration sound. Sounds easy enough, right? The problem is that the sound of the deceleration would be different depending on how fast the car was moving when you started to decelerate.

Open car.fla in the Chapter13 directory. In this example, we show how to handle race car–driving sounds from idle (not moving) to maximum speed and how to handle the sounds for acceleration or deceleration at any time. This is done with four sounds:

- A loop played for the idle.
- A loop played for the car when it is at maximum speed.
- An acceleration sound that plays from idle all the way up to maximum speed.
- A deceleration sound that plays from maximum speed all the way down to idle.

The acceleration and deceleration sounds are the same length. (In fact, the deceleration sound was actually made by reversing the acceleration sound in a sound-editing program.)

When the car accelerates, we play the acceleration sound. When the player instructs the car to decelerate, we check to see the position of the acceleration sound. We then use this information to figure out where to start the deceleration sound. Likewise, if while decelerating the player instructs the car to accelerate, we check the current position of the deceleration sound and use that information to determine where to start the acceleration sound.

Got that? Now let's inspect the ActionScript. First we use the following actions to create a sound object for each of the four sounds and to attach a sound to each object:

```
accel = new Sound();
accel.attachSound("accel");
decel = new Sound();
decel.attachSound("decel");
hi_loop = new Sound();
hi_loop.attachSound("hi_loop");
low_loop = new Sound();
low_loop.attachSound("low_loop");
```

And here are the functions that play the sounds:

```
1     function playAccel(offset) {
2            accel.setVolume(vol);
3            accel.start(offset);
4            accel.onSoundComplete = accelDone;
5            playing = "accel";
6     }
7     function playDecel(offset) {
8            decel.setVolume(vol);
9            decel.start(offset);
10           decel.onSoundComplete = decelDone;
11           playing = "decel";
12    }
13    function accelDone() {
14           accel.stop();
15           hi_loop.setVolume(vol);
16           hi_loop.start(0, 100000);
17    }
18    function decelDone() {
19           decel.stop();
20           low_loop.setVolume(vol);
21           low_loop.start(0, 100000);
22    }
```

The first function, playAccel(), is used to play the acceleration sound. All of these functions accept a parameter called offset that is used to offset the starting point of the sound they control. If the duration of the sound is 10 seconds and the offset is 3 seconds, then the ActionScript will skip the first 3 seconds of the sound and start playing it immediately. In line 4, we set an event handler for the acceleration sound. When that sound is finished playing, it calls the function accelDone(). This enables us to easily tell when the acceleration has finished playing, so we know when to start playing the maximum-speed sound loop. On line 7, the next function, playDecel(), plays the deceleration sound. When it has finished playing, it calls the function decelDone() so that the idle sound loop can start playing. These onSoundComplete events only fire if the sound is allowed to reach completion. If, for instance, the acceleration sound is stopped before it has finished playing, then accelDone() will not be called.

The final part of the ActionScript in this file captures all the user actions and handles the starting and stopping of sounds that result from those user actions. It also includes the controls for the bar, which is not really related to the functioning of the sounds.

```
_root.onEnterFrame = function() {
	if (playing == "decel" || playing == null) {
		bar._yscale = (1-
		➥decel.position/decel.duration)*100;
		if (Key.isDown(Key.UP)) {
			if (playing == null) {
				var start = 0;
			} else {
				var start = (accel.duration-
				➥decel.position)/1000;
			}
			decel.stop();
			low_loop.stop();
			playAccel(start);
		}
	}
	if (playing == "accel" || playing == null) {
		bar._yscale =
		➥accel.position/accel.duration*100;
		if (Key.isDown(Key.DOWN)) {
			if (playing == null) {
				var start = 0;
			} else {
				var start = (decel.duration-
				➥accel.position)/1000;
			}
			accel.stop();
			hi_loop.stop();
			playDecel(start);
		}
	}
};
```

This is an `onEnterFrame` event that executes two main conditional statements in every frame. They check to see if the car is currently accelerating or decelerating. If the car is decelerating (line 2), then the bar movie clip on the Stage is scaled to show what the car is doing. This movie clip has nothing to do with the sounds themselves; it is just giving us a visual idea of what is happening. The script then checks to see if the up arrow key is being pressed. If it is, the script starts the sound at position 0, or if the car is already in motion, it calculates what the sound offset should be. The *sound offset* is the reverse of the position of the deceleration sound. If the deceleration is 10 seconds long and is at the position of the third second, then the acceleration offset is 7 seconds. In lines 10 and 11, we stop sounds that could be playing, and in line 12, we start the deceleration sound by calling `playAccel()`. The second `if` statement (line 15) does the same thing as the first one, except that it checks to see if the car is currently accelerating. If the car is accelerating and the down arrow key is pressed, then the deceleration sound is played.

Generate an SWF from this file. Press the up arrow key. You should hear the car start to accelerate. If you let the acceleration reach maximum, then you will hear the maximum speed loop, hi_loop, start playing. At any time, you can press the down arrow key to have the deceleration sound kick in. If you let the deceleration continue to completion, the idle sound, low_loop, will play.

CREATING SOUND EFFECTS

If you are reading this, then you are probably not a professional sound designer. As such, you probably don't own a $2,000 microphone with tube preamp and top-notch digital conversion. However, chances are you do have a Sound Blaster card (from Creative Technology, Ltd.) or something similar and the $3 plastic microphone that came with your computer. This may very well be all you need to capture the necessary sound effects for your games. So let's set up shop! In the following section, we'll give you some practical advice from the trenches on proper setup, recording dos and don'ts, ways to make your own sounds, and where to find prerecorded sounds.

Setting Up

Before capturing sounds, take at least a few minutes to be sure that everything is set up properly for the task at hand. Make sure the microphone is properly plugged into your sound card and unmute the microphone in your sound manager/mixer. I recommend temporarily plugging in headphones where your speakers are because you are likely to spawn a feedback loop if you record while the speakers play back. (You are probably familiar with the loud shriek of feedback usually experienced at the high school dance or church picnic when someone points the microphone toward the speakers.) You can also just unplug the speakers while you record and then plug them back in later. It's up to you, but remember—they're *your* ears.

Use whatever sound-editing software you choose (see Appendix A, "Developer Resources"), and start by recording yourself speaking. Take note of how your microphone sounds, as this will be what determines how your sound effects will go into the computer. Does it pick up other sounds in the room? If so, try to isolate your recording area with blankets or any other reflection-absorbing (or echo-absorbing) material.

Also check proximity to the microphone—talk into it and note how close you are and what the sound is like at that point. For example, test as you move back in very small increments, saying, "Check 1 inch, check 3 inches, check 6 inches…" Most run-of-the-mill cheap computer microphones will not pick up much beyond 6 inches, depending on volume.

And that's the other big thing—volume. Set the volume level carefully so that you get your sound as loud as possible *without passing 0 dB* (usually indicated by a red line or clip on your decibel meter).

The Golden Rule of Digital Sound

Digital sound is measured in negative numbers going up to 0 dB (decibels). If the sound passes 0, digital clipping occurs. Digital clipping is like trying to run through a metal barred gate at top speed—and it sounds that bad, too, so the golden rule of digital recording is: Don't go over 0 dB! And don't be a cowboy thinking this is like *Ghostbusters* ("Don't cross the streams"). Even if the marshmallow monster is eating your sister, *don't* go over 0 dB. It might make a cool distortion sound on *your* computer, but it won't on most.

Recording

The second important rule of recording your own sounds (after the golden one discussed previously) is to always do several takes. Trust me: You may have absolutely nailed that punch-in-the-mouth sound effect, but the truth is, you don't know how good it really is until you've heard it over the background music and other sounds in your game. This is why you should have several takes to choose from. The more sound design you do, the more you realize how important it is to have several options. There are many complex factors at play when you start combining sounds (not to mention sound and animation), so don't be surprised if what you originally thought was the best take ends up being your worst, and vice versa. If there is only one take to choose from, then you could be in trouble.

Many beginners make the mistake of recording each take as a separate file. Although there is nothing wrong with this, the more productive way to go about it is to just hit Record and make your sound repeatedly in various fashions. This is where the editing software comes in really handy—you can just trim your big recording down to the parts you like and save/cut/paste the takes as separate files later.

When you're stockpiling takes, it's best to have a good variety, so if you usually swing from the right to make your swinging-punch sound, do two from the right and two from the left. Do two close to the microphone and two a little farther away. Again, you never know which will sound best until later, so it's better to have some choices.

"That's Not the Right Sound!"

I think we're all well aware that the punching sounds we hear in TV shows do not even closely resemble what a punch sounds like in real life. However, the way the mind perceives action in the two-dimensional world dictates that we need something a little more dramatic than the real thing to get the point across. This is the art of sound design—using your imagination to figure out how to give more emphasis or even depth to the sound (like in karate movies) so that the listener is right there with you. So don't be afraid to venture beyond the realm of what may seem logical and try a completely different sound to achieve what you're looking for.

Sound events in real life usually have a certain order, not just one simple sound. To make a punch sound more dramatic, we have a swinging sound followed by an impact sound, and maybe, to put the frosting on the cake, we add the "Uggh!" sound of the punch victim. These must be timed correctly in order to sound realistic. They may even have to overlap some. This brings us to the concept of *layered sounds.* A basketball game scene doesn't just have the sound of the ball bouncing. It may have squeaky sneakers, ball passes, bodies colliding, the crowd talking and cheering, and the like. The sounds all happen at different times, volume levels, and positions relative to the listener. Although the layering of sounds is really an advanced sound-design concept and is not for the faint-of-heart programmer who just needs a couple of sounds to add to the game, it still can be a very good thing to have in mind while you're designing.

Try to be consistent in matching the point of view with the acoustic space of your sounds. (It just doesn't work well to have a bar-scene punch followed by some guy yelling "Uggh!" in a hollow-sounding gymnasium.) Consider your scene carefully if you want effective sound in your game. Careful sound planning can pay off every bit as much as the hours spent perfecting subtleties in the GUI and gameplay.

The following are a few possibilities for home-grown sound effects that you may find helpful. Some are realistic, some are melodramatic and cartoony. It is up to the sound designer's imagination to effectively use these ideas and come up with more.

TABLE 12.1 **Sounds from Scratch**

Desired Sound	Materials with Which to Fake It
Arrow, swinging fist, or swinging anything	Swing various-sized sticks, wires, and so on about 6 inches from the microphone.
Bushes	Broom straw rustling.
Electric shock	Two blocks of wood covered in sandpaper; make one long stroke.
Boiling water	Use a straw to make bubbles in water.

Desired Sound	Materials with Which to Fake It
Crashes	Make a "crash box"—a wooden box (or cardboard for smaller crashes) filled with clangy metal things. Toss in some glass and even plastic containers for variety. Seal it up well, and beat it around to get the crash effect. If you were backstage in a live theater, you might see a 2-by-4-by-2-foot box attached to a crank that spins it.
Mud	Put some newspaper in a few inches of water and slosh around with your hands or feet.
Telephone voice	Use the equalizer in your sound-editing software to remove the bass. Some programs even have a preset for phone voice.
Fire	Open an umbrella really fast for a burst of flames. Crumple up thick cellophane near the microphone for the crackle.
Horses	Knock coconut shells together. Cover them with cloth for galloping on grass, and so on.
Gunshot	Slap a ruler against various surfaces, or fold a belt in half and snap it.
Thunder	The easiest, most common way of getting a large, boomy sound is to take a recorded sound (such as waving poster-board or really low piano notes) and just slow it down substantially with the sound editor, maybe adding some reverb to make it ring out.
Aircraft such as airplanes or spaceships	You can make a multitude of aircraft and space sounds using a garden-variety hair dryer. Just record the motor sound starting up and turning off, and then, with the sound-editing program, slow down the sound or speed it up—or try it in reverse!

Fact: Almost every sound in *Star Wars* was made by recording common items and then making common alterations and modifications to the sounds, such as slowing them down, reversing them, or adding reverb. Try these on your recorded sounds and see what you come up with. To some extent, it is even OK to use someone else's prerecorded sounds to play with and edit yourself; just be sure that you are making significant changes to the sounds because it's not cool to steal.

You can find a brief list of online sound resources in Appendix A, "Developer Resources."

Creating Music Loops

Much like tiles for the background of a web page or those in a tile-based world, a music or audio loop is an economical means of creating a larger sound or musical idea from a smaller one. The goal is to make the loop seamless and interesting. In most cases, there should not be any sense of beginning or end to your sound because this very quickly creates monotony. Looping sound has been in use since the early days of electronic music and *musique concrète* (a form developed in the early 1940s, based on the recording, mixing, and synthesizing of sounds found in nature). In the old days, loops were created by splicing the ends of a tape-recorded sound and piecing the start and end segments of the sound together with splicing tape. This looked like—you guessed it—a loop. The sound designer would then set the looped tape on the reel-to-reel and hit the Play button, and repeated sound was the result. Needless to say, this was a very time-consuming process, and any mistakes made in the cutting of the tape were very difficult to repair. Add to this the fact that there was no way to determine exactly where to cut the tape except by trial and error with a piece of chalk to mark potential cutting points.

Thanks to the awesome help of computers, this process has been made much easier, faster, and precise beyond aural perception. In digital audio, the basic process is still the same as it was with tape, only we now have the ability to "audition" the loops before making the cut, and of course there's the magical Undo button. I will discuss two ways of making looped sounds on the computer: The first one is with beat-/loop-creation software, and the other is by editing preexisting sound and music with digital-audio editing software.

Drum Loops

Drum loops are popular in games and on web sites right now. The style is derived from electronic dance music that's been trendy since the 90s. It is also the basis of most rap and hip-hop music. For people who are not necessarily musically-inclined, drum loops are really the best means of adding a sense of action to anything happening on the screen. The typical drum loop features three things:

- A repeated rhythmic drum pattern.
- A complementary bass line.
- Miscellaneous additional atmospheric sounds, such as ambient synthesized orchestral strings.

There are dozens, if not hundreds, of programs out there on the Internet for beat and loop creation. It is standard for these programs to open up to a default groove, which you can then edit to your liking. (Just don't use the default one in your game without changing it significantly first!) You can just open up the software and make a few adjustments to the default groove to create your beat. The start and end timing of the loop will already be set up when you save the sound from the program, and all you'll have to do is optimize it for Flash (more on this later).

My favorite software for beat creation is ReBirth (Propellerhead Software; `www.propellerheads.se`) (see Figure 13.1). It is very easy to learn and seamlessly sets up your beat; all you have to do is save it. The coolest thing about ReBirth is that it has "mods." Mods are essentially skins for the drum machine. However, these are not just graphical skins—these skins change the entire sound. You can instantly change the beat you just created from a driving rock sound to a jungle texture to anything else, just by changing the mod. The sounds change, but your beat remains intact. At first, this program may look overwhelming, but the cool thing is that the beats are already set up when you open the program; literally all you have to do is click a couple of buttons of your choice, and the beat is now your own. If this is not easy enough for you, there is a Randomize Pattern button in the menu that automatically reorganizes the beat.

The downside of ReBirth is its very high price. The Propellerheads make a smaller, less functional version, called ReBirth One, which is a little more accessible.

There are demo versions of these products on the web sites, so you can try them out and see if they fit your needs.

A list of popular (and more affordable) drum machines is included in Appendix A, "Developer Resources."

FIGURE 13.1
ReBirth.

Editing and Preparing Audio Loops

Before importing your audio file into Flash, it will most likely need to be prepared. Much as when preparing a GIF or JPEG graphics file, there are many adjustments that should be made with audio, the most important of which is file compression. Flash is capable of compressing the audio file for you, but in many scenarios, it is best to set up the compression before bringing the file into Flash so you can get the desired sound-quality-to-file-size ratio. There are countless audio-editing programs available. The professional standard is Sound Forge (Sony Pictures Digital Media Software; `mediasoftware.sonypictures.com`), but the one that many non-musical audio types use is Adobe Audition (formerly Cool Edit) (Adobe Systems Incorporated; `www.adobe.com/products/audition/main.html`).

Here's a basic checklist to use in preparing your audio for Flash or any other Internet use. Of course it's just a starting point, but it will give you some pretty good ideas and reminders.

- Length (2.5 seconds, for example).
- Volume (overall, as close to 0 dB as possible—not too loud, not too soft).

- **Dynamics (moment-to-moment volume level should be consistent).** This is the most common rookie oversight! Don't taunt your listeners with two seconds of quiet violin sounds and then blast them with a crash cymbal. They will hate you, and you might as well put your entire project on a neon-yellow background with white writing.
- **Sample rate and bit depth (22 kHz/8-bit, 44.1 kHz/16-bit, and so on).** The sample rate is a representation of how many times per second a sound is sampled for digital storage (just like the frame rate for video or animation). A sound sampled at 8 kHz will take up less memory than a 44.1 kHz sound but will be much noisier. Bit depth represents the chunk of numbers used to describe each sample. Eight-bit sound files take up less space than 16-bit but don't sound as good. For reference, CDs are 44.1 kHz and 16-bit. If you can sample your sound file at 44.1 kHz/16-bit without it becoming too large for your Flash project, by all means do so.
- **File type (WAV, AIFF, or MP3).** These are the recommended file formats for Internet use. The WAV and AIFF formats are uncompressed. The MP3 format is compressed, with a small amount of loss in audio quality.

To simplify the choices and numbers in the last two items in this list, the smallest file size with the poorest sound quality would be an MP3 at 8 bits and 11 kHz. The largest file size would be a WAV or AIFF at 16 bits or more and a sample rate of 44.1 kHz or more, and it would have superior sound quality.

Audio editors like Adobe Audition and Sound Forge enable you to edit your sound files graphically. In Figures 13.2 and 13.3, you'll see the "dashboards" of Sound Forge and Adobe Audition. A cursory study of these interfaces will show you their essentials.

As you can see from these images, both programs allow for extremely precise editing of the sound data. When checking the length of the data (item No. 1 from the list), keep in mind that you *must* check your loop to make sure it's continuous and clean. Both Adobe Audition and Sound Forge enable you to loop playback so that you can test the length for proper fit. There is really no way to ensure that your loop will be seamless except by good old-fashioned trial and error. However, I can give you a couple of tips. First, listen carefully to the very beginning and very end of the loop. How does the end work? Does it lead up to the beginning hit? Does the ending fade out? Is that what you wanted? If the sound is repetitive throughout (for example, "Boom boom bap, boom boom bap, boom boom bap"), you will be able to see that very easily on the editing screen. Take note of the timing (in seconds, tenths of seconds, and so on). Zoom in to make sure that the sound ends exactly before the next hit, and adjust as necessary. (You don't want it to be "Boom boom bap, boom boom bap, boom boom b—.") There are options for processing the sound to make it louder or softer, to pan left or right, and more. These programs enable you to adjust the sample rate and bit depth right there on screen, but you can also use the Save As command and choose the sample rate and bit depth there.

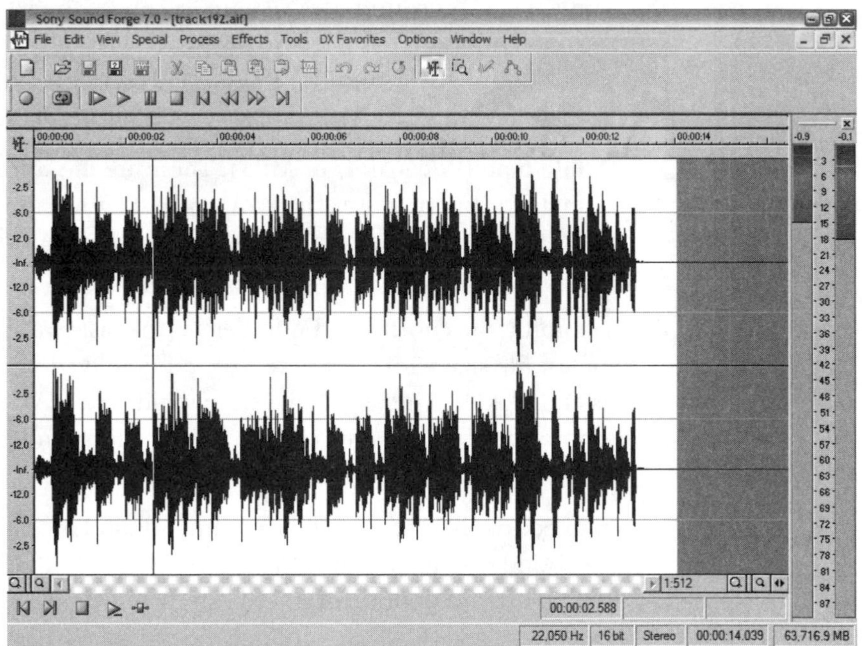

FIGURE 13.2
Sound Forge.

You can see a list of popular audio-editing software in Appendix A.

Sound is a very important part of a game. In this chapter, we have outlined several reasons why you should give sounds a lot of attention when developing your games. Hopefully you will take the time to look for or create sounds that fit well with your game.

FIGURE 13.3
Adobe Audition.

To maintain the most flexibility in your development process, it is good practice to import your sounds and loops at higher quality than you will need when publishing. For example, if you import a music loop as a 44.1 kHz , 16 bit Stereo .WAV file, you can then later experiment with different compressions to achieve a combination of high quality and low file size.

POINTS TO REMEMBER

- Sound effects and music can make a good game extraordinary.
- Sound effectively contributes to the environment and atmosphere of your game and can cause the game player to feel a certain way.
- You can compose or license songs specifically for your game.
- Well-crafted and well-chosen sounds are not usually noticed; that is the mark of a good sound track. Sounds that stand out are often sounds that do not belong.

- You can place a sound directly on a frame in the Timeline, or you can attach and play a sound using ActionScript. Each technique provides different advantages.
- Keeping all your sounds in one movie clip makes it easy to manage them and to add sound effects to your game whenever necessary.
- A sound on/off toggle and volume settings are features that users will appreciate.
- You can change the volume of a sound in a game based on dynamic values, such as the speed of an object or the change in momentum of an object (during a collision).
- With very little equipment (which you probably have already), you can create the majority of sound effects you need by yourself.
- When recording digital sound, don't go over 0 dB.
- Record more takes of a sound than you think are necessary, and keep them in the same file until you begin editing.
- Consider beefing up real-world sounds in a creative or dramatic manner to help convey a stronger image of the event.
- Try to match a sound's environment and acoustic properties to the kind of environment or room in which the action is supposed to be taking place.
- An audio loop is an economical means of creating a larger sound or musical idea from a smaller one.
- Run your file against a checklist before you import it into Flash to make sure it's properly compressed, has the right specs, and is as seamless as you want it to be.
- Import sounds at higher quality than you need. Use Flash's compression settings to adjust during publishing.

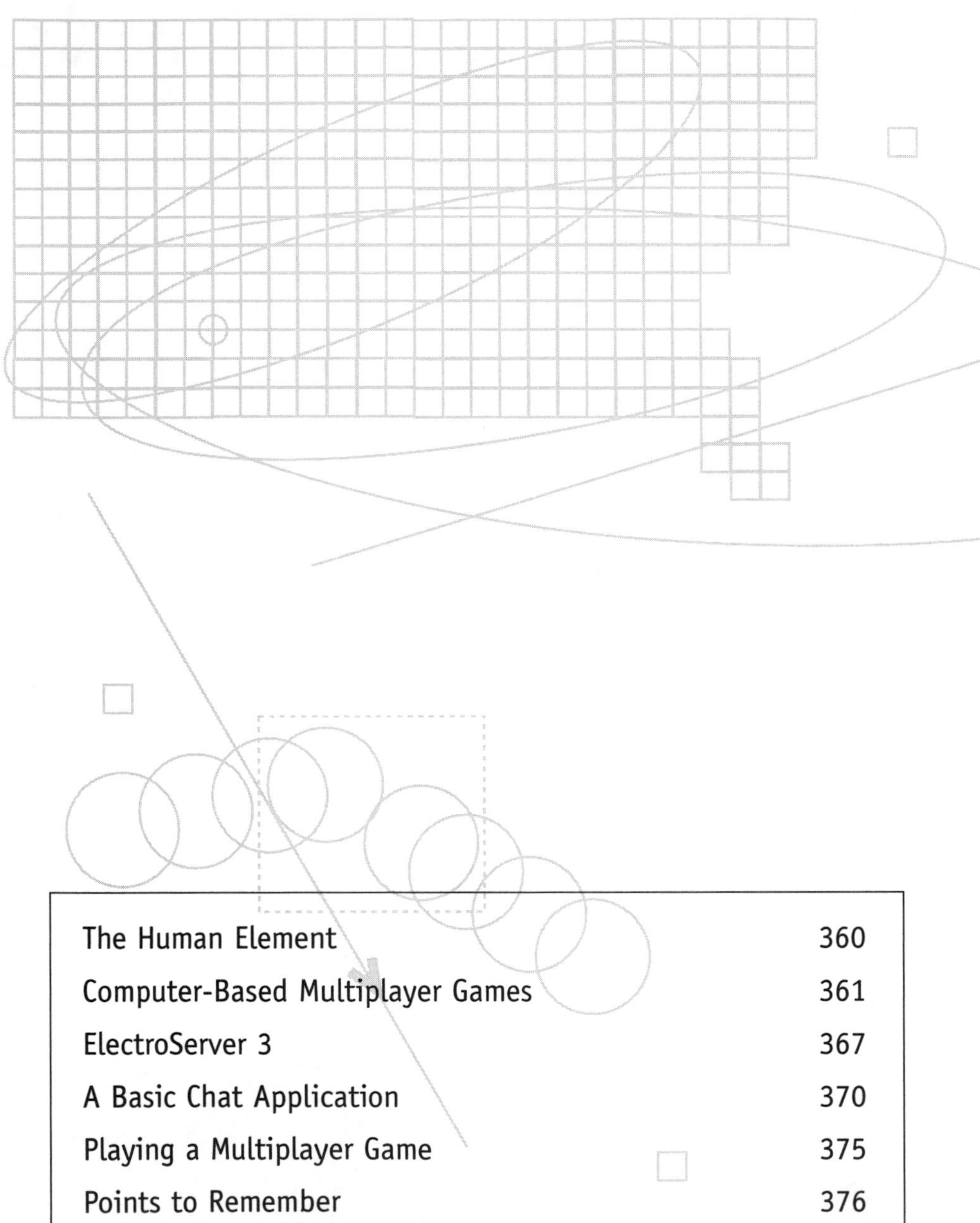

The Human Element	360
Computer-Based Multiplayer Games	361
ElectroServer 3	367
A Basic Chat Application	370
Playing a Multiplayer Game	375
Points to Remember	376

CHAPTER 14

Introduction to Multiplayer Games

Multiplayer games have become very popular over the last several years. In a multiplayer computer game a player can chat with other game players and enter into a game with one or more other players. Some games, such as massively multiplayer role-playing games (MMRPGs), enable thousands of people to play simultaneously. In this chapter, you will learn about the different types of multiplayer games and will be introduced to the concepts behind them. You will also be taken on a tour of a chat source file. You won't actually get into creating multiplayer games until the third section of this book.

The Human Element

In this day and age, when you hear the words "multiplayer game," you probably think "computer game." Technically, any game where more than one person can compete is a multiplayer game. This includes sports, board games, computer games, and maybe even politics!

What makes multiplayer games so popular? In my opinion, there are two primary reasons.

- **Social interaction**—People like to meet others, talk, and develop relationships. Most multiplayer games on the Internet have chat rooms in which these things occur. In many chat rooms, you will find many people that get to know each other and return frequently, sometimes several times a day, to talk and to play games.
- **The desire to win**—This is what drives many people to play games in the first place; they want to have fun, and they want to win. If you can beat another human (rather than a computer player), then you might feel good because you know that you played the game better than someone else did.

Of course there are many other possible reasons to play a multiplayer game (competing for money, wasting time at work, doing research as a game developer, and so on), but the two reasons listed above are the biggest.

Emergent Societies

Games such as *Everquest*, *Ultima Online*, and *Asheron's Call* are MMRPGs. At any given time, literally thousands of players are interacting with each other and the virtual world. A very interesting thing has happened as these players devote hundreds or thousands of hours to game play: They are forming social groups. A market value also develops for virtual items collected, earned, or stolen in these games. In one of the games, players can actually buy and sell virtual houses for real-life money. This was not programmed as part of the game.

A few people even make their real-life living by buying and selling virtual items in games. The longer that these games are around, the more like real societies they can become. I have even heard of wars occurring in the games where groups of players group together to defeat other players (which is usually not the intent of the games).

Computer-Based Multiplayer Games

From now on, the term multiplayer game refers to multiplayer games on the computer. Four types of computer-based multiplayer games exist.

- **More than one player on the same computer**—This type of game is not very popular, but they do exist. Both players can interact with the keyboard on the same computer simultaneously or by taking turns to play a game.
- **Email-based multiplayer games**—In this type of game, a player makes a move, and then an email is sent to the opponent. The opponent then makes a move and an email is sent back to the other person. When a player receives an email, he or she can view the progress of the game on the Internet (usually). Several email-based chess games exist.
- **Turn-based multiplayer games**—By the strictest definitions, a turn-based game is one in which only one player can make a move at a time. Games such as *Chess*, *Golf*, *Checkers*, and *Poker* are examples. With this basic definition, email-based games fit into this category. Usually though, the term turn-based multiplayer game is used with a game that is being played by two players at the same time. Usually these players can chat and play through a web page or a game that they installed on their respective computers.
- **Real-time multiplayer games**—In this type of game, players can make a move at any time. A car racing game or role-playing game (RPG) are common to this style. Real-time games are more difficult to create than turn-based games for reasons discussed later in this chapter.

In this chapter, we discuss the concepts behind both turn-based and real-time multiplayer games. The other two types of multiplayer games are covered other places in this book.

Socket-Servers

For players to play a multiplayer game or chat, their clients (the downloaded instance of the game) need to be able to communicate with each other. Have you ever wondered how everyone in a chat room can send and receive messages to everyone else in the room or directly to specific chatter? It begs the question, "How does Flash know where to send the chat message?"

Well, the answer is a socket-server. A socket-server is a piece of software that runs on a computer, usually the computer that your ISP uses to host your web site, and acts as an intelligent central routing system. When a client is loaded in a web page, such as a chat or multiplayer game, it immediately connects to a socket-server (see Figure 14.1). The socket-server sees you and all the other people who are simultaneously connected to it. It can send messages to the clients without being asked, and the clients can send messages to it.

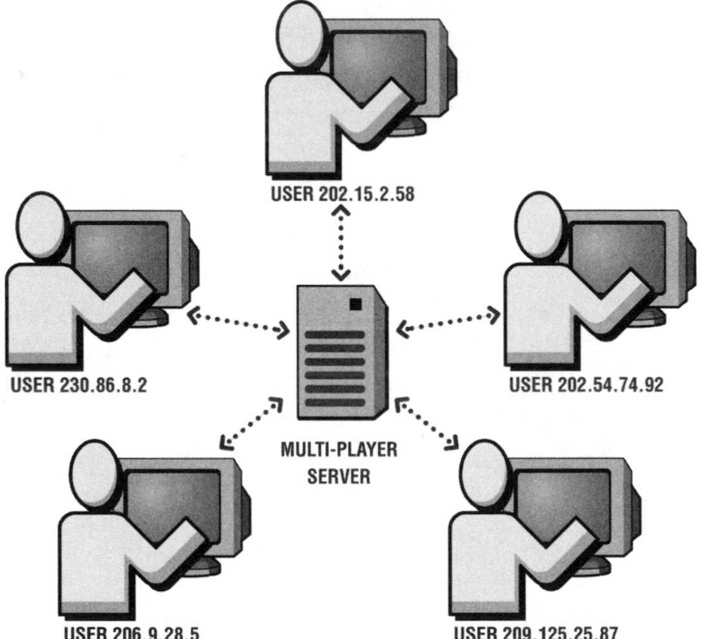

FIGURE 14.1
The client machines connect to the same server.

Different socket-servers are programmed to do different things, but most of them are intelligent enough to take an inbound chat message (a message that a client just tried to send) and send it to all the users in the same room. A room, as you probably know, is a group of users that can see each other. Socket-servers usually support multiple rooms. So there could be dozens or hundreds of rooms on a socket-server, each of which has a varied number of people chatting in them.

That is about where the similarities between most socket-servers end. Many socket-servers are created with extra capabilities, such as the capability to talk to a database or the capability to have one user exist in multiple rooms simultaneously, while others are just for basic chatting.

In this book, we use a socket-server called ElectroServer 3, sometimes just referred to as ElectroServer. ElectroServer 3 is very easy to use and has many special capabilities to help a developer create advanced multiplayer games. You will learn more about ElectroServer later in this chapter.

To recap so far:

- A socket-server sits in a remote location, usually on the same server as your web site, but for development purposes, you can run it locally.
- The socket-server intelligently routes incoming messages to connected users.
- Some socket-servers do more than message routing. They can give game developers many helpful options for developing advanced games.

Note that Macromedia has a product called Flash Communication Server MX. This is similar to a socket server, although it is not the same. It communicates using a proprietary protocol (not XML). This protocol, RTMP, allows for video and audio transfer.

Turn-Based Multiplayer Games

In this section, you will learn the fundamental concepts for turn-based multiplayer games. As you will see, they are not difficult.

In a turn-based multiplayer game, only one player can move at a time, as in the game of *Chess.* Conceptually, there is no limit to the number of players that can play in the same game. That limit comes from the game itself and what the Flash Player can handle. It doesn't make sense to have more than two players in a game of chess, but you might want ten players in a game like Monopoly.

Typically, turn-based multiplayer games created in Flash are *authoritative client.* That means that each Flash client calculates everything that happens in the game and keeps track of one hundred percent of the game.

To continue with the *Chess* example, the game file itself (on both players' machines) must calculate if a move is valid, if a piece was captured, or if the game is over. They also keep track of the state of the board.

As another example, take a game of pool. Player 1 shoots the cue ball, which hits five other balls. Lots of calculations were made when this player shot the ball. Player 1 does not send all the information to Player 2 about which balls were hit. All Player 1 must do is send the information about how hard to hit the cue ball and in what direction. Both clients can take this initial input and have the game play out what should happen. All the logic is done in both clients (See Figure 14.2).

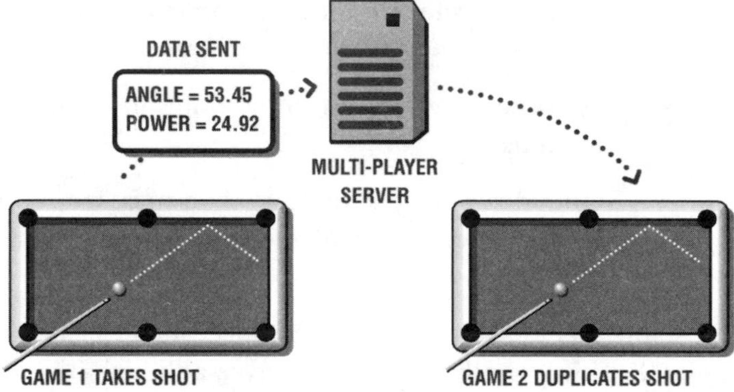

FIGURE 14.2
Authoritative client example.

In authoritative client games, a game player makes a move and then sends that move to the socket-server. The socket-server can then pass that move along to the other game players. When the other clients receive the move, those games make the move occur.

This type of multiplayer game is generally easier to create than a real-time multiplayer game because the socket-server can just blindly pass the move along. The socket-server doesn't care if the move was valid or even what game is being played.

Real-Time Multiplayer Games

In a real-time multiplayer game, a game player does not have to wait for his turn to make a move. Imagine a tank game where each player is guiding a tank around in an open desert. The goal is to shoot other tanks. The view is top-down, so you can see all the tanks. Occasionally ammo pops up on the map in certain areas. If a tank hits the ammo, then the tank can reload its weapons.

Sounds like a fun game. The problem comes when you start to think about how you are going to pull it off. The main issue is latency. Latency is the amount of time that it takes information to get from a client to the server. As you can probably guess, the larger the latency, the less real-time a game feels. Latency is different for every client because of the various paths that the information can take to get to that client. This problem doesn't come up much in most turn-based games—who cares if it takes one second for someone to receive a move in a game of chess? Big deal. But one second can make a huge difference in a real-time game.

When you take latency into mind, conceptual issues arise. If you see a tank at X=100 and Y=200 on the screen, you can't be one hundred percent positive that it's still there when you decide to shoot. If you shoot toward that tank and the projectile appears to barely clip the edge of the tank, should that register as a hit? That tank might actually have just started moving again, but you didn't get the update just yet. In another one-third of a second, you might have gotten the update.

So the question is, "With latency in mind, how do we know when a projectile actually hits something?" The answer is with an *authoritative server*: one centralized location that keeps track of, at minimum, everything that could be calculated differently by the different client machines. This centralized location is the socket-server. You must program logic into the socket-server that will keep track of the appropriate things for the game.

Before you get scared and close the book, let me assure you that extending the socket-server used with this book, ElectroServer 3, for use in a multiplayer game is easy. It is not covered in this book, but you can find more information here: `http://www.electrotank.com/ElectroServer/Articles.aspx`.

The idea is that the socket-server is no longer treated as just an information router. It now has a more intelligent purpose. It's like a game master making sure everything in the game is copasetic.

In the tank game example, the following are some things that would be best handled by the server:

- **Validating movement**—If a tank wants to move to a new location, then the proposed position is sent to the server where it is validated.

The server then broadcasts to everyone that the tank is moving. With normal latency, this can be done in a fraction of a second.

- **Shot creation**—When a tank wants to fire a projectile, it sends the proposed information to the server. The server then deducts from the tank's ammunition inventory and creates a projectile in memory and keeps track of its movement. The server then sends a message to all players to create a projectile on the screen at specific coordinates, moving at a certain angle. If the tank is out of ammunition, then no projectile is fired.
- **Collision detection**—The server keeps track of projectile position and checks for collisions in intervals. If a collision is found, then the server broadcasts information to the game players.
- **Power-up creation and detection**—Something that you can collect in a game is called a *power-up*. The server decides when and where to create ammunition power-ups. Also, it handles detecting which player picks up the power-up. If this detection occured on the client instead of the server, then you could run the risk of two players picking up the same power-up.

As you can see, real-time games are more complicated than typical turn-based games because of the logic added to the socket-server.

Please note that turn-based games can be authoritative server as well. In fact, some of them should be. It is just not that common yet. A good example of a game that should at least be partly authoritative server is poker. In this game, which client should shuffle the deck? The deck shuffling should be done on the server.

Avoid the Sucker Punch: Choosing a Real-time Game

Real-time games are possible using Flash and a good socket-server. But that does not mean that all real-time games are feasible. We have all seen good real-time multiplayer shooter games, role-playing games, and a few other unique games. But think for a minute about what you have not seen done over the Internet: hand-to-hand fighting games (such as *Mortal Kombat*), soccer, basketball, and so on. Games where the action actually surrounds two characters interacting with each other directly at a fast pace are not good candidates for a game to attempt.

Take *Mortal Kombat* for example. In a game like that, you can zip around on the screen and change directions several times per second. A game like this hinges on reaction time. When you can't guarantee that you are seeing an up-to-date version of the other character, then how can you be sure that you are reacting correctly? A player might punch, and the authoritative server registers that the punch hit you before you even saw the character make a fist. How can you block a punch that you didn't see coming?

With this in mind, it is best to choose a game where characters indirectly interact. Real-time shooters appear fast-paced, and they are, but you are tricked into thinking that what you are seeing is accurate. The game is sent updates about the most recent locations of the characters. Algorithms are used to predict what a player will do next based on that players recent history to make the game look smoother. The sucker punch discussed with *Mortal Kombat* is still possible here, but you have more of a chance in a game like this.

ElectroServer 3

ElectroServer 3 is a socket-server created by Electrotank (`www.electrotank.com`). Although it can be used to create just about any type of multi-user application, it was designed with multiplayer games and chat applications in mind. As such, ElectroServer 3 has several features that make creating multiplayer games and chats easy. In addition, ElectroServer 3 has some features that are required to make solid real-time multiplayer games.

ElectroServer 3 is a Java application. That means that it can run on any computer that can run the Java Runtime Environment (JRE), also known as the Java virtual machine. Windows 98/NT/ME/2000/XP, Macintosh, Unix, and Linux are among the supported operating systems.

Typically, a developer installs ElectroServer 3 on his own computer and develops and tests a chat or multiplayer game locally. When finished, the developer can then install ElectroServer 3 on the server on which the web content resides and upload the game or chat. For instance, the web content for `www.electrotank.com` and ElectroServer 3 are both installed on the same physical server.

To install and run ElectroServer 3 on a computer, the JRE version 1.4.1 or higher must be installed. Here are the steps that you need to take to get ElectroServer 3 up and running on your Windows computer.

1. Download and install the JRE (for Windows) by going to `http://www.java.com`. Look for "Download Software" or "Free Download" and click the link.

   The download and install of the JRE most likely will be automated after you click the link. Also, it will probably say something like "Java software" rather than JRE or Java virtual machine.

2. To install ElectroServer 3 on Windows, locate the file called InstallElectroServer3.exe on the CD-ROM and double-click it to install ElectroServer 3. Follow the series of prompts to complete installation.

   You have just installed ElectroServer 3.

3. To start ElectroServer 3, click Start > All Programs (or Program Files) > Electrotank > ElectroServer 3 > Start ElectroServer 3.

   If you installed the JRE properly, ElectroServer 3 should start up without any problem. The console window remains open as long as the server is running. If started properly, the console window should look like what is shown in Figure 14.3.

FIGURE 14.3
The ElectroServer 3 console window.

```
C:\WINDOWS\System32\cmd.exe
Successfully started command line listener

-=-=-=-=-=-=-=-
Initializing Web Server
Web server is enabled
Will listen on 127.0.0.1:8080
Directory listing is enabled
Root directory is set to: webserver-root\
Using 'webserver-docs\404.html' for 404 error template
Using 'webserver-docs\DirectoryListing.html' for directory listing template
Using 'webserver-docs\DirectoryListingDenied.html' for directory listing denied
template
Attempted to start web server...
Successfully started web server on specified address and port

-=-=-=-=-=-=-=-
Starting Chat Server
Chat server will listen on 127.0.0.1:9875
Attempting to bind chat server address...
Successfully bound chat server address
Client queue: input=1000, output=5000, msglimit=50
Thread pool started: min=1, max=10, keepalive=60000
Chat server listening for inbound connections...
```

You only need to run ElectroServer 3 when testing a chat or multiplayer game.

By default, ElectroServer 3 connects to the 127.0.0.1 IP address, which is the IP address for your own computer. Also, the default port on which ElectroServer 3 exchanges data is 9875. Both the IP and the port are configurable.

Note that the IP address 127.0.0.1 is only used for local testing. If you want ElectroServer 3 to run and be available for other users to connect to (which typically occurs after you've developed an application), then you will need to start it up on an IP address that others can see.

Some ElectroServer 3 Features

Unlike most socket-server, ElectroServer 3 was created specifically with multiplayer Flash games in mind. Here are some features that can assist you in creating a wide variety of multiplayer Flash games:

- **Room support**—This is a basic feature of just about all socket-servers. Every game can be played in its own room.
- **Room variable support**—You can store variables in the room on the server. This enables you to easily store information in a centralized location. You can store information such as `doorOpen = true`. If doorOpen is `true`, then all game players see a specific door as open.
- **Automatic user numbering**—You can set a room to number users. This enables you to know who belongs in a game and who does not. If five people join a game, but the game only should have three players, then numbers 1–3 can be easily picked as the game players, and the other two users are just spectators.
- **Server-side plug-in support**—ElectroServer 3 can have its functionality extended by writing code in Java or ActionScript and hooking it up to the server. This is essential for creating real-time multiplayer games.
- **Object transfer**—You can send an ActionScript object between clients. This makes it much easier to code a game. You can actually just take something, such as an array (or any data object), and send it directly to anyone else in the game.

A Basic Chat Application

In this section, we discuss everything that goes into making a basic Flash chat application with ElectroServer 3. First, we discuss the class files used, and then we discuss how it works.

The *ElectroServer* Class

As you know, Flash communicates with ElectroServer 3 to exchange information, which is what makes chatting and multiplayer games possible. This transferred information is XML-formatted. ElectroServer 3 expects to see XML formatted in a specific way to understand what was sent to it.

Flash and ElectroServer 3 can exchange at least 100 or so different types of XML formatted messages. These are used to do things such as create rooms, log in, send messages, and make a move in a game. If you had to program each Flash chat and game to understand these different XML packets from scratch, then you would have a lot of repeated work ahead of you. That is why I created the `ElectroServer` class. The `ElectroServer` class is an ActionScript class that makes communicating with ElectroServer 3 super easy.

As an example, with the `ElectroServer` class you can send a message to everyone in your room with one simple action:

```
ElectroServer.sendMessage("public", "Anyone want to play a
game?");
```

The method `sendMessage` handles the formatting of the message into the required XML format so that you don't have to worry about it. Also, when messages are received from the server, they are sent through the `ElectroServer` class, parsed, and made available to you as a developer in an easily usable format. For instance, by subscribing to the `messageReceived` event, you can have a specific function called when a chat message arrives. The chat message and the name of the person that sent the message are parameters of the event handler.

You will see more about `sendMessage` and `messageReceived` later.

The Chat

The files used here are found on the CD-ROM in Chapter 14. Chat.fla is the source file for the chat application. Also, there are three AS files that together make up the `ElectroServer` class.

Quick Functionality Walk Through

Start up ElectroServer 3. Open Chat.fla and test it by choosing Control > Test Movie. You will be asked to enter a username and password. A username is required, but the password is not. ElectroServer 3 supports moderators (users that can kick out and ban other users). If you enter a password, then ElectroServer 3 checks to see if you are a moderator. Thus, passwords are only for moderators and the server administrator.

Note that you can have users log in with a username and a password that is verified against a database. This is an advanced feature and can be accomplished using the ElectroServer database plug-in. You can learn more about that plug-in on the ElectroServer web site, `http://www.electrotank.com/ElectroServer/`.

After you enter a username and press the Login button, your username is sent to the server, where it is checked against a language filter. If it contains no forbidden words and does not already exist in the server, then you are successfully logged into the server. Otherwise, the server returns an error, and it is displayed.

When logged in, you will be taken to the screen where you can chat, see the user list, see the room list, and create a new room. You can switch to another room that already exists by clicking on it in the room list. You can bring up a window that will enable you to send a private message to another user by clicking on the user's name in the user list.

Overview of the FLA File

Now that you have tested the chat application, let's take a general look at the ActionScript that was used to create it. Close the Test Movie so that you view the FLA source again.

You will notice immediately that there are six frame labels. The first one is simply used as a loading loop for the movie. The Code frame label initializes the `ElectroServer` class and defines some event handlers for connecting to the server, logging in, and joining the first room.

The Connecting and Waiting frames are very similar in that they are only seen while waiting for a response from the server. This usually means that they are only shown for a fraction of a second.

The Login frame is self-explanatory. It is used to enable a user to enter a username and password, if necessary.

The Chat frame is where most of the code exists and where a user will spend most of the time. It is there to handle several methods and events such as sending and receiving chat messages, room list updates, user list updates, and changing rooms.

A Look at the ActionScript

In this section, we will take a look at the ActionScript behind the chat application.

Code Frame Label

The first line of ActionScript on this frame initializes the `ElectroServer` class.

```
var es:ElectroServer = ElectroServer.getInstance();
```

The `ElectroServer` class is what is called a singleton. This means that only one instance of it can exist at a time. You do not instantiate the class using the "new" keyword like you do with most classes. You access the class directly as listed above. That one line of ActionScript tells the `ElectroServer` class to create an instance of itself in memory (static instance) and return it. We named the instance `es`, so we can now access the `ElectroServer` class by the reference `es`. This initialization of the `ElectroServer` class only needs to happen once in an application.

If you scroll to the bottom of the frame, you will see that we set the IP address and the port on which the server runs. By default, ElectroServer 3 is installed and configured to connect the IP 127.0.0.1 on port 9875, so those are the values that we use at the bottom of this frame. If you change the IP and/or port that ElectroServer 3 uses, then you must also change the values in these lines of ActionScript.

The final line of ActionScript here tells the Flash movie to go to the frame labeled Connecting. That frame label executes the connect method of the `ElectroServer` class. But in order to capture the response from ElectroServer 3 (the response to the connection request), we must define an event handler. That is done on this Code frame. We assign a function to the `onConnection` event. (A function that is executed as the result of an event is called an event handler.)

In a similar way, you will notice that we have also assigned functions to the events that are fired as a result of trying to log in and join a room: `loggedIn` and `roomJoined`, respectively.

The function on this frame named `joinRoom` is called when a user is successfully logged in. The `joinRoom` function creates an object that describes the room and then passes it into the `createRoom` method of the `ElectroServer` class. The `createRoom` method takes an object because several default attributes of a room can be configured when creating the room, and those attributes can be changed on this object. See the HTML documentation of the `createRoom` method for more details.

One property to note is `zone`. Just as a room is a group of users, a zone is a group of rooms. You can specify any zone, and it will be created if it does not already exist. Zones are useful for organizing rooms on the server.

To recap, when the movie is one hundred percent loaded, it goes to the Code label. On this frame, several event handlers are defined, and then the movie is sent to the Connecting label where `es.connect()` is executed to establish a connection with ElectroServer 3. When a response is received, the `onConnection` event is fired, and if successful, the user is taken to the Login frame.

Login Frame Label

On this frame, there are two `TextInput` component instances, one for the username and one for the optional password. If the user enters a password, then ElectroServer 3 attempts to log the user in as a moderator. Moderator usernames and passwords are defined in the Configuration.xml file for ElectroServer 3. The Configuration.xml file is found in the install directory for ElectroServer 3.

When the user clicks the "Login" button, the username and password (if it exists) are passed into the `login` method: `es.login(username, password)`. When the movie receives a response from the server, the `loggedIn` event is fired. An event handler was assigned to this event on the Code frame label. If the login was a success, the `joinRoom` function is called, and a room is created for the user to join.

If the room that the user is trying to create already exists, then the `ElectroServer` class internally receives an error from the server and then will join the user to the room instead of creating the room. Next, the `roomJoined` event fires. If it is a success, then the user is taken to the Chat frame.

Note that you can create a persistent room through the Configuration.xml file, and then the user could just use the `joinRoom` method instead of the `createRoom` method.

Chat Frame Label

On this frame, there are two list components, one for the rooms and one for the users. Also, a `TextArea` component is used to display the chat messages and a `TextInput` component is used for writing new messages.

If you scroll to the ActionScript found at the bottom of the frame, you'll see that `showUsers` and `showRooms` are functions that were assigned to the `userListUpdated` and `roomListUpdated` events.

The `showUsers` function does two things. First, it grabs the user list (an array) from the `ElectroServer` class: `var userlist:Array = es.getUserList();`.

It then assigns this array as the data provider for the list component: `userListBox.dataProvider = userlist;`.

The user list array is an array of objects. Each object represents one user in the room. The objects have a `label` property that has a value of the user's name.

The room list is retrieved and displayed in exactly the same way as in the `showRooms` function. The only difference is the name of the method called, `getRoomList`. The `roomList` array is also an array of objects whose label is that of the room's name.

A function is assigned to the `messageReceived` event handler. This event is fired every time a chat message arrives. A chat message can be public or private. A public chat message is sent to the entire room. A private message is sent directly to you. The event handler accepts three parameters: `type`, `message`, and `from`. The `type` parameter is a string value of either "`public`" or "`private`", depending on what *type* of message it is. The `message` parameter simply contains the chat message text, and the `from` parameter contains the username of the person who sent the message. The way that the function takes this information and displays it in the chat window is straightforward if you look at the function.

You will notice that the `roomJoined` event handler is reassigned on this frame. This is because when a user is going to change rooms when they are already on this frame, we want to react in a different way. If they attempt to change a room and it is a success, then we do nothing. The other events will serve to update the screen appropriately (new room list and user list will arrive). However, if an error occurs, then we give a special popup displaying the error.

The function called `showPopup` on this frame can be called by many other functions and, when executed, will open a popup window (just a movie clip) and send it to a specific frame. There are different frames to handle things like creating a new room, joining a room, sending a private message, and a special frame for moderators.

To get a feel for how all of this works, you might want to take the time to go inside of the popup movie clip (look at the upper left corner of the Stage) and check out the ActionScript on each frame. You will see methods used such as `createRoom`, `joinRoom`, `sendMessage`, `kick`, and `ban`. They are all quite simple to understand.

For more information on the methods, properties, and events of the `ElectroServer` class, please view the HTML documentation files that were installed with ElectroServer 3.

Playing a Multiplayer Game

In this chapter, you have learned fundamental concepts concerning how multiplayer games work, you have been introduced to a specific socket-server (ElectroServer 3) that can be used for multiplayer games, and you have been walked through a working chat application. But you still have not seen code specific to multiplayer games.

You will not see any multiplayer game code in this chapter. Two multiplayer games are covered in this book: *Chess* and *Don't Fall*. In the *Chess* chapter, we will pick up where we left off in this chapter with code specific to playing a multiplayer game of *Chess.* We will cover:

- How a user can start a new game
- How another user can join that game
- How spectators can watch the game
- How each player makes a move and sends that move to the opponent and spectators

POINTS TO REMEMBER

- Multiplayer games are popular because they can be played with other humans.
- There are two main types of multiplayer games created with Flash: turn-based and real-time.
- Turn-based multiplayer games are typically authoritative client, which means that the game itself performs 100 percent of the logic.
- Real-time multiplayer games are typically authoritative server. This means that the server must perform custom logic for that game so that no client is confused about what is supposed to happen.
- Multiplayer games need a socket-server to exchange information. ElectroServer 3 is used in this book.
- The `ElectroServer` class is used as an integration layer between Flash and ElectroServer 3. It enables a developer to making API calls that in turn talk to ElectroServer 3.

PART III:
THE GAMES

Chapter 15
Word Search 381
Game Overview 382
Game Logic 387
Points to Remember 406

Chapter 16
Multiplayer Chess 409
Game Rules 410
Multiplayer Aspects of the Game 414
Game Code 417
Points to Remember 433

Chapter 17
501 Darts Game 435
Game Overview 436
Game Logic 438
Points to Remember 450

Chapter 18
Cone Crazy 453
Game Overview 454
Game Logic 454
Points to Remember 475

Look for these words

MOTHERBOARD
KEYBOARD
MONITOR
RESOLUTION
MOUSE
ELECTROTANK
CDROM
MACINTOSH
INTERNET
DESKTOP
MENU
ONLINE
NETWORK
ICON

Computer Terms

```
J G Y Z W S F C N A N O V P W R E
Z I D G X T D C I C O N Z S J B U
M B T G D R A O B Y E K A R A G L
L E H V D C G Z V C I X K O M N Y
I M N O I T U L O S E R N T D K V
R A Y U I D G V O V H M A I E R Z
J C G J E R O M H M Z Z T N D O A
Y I P O P A E Q O P P O O O D W A
U N I Y U O X O Y R Z I R M E T C
M T J Q Z B P G N T D Y T S R E X
Z O V G M R O C Y L M C C I R N R
L S U V D E T O M T I V E I J R Y
J H E S L H K E F T E N L S R E E
C K V Q E T S Z R D W W E R B T U
F X P L Z O E B V A G G F Z I N O
A M F I H M D G E T Q A G W R I R
M O E C E I L N N L K W F R I Y Z
```

RESTART SHOW ANSWERS BACK

Game Overview 382

Game Logic 387

Points to Remember 406

CHAPTER 15

Word Search

Word games are one of the most popular types of casual games on the Internet. *Word Search* is a word game in which you search for words hidden among what appears to be a random pool of letters. Although it's a very simple-looking game, *Word Search* requires some complicated ActionScript. If you have read through most of this book, then there shouldn't be any surprises in the code that pulls this game together. However, if you have just turned to this chapter, you'll probably need an intermediate-or-higher grasp of ActionScript to fully understand what is done here.

Prerequisites

Read Chapter 7, "Tile-Based Worlds." *Word Search* is not a tile-based world; however, you should be familiar with the tiling technique for adding movie clips to the Stage in a grid using nested loops. Also, you should be familiar with the simple math trick used to determine which tile a point is over.

Game Overview

As someone who loves physics, I usually like to create games that have a lot of physically realistic movement, like *Pool*, *Pinball*, or *Miniature Golf*. One day, though, I noticed my wife playing a word-search game from a tiny book she'd just bought. She jokingly asked me, "Why can't you make a game like this?" So I did, and this is it!

Before beginning the task of creating *Word Search*, I thought, how hard can it be? It turns out that although it wasn't too terribly difficult, it was much harder than I had initially thought. It took me quite a bit of time to come up with a plan for coding this game.

The game of *Word Search* is easy to understand. It has a grid of letters that can be any size. In this game, we use 17 by 17 (see Figure 15.1). A list of words can be found within this grid. Words may be positioned vertically, horizontally, or diagonally (and either spelled forward or backward in any of these directions). In this Flash *Word Search* version, I have enabled words in all directions except diagonal stretching from upper right to lower left.

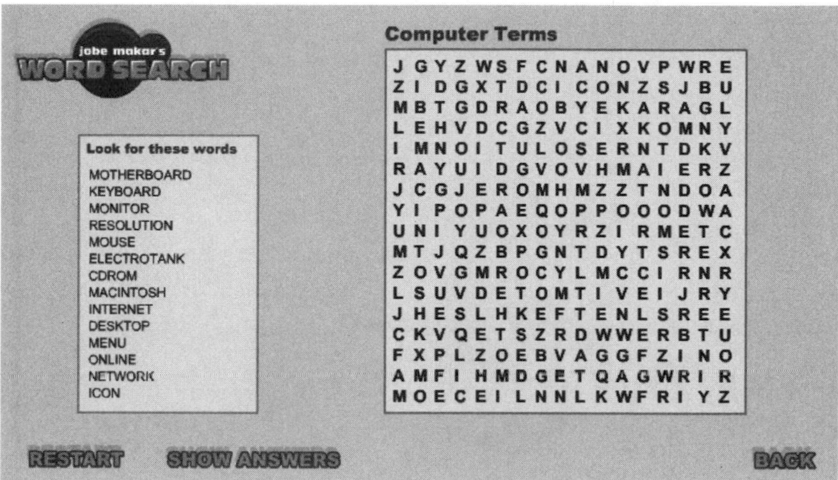

FIGURE 15.1
Word Search.

When playing a word-search game on paper, you typically circle a word when you find it, or you mark through it. You also mark it off the list so that you can easily see which words you still have left to find. It's the same in this Flash version. When you find a series of letters you want to select, you click and hold the first letter, and drag toward the last letter you want to include. As you drag, an oval is drawn along your path of movement. When you reach the last letter, you release the mouse button. If the letters you selected match a word from the word list, then the oval you drew stays on the grid, and the word from the word list is marked through and its color is changed. (If you've tried to select a group of letters that isn't on the word list, the oval disappears.)

Now that you have a basic understanding of how the core of the game functions, I'll tell you about the rest of the game. Open wordsearch.swf in the Chapter15 directory.

The first thing you see is the main menu (also called the *splash screen*). This is the screen from which the player should be able to reach all major areas of the game. This basic splash screen has just three buttons: Start Game, Instructions, and Credits (see Figure 15.2).

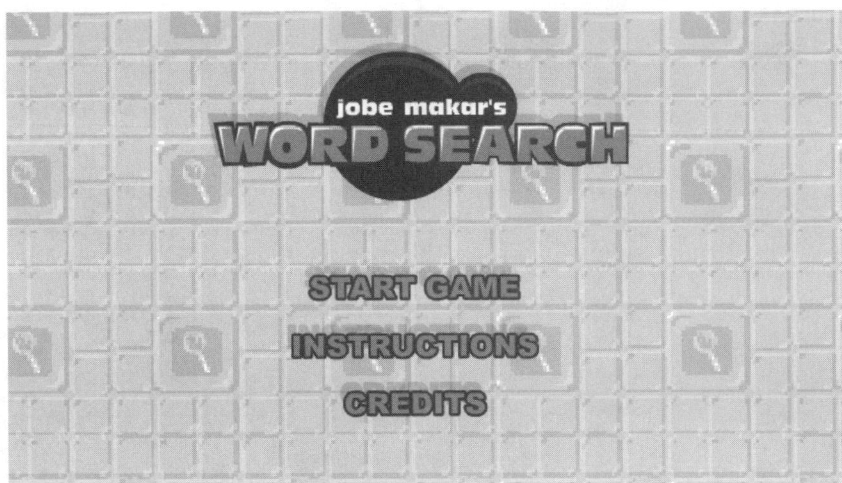

FIGURE 15.2
The splash screen.

Where is the Content for the Instructions and Credits Pages?

In wordsearch.fla, I have included all the graphical assets and ActionScript needed for the complete game of *Word Search*. However, I have left the credits and instructions screens blank because it will be easy enough for you to fill them in, and you can do it in your own way. Unless you take this game completely unmodified and put it on your web site, chances are you will have made enough changes to the way things work that you should write your own instructions on how to play the game. You can easily list the instructions for this game in a text field on the instructions page. On the credits page, you can list yourself and whoever helped you create the word lists (and even me if you want to!).

When you click Start Game, you are immediately taken to a new screen. On this screen, you can scroll through a roster of word lists. Each category contains 14 words that will be hidden in the *Word Search* grid. To select a category, click the category name and click the Play button. You are then taken to the game screen. A list of words is displayed on the left. Each of those words is hidden among the pool of letters in the grid. Unlike what happens in the paper version of this game, if you get stumped, you can click the Show Answers button (see Figure 15.3). This will make all the letters invisible except those that fall within a word from the word list.

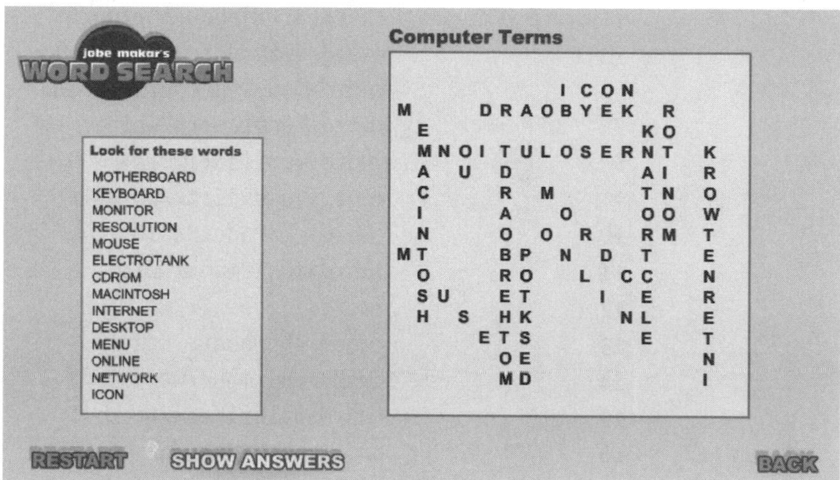

FIGURE 15.3
Showing the answers.

Every time a game starts, the grid is randomly created. The words are placed randomly and the filler letters are chosen randomly. The end result is this: You can play the same word list thousands of times and never get the same grid configuration. If you click Restart, the game will be restarted with a new grid configuration but with the same word list.

That's it for the basic tour of the game. There is one more important thing to note, though. The word lists are stored in a single XML file called wordlists.xml. Without much knowledge of XML, you can still modify the word lists very easily. You can add or remove lists, or just change what is there.

Open wordlists.xml from the Chapter15 directory. (As you probably know by now, you can open an XML file in almost any text editor.) The format of the XML in this file is very basic and should be easy to understand. The root node—the lowest level of the XML structure—is `<lists>`. There can be any number of `<list>` nodes that are children of `<lists>`. Each `<list>` contains 14 `<word>` nodes (to correspond to the 14-word format we've chosen for this game). The following is an example of what the entire XML file could contain if there were only two word lists.

```
<lists>
      <list category="Classic Films">
            <word>casablanca</word>
```

```
            <word>africanqueen</word>
            <word>wizardofoz</word>
            <word>bodysnatchers</word>
            <word>redplanet</word>
            <word>vertigo</word>
            <word>suspicion</word>
            <word>charade</word>
            <word>musicman</word>
            <word>lifeboat</word>
            <word>showboat</word>
            <word>thinman</word>
            <word>palerider</word>
            <word>blob</word>
      </list>
      <list category="Greek Mythology">
            <word>zeus</word>
            <word>hera</word>
            <word>hermes</word>
            <word>minerva</word>
            <word>apollo</word>
            <word>artemis</word>
            <word>aphrodite</word>
            <word>poseidon</word>
            <word>hades</word>
            <word>cronos</word>
            <word>gaia</word>
            <word>ares</word>
            <word>atlas</word>
            <word>demeter</word>
      </list>
</lists>
```

Other than my choices for classic films, this example file should be fairly easy to understand. You'll notice that there is an attribute called `category` on the `<list>` nodes. This is the name you will see in the scrolling list on the Start Game screen of the game. You should also note that it doesn't matter if the words are capitalized or lowercased (except in the category attribute) because in the game, all the letters are capitalized. Finally, you cannot use any characters in the <word> tags that are not letters. That means no spaces, dashes, numbers, or any symbols that are outside the realm of A–Z. As an example, "Wizard of Oz" is written here as wizardofoz. With this information, you can easily create your own word lists!

Game Logic

In this section, we will discuss the logic involved in all aspects of the game, from choosing a word-list category to generating the grid and selecting words. In certain cases we will specifically look at code, but in most cases I will explain what each function does without taking you through it line-by-line.

Choosing a Category

Before you can choose a category (which is just any one of the word lists in the wordlists.xml file), the file must be loaded and the information extracted. Let's look at the ActionScript on frame 1.

```
var doc:Object = new XML();
doc.ignoreWhite = true;
doc.load("wordlists.xml");
```

First we create an `XML` object called `doc` in which we want to load the file. Then we load it using the `load()` method of the `XML` class. Because we can't do anything in the game until this file is loaded, we add a condition to the pre-loader for the game. You can see this on frame 2 (see Figure 15.4).

```
var factor:Number
➥=(_root.getBytesLoaded()+doc.getBytesLoaded())/
➥(_root.getBytesTotal()+doc.getBytesTotal());
percent.text=Math.floor(factor*100)+"%";
if (factor>=1 && doc.loaded) {
     _root.gotoAndStop("Splash");
}
```

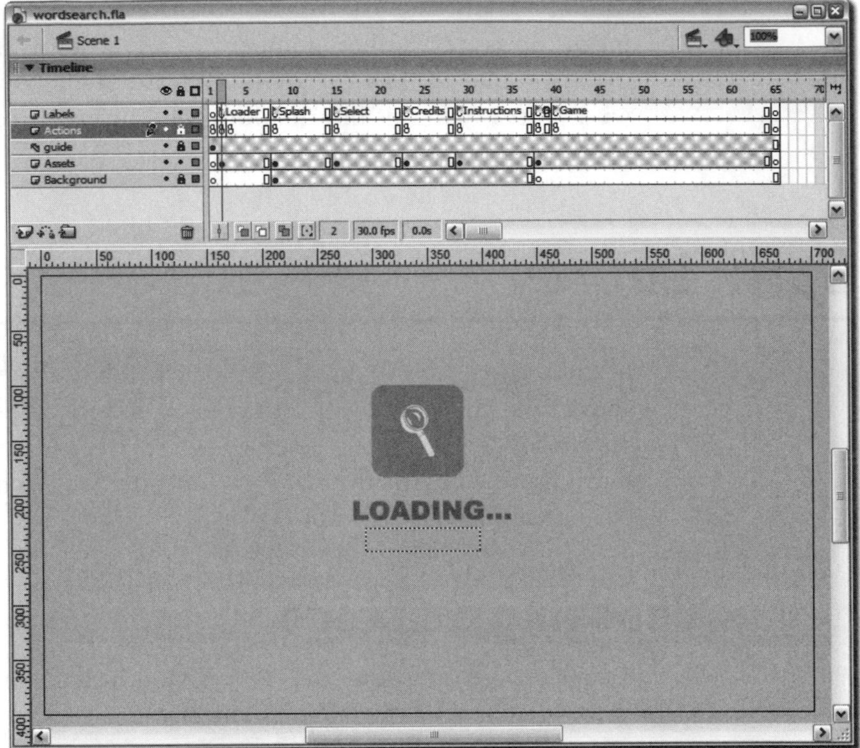

FIGURE 15.4
Loading.

Imagine that the XML file is very large, say 50 KB. Then adding this XML file to your pre-loader would be a necessity. If you did not, the game file would display the main menu, and the user could attempt to start playing a game before the words were even loaded! In line 1 of this code, we create a variable called `factor`. It is the total number of bytes loaded, divided by the total number of bytes in the file. When `factor` is multiplied by 100, the result is the percentage that has been loaded. So, for instance, if wordsearch.swf is 80 KB and wordlist.xml is 20 KB, then the denominator of that ratio is 100. If at one point wordsearch.swf has 60 KB loaded and wordlist.xml has 10 KB, then the numerator is 70. So then the percentage loaded at that time is (70/100)*100 = 70%. In line 3, we check to see if `factor` is greater than or equal to 1 and if `doc` is fully loaded. When `doc` is fully loaded, its `loaded` property is `true`. If both of these conditions are met, then everything is finished loading, and it is OK to proceed to the Splash frame. Otherwise, the playhead moves to the next frame and then back to this frame again for another check.

From the Splash frame, the user can click Start Game and be taken to the Select frame. Here we interpret the XML in the doc object and build and display the categories in a List component. Here are the first few lines of ActionScript:

```
1    var words:Object = new Object();
2    words.lists = new Array();
3    play_button._alpha = 50;
4    play_button.enabled = false;play_button
```

First we create an object called words. This object will be used to store the word lists and eventually will be used to store all the information about the game. In line 2, we create an array in the words object called lists. This array will contain one object for each category. The object will contain the list of words in that category, as well as the category's name. Next we set the _alpha property of play_button to 50. This is to give a visual indication that you cannot proceed until a category is chosen. Also, we set the enabled property of that button to false, which means that there will be no feedback when the user clicks on this button. When a category is chosen, play_button's _alpha is set back to 100, and the enabled property is set to true, allowing the user to interact with it.

Next, the following function is created and then executed:

```
function init() {
	var temp:Array = new Array();
	var temp:XMLNode = doc.firstChild.childNodes;
	var scrollingList:Array = new Array();
	for (var i = 0; i<temp.length; ++i) {
		var tempList:Array = temp[i].childNodes;
		var category:String =
		➥temp[i].attributes.category;
		var wordArray:Array = new Array();
		for (var j = 0; j<tempList.length; ++j) {
			var word:String =
			➥tempList[j].firstChild.nodeValue;
			wordArray.push(word);
		}
		words.lists.push({wordList:wordArray,
		➥category:category});
		scrollingList.push({label:category, data:i});
```

```
15          }
16          scrollList.dataProvider = scrollingList;
17      }
18      init();
```

This function steps through the XML in the doc XML object and extracts all the information we need. An array of words is created for each category (line 11) and then stored in an object that describes that category (line 13). Also stored in that object is a property called category that stores the category's name. This object is pushed into the lists array. For example, the object for the first category, Types of Fruit, is stored as the first element in the lists array, lists[0]. This object, lists[0], contains the property category whose value is "Types of Fruit", and an array called wordList, whose values are the words of the category. By the time the function gets to line 16, all the information from the XML has been extracted and stored properly. The List component on the Stage has an instance name of scrollList. In line 16, we set the data provider for this list by pointing it to the scrollingList array, which contains the name of each category. The List component then takes this information and automatically populates the list. Up to this point, you have seen the ActionScript needed to load the XML file, parse it, store the data logically, and display the categories in a list. Now let's show what happens when a user clicks on an item in the List component. An event handler was assigned to the change event of the List component, so when an item is selected, the following function is executed.

```
1       myHandler.change = function() {
2           play_button._alpha = 100;
3           play_button.enabled = true;
4           var categoryIndex:Number =
            ➥scrollList.selectedItem.data;
5           words.words = words.lists[categoryIndex].wordList;
6           words.category =
            ➥scrollList.getSelectedItem().label;
7       };
```

This event handler is called whenever a category is selected. First the play_button is given an _alpha value of 100 so that it appears to be enabled. Then we set the play_button enabled property to true. In line 4, we set a variable called categoryIndex. This variable stores a number—the number of the category that was selected in the list. Then, in line 5, we create an array in the `words` object called `words`. The value of this array is set by using `categoryIndex` and pointing to the `wordList` array on the object that represents that category. In short, this line creates an array of the words that will be in the game from the category selected. In line 6, we store a property on the `words` object called `category`. The value of `category` is the string name of the category selected. So, if "Types of Fruit" were selected, then `words.category` would be "Types of Fruit" (see Figure 15.5).

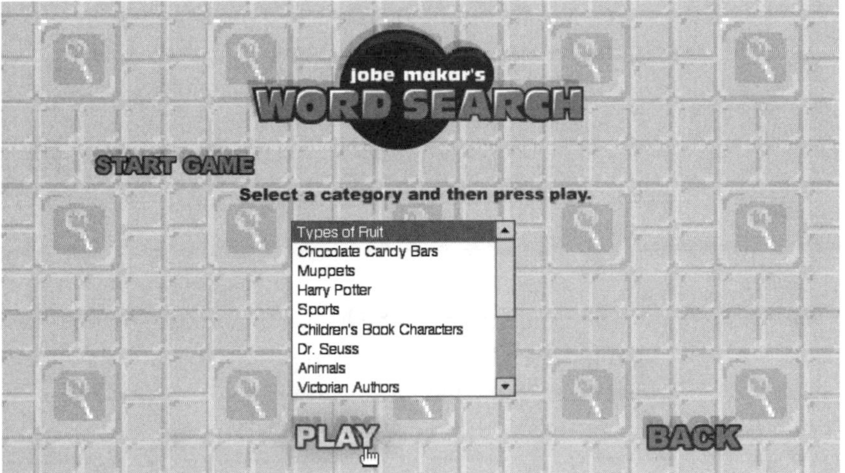

FIGURE 15.5
The "Types of Fruit" category being selected.

After a category has been selected, we have (as seen previously) an array of words called `words` and the name of the category both stored in the `words` object. We can now safely move the frames needed to build the board.

Generating the Grid

Creating the grid layout from the list of words is the toughest part of this game. Words can be written forward, backward, vertically, horizontally, or diagonally, and they can even cross through each other. The logic used to do all of this is not too complex—but it's not that easy, either! What is complex is the tall function, approximately 130 lines, that handles the bulk of this logic. In this section, we will pick up where we left off in the previous section and look at everything needed to create a unique word-search grid on the screen.

We left off in the previous section after a category was selected. When this is done, it is OK for the user to click the Play button. When Play is clicked, the game is taken to a frame called Generate. This frame contains all the movie clips needed for the game screen. Here are the two actions in this frame:

```
1    generating._visible=true;
2    play();
```

There is a movie clip instance on the Stage called `generating`. We set its `_visible` property to `true`. The first time you reach the Generate frame, the generate movie clip is already visible. However, when the game is restarted and this frame is visited again, generate is not already visible, so we make it visible with this action. We want this movie clip to be visible while the game is computing the grid layout so that the game player knows what is happening. Line 2 just tells the Timeline to keep playing. Two frames later, we reach the Game label and stop there.

The Game frame is the location of all the ActionScript that handles creating the grid, detecting word selections, and restarting the game. We will look at four functions in this section: `scrambleWords()`, `displayList()`, `createBoard()`, and `restart()`.

`ScrambleWords()` takes the word list in memory and randomly maps those words into the board layout. It is the large function mentioned previously and handles all the logic needed to create the grid in memory. This function does not perform any physical placement of movie clips or text fields on the Stage.

`CreateBoard()` takes the results from `scrambleWords()` and actually builds the board layout with all the movie clips, adding random letters to fill all the blank spaces.

`DisplayList()` creates the list of words on the left side of the screen. This function is also called whenever a correct word has been selected; it handles marking off a word in the list after it has been found.

`Restart()` simply removes all circle movie clips that have been created, if any, and then sends the movie back to the Generate frame label.

But first, let's look at the initial actions that need to happen to get this game going. The following ten lines of ActionScript, at the bottom of the Game frame, are not contained within a function.

```
1     scrambleWords();
2     if (scrambledOK) {
3           wordList.createEmptyMovieClip("lines", 1);
4           category.text = words.category;
5           generating._visible = false;
6           displayList();
7           createBoard();
8     } else {
9           restart();
10    }
```

When the Game frame is reached, these actions are performed. First, the `scrambleWords()` function is called. We will talk about that function in detail later, but for now, just assume the following: If `scrambleWords()` does its job successfully, then the variable `scrambledOK` is set to `true`. If it does not succeed, then `scrambledOK` is set to `false`. If `false`, then the game is restarted, and the movie will keep looping between the Game frame and the Generate frame until `scrambleWords()` does its job successfully. (We will talk about what determines success later.) If `scrambledOK` is `true`, then lines 3–7 are executed. Line 3 creates an empty movie clip within the `wordList` instance. The `wordList` movie clip is the one that will contain the list of words that are in the grid. The empty movie clip, called `lines`, is where the lines will be drawn through any words in the list that have been selected in the grid. We will discuss this in the next section. In line 4, we simply display the name of the category in a text field. Next, we set the visibility of the generating movie clip to `false` because the generating is finished. We execute the `displayList()` function so that the list of words is shown on the left, and then we call the `createBoard()` function so that the grid is made visible on the screen. You may recall that before `createBoard()` is called, the board exists only in memory.

What you have just seen is the big picture. First we attempt to create the board in memory. If we can't, then we restart and try again. If we can, then the board is created on the Stage.

scrambleWords()

Now let's look at what the scrambleWords() function does. Here is pseudo-code that represents what is done in the function:

```
set maxTime to 3000
set scrambledOK to true
create two-dimensional letters array
create listings array
set now to getTimer()
for each word in words.wordList
      randomly choose alignment
      randomly choose direction
      set tempWord from the word
      set wordLength to tempWord.length
      push object which stores tempWord, direction, and
      ➥alignment onto listings
      if direction is backward
            reverse tempWord
      if alignment is horizontal
            set notDone to true
            while notDone
                  row = random row
                  startx = random(boardsize-wordlength)
                  notDone = false
                  for each letter in tempWord
                        set tempLetter to current letter
                        if grid spacing contains
                        ➥something and it's not tempLetter
                              notDone=true
                  if notDone is false
                        store the word letters in the
                        ➥letters array
                  if getTimer() - now > maxTime
                        set scrambledOK to false
                        break
      else if alignment is vertical
            set notDone to true
            while notDone
                  column = random column
```

```
            startY = random(boardsize-wordlength)
            notDone = false
            for each letter in tempWord
                set tempLetter to current letter
                if grid spacing contains
                ➥something and it's not
                ➥tempLetter
                    notDone=true
            if notDone is false
                store the word letters in the
                ➥letters array
            if getTimer() - now > maxTime
                set scrambledOK to false
                break
    else if alignment is diagonal
        set notDone to true
        while notDone
            startX = random(boardsize-wordlength
            startY = random(boardsize-wordlength)
            notDone = false
            for each letter in tempWord
                set tempLetter to current letter
                if grid spacing contains
                ➥something and it's not
                ➥?tempLetter
                    notDone=true
            if notDone is false
                store the word letters in the
                ➥letters array
            if getTimer() - now > maxTime
                set scrambledOK to false
                break
```

This function is pretty well-commented in the actual ActionScript in the FLA file. With the explanation of the pseudo-code given here and the function itself, you should be able to understand what is going on in `scrambleWords()`.

First we set a variable called `maxTime` to `3000`. This number serves as a cutoff for the amount of time we will allow the function to run. In this function, we place words randomly. But if you've ever tried to make your own word jumble or crossword puzzle on paper, you'll know that this procedure is not foolproof; sometimes the script places words in positions that make it impossible to place any more words! In the case of the code we've written for this particular game, the loops in `scrambleWords()` would continue indefinitely, looking for available slots that do not exist. To prevent this from happening, we set this `maxTime` variable. During every `while` loop, we check to see how long the function has been running. If it has been running for a longer time than `maxTime`, then we break out of the loop and the function. This is when we would consider the `scrambleWords()` function not to have been successful, and as a result, the `restart()` function will be called.

Next, we set `scrambledOK` to `true`. This variable is set to `false` if `maxTime` is ever reached. We then create a two-dimensional array called `letters` on the `words` object. Each element in this array corresponds to a letter in the grid. The letters are inserted into the array as we place the words. At the end of the `scrambleWords()` function, the only letters in the array are the ones from the words, so there are many blank elements. It is not until the `createBoard()` function is called that we fill in the remaining empty spaces.

In line 4, we create an array called `listings`. This array will contain one element for each word that is placed in the grid. The element is an object that stores information about the word. Next, we set a variable called `now` to store the current time. We can use that later to determine how long the function has been running.

The rest of the code, lines 7–58, is performed for each word in the `wordList` array. We randomly choose an alignment for a word (horizontal, vertical, or diagonal). Then we randomly choose a direction for the word to be spelled (forward or backward). Then, in line 9, we create a variable called `tempWord`, which stores the current word. We also create a variable, called `wordLength`, to store the length of the word. In line 11, we create an object that stores `tempWord`, the alignment, and the direction of the word and pushes it onto the `listings` array. This array is used later to determine if a word has been selected. We will see more of this in the next section. If the direction randomly chosen is backward, then we reverse the order of the letters in `tempWord` (line 12).

What happens next depends on the alignment that's been randomly chosen. There is a giant conditional with one branch for each of the three possible alignments. Each branch works quite similarly. I will explain what happens in the horizontal branch and then mention the minor differences in the other two branches.

If the script has chosen horizontal alignment, then the "horizontal branch" (lines 15–28) is executed. We set a variable called `notDone` to `true`. Then we execute a `while` loop that will keep looping until `notDone` is no longer `true`. In the loop, we randomly choose a row for this word to appear in. We then randomly choose an *x* position for the word's starting point. This random starting position isn't *completely* random, though; we base it on the width of the grid minus the length of the word. So if the grid's width is 20 and the word's length is 7, then we can start the word on row 13 or earlier. At this point, we have a row in which to place the word and a starting *x* position, which is the equivalent of choosing a random column. Next, we loop through each letter in `tempWord` and compare the letter with the grid spacing in which this letter can be placed. If that space contains nothing, or if it already contains this same letter, then we continue on and check the next letter. However, if we find a letter in that grid spacing other than the one that we are currently using, then we abort this loop and start over with new random starting positions. The script runs through this loop until it finds an acceptable position in the grid. If the loop takes too long (as previously discussed), then the entire function is aborted and the `restart()` function is called.

The `scrambleWords()` function is well-commented throughout the ActionScript, so don't worry about being able to follow along with it.

The branches of the conditional that handle vertical and diagonal alignments are very similar. The vertical alignment randomly chooses a column and then randomly chooses a starting *y* position based on the grid size and the length of `tempWord`. The `while` loop is then performed in the same way as it was for the horizontal alignment. For the diagonal branch of the conditional statement, the only difference is in choosing the starting position; both the starting *x* position and the starting *y* position are chosen from random numbers, based on the grid size and the word length.

createBoard()

The `createBoard()` function takes the randomly-placed words from the `scrambleWords()` function and places movie clips on the screen to represent them. Then, if a grid spacing is blank (as most of them are), `createBoard()` assigns a random letter to that position.

```
1   function createBoard() {
2       path = board;
3       path.depth = 0;
4       path.circles = 0;
5       gridSpacing = 17;
6       for (var i = 0; i<boardSize; ++i) {
7           for (var j = 0; j<boardSize; ++j) {
8               var clipName:String = "letter"+i+"_"+j;
9               path.attachMovie("letter", clipName,
                ➥++path.depth);
10              path[clipName]._x = i*gridSpacing;
11              path[clipName]._y = j*gridSpacing;
12              var tempLetter:String =
                ➥words.letters[i][j].toUpperCase();
13              if (tempLetter == undefined ||
                ➥tempLetter == "") {
14                  tempLetter = chr((random(26)+65));
15                  words.letters[i][j] = tempLetter;
16                  path[clipName].dummy = true;
17              }
18              path[clipName].letter.text = tempLetter;
19          }
20      }
21  }
```

In line 2, we create a reference to the board movie clip called `path`. The `board` instance is where we will attach all the movie clips to hold the letters. It will also contain the circles when they are drawn. Next, we set the variable `depth` to `0` in the `board` movie clip using the `path` reference. This number will be incremented for every movie clip attached and used to assign each of those movie clips a unique depth. In line 4, we set `circles` to `0`. When circles are drawn in the board instance to select a word, a new movie clip is created to hold that circle, and this variable is incremented. After the game is over, we can then easily remove all the circles because this variable tells us how many there are. In line 5, we create a variable called `gridSpacing`. This will represent the distance we need to have between the registration points of each letter. The registration point is the top-left corner of the movie clip called letter, which will be attached for each letter. It has a linkage identifier name of `letter`.

Next, we perform a nested loop to make the grid. In line 8, we create a name for each movie clip we are about to attach. We'll use the same naming convention as we did in Chapter 7, but with a slight variation: We'll use "letter" instead of "cell" as the naming stem, and we'll start the counting from 0 instead of 1. (It is common, when accessing arrays, to count from 0 because array values start at index 0.) For instance, `letter3_5` is found in column 4 and row 6. Next, we add the new instance of the letter movie clip to the grid and position it. In line 12, we set a local variable called `tempLetter` from the element sitting in the corresponding spot in the two-dimensional array called `letters`. If that spot was occupied by a letter from one of the randomly-placed words, then it will contain a letter. Otherwise, it will contain nothing.

In line 13, we check to see if a letter in column `i` and row `j` exists. If it doesn't, we generate one randomly. Every character—even tabs and carriage returns—can be represented by a numeric value. This number is called an ASCII value. The ASCII numbers 65–90 represent the letters A–Z (A=65, B=66, and so on). The ASCII numbers 97–122 represent the letters a–z. Flash contains a function called `chr()` that returns a letter from an ASCII value. So, `chr(65)` returns "A." Using this expression, `chr((random(26)+65))`, we can have a random letter from A to Z returned (line 14). That is how we populate the blank grid spacings (see Figure 15.6). In line 15, we take this new letter and store it in the two-dimensional `letters` array. Then we store a variable called `dummy` on the new letter movie clip with a value of `true`. We use this variable later when determining if selected text belongs to a word.

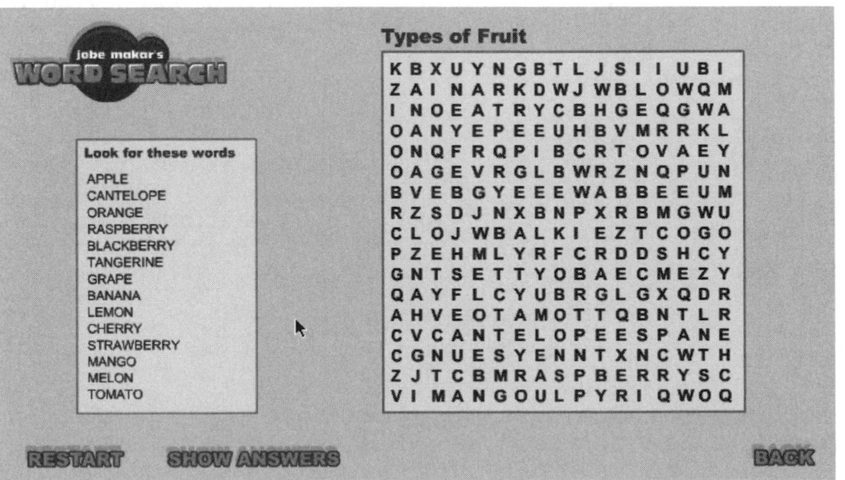

FIGURE 15.6
The populated grid.

displayList()

This function handles the creation of the list of words to be displayed on the left side of the game screen. If a word has been selected in the game, it is crossed out in this area.

```
function displayList() {
	_root.tempFormat = new TextFormat();
	_root.tempFormat.font = "arial";
	_root.tempFormat.size = 12;
	var tempValue:String = "";
	for (var i = 0; i<words.listings.length; ++i) {
		var tempWord:String = words.listings[i].word;
		if (!words.listings[i].found) {
			tempValue += "<font
			➥color=\"#000099\">"+
			➥tempWord+"</font><br>";
		} else {
			tempValue += "<font
			➥color=\"#009999\">"+
			➥tempWord+"</font><br>";
			_root.wordList.list.htmlText = tempValue;
			var width:Number =
			➥_root.tempFormat.getTextExtent
			➥(tempWord).width+15;
			var y:Number =
			➥_root.wordList.list.textHeight-5;
			_root.wordList.lines.lineStyle(2,
			 ➥0x990000, 100);
			_root.wordList.lines.moveTo(0, y);
			_root.wordList.lines.lineTo(width, y);
		}
	}
	_root.wordList.list.htmlText = tempValue;
}
```

It's not hard to understand the big picture of what this function does. It uses HTML-formatted text to display the word list in an HTML text field. If a word has not yet been selected, it appears as one color; if it has, it appears as another color with a line marked through it. In this function, we loop through the list of words in the `listings` array. If you remember, the `listings` array contains objects that represent each word. If there is a property on a word object called `found` that has a value of `true`, then the word has been marked as found.

In the first few lines, we create a new text format. This text format is not to be applied directly to a text field. We create it for the sole purpose of being able to use the `getTextExtent()` method of the `textFormat` class. With `getTextExtent()`, we can find out how wide a certain phrase of text will be. We use that information when drawing a line through a word to cross it out (lines 13–17).

After every word in the `listings` array has been inspected and formatted in the `tempValue` variable, we set this value in the text field (line 20).

restart()

This function was discussed briefly at the beginning of this section. It is very short and simple. It removes all the circle movie clips and then sends the movie back to the Generate frame label.

```
1      function restart() {
2            for (var i = 0; i<=board.circles; ++i) {
3                  board["circle"+i].removeMovieClip();
4            }
5            _root.gotoandPlay("Generate");
6      }
```

The `for` loop uses the value of the `circles` variable to know how many circle movie clips need to be removed. In line 5, the movie is instructed to go back to the Generate frame label. The game has now been restarted (see Figure 15.7).

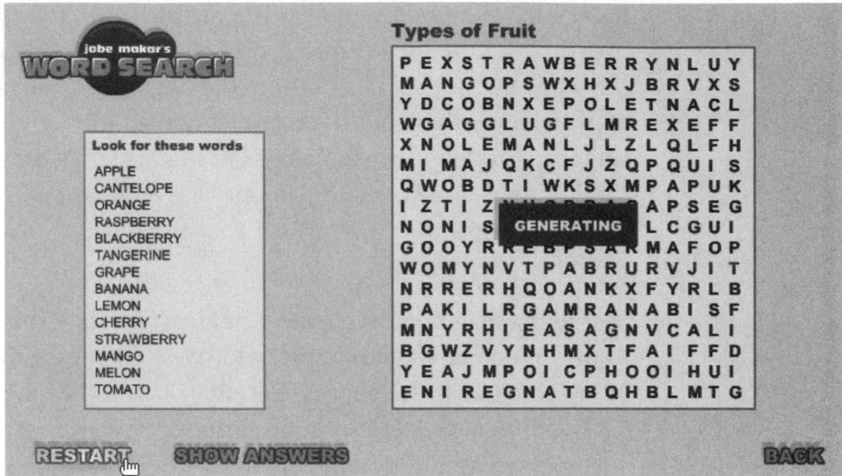

FIGURE 15.7
"Generating" is displayed as the game restarts.

Detecting a Choice

When you click anywhere on the grid, a blue circle appears. If you keep the mouse button pressed and move the mouse around, one end of the circle (or, more accurately, the oval) stays pinned in the original spot but can freely rotate. The other end of the oval stretches to match your mouse position. The result is that you appear to be circling a group of letters. I am not going to discuss the ActionScript needed to move this circling movie clip around; I think you'll easily be able to understand it by looking at the ActionScript on the `circler` movie clip. (There's an instance of that movie clip to the left of the Stage in the main Timeline on the Game frame.) What you should know, though, is that when you (as a user) attempt to select text, the `circler` movie clip calls the `selected()` function and passes in the mouse's initial and end positions. From these two positions, the `selected()` function can tell which letters were selected. It then checks these selected letters against the list of words, using a function called `checkList()`. If the word is found, then a permanent circle is created around the word, and the `displayList()` function is called to update the list, now showing the found word crossed out.

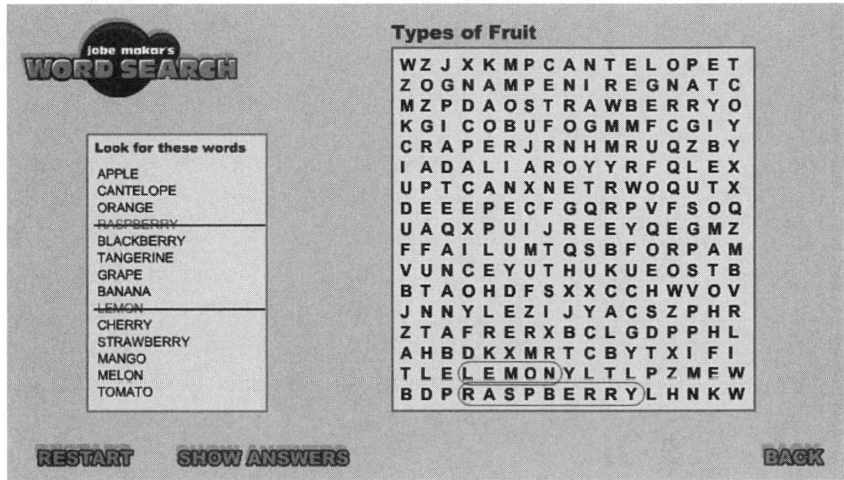

FIGURE 15.8 The selected words are circled and crossed out on the list.

Here is the selected function:

```
function selected(downX:Number, downY:Number, upX:Number,
➥upY:Number) {
      var x1:Number = Math.floor(downX/gridSpacing);
      var y1:Number = Math.floor(downY/gridSpacing);
      var x2:Number = Math.floor(upX/gridSpacing);
      var y2:Number = Math.floor(upY/gridSpacing);
      var tempWord:String = "";
      if (y1 == y2) {
                  if (x2>x1) {
                  for (var i = x1; i<=x2; ++i) {
                        tempWord += words.letters[i][y1];
                  }
            } else if (x1>x2) {
                  for (var i = x2; i<=x1; ++i) {
                        tempWord += words.letters[i][y1];
                  }
            }
      } else if (x1 == x2) {
            if (y2>y1) {
                  for (var i = y1; i<=y2; ++i) {
                        tempWord += words.letters[x1][i];
                  }
            } else if (y1>y2) {
```

```
            for (var i = y2; i<=y1; ++i) {
                tempWord += words.letters[x1][i];
            }
        }
    } else if (x1 != x2 && y1 != y2 && Math.abs(x1-x2)
    ➥== Math.abs(y1-y2)) {
        var xSign:Number = (x2-x1)/Math.abs(x2-x1);
        var ySign:Number = (y2-y1)/Math.abs(y2-y1);
        var steps:Number = Math.abs(x2-x1);
        for (var i = 0; i<=steps; ++i) {
            tempWord +=
            ➥words.letters[x1+xSign*i][y1+ySign*i];
        }
    }
    if (tempWord != "") {
        if (checkList(tempWord)) {
            var x1:Number =
            ➥x1*gridSpacing+gridSpacing/2;
            var x2:Number =
            ➥x2*gridSpacing+gridSpacing/2;
            var y1:Number =
            ➥y1*gridSpacing+gridSpacing/2;
            var y2:Number =
            ➥y2*gridSpacing+gridSpacing/2;
            var rise:Number = y2-y1;
            var run:Number = x2-x1;
            var angle:Number = Math.atan2(rise,
            ➥run)*180/Math.PI;
            var distance:Number =
            ➥Math.sqrt(rise*rise+run*run);
            var name:String =
            ➥"circle"+(++board.circles);
            board.attachMovie("circler", name,
            ➥++board.depth);
            var clip:MovieClip = board[name];
            clip._x = x1;
            clip._y = y1;
            clip._rotation = angle;
            clip.right._x = distance;
            clip.lineStyle(0, 0x000099, 100);
```

```
53                      clip.moveTo(0, 9.3);
54                      clip.lineTo(distance, 9.3);
55                      clip.moveTo(0, -9.3);
56                      clip.lineTo(distance, -9.3);
57                      clip._alpha = 50;
58                      displayList();
59              }
60          }
61      }
```

First, we determine from the mouse positions the grid spacings that the mouse was over when the mouse button was pressed and when it was released. (This is a simple math trick that was explained in Chapter 7; "spacing" from that chapter works the same as "grid spacing" here.) We then check the coordinates of these spacings against three conditions. There are three valid relative positions of these coordinates: They can be in the same column (vertical); that is, `x1` is the same as `x2`. They can be in the same row (horizontal); that is, `y1` is the same as `y2`. Or they can be diagonal, in which case the absolute value of the difference in `x1` and `x2` is the same as the absolute value of the difference in `y1` and `y2`. If none of these conditions are met, then the selected letters are not a valid choice. If one of these conditions is met, then the user has made a selection in an appropriate way, but we still need to check if the letters form a word in the word list.

In each of these three conditions, we use `for` loops, moving from the starting position to the end position, to build the selected word from the individual letters. We store this built word as `tempWord`. In line 35, we check to see if `tempWord` has a string value. If it doesn't, then the function is over, and the user sees nothing happen (except that the circle that he or she attempted to draw disappears). If `tempWord` has a value, then we check it against the list of words using the function called `checkList()`. This function just loops through the available words and checks it in both forward and reverse directions. If the word matches, then a result of `true` is returned; otherwise `false` is returned. If `true`, lines 37–58 are executed. They add an instance of the `circler` movie clip and draw a circle around the selected text using Flash's drawing API. This leaves a permanent circle on the board to mark what the user has already found. In line 58, the `displayList()` function is called. This rebuilds the list on the left side of the screen so that it shows the newly found word crossed out.

You have seen the majority of what makes this game work. There are several little functions used to handle things like mouse-down and mouse-up events that we aren't discussing in this chapter, but that should be easily understood.

Points to Remember

- Word games are one of the most popular types of games on the Internet.
- Externalizing content into an XML file makes the game easy to modify and update.
- Flash components like the `List` component make scrolling lists very easy to create.
- Keeping track of how long a loop has been running is a good way to determine if a loop is taking too long. In our case, we restart the game if it takes too long to generate the board.
- The Flash drawing API can come in handy for tasks like drawing circles around words and crossing out words in a list.

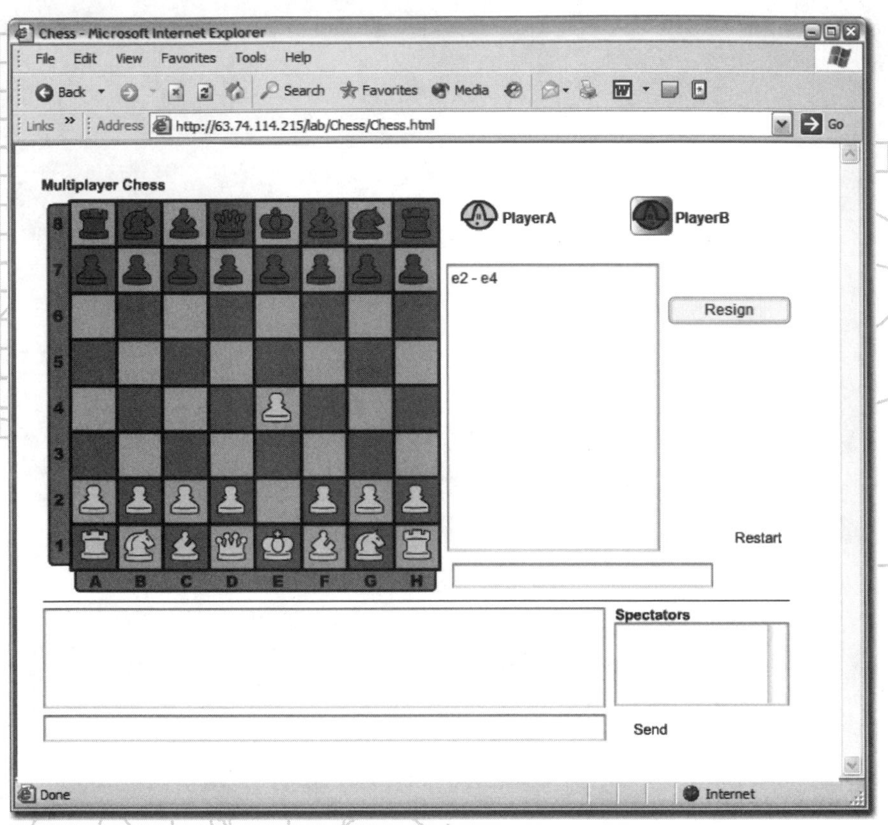

Game Rules 410

Multiplayer Aspects of the Game 414

Game Code 417

Points to Remember 433

CHAPTER 16

MULTIPLAYER CHESS

CREATED MORE THAN 1500 YEARS AGO, *CHESS* IS ONE OF THE OLDEST AND most popular skill games. It is a game whose rules can be learned fairly easily but can take years to master. In this chapter, we discuss the complete rules of the game of *Chess* and the logic used to create a multiplayer version of the game.

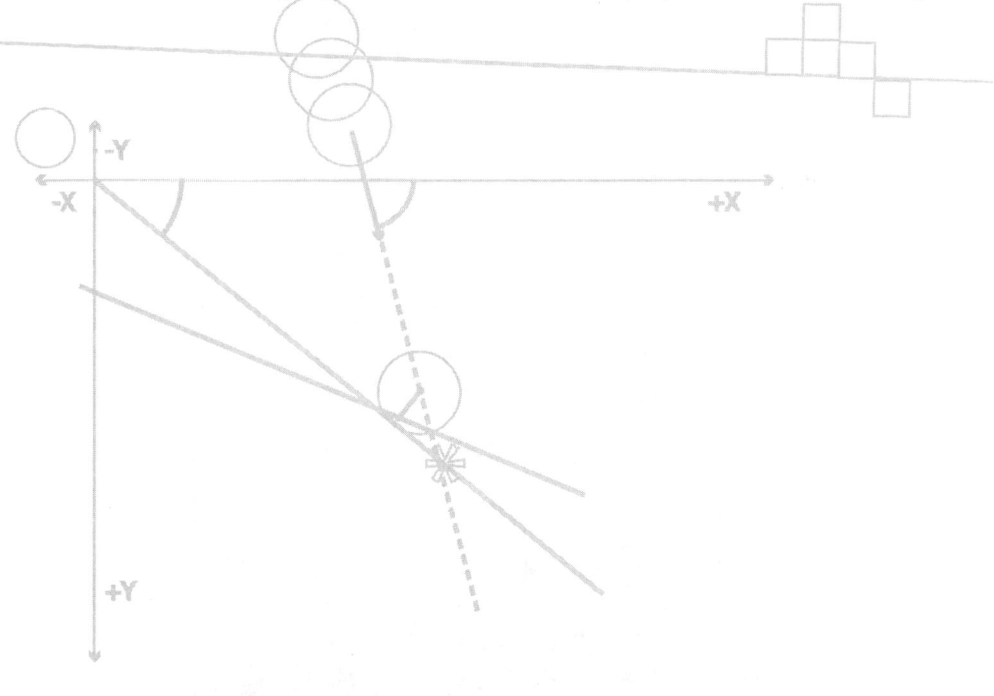

Prerequisites

Chapter 14, "Introduction to Multiplayer Games"

Chapter 7, "Tile-Based Worlds"

Game Rules

The complete rules of chess are fairly complex. This game has been programmed to meet all official chess rules.

Chess is played by two players on a board of 64 squares (tiles). Each player starts with 16 pieces of a certain color. Traditionally, one player has all white pieces and the other player has all black pieces. *Chess* is a turn-based multiplayer game. The white player takes the first move of the game. The black player then makes a move. The players alternate moves until an end state has been reached. We'll discuss the various end states later.

The rows of a chess board are numbered 1 through 8. The columns are labeled A through H. Tiles are referred to by column and row (for example, E7) (see Figure 16.1).

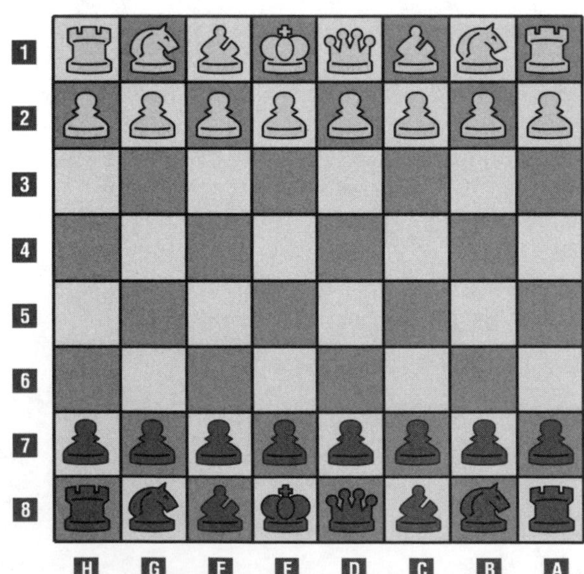

FIGURE 16.1
Rows and columns of chess board.

Every turn, a player can move one piece one time. Even though a player starts with 16 pieces, only 6 types of chess pieces exist. Each type of piece has unique rules that apply to it. These rules govern the way in which the piece can move, conditions under which they can capture another piece, and other unique qualities.

Here are the pieces:

- **Rook**—The rook can only move vertically or horizontally on the chess board. It can capture any enemy piece on a tile along its path without moving through another piece. The rook is shown in Figure 16.2.
- **Bishop**—The bishop can only move diagonally. It can capture any enemy piece on a tile along its path without moving through another piece. The bishop is shown in Figure 16.3.
- **Queen**—The queen is like the rook and bishop combined. It can move horizontally, vertically, or diagonally. It can move in only one direction per move. It can capture any enemy piece that it encounters along its path, without moving through that piece. The queen is shown in Figure 16.4.
- **Knight**—The knight can move either one space horizontally and two vertically in one move or two horizontally and one vertically. The knight jumps to a destination tile, even if the tiles along the way are filled. If the destination tile is filled with an enemy, then the knight captures that piece. The knight is shown in Figure 16.5.

FIGURE 16.2
The rook.

FIGURE 16.3
The bishop.

FIGURE 16.4
The queen.

FIGURE 16.5
The knight.

- **Pawn**—Unless it's capturing a piece, a pawn can only move directly forward (meaning toward the opponent's starting position), one tile per turn. On its first move of the game, a pawn can move forward either one or two tiles. A pawn can capture an opponent's piece if it is in one tile diagonal and forward of the pawn. Under no circumstances can a pawn move backward. If a pawn reaches the other end of the board, then that pawn must be changed to a rook, knight, bishop, or queen. It is the player's choice, but it must be changed to one of those pieces. Changing a pawn to another piece is known as *promotion*. A pawn can also capture a piece under a special scenario called *en passant*. If player1 moves a pawn two spaces on its first move, and then player2 moves a pawn to be directly side-by-side with player1's pawn, then on player1's next turn, he can capture player2's pawn. Player1's pawn is moved forward one position and horizontally one position toward the pawn being captured. Player1's pawn does not end up in the tile of pawn that it captured. The pawn is shown in Figure 16.6.
- **King**—The king can move one space in any direction and can capture any enemy piece that sits in the destination tile. This piece also can perform a move called *castling*, to the left or right. A king castles with a rook and can only do so if no pieces are between that rook and the king and neither piece has yet been moved. To castle left, the king is moved from E1 to G1 and the rook is moved from H1 to F1. To castle right, the king is moved from E1 to C1, and the rook is moved from A1 to D1. The king is shown in Figure 16.7.

FIGURE 16.6
The pawn.

FIGURE 16.7
The king.

A few rules were not mentioned in this list that apply to all moves. To describe those rules, the goal of the game must be discussed. The goal of the game is for a player to place his opponent's king in *checkmate*. A king is placed in *check* when, on the opponent's following turn, he could possibly capture the king. Checkmate occurs when it is impossible for a player to remove his king from check.

These are the additional rules:

- A player cannot make a move that will place his king in check. Therefore, a king can never move into an adjacent tile as the opponent's king.
- Only one piece can exist in a tile at a time.
- A player cannot capture his own piece.
- A king cannot be castled to remove himself from check. A king cannot castle if any of the tiles through which it will move are threatened.
- If a player is in check, then he must remove himself from check.

The game is over when an end state is reached. The following are the types of end states and the conditions under which they occur:

- **Checkmate**—As discussed previously, checkmate occurs when a king is in check and there exists no move that would remove that king from check.
- **Stalemate**—A stalemate occurs when a player can make no legal moves and is currently not in check.
- **Draw**—A draw occurs under one of three separate conditions. If there are only two pieces left on the chess board, two kings, then a draw has been reached. If the same game state is reached three times, then the game is a draw (A game state is the exact layout of the board). If 50 moves occur during which no pawn is moved and no piece is captured, then the game is a draw.

As you have seen, the game of chess has many rules. It is such a complex game to play that creating a computer-based artificial intelligence opponent is very difficult. We do not do that in this chapter. We simply program the logic that enables two humans to play against each other without cheating.

MULTIPLAYER ASPECTS OF THE GAME

The FLA file built for this chess game contains a chat application as well as the game itself. In this section, you'll be walked through the process of using the game file to start and play a game of chess.

In Chapter15 on the CD-ROM, you will find Chess.fla. Open this source file. Publish an SWF from it. Start ElectroServer 3 (see Chapter 14, "Introduction to Multiplayer Games," for help on this).

Open two instances of the Chess.swf file that you just created. In both windows, log in using any usernames. We'll refer to them as PlayerA and PlayerB.

Both SWF instances should be showing a chat room (see Figure 16.8). On this screen, you can chat, create a new room, send a private message to another user, or create a new game.

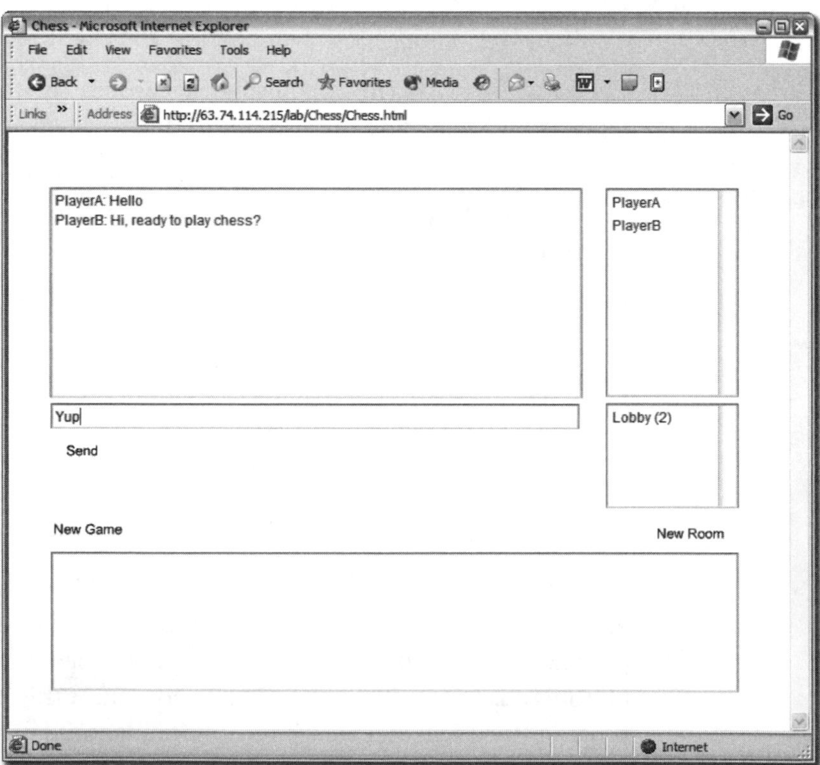

FIGURE 16.8
A chat room.

For two players to play a multiplayer game of chess, one player must create a new game. The other player will then see a visual representation of this new game and can elect to join the game.

In PlayerA's window, click on the New Game button. A pop-up window will appear with options about the game that you want to create (see Figure 16.9). In this pop-up window, you must give your game a name. You also can give the game a password if you so desire. Giving a game a password helps ensure that only someone who knows the password can join the game (either to watch or play).

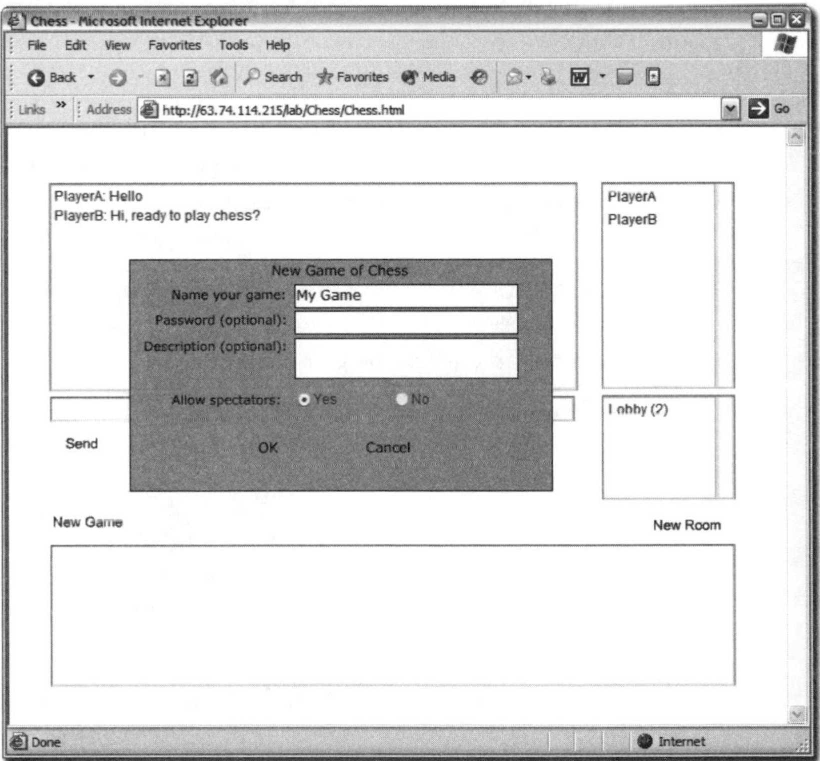

FIGURE 16.9
The pop-up window.

The radio button at the bottom of the pop-up window that says Allow Spectators can be set to Yes or No. If you choose Yes, which is the default value, then at any time throughout the game, another user can join the game and watch. If you choose No, then only the game players are allowed access to the game.

In PlayerA's window, create a new game called "My Game" and leave the other options with their default values.

PlayerA is taken to a new screen, the game screen, where he is shown the chess board and a new pop-up message indicating that another player has not yet joined. On PlayerB's screen, a game icon appears. This icon shows the name of the game as well as the number of game players that have joined.

Click on the game icon. A pop-up window appears to give you the choice to join the game. If the game is password-protected, then you can enter the password in this pop-up window. You can choose to join the game as a player or as a spectator. If you join as a player, then you will become PlayerA's opponent.

Have PlayerB join the game as a player. In PlayerA's window, you will now see a message indicating that a game player has joined. PlayerA is then given a Start button to click, while PlayerB is shown a message indicating that the game will begin when PlayerA starts it.

In PlayerA's window, start the game. The pop-up windows will go away on both user's screens. White moves first in chess, and in this game, the person who created the game is white, so PlayerA has the first move.

To make a move, simply click a piece and drag it to a destination tile. When ready, release the mouse. If the move is valid, the piece will be moved to that location (See Figure 16.10).

In PlayerA's window, move a piece. In PlayerB's window, you will see that the piece that PlayerA moved is animated from its starting position to the destination tile. PlayerB can then make a move.

When a move is made and validated, the move is sent to the opponent so that it can be displayed. Also, if any spectators are in the room, the move is sent to them. Spectators do not see any animation; the pieces just appear in their destination tiles.

Now, open a third SWF instance and log in. We'll call this person Watcher. When Watcher reaches the chat screen, he sees a game icon. When Watcher clicks the icon, he receives a pop-up window asking if he wants to join. The "Spectator" option is already selected because he cannot join as a player.

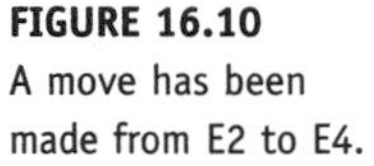

FIGURE 16.10
A move has been made from E2 to E4.

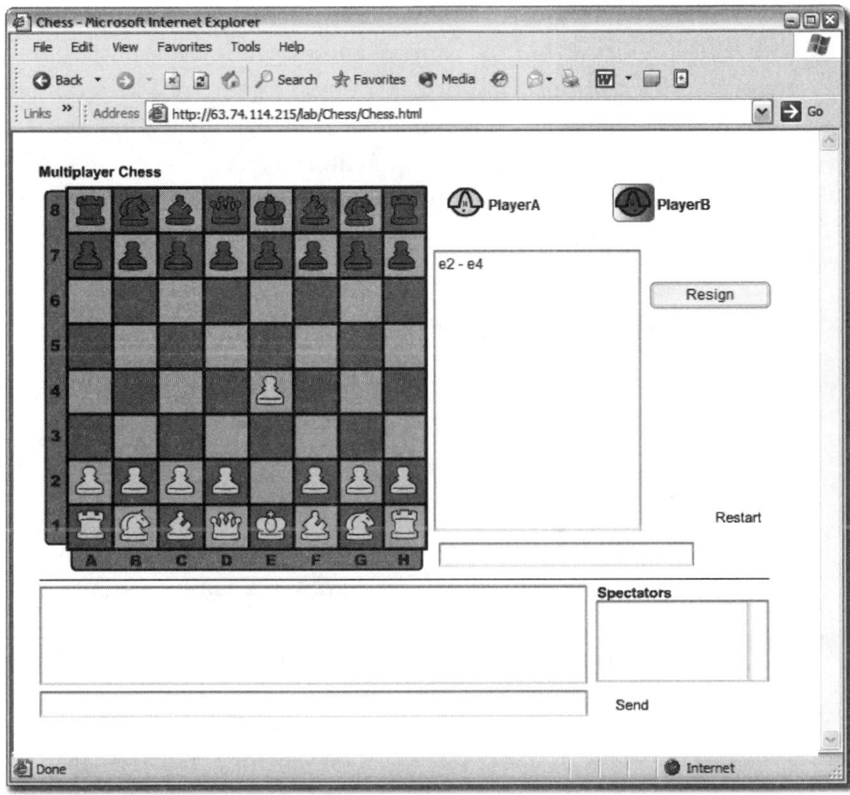

Join Watcher to the game as a spectator. When Watcher joins the game, he is shown the current state of the board and the move history. When more moves are made, Watcher receives updates to the board.

Game Code

You just learned how a game is created from the chat room, started, and played. In this section, we discuss the logic used to accomplish these features. In the directory that contains the game source files, you'll notice that there are six class files. Three of those class files are part of the `ElectroServer` class, as discussed in Chapter 14, "Introduction to Multiplayer Games." The other three class files were created specifically for this game.

The ActionScript used to make this game multiplayer is not very complicated, but the game of chess itself is complicated. In total, this game comprises about 2,000 lines of code (not including the ElectroServer class). The code that makes this game multiplayer is around 200 lines. The large quantity of ActionScript for the game itself is necessitated by the many rules and the extensive logic required to make sure the players can play properly without cheating.

Multiplayer Logic

First we'll discuss the logic used to create a game room and enter the game. Then we'll discuss the logic used for sending moves.

Creating a Game

When a new game is created, a new room is created. A game is a room. As far as ElectroServer 3 knows, a game room and a regular room are no different. When a room list update is received by a Flash client, it can display the rooms and game rooms separately because the attribute on the room object called isGameRoom enables us to detect if it is a game room. If isGameRoom is true, then the room is a game room. To see this in use, check out the showRooms function on the Chat frame label.

On the Chat frame label, there is a movie clip in the top left corner of the Stage with an instance name of popup. This movie clip contains several frame labels that are used to handle different options such as creating a game, sending a private message, or joining a game. On the New Game frame label, you can find the ActionScript used to create a new game. Here are some lines of ActionScript from the ok function found on that frame.

```
var gameRoomOb:Object = new Object();
gameRoomOb.roomName = roomName.text;
gameRoomOb.password = pass.text;
gameRoomOb.attributes = new Object();
gameRoomOb.attributes.allowSpectators = allowSpectators;
gameRoomOb.attributes.numPlayers = 2;
gameRoomOb.attributes.playersArrived = 1;
gameRoomOb.FloodingFilterEnabled = false;
_parent.es.createGameRoom(gameRoomOb);
```

To create a new game, you must call the createGameRoom method of the ElectroServer class. An object containing information on the room to be created is passed into the createGameRoom method. The only required property on this object is roomName. The password property can be left empty.

It is interesting to note the attributes object. Every room, including game rooms, have a description field associated with them on the server. The ElectroServer class serializes the attributes object and stores it as the room description on the server. That enables us to store variables associated with a room on the server that can be seen by people who are not in the room. For instance, the playersArrived property stores the number of game players that have entered the game room. Users in the chat room see an icon that represents the game. This icon shows how many game players have entered the room. You might wonder how we get that information—it's from the serialized data associated with the room.

You can store any variables or arrays in the attributes object that you want to. This feature enables you to display customized icons in a chat room. As you can see in this code, we create three properties on the attributes object. The allowSpectators property is either true or false. If a user clicks on the game icon and allowSpectators is false, then that user will not be permitted to join as a spectator. If the game room is already full and allowSpectators is false, then the user is not permitted to join at all.

Serialization

When data is serialized, it is represented as a string. The ElectroServer class takes an object and serializes it as XML. The object and all of its properties are represented by the XML document. That XML document can then be sent to other users or stored on the server in a database or in a text file for later use. That string can be deserialized at any time in the future to get the original object back.

Serialization makes things easier for us as game developers. As you will see later, the ElectroServer class has a method called sendMove that is used to send a game move to an opponent. This method uses serialization. You can build a simple or complicated object to send to your opponent.

Also take note of the FloodingFilterEnabled property. This is a property that can be set for any room. It is a good idea to set FloodingFilterEnabled to false for games. The default value is true, which means that by default the room detects flooding. Flooding is when a user sends many chat messages in a short amount of time. In a game, you are often expected to send many messages in a short amount of time. You can permanently disable the flood filter in the Configuration.xml file found in the install directory for ElectroServer 3. If the filter is not disabled and a user sends messages too frequently in a game, then the server will automatically kick the user from the server.

Showing the Game Icons

When a game is created, it is represented by an icon displayed on the main chat screen. This icon displays the name of the game and a text field containing information about the number of game players in the game. Because chess is only a two player game, you will only see this field say "1/2" or "Full." The string "1/2" means that the room current has one game player out of the two game players that it needs.

When a room list update is received, the showRooms function is called. This function calls the getRoomList method of the ElectroServer class. That method returns an array of all the rooms in your zone. Every element in the list is an object representing a room. As rooms are looped through in the showRooms function, any game rooms found are pushed into an array called gameRoomList. At the end of the showRooms function, another function called showGameRooms is called.

The showGameRooms function loops through the gameRoomList array and displays an icon for each game room. In addition to creating an icon and displaying it, a reference to the room itself is stored in the icon movie clip. When the icon is clicked, it takes this room reference and passes it into the gameClicked function.

The gameClicked function displays the Join Game frame of the popup movie clip. If the room is full, then it only lets the user join the game as a spectator if allowSpectators is true.

Joining a Game

When the gameClicked function is clicked, the Join Game frame of the popup movie clip is displayed. On this frame, a user can choose to join the game as a spectator or as a game player. Also, if the game is password-protected, then the user can enter the password here. Here are a few lines of ActionScript from the ok function on the Join Game frame of the popup movie clip.

```
_parent.joiningGame = true;
 if (IsPasswordProtected) {
       var password = pword_clip.password.text;
 } else {
       var password = "";
 }
 _parent.es.joinGame(roomName.text, password, joinType);
```

First we set a variable on the main Timeline called `joiningGame` to `true`. We do this so that when the `roomJoined` event is fired, we know that it is the response to joining a room, so we take the user to the Game frame label.

If the game room is password-protected, then we display a field where the user must enter a password.

The final line of ActionScript calls the `joinGame` method of the `ElectroServer` class. It passes in the name of the game to join, the password (which may not be needed), and the variable `joinType`. The variable `joinType` is a string that can be either "`player`" or "`spectator`".

Autonumbered Users

By default, a game room assigns numbers to game players and no numbers to spectators. This is a very useful feature. Users are numbered starting with 0 and increasing by 1 for every game player joined, so the person who creates the game has a number of 0, and the next game player to join has a number of 1. As people join a room (or game), everyone receives user list updates. If a user has a number, then this number is sent with the user list update.

In the game of chess, we can only have two players. Imagine that player 1 has created a game and is waiting for another player to join. Now three other users click on the game icon simultaneously and attempt to join as a game player. How do we know who should be the game player? Well, whoever ends up having a player number of 1 would be the person who gets to play. The other two users are numbered but are treated as spectators because the game player position was filled.

Starting the Game

We'll call the user that started the game PlayerA, user 0 (because that is the user's number), or the game master. PlayerA's opponent will be referred to as PlayerB or user 1.

When PlayerA creates the game, he is immediately taken to the Game frame label. On this frame, some ActionScript handles capturing chat messages, sending room list updates, and determining when there are enough players to start the game.

Also on this frame is a movie clip called `game_clip`. This movie clip contains all the ActionScript used to play the game.

The function on this frame called `showUsers` is called whenever the user list is updated. This function loops through the entire user list and populates two arrays: `playerList` and `spectatorList`. When PlayerA executes this function and the `playerList` contains the total number of people needed to play the game (which is two), then PlayerA executes `sendStartMove`.

The function `sendStartMove` simply calls the start function in the `game_clip` movie clip. That function displays a pop-up window for PlayerA to view. This pop-up window informs PlayerA that another player has joined the game and the game can now be started.

When PlayerA clicks the Start button, this function is executed:

```
function startClicked() {
      var moveOb:Object = new Object();
      moveOb.action = "start";
      sendMove(moveOb);
      startGame();
      popUp("1");
}
```

This function constructs an object to send to the opponent and then sends it. You can send any object that you want to another game player, but it is best to come up with some sort of basic structure. In this game, every object that is sent has an `action` property. This property contains a string that is used by the client receiving the move to determine what to do. In the case of this start move, the `action` property is the only one needed.

In line 4, the sendMove function is executed. That function takes the object that is passed in and sends it to the opponent.

Here is the sendMove function:

```
function sendMove(moveOb:Object) {
        es.sendMove([opponentName], moveOb);
}
```

This function simply sends a game move directly to your opponent.

The *sendMove* method

The sendMove method of the ElectroServer class enables you to send an object to one or more other users. This method takes two parameters. If the first parameter is "all", then it sends the object (which is the second parameter) to everyone in the room. If the first parameter is an array, then it sends the move to every user specified in the array.

```
var moveOb:Object = new Object();
moveOb.action = "start";
es.sendMove("all", moveOb);
```

These three lines of ActionScript create an object and send it to everyone in the room.

```
var users:Array = ["mike", "jobe", "ben"];
var moveOb:Object = new Object();
moveOb.action = "start";
es.sendMove(users, moveOb);
```

These four lines create an object and then send it to three specific users.

The object is serialized as XML, sent, received by other users, deserialized, and then used. When a move object is received, the moveReceived event is fired.

The *moveReceived* Event

As we have discussed, a move can be sent to one or more users at a time or can be sent to the entire game room. By sending a move, a serialized object is sent. This data passes through ElectroServer 3 and is routed to the appropriate users. When a user receives a move, the moveReceived event of the ElectroServer class is fired.

On the Game frame label in the root Timeline, we assign an event handler to the moveReceived event.

```
es.moveReceived = function(type:String, moveOb:Object,
➥from:String) {
	game_clip.moveReceived(moveOb, from);
};
```

This function is executed when a move is received. Three parameters are passed in. The first is a string whose value is either "public" or "private". If "public", then the move was sent to everyone in the room; otherwise it was sent to specific users. The second parameter is the object that was sent. It contains the move information. The third parameter is a string containing the username of the person that sent the move in the first place.

As you can see in the second line of this ActionScript, we pass the object and the name of the user that sent the object into a function called moveReceived in the game_clip movie clip.

Inside the game_clip movie clip is the moveReceived function:

```
function moveReceived(moveOb:Object, from:String) {
	//The type of move
	var action:String = moveOb.action;
	if (gamePlayer) {
		if (action == "move") {
			//Normal chess move
			var x1:Number = moveOb.x1;
			var y1:Number = moveOb.y1;
			var x2:Number = moveOb.x2;
			var y2:Number = moveOb.y2;
			starting_tile = chess.getTile(x1, y1);
			ending_tile = chess.getTile(x2, y2);
			if (moveOb.promote) {
				promotePiece = true;
				thePromotionPiece =
				➥moveOb.promotionPiece;
			} else {
				promotePiece = false;
			}
			animateMove();
```

```
            } else if (action == "start") {
                //start the game
                startGame();
                popUp("1");
            } else if (action == "restart") {
                _root.gotoAndStop("Refresh");
            } else if (action == "request state") {
                //A spectator requested the current
                ➥state of the game
                sendState(from);
            }
        } else if (!gamePlayer) {
            //Spectator received a move
            if (action == "board update") {
                //Normal move during the game
                updateBoard(moveOb.chessActions);
            } else if (action == "board state") {
                //Just joined the game, this displays
                ➥the board state
                showBoardState(moveOb);
            }
        }
    }
```

First, the move action is extracted from the object. This action is a string describing what the move represents, such as a move to start the game, a request of the entire board state (which would be requested by a spectator), or an actual in-game chess move.

This function has an `if` statement that allows the function execution to continue on one of two paths. If `gamePlayer` has a value of `true`, the client is one of the two players of the game. Otherwise, the client is just a spectator.

A game player can receive these possible moves:

- **move**—This type of move is a normal game move, such as a chess piece moving from one tile to another.
- **start**—This move is received by PlayerB after PlayerA clicks the Start button in the pop-up window. It tells PlayerB to close the pop-up window and to start the game.

- **restart**—When this action is received, the game is completely restarted.
- **request state**—This move is received by PlayerA and is a request from a spectator that just joined the game. PlayerA then sends information to that spectator on the current state of the board so that it can be displayed properly.

A spectator can receive these possible moves:

- **board update**—This move contains a list of actions that the spectator client should perform to show the most up-to-date board. It tells a client which piece to move, which piece is captured (if any), and other extra information. Extra information includes: the line of history text to add or if something special happens such as promotion or castling.
- **board state**—When a spectator first joins the game, he sends a move to PlayerA requesting the state of the board. PlayerA's response is captured here. Based on the information sent by PlayerA, the board is appropriately displayed.

Game Logic

Three classes were created for this game. They are `Tile`, `ChessPiece`, and `ChessBoard`. Before discussing these classes, we'll mention a few pieces of terminology.

Every tile that a chess piece has the capability to move to on the next turn is *threatened* or *hot*. All pieces start off *alive*. When captured, a piece is *dead*.

Tile class

Every instance of the `Tile` class represents one of the 64 tiles on the chess board. A tile knows if it is threatened. If it is threatened, a tile knows every chess piece that is threatening it. A tile also knows if it contains a chess piece. It has the capability to capture a chess piece, and it knows which row and column it belongs to.

Here are a few important methods to note:

- `getPiece()`—This method returns the chess piece (and instance of the `ChessPiece` class) that is currently contained in the tile, if any.

- `getColumn()`—Returns a number representing the column that it's in.
- `getRow()`—Returns a number representing the row that it's in.
- `isFilled`—Returns `true` if it contains a piece and `false` if it doesn't.
- `isWhiteHot`—Returns `true` if it is threatened by a white piece and `false` if it is not.
- `isBlackHot`—Returns `true` if it is threatened by a black piece and `false` if it is not.
- `getWhiteThreats()`—Returns an array of all white pieces that are threatening it.
- `getBlackThreats()`—Returns an array of all black pieces that are threatening it.
- `addPiece()`—Adds a chess piece to the tile.
- `removePiece()`—Removes a chess piece from the tile.
- `capturePiece()`—Captures the piece that is currently contained in the tile.

ChessPiece class

An instance of the `ChessPiece` class is used to represent each of the 32 pieces on a chess board. A chess piece knows what tile it's on, which tiles it is threatening, what type of piece it is, what color it is, the movie clip that represents it, and if it's alive or dead.

Here are a few important methods of the `ChessPiece` class to note:

- `getType()`—This returns a string representing the type of chess piece. This can be "pawn," "knight," "rook," "bishop," "king," or "queen."
- `getTileThreats()`—Returns an array of tiles that the piece is threatening.
- `clearTileThreats()`—Loops through every tile that it's threatening and removes the threat.
- `addTileThreat()`—Adds a tile to the list of tiles that the piece is threatening.
- `getColor()`—Returns either "white" or "black."

- `getAlive()`—Returns `true` if the piece is still alive or `false` if it has been captured.
- `changeType()`—Changes the type of chess piece that it represents. This method is only called if it is a pawn and has been promoted.
- `getID()`—Every chess piece has a unique id (1 through 32). The id is used for naming the movie clip that represents it. It is also used by spectators to easily update the state of the board.

ChessBoard class

Only one instance of the `ChessBoard` class exists per game. It is the largest of the three classes, totaling about 1200 lines of ActionScript. This class handles all the game logic and initialization. It creates the 64 `Tile` class instances and the 32 `ChessPiece` class instances and handles validation of chess moves, updating piece positions, and checking for the possible end game states.

Most of the methods of the `ChessBoard` class are used internally. Here are the methods called externally from the first frame in the Actions layer in the `game_clip` movie clip.

- `Initialize()`—When this method is called, the class builds 64 `Tile` instances (one for each tile on the game board) and 32 `ChessPiece` instances (one for each piece). It also places the chess pieces on their appropriate initial tiles and resets the game history.
- `setPieceIdentifier()`—This method accepts a string as a parameter corresponding to a linkage identifier. This linkage identifier is for the movie clip that contains the chess pieces. In Chess.fla, a movie clip called "pieces" contains 12 frames corresponding to the 6 different chess pieces of two different colors.
- `setBoard()`—A reference to the timeline where the chess pieces are to be attached is passed in. When the board is initialized, it creates 32 chess pieces and places them in this timeline.
- `setTileWidth()`—This method is used to set the pixel width of the tiles. The value is passed in.
- `setReverse()`—Both players see their own pieces at the bottom of the board. The default layout is for the white pieces to be displayed at the top of the board. So, for the white player to see his pieces at

the bottom, setReverse is called and true is passed in. If false is passed in, then black is shown on the bottom.

- getTile()—This method returns a reference to a tile. The column and row of the tile are passed in, such as getTile(5,7).
- getHistory()—This returns a preformatted string that can be displayed in a text field. This string contains the move history for the game.
- getLatestHistoryAddition()—This returns the most recent piece of history added to the history string.
- move()—This method is called when you want to make a move. It can be used in two separate ways. In the first way, you can pass in a reference to the starting tile and the destination tile, and it will detect the piece to move and move it. If needed, it will also capture a piece on the destination tile. The other way that this method can be used is to promote a pawn to a new piece. We'll discuss this later.

When the move method is called, a reference to the starting tile and the destination tile are passed in. Here is an example of the move method in use with an instance of the ChessBoard class called chess.

```
var starting tile:Tile = chess.getTile(5,7);
var ending tile:Tile = chess.getTile(5,5);
var result:Object = chess.move(starting tile, ending tile);
```

The first two lines create variables that store a reference to the starting tile and the destination tile. The third line of ActionScript passes the references into the move method of the ChessBoard class and captures the results as the result object.

Here is what happens when the move method is called:

First, based on the starting tile, the chess piece that is being moved is determined. Then a check is run to see if the move that is about to be performed is legal. If it is legal, then the move is performed in memory. After the move is made, a check is run to see if the color that just moved placed its own king in check. If it did, then the move is undone.

If the move placed the opponent's king in check, then we run some code to see if a checkmate game state has been reached. If no one is in check, then we check to see if the game is now a stalemate. If there is no check and no stalemate, then we check to see if either of the other two end game states have been reached. As a reminder, they are: if there are only two pieces left on the board, then a draw has been reached. If 50 moves have passed with no pawn moving or piece being captured, then a draw has been reached.

If no end game state has been reached and the move was valid, then it is visually updated on the screen, and a bit of history is added to the history text.

Finally, an object is constructed to return. This object contains several properties used to explain what happened. Here are the properties of this object:

- `success`—This is either `true` or `false`. If `true`, then the move was made.
- `history`—This contains the entire game history as a string.
- `checkmate`—This is either `true` or `false`. If `true`, then the game is over due to a checkmate.
- `stalemate`—This is either `true` or `false`. If `true`, then a stalemate has occurred, and the game is over.
- `draw`—This is `true` if the game reaches the same state three times. The game is over if `true`.
- `stall`—This is `true` if 50 moves have transpired with no pawns being move or pieces being captured.
- `insufficient`—This is `true` if only two pieces are left in the game.
- `promote`—If `true`, then a pawn needs to be promoted. It is not promoted yet because user input is needed. A reference to the pawn that is to be promoted is stored as a property called `pawnToPromote`.
- `pieceCaptured`—If `true`, then a piece was captured. The id of the captured piece is stored on the object as `capturedPieceID`. This is only used for the benefit of broadcasting an update to spectators.
- `castled`—If `true`, then the castling move has occurred. Information about the castling move is stored as `castleInfo` on the object.
- `enpassanted`—If `true`, then an *en passant* move has occurred. This is used to send an update to the spectators.

The Rest of the Frame Actions

In this section, we discuss what is going on with the ActionScript on the Actions and Spectator Actions layers in the `game_clip` movie clip. Most of the ActionScript is straightforward.

Approximately the first 30 lines of ActionScript in the Actions layer is composed of initializing variables and arrays that will be used throughout the game. These variables and arrays are used to store information such as the names of the two game players, if the user is a player, and a list of all spectators.

Next, you see this ActionScript.

```
1     if (myNum == 0) {
2            myColor = "white";
3            gamePlayer = true;
4            whitePlayer_txt.text = myName;
5     } else if (myNum == 1) {
6            myColor = "black";
7            gamePlayer = true;
8            blackPlayer_txt.text = myName;
9     }
10    if (myColor == "white") {
11           //flip the row and column ids
12           rowAndColumnClip.gotoAndStop(2);
13           boardReverse = true;
14    }
```

In the variable initialization (the first 30 lines in the .fla file), a variable called `myNum` was created. Its value is the automatic number assigned to the player by ElectroServer 3. The person that created the room (the "white" player) was given a number of 0. The next game player to join, "black," is given a number of 1. This code sets the value of `myColor` to either "`white`" or "`black`," depending on the number of the player. It also sets the player's own name into the appropriate text box.

By default, the value of `gamePlayer` is `false`. If the user's number is 0 or 1, then that user is a game player, and the value of `gamePlayer` is set to `true`. This is done in lines 3 and 7.

In lines 10–14, the board is flipped if the game player is the white player. Each player should see his own pieces at the bottom of the board. By default (that is, without flipping the board), the black pieces are on the bottom, so when the player is white, we need to flip the board. To do that, we send the move clip `rowAndColumnClip` to frame 2. The chess board itself is symmetric, so flipping it makes no visual difference. By flipping it, we are flipping the row and column numbering, and we are flipping where the pieces are initially places on the screen.

Next, the `ChessBoard` class instance is created and configured.

```
1       var chess:ChessBoard = new ChessBoard();
2       chess.setReverse(boardReverse);
3       chess.setPieceIdentifier("pieces");
4       chess.setBoard(board_mc);
5       chess.setTileWidth(tileWidth);
6       chess.initialize();
```

In line 1, we create a `ChessBoard` class instance and give it a reference name of `chess`. Then we set the `reverse` property based on the `boardReverse` variable. The `boardReverse` variable is `false` if the player is black and `true` if the player is white. Next, we set the linkage identifier that is used for the movie clip that contains all the chess pieces. Then, in line 4, we pass in a reference to the timeline to which the chess pieces should be attached. In line 5, the width of the chess tiles is set. Using the tile width, the `chess` class can properly place the chess pieces on the board. Finally, the `chess` class is initialized. Initializing the class builds the tiles and chess pieces and places the pieces on the screen.

On the Actions layer, we define event handlers for `onMouseDown`, `onMouseUp`, and `onMouseMove`. When the mouse is pressed down, we detect which tile it is over. If that tile contains a piece of that player's color, then it is picked up. When the mouse is moved while the player is holding a piece, the piece follows the mouse. When the mouse button is released while the player is holding a piece, the tile over which this occurred is detected and the `move` method is called.

If the move is a success, it is sent to the user's opponent and the spectators.

When a move is received by a player, the piece being moved is animated from the starting tile to the end tile. When it reaches the end tile, the `move` method is called to update the game board in memory.

Here is a quick recap of the entire game:

- PlayerA creates the game room and is given a number of 0.
- PlayerB joins the game and is given a number of 1.
- When PlayerB detects the presence of PlayerB, the game is started.
- PlayerA makes a valid move and sends that move information to PlayerB and to the spectators.
- PlayerB receives the move and animates the piece from its starting position to its end position. When a spectator receives a board update, no animation occurs; the board is just updated.
- When a move is made, the history is updated to reflect the move.
- When an end state of the game is reached, no further moves can be made.

You should now have a good idea of how this two player multiplayer turn-based game of chess works.

POINTS TO REMEMBER

- When a new game is created, an icon appears in the main chat area.
- A user can click on the game icon to join the game as a player or a spectator.
- Game players are automatically numbered by ElectroServer 3.
- The users numbered 0 and 1 are the game players. This is how you can detect who should be permitted to make a move.
- The chess game is comprised of three classes: `Tile`, `ChessPiece`, and `ChessBoard`.
- The `sendMove` method of the `ElectroServer` class is used to send objects to other players and spectators in a game.
- A spectator can join the game at any time and see the current state of the board.

Game Overview 436

Game Logic 438

Points to Remember 450

CHAPTER 17

501 Darts Game

Ah, Darts. The age old game of skill that challenges your ability to throw colorful, needle-sharp objects across the room, stick them in a desired spot on a board, and obtain certain game goals. Numerous games and variations on the darts theme exist, and one of the most popular competition games is *501 Darts*.

We've created a single player version of this popular game using Flash MX 2004, and in this chapter, we will take a close look at all the logic and code used to create the game.

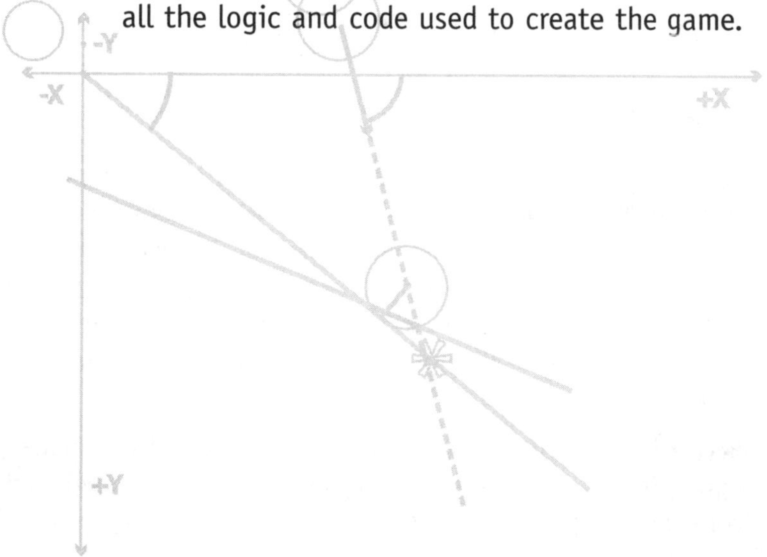

Prerequisites

Chapter 3, "Game Math"—We use some simple trigonometry when calculating the angle between the dart and the board center. This is used when figuring the point values for the dart hit.

The reader should be familiar with basic handling of attached assets. This game uses attached movie clips and sounds.

The user should be familiar with using objects to store data. This game sets up objects as controllers and uses them to control the darts in their various modes during play.

Game Overview

501 Dart Challenge is a simple, quick, easy-to-play classic darts game that challenges the player to whittle away the 501 points down to zero by subtracting the point values hit by the dart throws. This game, along with its sister games 301, 701, and so on, is commonly used in dart tournaments.

Game Play

501 Darts is one of many derivatives of the '01' theme. Other games include 301, 701, 901, 1001, and so on, and all follow the same simple game play. In a multiplayer environment, each player starts out with x01 points, each dart throw is subtracted from the player's score, and the first person to reach zero exactly wins. This is called *Closing Out.* If a player throw exceeds the point value needed to close out, this is called a *Bust,* and no points are subtracted for the throw.

Because our version is a single-player game, we will still challenge the player to close out in as few throws as possible, but we will add some competition by saving their best score and challenging them to beat it.

Scoring

Scoring in darts can seam a bit confusing and intimidating, but it is actually quite simple. The confusion is mostly due to the problem of doing those few simple math calculations in your head while your friends impatiently stare and wait for you to tally your score. Ok, that could just be me. Anyway, our game will do the math automatically, so that won't be a concern. We just need to know how the score board works.

The darts board is divided into 20 pie-shape wedges, with the 20-point wedge at the top, and then proceeding clockwise, it goes 1, 18, 4, 13, 6, 10, 15, 2, 17, 3, 19, 7, 16, 8, 11, 14, 9, 12, 5 and then back to 20 at the top (see Figure 17.1). Personally, I don't see any pattern there, but that's the way it is. The wedges' base point value is defined by these numbers.

FIGURE 17.1
The traditional darts board.

The entire board is then divided into rings. Starting from the outside, the board has a small ring known as the *Double Point Ring*. Any hit in this ring scores double the base value of the wedge.

Further in, around half-way to the center, there is another small ring known as the *Triple Point Ring*. Any hit in this ring counts triple the base value of the wedge.

In the center, there is a small area known as the *Bull's-Eye*. This area is not associated with a numbered wedge and can often have different point values, based on the game being played. For our game, we will be giving 25 points for a hit in this area.

Game Logic

Overall, the code needed to create this game is fairly simple. We'll go through it piece-by-piece in sections. We'll start with code that is used before the game for loading and setup (you always need a certain amount of this). Then we'll examine the code used for playing the game, including aiming, throwing, and scoring. Finally, we'll go over the code used after the game is played.

Open the Flash file 501Darts.fla from the CD and follow along.

Before the Game

As I mentioned, you will always need a certain amount of code for setup purposes before you can work on the playable part of the game. Some of these pieces are used in every game, so it is good practice to have some generic code snippets that you can reuse for all your games.

Saved High Score

On the first frame, we make an attempt to load a saved high score from the local `SharedObject`.

The following code sets up the `SharedObject` that we'll use to save the player's best score. If the player has already saved a score in the object, this line sets up a reference to the data.

```
//SET UP THE SHARED OBJECT TO HAVE OUR BEST SCORE
var myGameData:SharedObject =
➥SharedObject.getLocal("myGameData");
```

This code then checks to see if any high score data is available. If so, it retrieves our high score and stores it in a variable called `highScore`.

```
//CHECK FOR HIGH SCORE
if (myGameData.data.savedHighScore){
      var highScore:Number =
      ➥myGameData.data.savedHighScore;
}
```

Loading Progress Bar

The first thing people see when they load your game shouldn't be a blank screen. If your game requires many assets to be loaded, you should make a loading progress bar be visible as soon as possible. This particular game is only around 27 KB, so a loading bar is probably not even needed, but it is very simple to include, so let's take a look anyway.

All you need to create a nice loading bar is a movie clip the length and shape of your desired loading bar when fully loaded. In this game, the clip is called loadingbar. This clip goes in the first frame of our movie, where we include the following ActionScript to control it.

```
//WAIT FOR LOADING
loadingbar.onEnterFrame = function(){
if(_root.getBytesLoaded() >= _root.getBytesTotal()){
        _root.gotoAndPlay("init");
}else{
        this._xscale=
        ➥((_root.getBytesLoaded()/_root.getBytesTotal()) *
        ➥100);
}
}
```

This code attaches an `onEnterFrame()` script to the loadingbar movie clip. Each frame, this script compares the loaded bytes to the total bytes. If all the bytes are loaded, the playhead is moved to the "init" frame where we get ready for the game. If the loading is not complete, the scale of our loadingbar movie clip is changed to represent the current load progress.

After the movie has finished loading, the loading bar moves the playhead to the "init" frame. This frame is where we do all of the required setup and define the functions that we will be using for the gameplay itself.

Setup

We need to initialize a few things before we can play the game. First, we set up a couple sounds that we need. In the Library, these two sounds have "Export For ActionScipt" selected in the Linkage Properties panel. Now they are available for attaching to our newly-created `Sound` objects. Later we will use the `.start()` command to play these sounds.

```
//INIT SOUNDS
var Snd_alert_good:Sound = new Sound();
Snd_alert_good.attachSound("alert_good");

var Snd_alert_bad:Sound = new Sound();
Snd_alert_bad.attachSound("alert_bad");
```

We then create the dart scaling array. Basically, this sets up a simple array with an entry for each distance step, containing a scale factor for that distance. This is a very simple but efficient way to simulate the scaling of objects as they move away from the camera. For example, an object at a distance of zero would not be scaled at all (100 percent); the next step multiplies that scale by .998, resulting in a slightly smaller object at distance 1, and so forth.

This method is a little faster than doing the calculations each frame during play, and for most cases, it looks just as good.

```
//BUILD SCALING ARRAY FOR DART
var perspective_scalefactor:Number = 0.998;
var scale:Number = 100;
var max_dist:Number = 500;
var scalearray:Array = new Array();
for(var dist:Number = 0; dist<= max_dist; dist++){
      scale *= perspective_scalefactor;
      scalearray.push(scale);
}
```

On this screen, we display the help and intro graphics for the game. The user must click the [PLAY] button to start the game.

Playing the Game

Now for the code that we will use to actually play the game. We'll need to aim the dart, throw it, track its movements in space until it eventually hits the dart board, and then calculate the point value for the throw.

Because the game consists of different modes (aiming, throwing, flying), we define a controller object. We use this object to define actions that we can attach to the darts for controlling the different dart modes.

These controller definitions are on the "init" frame.

```
var controller:Object = new Object();
```

Aiming the Dart

The aim controller simply moves the movie clip to which it is attached to the mouse position. This function is assigned to the onEnterFrame() event of our dart clip while the user is aiming.

```
//AIM CONTROLLER
controller.aim = function(){
      this._x = _xmouse;
      this._y = _ymouse;
}
```

Releasing the Dart

Releasing the dart consists of two events. The user clicks the mouse and releases it in a new position. We will use the two positions as well as the elapsed time between the click and release to determine flight path and dart speed.

The first dart controller is attached to the onMouseDown() event while the player is aiming. This controller just records the mouse position and time when the mouse is clicked.

```
//RELEASE CONTROLLER 1 (PRESS)
controller.shoot_click = function(){
      this.startTime = getTimer();
      this.start_x = _xmouse;
      this.start_y = _ymouse;
}
```

After the mouse is clicked, it will be released to initiate the dart throw. This controller is attached to the onMouseUp event during aiming and captures the mouse position and time when the mouse is released. This data, along with the onMouseDown data, is used to initiate the thrown dart.

```
//RELEASE CONTROLLER 2 (RELEASE)
controller.shoot_release = function(){
      this.endTime = getTimer();
      this.end_x =  _xmouse;
      this.end_y =  _ymouse;
```

Now that we have the data from both the mouse press and release, we calculate the offsets, speed, and distance between the two actions.

```
//CALCULATE OFFSETS
var xoffset:Number = Math.abs(this.start_x -
➥this.end_x) + 1;
var yoffset:Number = Math.abs(this.start_y -
➥this.end_y) + 1;
var distance:Number = Math.sqrt(Math.pow(xoffset,2)
➥+  Math.pow(yoffset , 2));
var elapsedTime:Number = this.endTime -
➥this.startTime;
var speedfactor:Number = (distance/elapsedTime*10)-
➥10;
```

After we've done that, it's time to create the dart that will be thrown. Just duplicate the aiming dart for this, then assign it variables for the flight path and starting position.

The flight path variables (fall, speed, lift, and lateral offset) are all derived from the offsets and speed that we just calculated. In this game, the fall, speed, and lift values were tweaked many times through trial and error to achieve the desired effect.

When tweaking certain variables, it can take many many trials and adjustments to achieve the desired effect. This is part of the process, so plan to spend some time on it. Sometimes this fine tuning can really take your game to the next level. Also don't be afraid to try values that seam unreasonable, as doing so can result in discovering a cool effect that you didn't expect.

```
//CREATE AIRBORN DART
duplicateMovieClip(this, "dart_hit", 1);
 _root.game.dart_hit.fall = 7;
 _root.game.dart_hit.speed = 40 + speedfactor;
 _root.game.dart_hit.lift =
 ➥_root.game.dart_hit.speed*.8;
 _root.game.dart_hit.lateraloffset = (this.start_x -
 ➥this.end_x)*0.15;
 _root.game.dart_hit.pos_x = this.end_x;
 _root.game.dart_hit.pos_y = this.end_y;
 _root.game.dart_hit.pos_z = 0;
```

Through user testing, we found that some people do it backward (clicking high and dragging down to release). No problem; just reverse the lateral offset if that happens.

```
        //ACCOUNT FOR PEOPLE THAT MIGHT DO IT BACKWARDS –
➥IT HAPPENS
        if (this.start_y>this.end_y){
            _root.game.dart_hit.lateraloffset *= -1;
        }
```

Finally, to throw the dart, we assign the "fly" controller to the newly-created darts (detailed in the next section). Because the dart has now been thrown, we need to hide and disable the aiming dart, which will be re-enabled after the current dart hits the board.

```
1       //HIDE AIMER DART AND THROW DART
2        root.game.dart_hit.onEnterFrame = controller.fly;
3        root.game.dart._visible = false;
4        root.game.dart.onMouseUp = null;
5   }
```

Flying

On line 2 (in the previous section), we assign the fly controller to the onEnterFrame() event of the dart clip that has just been thrown. This code executes every frame while the dart is in flight; let's take a close look.

```
    //FLY CONTROLLER
    controller.fly = function(){
```

The first thing the function does is translate the dart's *x*, *y*, and *z* coordinates according to the flight path data that was defined by the shoot_release controller.

```
        //TRANSLATE DART
        this.pos_x += this.lateraloffset;
        this.pos_y -= this.lift;
        this.pos_z += this.speed;
```

Next, using the scaling array that we set up in the "init" frame of the movie, it's time to apply the scaling and translate the actual dart sprite to the correct position on the screen.

```
//SCALE AND POSITION
var scalefactor:Number =
➥_root.scalearray[Math.round(this.pos_z)];
this._xscale = scalefactor;
this._yscale = scalefactor;
this._x = this.pos_x
this._y = (this.pos_y * (scalefactor * .01));
```

To create a realistic flight path, we'll adjust the lift and speed a little each frame. This gives us the effect of gravity and drag. When the dart is first thrown, the lift is a fairly large number, so the dart flies upward, but as in real life, what goes up must come down, so we subtract the fall value each frame, and the dart's height is gradually decreased.

```
//ADJUST DYNAMICS
this.lift -= this.fall;
this.speed *= 0.96;
```

Now that the new dart position has been defined, it's time to check for a hit. Not only do we check for the dart to reach the distance of the wall, but we also must check for a dart that was not thrown hard enough to make it to the wall. We can assume that if the *y* value exceeds 2000, the dart is only falling and has no chance of hitting the board. (Actually, this number doesn't need to be that big, but it is just a bit more fun to delay the hit a second after the dart falls off screen.)

```
//CHECK FOR HIT
if((this.pos_z >= _root.boardDist) ||(this.pos_y >=
➥2000)){
```

When a hit is detected, we move the playhead on the dart clip to the "hit" frame. This frame starts a simple animation of the dart sticking into the board (or wall). Also, the "hit" frame contains a frame sound of the dart hitting.

```
//PLAY HIT ANIMATION
this.gotoAndPlay("hit");
```

Using the `getScore()` function detailed in the next section, we obtain the point value for the hit and then attach our point_display movie clip to the Stage and assign it the point value. This clip is a simple text animation of the point value. The last frame of the clip contains the code `this.removeMovieClip();` which removes the clip from the movie. We will attach a new one with each hit.

```
//GET SCORE
var pointvalue:Number = _root.getScore(this._x,
➥this._y);
//DISPLAY SCORE
_root.game.attachMovie("point_display" ,
➥"point_display", 3);
_root.game.point_display._x = this._x;
_root.game.point_display._y = this._y;
_root.game.point_display.pointvalue = pointvalue;
```

At this point, we increment the throw count and check the status of the game to decide what to do next. Line 4 checks to see if the new score is equal to zero. If so, this is a Close Out. We display the appropriate alert text and play the good alert sound. Line 10 sets an interval function to move the playhead to the "game_over" frame after 1500 milliseconds (1–1/2 seconds). If you were to advance to the screen right away, the player wouldn't have time to give themselves a pat on the back and admire their final precise shot.

```
1     //INCRIMENT THROW COUNT
2     _root.throws++;
3     //CHECK STATUS
4     if(_root.score - pointvalue == 0){
5           //CLOSE OUT
6           _root.score = 0;
7           _root.alerttext = "CLOSED! YOU GOT IT!!";
8           _root.alert.gotoAndPlay(2);
9           _root.Snd_alert_good.start();
10          var intervalID =
            ➥setInterval(function(){gotoAndPlay("game_
            ➥over");clearInterval( intervalID );}, 1500);
```

If the resulting score is below zero, this is a Bust. Again, we display the appropriate alternate text, this time with the bad alert sound. In keeping with the rules of the game, the player's point value is not changed, but the game goes on, so the aiming dart is made visible, and the release controller is again attached to the onMouseUp() event.

```
        }else if(_root.score - pointvalue < 0){
                //BUST
                _root.alerttext = "BUST! (MUST CLOSE OUT
                ➥EXACTLY)";
                _root.alert.gotoAndPlay(2);
                _root.Snd_alert_bad.start(0,2);
                _root.game.dart._visible = true;
                _root.game.dart.onMouseUp =
                ➥controller.shoot_release;
```

If the shot doesn't result in either a Close Out or a Bust, it is treated as a regular shot. The point value is subtracted from the total, no alert messages are shown, and regular play is continued.

```
        }else{
                _root.score -= pointvalue;
                _root.game.dart._visible = true;
                _root.game.dart.onMouseUp =
                ➥controller.shoot_release;
        }
```

In any event, if the dart hits the wall, the fly controller must be disabled. This is easy—just reassign the onEnterFrame event to null.

```
        //DIABLE THIS DART
        _root.game.dart_hit.onEnterFrame = null;
    }
    }
```

getScore()

For each dart hit, we need to calculate the point value for that throw (see Figure 17.2). This function is called by the fly controller when the dart hits the wall and returns the point value for that throw.

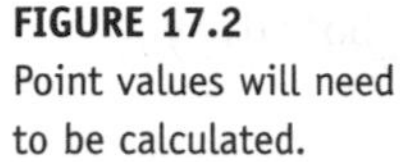

FIGURE 17.2
Point values will need to be calculated.

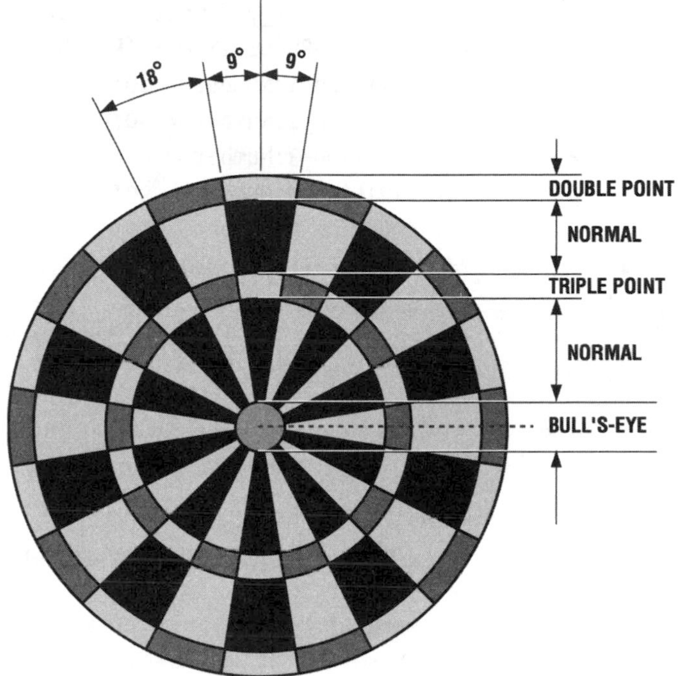

Many point possibilities exist for a throw, with the 20 wedges, Double and Triple Rings, and the Bull's-Eye, so we'll need an elegant way to obtain a score based on the dart's landing position. The solution is not too complicated.

For the function to work, we pass in the point where the dart hits (just an *x* and *y* value).

```
1      function getScore(darthit_x, darthit_y){
```

First, we identify the center of the dart board and assign the values for the division rings and the wedge values. Lines 5–9 define the distance from the center to each ring division. These values were measured during development and hard-coded. If you want to move and scale the board during run-time, these values should be dynamically generated. Line 11 defines the wedge base values in an array.

```
1             //IDENTIFY CENTER OF BOARD
2             var boardcenter_x:Number = _root.dart_board._x;
```

```
var boardcenter_y:Number = _root.dart_board._y;
//DEFINE BOARD DIVISIONS (RINGS)
var division_1:Number = 10;
var division_2:Number = 50;
var division_3:Number = 60;
var division_4:Number = 90;
var division_5:Number = 100;
//DEFINE SLOT POINT VALUES
var slotArr:Array = new
➥Array(20,1,18,4,13,6,10,15,2,17,3,19,7,16,8,11,14
➥,9,12,5,20);
```

Next, we use the dart center point and the hit point data to calculate the angle and distance (or tangent) between the two points.

```
// CALCULATE OFFSETS
        var xoffset:Number = darthit_x - boardcenter_x;
        var yoffset:Number = darthit_y - boardcenter_y;
        var tangent:Number =
        ➥Math.sqrt(Math.pow(Math.abs(xoffset),2)+Math.pow(
        ➥Math.abs(yoffset),2));
        var angle:Number =
        ➥(Math.atan2(yoffset,xoffset)*180/Math.PI)+90;
        if(angle<0){angle = 360+angle;}
```

With the angle, it is easy to calculate the slot that we are in. Because we know that the wedges are at 18 degree angles (360 degrees divided by 20 wedges) and that the top wedge is split, we can use this formula to arrive at the slot the dart lands in.

```
var slot:Number = Math.floor((angle+9)/18);
```

Knowing the slot, or wedge, it's only a matter of evaluating the distance from the board center to arrive at the final point value for our throw.

```
// ASSIGN POINT VALUE
if(tangent<=division_1){pointvalue =25;}
else if(tangent<=division_2){var
➥pointvalue:Number=slotArr[slot]*1;}
```

```
            else if(tangent<=division_3){var
            ➥pointvalue:Number=slotArr[slot]*3;}
            else if(tangent<=division_4){var
            ➥pointvalue:Number=slotArr[slot]*1;}
            else if(tangent<=division_5){var
            ➥pointvalue:Number=slotArr[slot]*2;}
            else {var pointvalue:Number=0;}
            ➥Then return that value, and this step is finished.
            return pointvalue;
    }
```

After the Game

Like the pre-game elements, a bit of content and logic always comes into play after the game is over. There's not much here really, mainly the GAME OVER screen, where we display the final results of the game along with a button to play again.

Also, this is where we update the player's saved high score data if he or she did better this time.

Updating Saved High Score

If the player's new score is better (in this case, lower) than the score we have saved for him or her, we need to update it. Lines 3 and 4 set the object data, and line 5 actually saves the data.

```
1    //UPDATE THE HIGH SCORE IF THE PLAYER DID BETTER THIS TIME
2    if(throws <= highScore){
3           highScore = throws;
4           myGameData.data.savedHighScore = highScore;
5           myGameData.data.flush();
6    }
```

That's the game. Experiment by changing the graphics and sound and flight parameters, to see how these changes affect the feeling of the game.

Points to Remember

- Math is your friend. Even in a simple game like this, we use a certain amount of math to help us determine the hit angle.
- Simple features like saving the player's personal high score can add a lot of fun to a game.
- Whenever possible, develop code elements such as loading bars, score savers, and so on in generic terms so that they can be reused in your other projects.
- Controller objects can be used to define different behaviors for your game elements.
- Try making variations on this game by changing the initial score variable from 501 to 301 for a shorter game or 701 for a longer game.
- It is possible to close out a game of *501 Darts* in 9 throws. You won't do it, but it is possible.

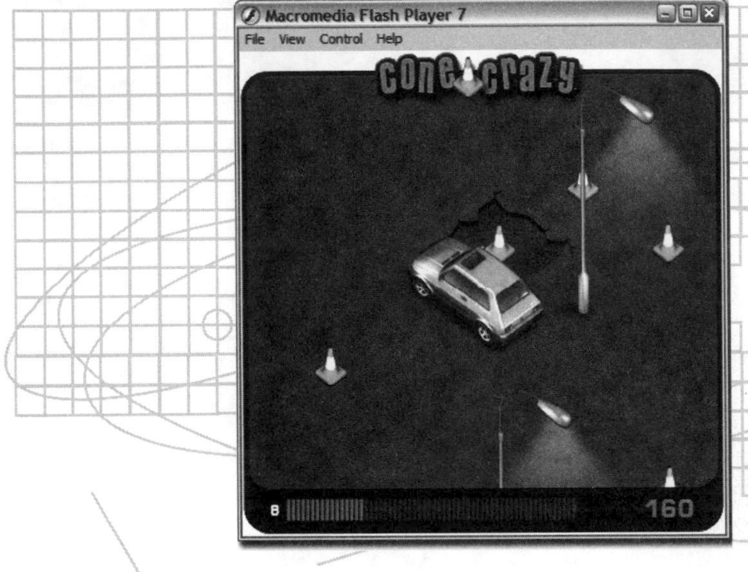

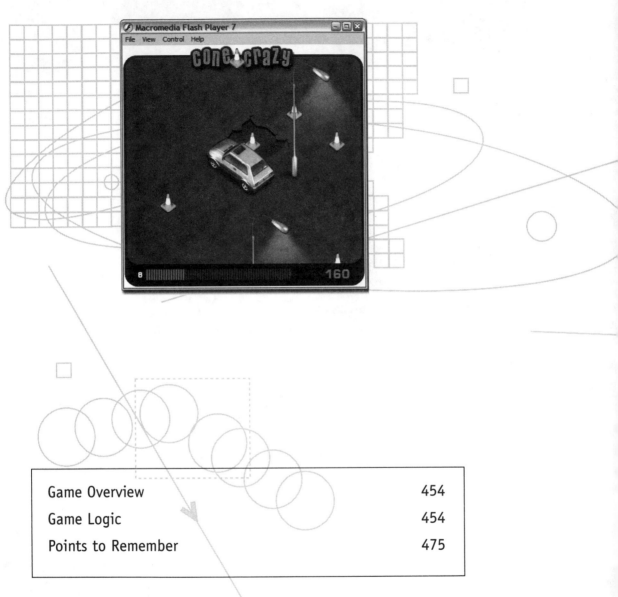

Game Overview	454
Game Logic	454
Points to Remember	475

CHAPTER 18

Cone Crazy

Cone Crazy is a little game we made up to demonstrate some techniques for creating effective tile-based games. The game and code described in this chapter will serve as a good basis for you to create your own tile-based game. These kinds of games are very powerful and easily expandable. I recommend that after you have established a basic understanding of the working of this game, you try adding your own objects and effects. Have fun! If you break something, you can always start over with the original files included on the CD.

Prerequisites

Chapter 3, "Game Math"—We use some simple trigonometry for calculating angles of travel for both the car and the cones.

The reader should be familiar with multi-dimensional arrays. These are used to define the game level.

The reader should be familiar with basic handling of attached assets. This game uses attached movie clips and sounds.

The reader should be familiar with using objects to store data. This game sets up objects as controllers for just about everything.

Game Overview

Cone Crazy positions you in a little red car in the middle of a large paved area full of cones, light poles, and fire hydrants. Your objective is that knock down as many cones as you can before the 30-second timer expires. There are two kinds of cones: the 10-point orange cones and the less frequent 50-point yellow cones. Watch out for the poles and hydrants though; they'll stop you dead in your tracks. There are no rules; just drive around like you've gone *Cone Crazy*!

Game Logic

Here's where we dissect the logic for this game. This game is fairly complicated, so there is a lot of information here. It is broken down into small chunks with commentary, so it shouldn't be too difficult to follow.

Before the Game

Before we even set up the game, we have a few standard tasks to take care of—namely, the loading bar and initialization of a few sounds.

Loading Progress Bar

This is pretty standard loading bar code. It's also portable, so you can use it in all your games.

```
//WAIT FOR LOADING
loadingbar.onEnterFrame = function(){
if(_root.getBytesLoaded() >= _root.getBytesTotal()){
      _root.gotoAndPlay("init");
}else{
      this._xscale=((_root.getBytesLoaded()
      ➥/_root.getBytesTotal()) * 100);
}
}
```

Initialize Sounds

When calling sounds with code, you first need to set them up. This code sets up two sound objects and attaches one of our hit sounds to each one. These sounds must be exported for ActionScript in the Linkage Properties dialog box.

```
//INIT SOUNDS
var Snd_hit:Sound = new Sound();
Snd_hit.attachSound("hit_1");
var Snd_hit2:Sound = new Sound();
Snd_hit2.attachSound("hit_2");
```

Setup

With a tile-based game (or any game where things are happening dynamically), there is a good bit of setup required before the game can be played. This defines the tiles, objects and their actions, defines the game level, and initializes the variables that govern the game.

Tile/Object Definitions

The power of a tile-based game is that a large and/or complex game level can be made up of just a few tiles. These tiles need to be defined before building the game world.

The method that we use in this game is to set up separate code objects for each tile and object in the game. These code objects define everything about the individual elements, including any variables, effects, and actions.

For this game, we have two distinct tile types:

- **B (blktop)**—This is a plain black top road surface.
- **P (pothole)**—A pothole tile that slows the car down.

These tiles make up the surfaces that the player will be driving on, so they'll need to contain information about themselves that the car can reference during play. Here is a sample format for a tile object. This code is not actually found within the game, but it is provided as an example of the way we will be formatting our tile objects.

```
var sampletile:Object = new Object();
sampletile.clip = "tile_sample";
sampletile.oktodrive = true;
sampletile.effects = new Object();
sampletile.effects.bumpy = 0;
sampletile.effects.drag = 0;
```

In addition to the tiles, the game contains distinct objects and obstacles. In this game, there are four distinct object types:

- **C (cone)**—Regular cone worth 10 points when hit
- **S (sp_cone)**—Special cone worth 50 points when hit
- **L (lightpole)**—Light pole obstacle
- **H (hydrant)**—Fire hydrant obstacle

Each type is defined by a code object containing information about itself and actions that are called when hit. Here is an example of how these objects are defined. Again, don't look for this code in the file; it's just an example of the format used.

```
var sampleobject:Object = new Object();
sampleobject.clip = "obj_ sampleobject";
sampleobject.doWhenHit = function(speed, angle, tile){
//ACTIONS THAT HAPPEN ONCE WHEN HIT
};
```

```
sampleobject.doAfterHit = function(){
//ACTIONS THAT HAPPEN CONTINUALLY AFTER HIT
};
```

Those are only examples of the format for the objects that define our world. We'll go through the actual game code used to set up and govern these objects in "Playing the Game" section later in this chapter.

Laying Out the World

After we've defined the code objects that make up our game world, we need to lay out the world itself. In this game, we have divided the layout into two separate multi-dimensional arrays: one array for the tiles, and a separate array for the objects. For this game, both arrays describe a 12×12 grid.

The tile array looks like this:

```
//CONSTRUCT OUR WORLD MAP
var map:Array = new Array();
map[0] = [B,B,B,B,B,B,B,B,B,B,B,B];
map[1] = [B,B,B,B,B,B,B,B,B,B,B,B];
map[2] = [B,B,B,P,B,B,B,B,P,B,B,B];
map[3] = [B,B,B,B,B,B,B,B,B,B,B,B];
map[4] = [B,B,B,B,B,B,B,B,B,B,B,B];
map[5] = [B,B,B,B,B,B,P,B,B,B,B,B];
map[6] = [B,B,P,B,B,B,B,B,B,B,B,B];
map[7] = [B,B,B,P,B,B,B,B,B,B,B,B];
map[8] = [B,B,B,B,B,B,B,B,B,B,B,B];
map[9] = [B,B,B,B,B,B,B,B,B,B,B,B];
map[10] = [B,B,B,B,B,B,B,P,B,B,B,B];
map[11] = [B,B,B,B,B,B,B,B,B,B,B,B];
map[12] = [B,B,B,B,B,B,B,B,B,B,B,B];
```

Each entry in the array contains another array, resulting in rows and columns for our world, with rows increasing along the *z* axis and columns increasing along the *x* axis. Each value is a reference to one of our predefined tiles. For instance, a lookup into `map[2][8]` would return the tile object `P`, which contains data to describe a pothole.

We are using single-letter objects for no other reason than to make it easier to understand the array data visually.

The same methods are used to define the in-game objects such as cones and obstacles.

```
//ADD INDEPENDANT OBJECTS
var objects:Array = new Array();
objects[0] = [0,0,0,0,0,0,0,0,0,0,0,0];
objects[1] = [0,S,0,C,0,C,C,0,0,S,0,0];
objects[2] = [0,C,0,0,H,0,0,0,C,L,0,0];
objects[3] = [0,C,C,C,0,0,C,0,0,0,C,0];
objects[4] = [0,C,0,0,C,S,0,0,0,C,C,0];
objects[5] = [0,L,C,0,0,0,C,L,0,C,0,0];
objects[6] = [0,0,0,S,C,C,C,C,0,C,0,0];
objects[7] = [0,L,0,0,0,C,0,C,0,0,H,0];
objects[8] = [0,C,C,C,C,0,L,0,C,0,C,0];
objects[9] = [0,C,S,C,0,0,C,C,C,0,H,0];
objects[10]= [0,0,C,C,0,0,C,S,C,0,0,0];
objects[11]= [0,C,C,C,0,S,C,C,C,0,L,0];
objects[12]= [0,0,0,0,0,0,0,0,0,0,0,0];
```

These references to the tile and object definitions make it easy for us to quickly access information about specific tiles and in-game objects.

Initializing Variables

Now it's time to define the variables we'll be starting with. We use separate code objects to define world, screen, and player variables.

Our `world` object holds data about the world. This is our in-game system that we use for almost all the game logic. Here we set the tile width, height, and total dimensions of the world.

```
//WORLD VARIABLES
var world:Object = new Object();
world.tile_width = 10;
world.tile_height = 10;
world.totaldepth = world.tile_height*map.length;
world.totalwidth = world.tile_width*map[0].length;
```

The `screen` object contains information used for rendering the game to the screen. The `keepplayerat` variables are used to pan the game view to keep the player at these coordinates.

```
//SCREEN VARIABLES
var screen:Object = new Object();
screen.scroll_x = 0;
screen.scroll_y = 0;
screen.keepplayerat_x = 200;
screen.keepplayerat_y = 200;
```

Finally, the player object contains data used when dealing with the player car. This data includes the starting position of the car and dynamic properties such as maximum speed, acceleration rate, turning rates, and so on. Having these variables defined here makes it very easy for us to tweak the game and maximize game play. The allowturns variable is used to temporarily disable turning after a collision with an obstacle.

```
//PLAYER VARIABLES
var player:Object = new Object();
player.car_x = 55;
player.car_y = 0;
player.car_z = 55;
player.speed = 0;
player.maxspeed = 2;
player.accelrate = .2;
player.decelrate = .9;
player.angle = 0;
player.anglechange = 0;
player.maxanglechange = 10;
player.anglechangerate = 7;
player.allowturns = true;
```

WorldToScreen() Conversion

Because our world coordinate system is different from Flash's screen coordinate system, we'll need a conversion function that can quickly convert world coordinates to screen coordinates for sprite placement and rendering.

This function accepts world *x*, *y*, and *z* and returns screen *x* and *y*. A more mathematically-correct function can be found in Chapter 8, "The Isometric Worldview," but because this game has a constant view, we can use this hard-coded function to get the same results with a little more control and performance.

```
function WorldToScreen(world_x, world_y, world_z) {
      x = Math.round((world_x*7)+(world_z*5)*1.4);
      y = Math.round((-(world_z*5)+(world_x*7)*.71426) -
      ➥(world_y*5));
      return [x, y];
}
```

Constructing the World

Now that we have defined our tiles, objects, and level layout, we can complete our game preparation by constructing our game world. For this we use nested loops. The first loop cycles through the world rows. For each row, the nested loop cycles through the columns in the current row. You'll find this in the ACTIONS layer on frame 11.

The code contained in our nested loop is executed for each tile in our grid. Let's take a closer look.

```
for (var row:Number = 0; row<_root.map.length; row++){
for(var col:Number = 0; col<_root.map[row].length;
➥col++){
```

First, we'll go through the construction of the tiles. Before we construct a tile and add it to our game, we need to make sure that the tile is valid. Line 2 of the following code checks this. If it is not valid, the `continue;` statement omits the rest of the loop and continues with the next tile. Lines 6, 7, and 8 define the tile's coordinates in our world system. These are then used in line 10 to calculate the depth of the new tile. Finally, line 18 actually attaches the clip to the Stage.

```
1       // **** TILES ****
2       if(!_root.map[row][col]||_root.map[row][col]==0)
        ➥{continue;}
3       //NAME TILE
4       var the_tile:String = "tile_"+row+"_"+col;
5       //GET WORLD POSITION
6       var world_x:Number = world.tile_width*col;
```

```
7     var world_y:Number = 0;
8     var world_z:Number = world.tile_height*row;
9     //ATTACH CLIP
10    var newdepth:Number =
      ➥Math.floor(((world.totaldepth-
      ➥world_z)*1000)+(world_x));
11    root.game.attachMovie(_root.map[row][col].clip,
      ➥the_tile, newdepth, _root.map[row][col]);
```

Notice that in line 11, where the `attachMovie()` command expects a clip name, we are getting the clip name by addressing the information through the object found at desired position in our map array. For example, if we were attaching a tile for row 2 and column 3, then the object found at `_root.map[2][3]` would be P. The clip name would also be accessible from the P object using `P.clip`, but we can access it directly using `_root.map[row][col].clip`.

The next step is to position the tile sprite on the Stage. To do this, we'll need to convert our world coordinates to a screen position using the function that we described previously. The results of the conversion are returned in an array, which we then use to position the newly-created tile clip.

```
//POSITION CLIP ON SCREEN
var temp:Array = _root.WorldToScreen(world_x,
➥world_y, world_z);
_root.game[the_tile]._x = temp[0];
_root.game[the_tile]._y = temp[1];
_root.game[the_tile].swapDepths(temp[1]+temp[0]);
```

Next, we follow similar steps to attach any objects that we've defined for the current row and column.

```
// **** OBJECTS ****
if(!_root.objects[row][col] ||
➥_root.objects[row][col]==0){continue;}
//NAME OBJECT
var the_object:String = "object_"+row+"_"+col;
//GET WORLD POSITION
var world_x:Number = world.tile_width*col +
➥(world.tile_width/2);
```

```
            var world_y:Number = 0;
            var world_z:Number = world.tile_height*row +
            ➥(world.tile_height/2);
            //ATTACH CLIP
            var newdepth:Number =
            ➥Math.floor(((world.totaldepth-
            ➥world_z)*1000)+(world_x));
            _root.game.attachMovie(_root.objects[row][col].
            ➥clip, the_object, newdepth,
            ➥_root.objects[row][col]);
            //POSITION CLIP ON SCREEN
            var temp:Array = _root.WorldToScreen(world_x,
            ➥world_y, world_z);
            _root.game[the_object]._x = temp[0];
            _root.game[the_object]._y = temp[1];
            _root.game[the_object].pos_x = world_x;
            _root.game[the_object].pos_z = world_z;
```

The only significant difference between our treatment of tiles and the game objects that sit on them is that the objects need to be registered to the tile that they sit upon. The reason that we do this is so that we can use the current tile reference to check for objects. The benefits are huge. This method enables us to perform our collision checks selectively—we only need to check for collisions on the object sitting on the current tile. Thus, even if the game has hundreds of objects, we only perform one check per frame. This is vital for smooth performance.

```
            _root.game[the_tile].object =
            ➥_root.game[the_object];
      }
    }
```

Adding the Player Car

At this point, the world tiles and objects are all initialized. Now we'll add the player car. Our car is made up of 35 images, each rotated 10 degrees from the last. Each image is placed on a separate frame. During the game, we'll use the angle of the car to select the proper frame to which we should move the car's playhead.

The car images for this game are generated by rendering a 3D model. In the 3D scene, the car model is rotated once fully over 36 frames. Each frame is then rendered and saved as an image file. The last step is to scale and trim all these image files for importing into Flash, where they are sequenced in our `player` object. Our main loop then jumps to the proper rendered frame to reflect the current car angle. Using prerendered image files this way is a lot of work, but taking these extra steps can make a big difference in your final game.

The car also has a collider clip that is hidden and used for collision detection. This collider clip has the same number of frames as the car, and its playhead is controlled in the same way.

```
var newdepth:Number = Math.floor(((world.totaldepth-
➥player.car_z)*1000)+(player.car_x));
game.attachMovie("player", "player", newdepth, player);
var temp:Array = WorldToScreen(player.car_x,
➥player.car_y, player.car_z);
game.player._x = temp[0];
game.player._y = temp[1];
game.player.stop();
game.player.car_collider.stop();
game.player.car_collider._visible=false;
```

We also initiate coordinates for a focus point. This point moves in accordance with the car's direction and speed so that we can focus the view for a nice panning effect. The reason we use a separate focus point rather than just using the car's position is so that we can move the focus point ahead of the car as we go, depending on speed, and in turn focus the view a little ahead of the car's path. Otherwise, it becomes very difficult to see where you are going.

```
_root.focus_x = temp[0];
_root.focus_y = temp[1];
```

Playing the Game

At this point, we've set up everything needed to start the game. Earlier in this chapter, we discussed the format for these elements but breezed over the actual tile and object definitions. I thought it would be more appropriate to discuss them here because the code defined in them is really what drives game play.

The Tiles

Let's start with the tiles. The tiles don't really do a lot during play other than make information available to the car as it drives over them. Thus, the code used to define a tile is pretty short.

The following code defines our pothole tile.

```
1       //POT HOLE
2       var P:Object = new Object();
3       P.clip = "tile_pothole";
4       P.oktodrive = true;
5       P.effects = new Object();
6       P.effects.bumpy = 5;
7       P.effects.drag = .08;
```

Line 2 sets up the object that holds the tile definition. Line 3 identifies the movie clip used to display the tile visually. This clip tile_pothole has been Exported for ActionScripting in the Linkage Properties dialog box so that it is ready to be used by our code.

Lines 4–7 define attributes about the tile that the car will use to define its behavior as relates to the tile. Line 4 simply tells the car whether it is ok to drive on this tile. This is used in the player loop to validate the car's movements. You'll see when we dissect the player script how we use this.

Line 5 sets up another object to hold information about the tile's effects. In this game, we have two effects, bumpy and drag. Bumpy is used by the player loop to jitter the car up and down. It's mainly for visual effect and has little to do with the game play. The second effect, drag, does a little more. Also used by the player, this effect tells the player to slow down and can be a real drag—hence the name.

The Objects

Objects are defined in much the same way as tiles. There are two categories of objects in this game, static objects that don't move (hydrant and light pole) and dynamic objects that you can hit that will go flying (cones). Like the tiles, these objects have the `clip` variable to hold a reference to the movie clip used to represent it. Unlike tiles, the object definitions hold functions that are called by the player when an object is collided with. This is the `doWhenHit()` function.

Let's look at a static object first. Here is the code for a hydrant.

```
1    //HYDRANT
2    var H:Object = new Object();
3    H.clip = "obj_hydrant";
4    H.doWhenHit = function(speed, angle, tile){
5          //DO HIT SOUND
6          if(Math.abs(_root.game.player.speed) >=
           ➥.5){_root.Snd_hit.start();}
7          //BACK UP TO LAST POSITION BEFORE HIT
8           root.game.player.car_x = _root.game.player.car_x +
            ➥(-speed * Math.sin((angle)*Math.PI/180));
9          _root.game.player.car_z = _root.game.player.car_z +
           ➥(-speed * Math.cos((angle)*Math.PI/180));
10         _root.game.player.speed = -
           ➥(_root.game.player.speed*.8);
11   };
```

Line 4 defines the function that is called by the player when this object is hit. Notice that it is given the speed and angle of the car as well as the tile that it is hit on. Line 6 plays the hit sound if the speed is greater than 0.5. If the speed is less than that, it is barely a hit, so the big clang sound seams out of place. Lines 8 and 9 translate the car to its last position (before the hit), and line 10 reverses the direction so that the car appears to bounce back after the impact.

For dynamic objects, we include an extra script called `doAfterHit`. This script is attached to the `onEnterFrame` event of the object in question and controls the object for the remainder of its life span. The `doWhenHit` function is a little different too because cones react differently to being hit by a car than a hydrant does. Here is the code for a cone.

```
//CONE
var C:Object = new Object();
C.clip = "obj_cone";
C.doWhenHit = function(speed, angle, tile){
```

When a cone is hit, the first things we do is play the hit sound and increase the score and hit count.

```
      _root.Snd_hit2.start();
      _root.score += 10;
      _root.cones_hit++;
```

Then we prepare the cone for its hit reaction. Line 1 in the following code sets the speed of the cone, while lines 2–5 set the angle of the cone. We add a little randomness to this so that the collision responses look more natural. After we have the angle, lines 6 and 7 move the playhead of the cone clip to the proper frame to reflect the angle.

```
1           this.speed = speed*1.8;
2           this.angle = angle + (random(30)-15);
3           //ADD SOME RANDOMNESS
4           if(this.angle<0){this.angle = 360 + this.angle;}
5           this.angle %= 360;
6           var frame:String = "hit_" +
            ➥45*Math.floor(this.angle/45);
7           this.gotoAndStop(frame);
```

Next, we slow the car down a bit for effect on line 1 in the following code. Line 2 attaches the actions for the cone's behavior after a collision to the `onEnterFrame` event of the cone.

Line 4 then un-registers the object from the tile it was sitting on. This keeps us from checking for collision on this object again because it has already been knocked down.

```
1           _root.game.player.speed*=.8;
2           this.onEnterFrame = this.doAfterHit;
3           //UNREGISTER OBJECT FROM TILE
4           tile.object=null;
5     };
```

Because this next function has been attached to the `onEnterFrame` event of the cone, it is executed every frame as the cone goes flying.

```
1     C.doAfterHit = function(){
```

If this `if` statement returns `true`, the cone is still moving. Lines 2–10 in the following code translate and render the tile according to its speed and angle. Line 11 slows the cone down a little each frame until it eventually stops. When that happens, the `if` statement on line 1 fails. We pick up that condition a little later.

```
if(Math.abs(this.trans_x)+Math.abs(this.trans_z) >=
➥.01){
        this.trans_x =
        ➥this.speed*Math.sin((this.angle)*
        ➥Math.PI/180);
        this.trans_z =
        ➥this.speed*Math.cos((this.angle)*
        ➥Math.PI/180);
        this.pos_x += this.trans_x;
        this.pos_z += this.trans_z;
        var temp:Array =
        ➥_root.WorldToScreen(this.pos_x, 0,
        this.pos_z);
        var newdepth:Number =
        ➥Math.floor(((world.totaldepth-
        (this.pos_z+8))*1000)+(this.pos_x));
        this.swapDepths(newdepth);
        this._x = temp[0];
        this._y = temp[1];
        this.speed *= .8;
```

As the cone travels, it has the capability to knock down other cones. We use the same procedure here as we do when checking the car for collisions. In the next block of code, lines 2–4 identify the tile the cone is on at any give time. Line 5 looks for the object registered with the current tile. If there is an object on the tile, lines 8 and 9 check for a collision using Flash's `hitTest` function. If a collision occurs, line 12 calls the `doWhenHit` function on the newly-hit cone, and then all this is repeated for the newly-hit cone.

```
1       //GET TILE
2       this.t_row = ➥Math.floor(this.pos_z/
        ➥_root.world.tile_height);
3       this.t_col = ➥Math.floor(this.pos_x/
        ➥_root.world.tile_width);
4       this.t_tile =
        ➥_root.game["tile_"+this.t_row+"_"+
        ➥this.t_col];
5       this.t_object = this.t_tile.object;
```

```
            //CHECK FOR COLLISION
            if(this.t_object){
                  var temp:Array =
                  ➥WorldToScreen(this.t_object.pos_x, 0,
                  ➥this.t_object.pos_z);
                  if (this.hitTest(temp[0]+_root.game._x,
                  ➥temp[1]+_root.game._y, true)){
                        //UNREGISTER OBJECT FROM TILE
                        this.t_object=null;
                        //TELL OBJECT IT HAS BEEN HIT
                        this.t_object.doWhenHit
                        ➥(this.speed, this.angle,
                        ➥this.t_tile);
                  }
            }
```

As mentioned, when the cone stops moving, it fails the `if` condition we mentioned earlier. In this event, we get rid of the object. The first step is to lessen the alpha property of the movie clip slightly. When the alpha reaches zero, it's time to have this clip remove itself using `removeMovieClip()`.

```
      }else{
            this._alpha -= 5;
            if(this._alpha <=0){this.removeMovieClip();}
      }
};
```

The Player

Our tiles and objects are set up, and it's time to drive around like a madman running down cones. Let's jump to the ACTIONS layer on frame 20 and examine the main loop of the game. This code is executed once every frame.

```
game.player.onEnterFrame = function(){
```

The first step in this function is to process user input and adjust the car's speed and angle accordingly. We have defined the limits for these adjustments in the `player` object back in the "Initializing Variables" section.

```
// **** USER INPUT ****
//FORWARD AND REVERSE
if(Key.isDown(Key.UP)) {
     this.speed = Math.min(this.maxspeed,
     ➥this.speed + this.accelrate);
}else if(Key.isDown(Key.DOWN)) {
     this.speed = Math.max(-this.maxspeed,
     ➥this.speed - this.accelrate);
}else if (Math.abs(this.speed) <= .1){
     this.speed = 0;
}else{
     this.speed *= this.decelrate;
}
//ADJUST FOR DRAG
if(this.car_tile.effects.drag){
     this.speed -= (this.speed *
     ➥this.car_tile.effects.drag);
}
//TURNING
if(Key.isDown(Key.RIGHT) && this.allowturns==true){
     this.speedpercent = this.speed/this.maxspeed;
     this.anglechange =
     ➥Math.min(this.maxanglechange,
     ➥this.maxanglechange * this.speedpercent);
     this.angle += this.anglechange;
}else if(Key.isDown(Key.LEFT) &&
➥this.allowturns==true){
     this.speedpercent = this.speed/this.maxspeed;
     this.anglechange = Math.max(-
     ➥this.maxanglechange, -this.maxanglechange *
     ➥this.speedpercent);
     this.angle += this.anglechange;
}
if(this.angle<0){this.angle = 360 + this.angle;}
this.angle %= 360;
```

At this point, we have the car's speed and angle and can project the position that the car would end up at next frame. After we have the car's position, we further project the bumper's position (either front or back, depending on the direction we are going). This projected position is used to validate the next move.

Notice that the projected variables have a `t_` preceding them. This is because they are temporary until we can validate them.

```
// **** VALIDATE AND UPDATE POSITIONS ****
//GET STEP FACTOR
this.stepfactor_x =
➥Math.sin((this.angle)*Math.PI/180);
this.stepfactor_z =
➥Math.cos((this.angle)*Math.PI/180);
//PROJECT NEW CAR POSITION
this.t_car_x = this.car_x + (this.speed *
➥this.stepfactor_x);
this.t_car_z = this.car_z + (this.speed *
➥this.stepfactor_z);
//PROJECT BUMPER POSITION
if(this.speed>=0){
      this.t_bumper_x = this.t_car_x +
      ➥6*this.stepfactor_x;
      this.t_bumper_z = this.t_car_z +
      ➥6*this.stepfactor_z;
}else{
      this.t_bumper_x = this.t_car_x + -
      ➥6*this.stepfactor_x;
      this.t_bumper_z = this.t_car_z + -
      ➥6*this.stepfactor_z;
}
```

Now that we have the position, we can identify the tile that we'd be over and make sure it is ok to drive on it. This check is performed on line 11 in the following code. If it is NOT ok to drive on it, the car's direction is reversed. Line 15 disables turning for 250 milliseconds and skips the rest of the function this time around. Stopping the turning for one-fourth of a second helps the feel of the game.

```
1      //GET CAR TILE
2      this.t_car_row =
       ➥Math.floor(this.t_car_z/_root.world.tile_height);
```

```
this.t_car_col =
➥Math.floor(this.t_car_x/_root.world.tile_width);
this.t_car_tile =
➥_root.game["tile_"+this.t_car_row+"_"+
➥this.t_car_col];
//GET BUMPER TILE
this.t_bumper_row = ➥Math.floor(this.t_bumper_z/
➥_root.world.tile_height);
this.t_bumper_col =
➥Math.floor(this.t_bumper_x/_root.world.tile_width);
this.t_bumper_tile =
➥_root.game["tile_"+this.t_bumper_row+"_"+
➥this.t_bumper_col];
this.t_bumper_object = this.t_bumper_tile.object;
//CHECK NEW POSITION FOR DRIVABLE TILE
if(!this.t_bumper_tile.oktodrive){
      this.speed = -(this.speed*.8);
      this.allowturns=false;
      clearInterval(intervalID);
      var intervalID=setInterval(
      ➥function(){_root.game.player.allowturns=true;
      ➥clearInterval(intervalID);}, 250 );
      return;
}
```

If the move is ok, then the temporary variables are copied to the actual variables.

```
//MOVE IS OK- UPDATE PLAYER POSITION & TRANSFER
➥TILE INFO
this.car_x = this.t_car_x;
this.car_z = this.t_car_z;
this.bumper_x = this.t_bumper_x;
this.bumper_z = this.t_bumper_z;
this.car_row = this.t_car_row;
this.car_col = this.t_car_col;
this.car_tile = this.t_car_tile;
this.bumper_row = this.t_bumper_row;
this.bumper_col = this.t_bumper_col;
```

```
        this.bumper_tile = this.t_bumper_tile;
        this.bumper_object = this.t_bumper_object;
        this.bumper_local_x = this.bumper_x %
        ➥_root.world.tile_width;
        this.bumper_local_z = this.bumper_z %
        ➥_root.world.tile_height;
```

We then check for collisions on any objects that could be on the tile. Again, we use the `hitTest` function to do this. We are actually checking for a collision against the code position and a movie clip called car_collider that is part of our car movie clip. We can't use the car itself because it is made of a larger bitmap, so its boundaries are much larger than the area of the car that can collide with anything. If we find a collision, we call the `doWhenHit` function of the collided object.

```
        // **** OBJ COLLISIONS ****
        if(this.bumper_object){
              var temp:Array =
              ➥WorldToScreen(this.bumper_object.pos_x, 0,
              ➥this.bumper_object.pos_z);
              if (this.car_collider.hitTest(temp[0]
              ➥+_root.game._x, temp[1]+_root.game._y,
              ➥true)){
                    //TELL OBJECT IT HAS BEEN HIT
                    this.bumper_object.doWhenHit
                    ➥(this.speed, this.angle,
                    ➥this.bumper_tile);
              }
        }
```

With all the movement and collision logic out of the way, we move the actual car and focus point. Lines 10 and 11 are responsible for keeping things at the proper depths. Lines 12 and 13 adjust the playhead on the car and collider clips to reflect the car's angle. Line 16 uses the tile's bumpy effect to jitter the car up or down randomly.

```
1       // **** RENDER ****
2       //MOVE FOCUS DOT
3       this.pan_pos_x = this.car_x +
        ➥7*this.speed*this.stepfactor_x;
4       this.pan_pos_z = this.car_z +
        ➥7*this.speed*this.stepfactor_z;
```

```
        var temp:Array = WorldToScreen(this.pan_pos_x, 0,
        ➥this.pan_pos_z);
        _root.focus_x= temp[0];
        _root.focus_y= temp[1];
        //MOVE CAR
        var temp:Array = WorldToScreen(this.car_x,
        ➥this.car_y, this.car_z);
        var newdepth:Number =
        ➥Math.floor(((world.totaldepth-
        ➥this.car_z)*1000)+(this.car_x));
        this.swapDepths(newdepth);
        var frame:Number = Math.round(this.angle*.1)+1
        this.gotoAndStop(frame);
        this.car_collider.gotoAndStop(frame);
        this._x = temp[0];
        this._y = temp[1]+random(this.car_tile.effects.bumpy*
        ➥Math.abs(this.speed));
}
```

The Timer

To add fun to the game, we have a 30 second timer. This code is also found on the ACTIONS layer of frame 20 and could be used easily in any game. This timer counts down 30 seconds, and when time reaches zero, advances the playhead to the "game_over" frame. On every frame, the timer scales itself to reflect the amount of time left.

```
timer.gameStartTime = getTimer();
timer.gameDuration = 30000;
timer.gameTimerStarted = false;
timer.display = 30;
timer.onEnterFrame = function(){
        gameTimeLeft = this.gameDuration -(getTimer() -
        ➥this.gameStartTime);
        if(gameTimeLeft <=0){
                //OUT OF TIME
                timer.display = 0;
                this._xscale = 0;
                _root.timer.onEnterFrame = null;
                _root.game.player.onEnterFrame = null;
                _root.gotoAndPlay("game_over");
```

```
        }else{
              secondsleft = Math.ceil(gameTimeLeft/1000);
              timer.display = secondsleft
              this._xscale =
              ➥(secondsleft*1000)/this.gameDuration * 100;
        }
  }
```

Automatic Panning

You may have noticed that the world is much larger than the display screen for this game. This means we need some way to pan around to keep the action in view. For this, we attach an `onEnterFrame` script to the game movie clip so it gets updated each frame. This is the clip that holds everything in the playable game, so if we move it around, all the action will move with it.

To keep the motion looking smooth, this function only moves the display two tenths of the distance needed to center the focus point. In the ACTIONS layer of frame 11, we handle all the panning logic. You can see this in lines 3 and 4. The end result is a smooth, easy panning effect.

```
1     game.onEnterFrame = function(){
2           var ideal_x:Number = _root.screen.keepplayerat_x -
            ➥_root.focus_x;
3           var ideal_y:Number = _root.screen.keepplayerat_y -
            ➥_root.focus_y;
4           var step_x:Number = Math.floor(this._x + (ideal_x-
            ➥this._x)*.2);
5     var step_y:Number = Math.floor(this._y + (ideal_y-
      ➥this._y)*.2);
6           this._x = step_x;
7           this._y = step_y;
8     };
```

After the Game

After the timer determines the end of the game, it takes us to the "game_over" frame. This frame simply displays the game over message and gives the user the option to play again.

Points to Remember

- Like most games, math plays an important role. Place a bookmark in the math chapter of this book. You'll need it.
- Use the power of objects to define and govern your in-game elements.
- It is ok to use Flash's collision detection functions. Sometimes using these can be more efficient than doing all the math yourself.
- Little features like smooth panning can really enhance the user experience.
- Always align your bitmaps on even pixels. This improves performance and visual quality.
- Any movie clips or sounds that will be attached with code must be set up with Export for ActionScript in the Linkage Properties dialog box.

APPENDICES

Appendix A
Developer Resources 479
General Game Resources 480
AI 481
Isometric 482
Math 483
Physics 484
Audio Resources 485

Appendix B
Other Games 489

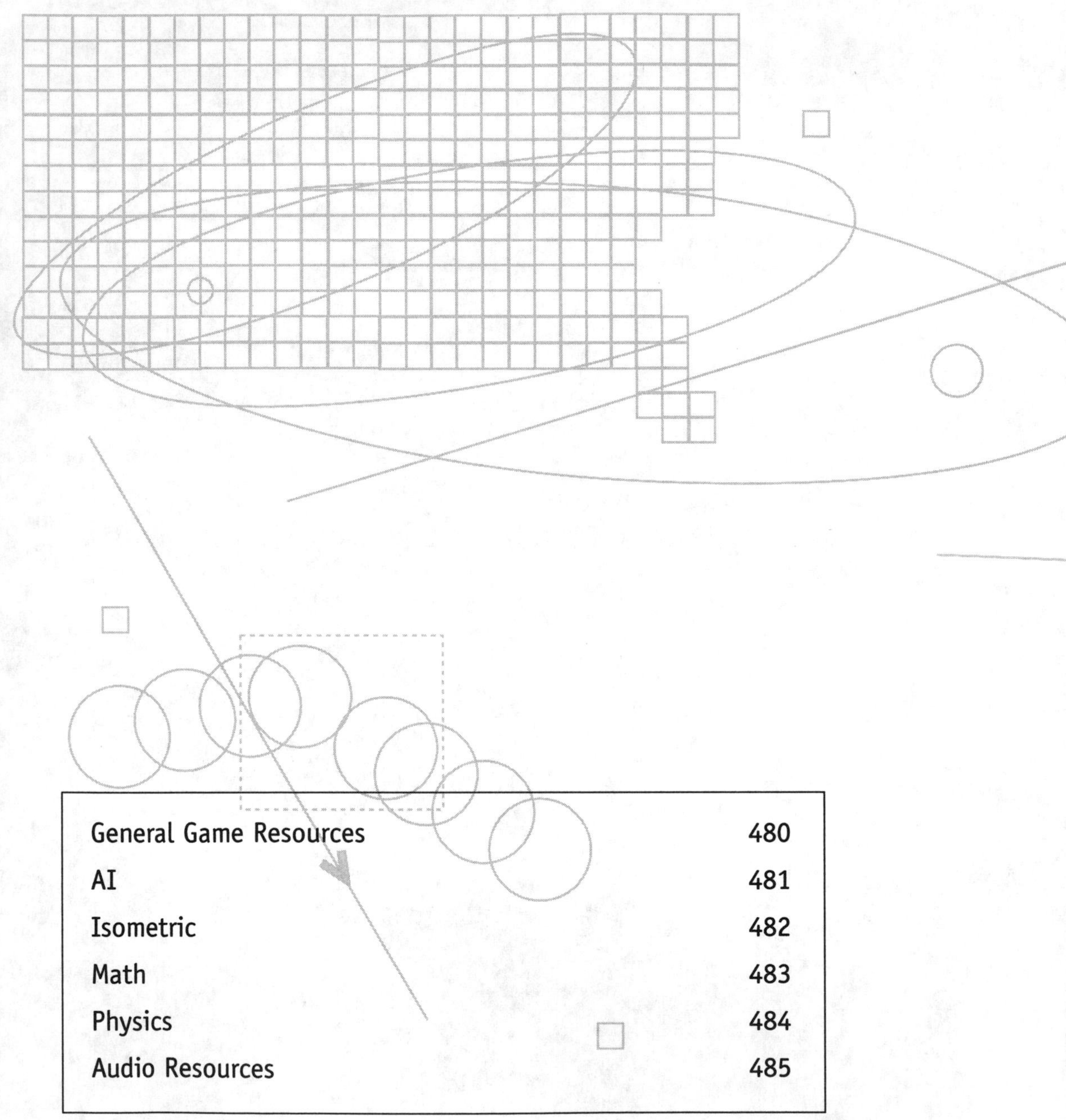

General Game Resources 480

AI 481

Isometric 482

Math 483

Physics 484

Audio Resources 485

APPENDIX A

Developer Resources

In this appendix, you'll find out where you can get more information about a variety of game-related topics, including online communities, books, and web sites on the elements of game design and audio resources.

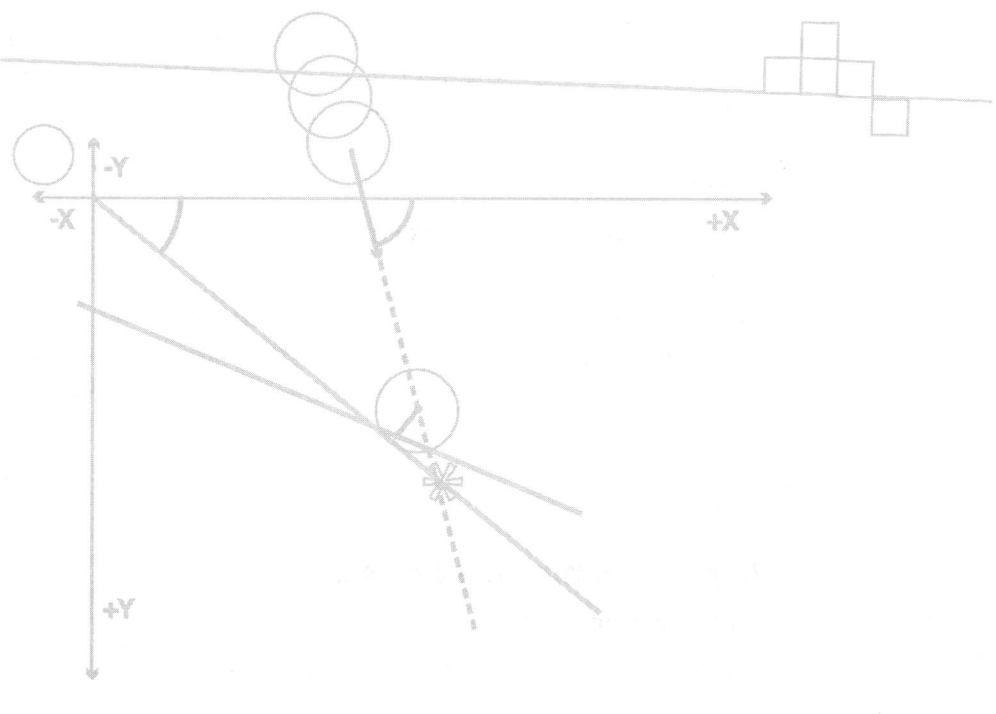

General Game Resources

On the Web

Gamasutra

`www.gamasutra.com`

This is the most popular game-development resource site in the world. It is focused on game development on all types of platforms. You will find some amazing articles on a variety of game-specific topics (some of these references are included later in this appendix).

GameDev.net

`www.gamedev.net`

After Gamasutra, GameDev.net is the most popular game-development resource site. It also contains many interesting articles and features, as well as user forums where you can discuss issues with other developers.

Flashkit

`www.flashkit.com/board/index.php`

Flaskit is a Flash resource site. On this site, you can find source files and over a dozen specific forums on various Flash topics. You will find the most active forum on the Internet for Flash gaming on this page. It is a great place to ask questions or just to see what other people are up to.

Books

Game Programming Gems 3

Edited by Dante Treglia

Charles River Media (ISBN: 1-58450-233-9; $69.95; `www.charlesriver.com`)

This book contains numerous techniques developed by programmers in the game-design industry. While it is not Flash-specific, it does present many ideas and techniques that can be used in Flash games.

AI

On the Web

"Smart Moves: Intelligent Pathfinding"

www.gamasutra.com/features/19970801/pathfinding.htm

This article gives a brief rundown of all the major pathfinding algorithms and then discusses A* in detail. I learned A* from a variety of articles, but this one helped me the most. Check out the downloadable demo; it contains an amazing little program that lets you design maps and perform any of about ten pathfinding searches. You can build a map and try pathfinding with A*, tracing, and more. Also, you can slow down the search and watch *how* it searches to better understand the algorithms. (You need to join the site to access the article; membership is free.)

"Amit's Thoughts on Path-Finding"

theory.stanford.edu/~amitp/GameProgramming/

This is another A* article. It comes highly recommended and appears to be very thorough.

It definitely helps to read several different articles on a confusing topic so that you can fully understand it."

"A* Algorithm Tutorial"

www.geocities.com/jheyesjones/astar.html

Yet another A* article.

"Toward More Realistic Pathfinding"

www.gamasutra.com/features/20010314/pinter_01.htm

While A* always gives the path with the lowest score, it does not always look natural. This Gamasutra article provides a look into how you can make pathfinding paths look more realistic.

"The Game AI Page"

`www.gameai.com`

This web site is dedicated to AI in games. You can find information on a lot of AI topics, including links to other useful web sites.

"Scrabble—Source Code"

`www.gtoal.com/wordgames/scrabble.html`

Yes, there is actually a web site dedicated to the AI involved in computerized games of *Scrabble*. Check it out.

Books

AI Game Programming Wisdom

Edited by Steve Rabin

Charles River Media (ISBN: 1-58450-077-8; $69.95; `www.charlesmedia.com`)

This book has proved to be one of my most valuable purchases. It is a collection of articles from expert game programmers. You will find great ideas on handling AI for enemy behavior, pathfinding, racing games, and many more interesting topics.

Isometric

On the Web

"Introduction to Isometric Engines"

`www.gamedev.net/reference/articles/article744.asp`

This article provides a fairly in-depth introduction to isometric views. Although it is the most popular online resource I could find on this topic, I don't think it is presented very well. However, if you first read Chapter 8, "The Isometric View," in this book, you may find this article of some use.

"Isometric Basics"

www.xaraxone.com/guest/guest05/index.htm

Graphic artists, this link's for you! This is an excellent article on how to create graphics for an isometric world.

"Tiled Terrain"

www.gamasutra.com/features/20011024/peasley_01.htm

This article shows how to graphically create tiles for a tile-based world in isometric and other kinds of games.

Books

Isometric Game Programming with DirectX 7.0

By Ernest Pazera, edited by Andre LaMothe

Premier Press, Inc. (ISBN: 0-76153-089-4; $59.99; www.premierpress-books.com)

This book comes highly recommended from some of my colleagues. It discusses many isometric-gaming topics that can be applied to games in Flash.

Math

On the Web

"Eric Weisstein's World of Mathematics"

http://mathworld.wolfram.com/

This web site is like a giant comprehensive math book—you can find information on just about any math topic here.

Books

CRC Standard Mathematical Tables and Formulae, 30th Edition

By Daniel Zwillinger

CRC Press (ISBN: 0849324793; $51.95; `www.crcpress.com`)

A must-have for anyone who uses math frequently. It does not teach any math; it's just the most comprehensive math reference I have ever seen. It is a required book for many hard-science degree programs.

Schaum's Outline of Trigonometry

By Robert E. Moyer and Frank Ayres, Jr.

McGraw-Hill (ISBN: 0070068933; $15.95; `www.mcgrawhill.com`)

The *Schaum's Outline* books are like *Cliffs Notes* for math and science. They are concise references in an easy-to-use format.

Physics

On the Web

At this time, I have not seen any physics resources on the web that I think are worth recommending. If you find any, let me know!

Books

Physics for Game Developers

By David M. Bourg

O'Reilly & Associates (ISBN: 0596000065; $39.95; `www.oreilly.com`)

The title tells it all: This book was written as a physics reference for game developers. You can find information on gravity, collision detection, and many more very advanced physics topics and how they can be applied in games. This book is intended for people with a basic college-level science background.

Physics for Scientists and Engineers with Modern Physics, 5th Edition

By Raymond A. Serway and Robert J. Beichner

International Thomson Publishing (ISBN: 0030317169; $142.95; www.thomson.com)

This book is the best college-level introduction to physics. It presents the most fundamental physics concepts in a way that is understandable even to those with a minimal math background. If you are interested in learning physics, this is the book to get. After you have mastered these concepts, you can move on to the book mentioned above.

Audio Resources

Sound Libraries

SoundEffects

Vilkki Studios (Both free and fee-based; www.stonewashed.net/sfx.html)

Absolute Sound Effects Archive

GRSites.com (www.grsites.com/sounds/)

Ultimate Sound and Music Archive

Advances.Com (Both free and by subscription; www.ultimate-soundarchive.com)

Drum Machines

Dream Station

Audio Simulation ($49; `www.audio-simulation.de`)

Highly recommended.

Fruityloops

Image-Line Software ($49–$139; `www.fruityloops.com`)

Tough learning curve, but affordable and very powerful.

eJay

eJay (`http://www.ejay.com/`)

Great for beginners, value priced. There are several software products geared toward different styles of music, such as techno and hip hop. All of them have great drum capabilities.

HammerHead

ThreeChords.com (`www.threechords.com/hammerhead`)

The simplest drum machine imaginable. Free!

Audio-editing Software

Sound Forge

Sonic Foundry ($399.96 and $499.96; `www.soundforge.com`)

Industry standard for professional audio; most powerful and simple.

WaveLab

Steinberg Media Technologies ($600, `www.steinberg.net`)

Very similar to Sound Forge, with native VST support.

Adobe Audition

Adobe ($299, http://www.adobe.com/products/audition/main.html)

Best value and price, most popular for both professionals and nonprofessionals.

Audacity

SourceForge.net (Free; http://audacity.sourceforge.net)

For Windows, Macintosh, Linux, and Unix!

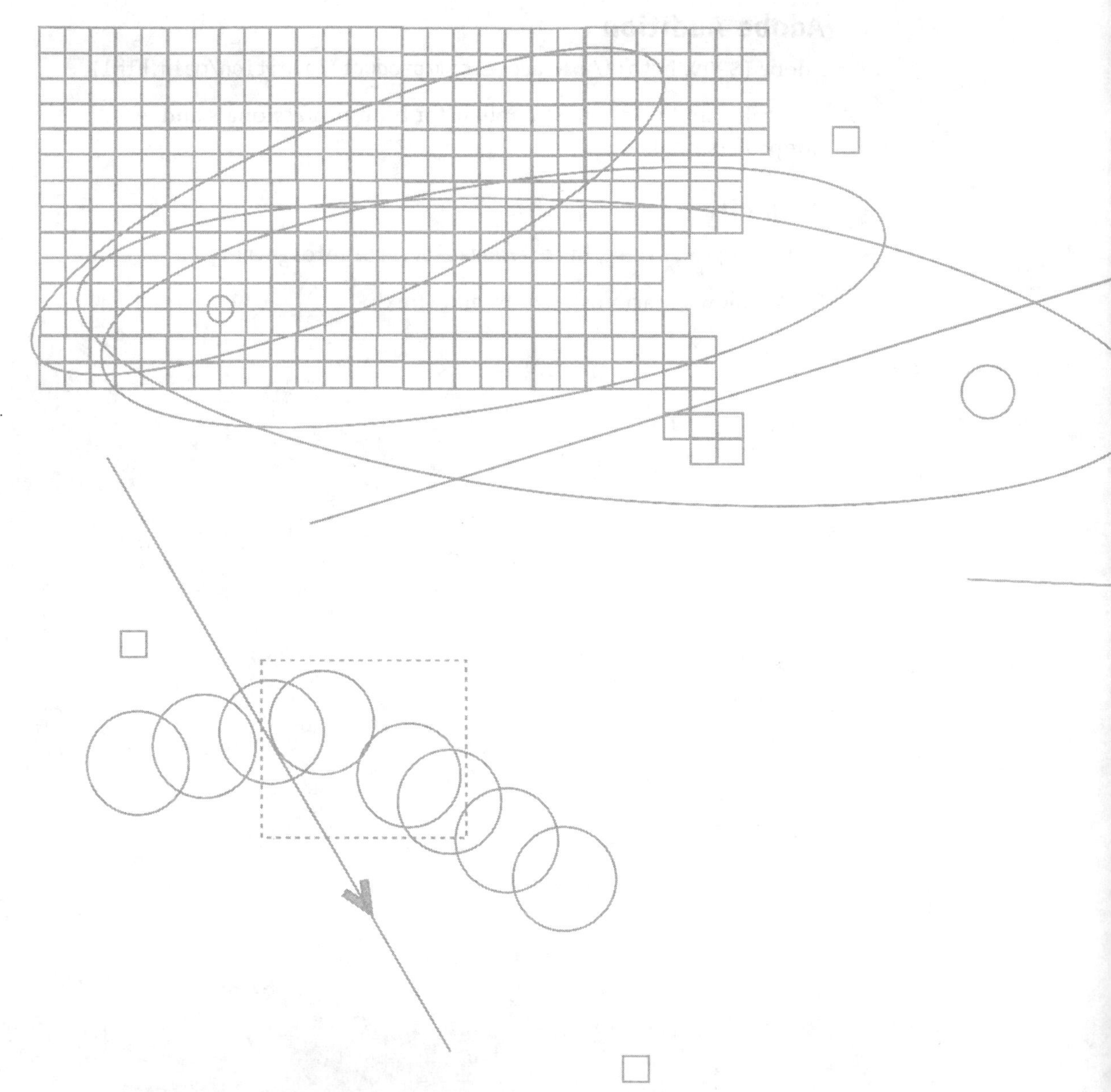

APPENDIX B

OTHER GAMES

WHILE WRITING THIS BOOK, WE RAN ACROSS SEVERAL OLD GAME OR OTHER game-related source files just sitting around. Some of the files illustrate a concept, such as 3D in games, while others are unfinished game engines. The games, partial games, and game-related files are all included in the Extras directory on the CD and are described briefly here. Enjoy!

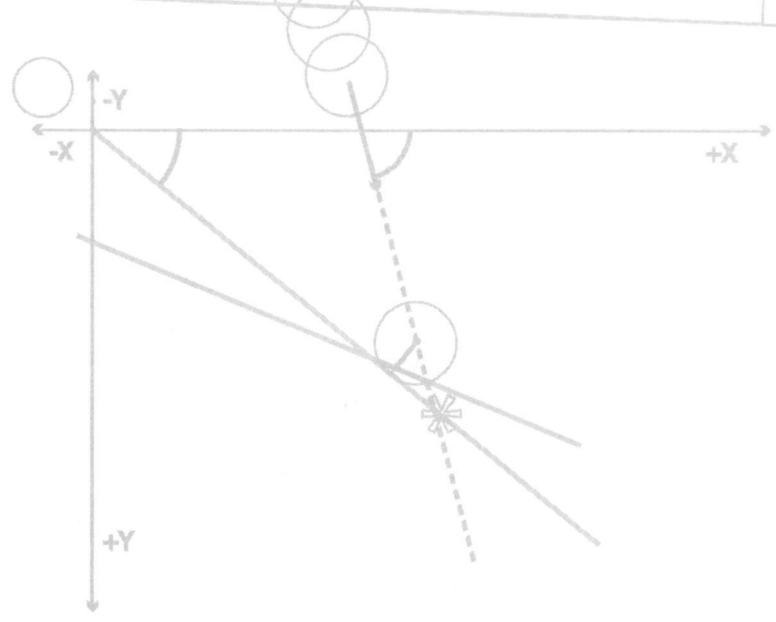

3D_race

Flash MX

I created this file to show that a 3D racing game in Flash is possible. This file contains only the most basic level of the game—a limited 3D engine you can use to move through an environment. It is a good starting point for learning how to create 3D racing games.

Cards

Flash MX

Jennifer Rosenthal created this deck of playing cards. Most decks in Flash games are imported as JPEGs or GIFs and have a total file size of a few hundred kilobytes. These vector cards weigh in at just under 8 KB!

Fox and Geese

Flash 5

This simple puzzle game was created with Flash 5. It is just waiting for someone to give it nice graphics. The rules are easy to understand and are included in the game.

Iso_maze

Flash MX

This is one of my successful simple experiments. In Chapter 11, "Artificial Intelligence," we discuss random maze generation. In this file we use the random-maze-generation algorithm but display it as an isometric maze. You can move a ball around through the maze.

Projectile_motion

Flash MX

In Chapter 3, "Game Math," and Chapter 4, "Basic Physics," we covered all the information needed to develop projectile motion in Flash. Here is a simple working example of how it is implemented.

RaiseTheBlocks

Flash 5

This game was created with Flash 5. It is an isometric grid of 25 blocks. The goal is to raise all the blocks. When you click one block, the height of that block and its vertical and horizontal neighbors changes. If the blocks are raised, then they lower; if they are low, then they rise. The object is to raise them all. It's a very tough puzzle!

Shared_object_highscore_list

Flash MX

This directory contains a well-documented example of a high score list that uses local shared objects. Its main use is for offline games.

Ship

Flash MX

You are probably familiar with top-down-view games such as *Asteroids* in which a spaceship can be controlled with the arrow keys. It rotates and you can shoot. This file contains the absolute basics needed to make something like that work.

Shuffle_deck

Flash MX

As a member of many Flash resource sites, I have seen the issue of shuffling a deck of cards come up frequently. In this file there are no graphics, just a function that handles taking a deck of cards in memory and randomly shuffling it in the fastest possible way.

Tic_tac_toe_ai

Flash 5

This is a nice file created in Flash 5. It contains a simple AI computer opponent so you can play tic-tac-toe against the computer!

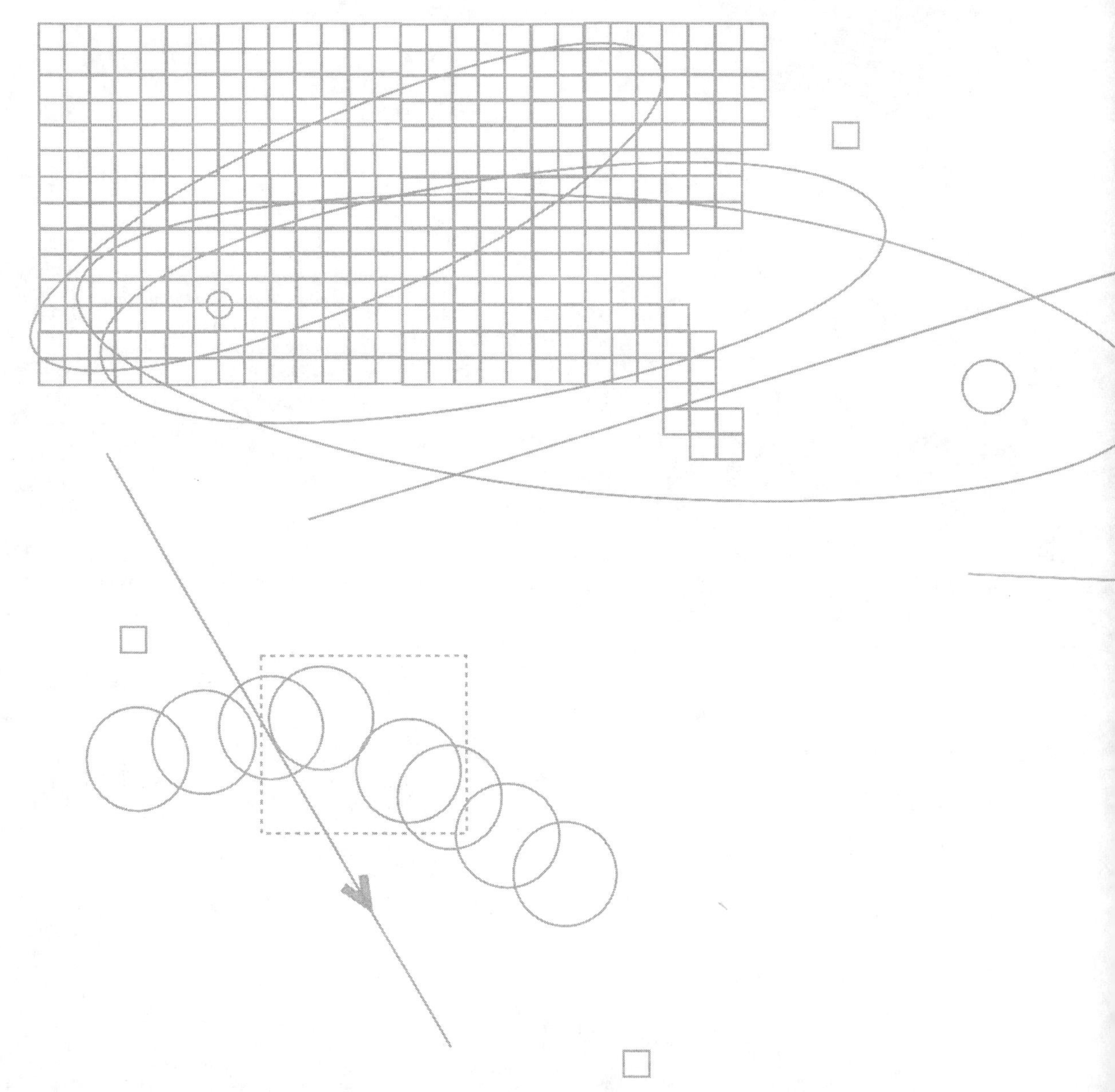

INDEX

Symbols

0db, 346
3D, 9, 212
  isometric view. *See* isometric view
  z-sorting. *See* z-sorting
3D engines, 212
501 Dart Challenge, 436
  game logic, 438, 440
    aiming darts, 441
    flying darts, 443-446
    getScore( ), 446-449
    releasing darts, 441-443
  game logic
    after the game, 449
    before the game, 438-440
  game play, 436
  scoring, 437

A

A*, 296-303, 307
  implementing, 303-307
accelDone( ), 343
acceleration, 78
  applying with ActionScript, 79-81
  controlling volume of sound effects, 341-345
action games, 13
ActionScript
  applying
    acceleration, 79-81
    speed, 73-77
  for ElectrotServer 3
    chats, 372-375
  enemy ActionScript, 284-288
  evolution of, 176
  Flash Studio Pro, levels, 260
  for loops, 107
  for mazes, AI, 290-294
  HighScoreList class
    Init frame, 271-274
  Key class, 81
  managing sound effects, 338
    controlling sound-based factors other than speed, 340-341
    controlling sound based on object speed, 338-340
    volume control through acceleration, 341-345
adding
  characters to tile-based worlds, 197-203
  player cards for Cone Crazy game, 462-463
Adobe Audition, 353
advanced shapes, collision detection with, 147-148
adventure games, 13
age groups, 23-24
AI (artificial intelligence), 11, 277-278
  creating, 281
    drawbacks and solutions, 284
    rules for controlling characters, 282-284
  custom logic, 280
  difficulty range, 280
  enemy ActionScript, 284-288
  enemy behavior, 279
  level generation, 279
  mazes, 288
    ActionScript, 290-294
    rules for, 289-290
    visual implementation of, 295
  neural networks, 279
  pathfinding, 278, 295-296
    A, 296-307*
  testing, 284
  turn-based games, 280
aiming darts, 501 Dart Challenge, 441
algorithms, 11
  pathfinding, 295-296
    A, 296-307*
allowSpectators property, 419
alpha channels, optimizing images, 324
angle gamma, 136

angles, 48-50
anti-aliasing, optimizing images, 324
applying conservation laws, 165-167
  circle-circle collision reactions, 169-175
  rectangle-rectangle collision reactions, 167-168
arrays, 62
artificial intelligence. *See* AI
ASP (Active Server Pages), high score lists. *See* high score lists
attachMovie( ), linkage identifiers, 106
attachSound( ), 334
audiences, 22. *See also* demographics
  playback specifications, 24-25
    Flash version, 25-26
    screen size, 26-27
    speed, 25
  understanding, 22
audio editors, 353
audio loops, editing and preparing, 352-355
authoritative clients, 363
authoritative server, 365
automatic panning, Cone Crazy, 474
autonumbered users, 421
avatar-chat, 11
avatars, 11

B

baddyAI( ), 284-288
ball-wall, 153
ball2BallReaction( ), 173
ballLineReaction( ), 161
bishops, chess, 411
bitmap graphics, 314-315
  versus vector graphics, 312
bitmap smoothing, optimizing images, 324
bonuses, 33
bouncing objects off of walls, 153
  circle-line collision reactions, 159-162
  object-wall collision reactions, 153-158
bounding boxes, 99
buildCharacter( ) function, 237-238
buildFlorr( ), 232
buildGrid( ) function, 187-188, 206
buildWorld( ) function, 236

C

calculateDepth( ), 225, 231
camera views, chase, 9
captureKeys( ), 226
Cartesian coordinate system, 44
  angles, 48-50
  coordinates, 45-48
casino games, 13
castling, 412
categories, choosing in Word Search, 387-391
cells. *See* tiles
challenge games, 35
chanting tile attributes based on object impact, 196-197
characters
  adding to tile-based worlds, 197-203
  AI, rules for controlling characters, 282-284
  developing, 29
  moving in isometric worlds, 235-245
chase, 9
chat applications, ElectroServer 3, 370-371
  ActionScript for chats, 372-375
  FLA files, 371-372
Chat frame, 372
Chat frame label, ElectroServer 3, 374
chat rooms, playing chess, 414
cheaters, 264
checkmate, chess, 413
Chess
  chat rooms, 414
  game code, 417-418
    ChessBoard class, 428-430
    ChessPiece class, 427-428
    frame actions, 431-433
    Tile class, 426-427
  game pieces, 411-412, 427-428
  gameboard, 428-430
  logic, 426
    creating games, 418-420
    joining a game, 420-421
    moveReceived event, 423-426
    showing game icons, 420
    starting the game, 422-423
  possible moves, 425
  rules, 410-413
  spectator moves, 426
  tiles, 426-427
  using the game file to start and play a game, 414-417

ChessBoard class, 428-430, 432
ChessPiece class, 427-428
choices, detecting in Word Search, 402-405
choosing categories, Word Search, 387-391
circle-circle collision detection, 115
  frame dependent, 116-118
  frame independent, 118-125
circle-circle collision reactions, 152, 169-175
circle-line collision reactions, 152
  bouncing objects off of walls, 159-162
CircleToCircleDetection, 118
class files, 255-256
classes
  ChessBoard, 428-430, 432
  ChessPiece, 427-428
  ElectroServer, 370
    serialization, 419
  HighScoreList, 269-271
    ActionScript, 271-274
  Isometric, 224
  Key, 81
  SharedObject, saving game data, 36-37
  Tile, 426-427
clients, 11
  authoritative clients, 363
code. *See* game code
collider clips, 463
collision detection, 11
  with advanced shapes, 147-148
  circle-circle, 115
    frame dependent, 116-118
    frame independent, 118-125
  frame-independent collision detection, 137
  hitTest( ), 98-100
    movie clip-movie clip collisions, 100-102
    movie clip-point collisions, 103-106
    shape-point collisions, 107-109
  line-line, 126
    determining if line segments intersect, 131-134
    equation of lines, 126-129
    intersecting lines, 129-131
  math, 99
  point-circle, 112-115
  point-rectangle, 142-144
  rectangle-rectangle, 145-146
  using math, 110-111
    circle-circle collision detection, 115
    circle-circle collision detection (frame dependent), 116-118
    circle-circle collision detection (frame independent), 118-125
    circle-line collision detection, 135-142
    line-line collision detection, 126-129
    point-circle collision detection, 112-115
    point-rectangle collision detection, 142-144
    rectangle-rectangle collision detection, 145-146
collision reactions, 12, 152-153
  circle-circle collision reactions, 152
  circle-line collision reactions, 152
  object-wall collision reactions, 152
  rectangle-rectangle collision reactions, 152
collisions, 98
  conservation laws, 165-167
    circle-circle collision reactions, 169-175
    rectangle-rectangle collision reactions, 167-168
  elastic collisions, 164
  inelastic collisions, 164
  momentum, 164
  movie clip-movie clip collisions, 100-102
  movie clip-point collisions, 103-106
  shape-point collisions, 107-109
color formats, 314
competition, 35-36
compression, 317
  Flash's settings, 320
  lossless compression, 318-319
  lossy compression, 320
    JPEG, 321
  schemes, 318
compressions, lossless comporession, 321-322
concept of games, 27-28
  characters, 29
  developing themes, 28-29
  flow, 30-31
  storylines, 29
Cone Crazy
  end of the game, 474
  game logic, 454-455
    adding player cars, 462-463
    constructing the world, 460-462
    automatic panning, 474
    objects, 464-468
    players, 468-470, 472-473
    tiles, 464
    timers, 473-474

game logic for setup, 455
initializing variables, 458-459
laying out the world, 457-458
tile/object definitions, 455-457
worldToScreen( ) conversion, 459-460
overview of, 454
conservation laws
applying, 165-167
circle-circle collision reactions, 169-175
rectangle-rectangle collision reactions, 167-168
energy, 164-165
momentum, 164-165
consoles, 12
constant of universal gravitation, 88
constructing worlds for Cone Crazy game, 460-462
container objects, 122
controlling
characters, AI, 282-284
sound
based on factors other than speed, 340-341
based on object speed, 338-340
volume through acceleration, 341-345
conversion functions, worldToScreen( ), 459-460
converting degrees to radians, 50
coordinate systems
Cartesian coordinates, 44-48
isometrics, 215-220
correlative cues, 223
cosine, 55-57
cost, A*, 298
createBoard( ), 392, 397-399
createMaze( ), 293
cues, correlative cues, 223
custom logic, 280

D

darts, 501 Dart Challenge
aiming, 441
flying, 443-446
releasing, 441-443
decelDone( ), 343
deconstructing isometric worlds, 234-245
degrees
angles, 49
converting to radians, 50
demographics, 23-24. *See also* audiences
depth, 229
tiles, 231
designing
games
concept of, 27-28
developing characters, 29
developing themes, 28-29
flow, 30-31
storylines, 29
tile-based worlds, 182
scaling tiles, 184-185
seamless tiles, 183-184
views, 182
destroying tile-independent objects, 196
detecting choices, Word Search, 402-405
difficulty levels, 32-33
difficulty range, AI, 280
digital clipping, 346
digital sound, 346
displacement, vectors, 62
displayList( ), 392, 400-401
doAfterHit, 465
doWhenHit( ) function, 464, 472
drawbacks of AI, 284
draws, chess, 413
drum loops, 350-351

E

Easter eggs, 34
editing audio loops, 352-355
editors, level editors, 250
educational games, 13
elastic collisions, 164
electronic music, 350
ElectroServer 3 (Electrotank), 367-369
chats, 370-371
ActionScript, 372-375
FLA files, 371-372
installing, 368
ElectroServer class, 370
serialization, 419
Electrotank, 264
ElectroServer 3, 367, 369
ActionScript, 372-375
chats, 370-371
FLA files, 371-372
installing, 368
email-based multiplayer games, 361
en passant, 412, 430

encryption, 264
enemies, ActionScript, 284, 286-288
enemy behavior, 279
energy, 163
  conservation laws, 164-165
  kinetic energy, 163
equation of lines, line-line collision detection, 126-129
events, moveReceived, 423-426
executables, creating enhanced executables, 256-257
  Flash Studio Pro, 257-260
expanding nodes, A*, 298

F

faking sounds, 347-349
feelers, 239
file types, 312
  graphics, 315-317
files
  class files, 255-256
  FLA files, ElectroServer 3, 371-372
  local files, saving game data, 38
  naming, 334
filters, language filters, 371
findIntersection( ), 133
first person, 9
first-person shooter games, 13
FLA files, ElectroServer 3, 371-372
FLA source file, 12
Flash, versions of (playback specifications), 25-26
Flash pen, 129
Flash Studio Pro, 256-260
FloodingFilterEnabled property, 420
flow of games, 30-31
flush( ) method, 37
flying darts, 501 Dart Challenge, 443-446
for loops, 107
force, vectors, 62
frame actions, chess, 431-433
frame dependence, circle-circle collision detection, 115
frame independence, 115
frame rate, 75
frame-independent circle-circle detection, 118-125
frame-independent collision detection, 137
frames, sound on, 334
  on/off toggles, 335-337
  setting volume for, 337-338
friction, 90
  good-enough friction, 92-93
  real friction, 90-92
fromXML( ) method, 256
fscommand function, 256-257
fun
  audiences, understanding, 22
  concept and flow of games, 27-28
    characters, 29
    developing themes, 28-29
    flow, 30-31
    storylines, 29
functions
  accelDone( ), 343
  attachSound( ), 334
  baddyAI( ), 284, 286-288
  ball2BallReaction( ), 173
  ballLineReaction( ), 161
  buildCharacter( ), 237-238
  buildFloor( ), 232
  buildGrid( ), 187-188, 206
  buildWorld( ), 236
  captureKeys( ), 226
  CircleToCircleDetection, 118
    for Cone Crazy games, 459-460
  createBoard( ), 392, 397-399
  decelDone( ), 343
  displayList( ), 392, 400-401
  doAfterHit, 465
  doWhenHit( ), 464, 472
  findIntersection( ), 133
  fscommand, 256-257
  gameClicked( ), 193
  generateXML( ), 204
  getFrame( ), circle-line collision detection, 139
  getScore( ), 501 Dart Challenge, 446-449
  hitTest, 472
  initializeBall( ), 198
  moveBall( ), 198-199
  moveCharacter( ), 242
  onEnterframe, 195
  playAccel( ), 343
  playDecel( ), 343
  playSound( ), 334-335, 338, 341
  pointRectangleDetection( ), 144
  positionCharacter( ), 239

RectangleRectangleDetection( ), 146
restart( ), 392, 401
scrambleWords( ), 392, 394-397
selected( ), 402-403
sendMove, 423
sendStartMove, 422
setInterval, 196
showGameRooms, 420
showPopup, 375
showRooms, 420
showUsers, 422
worldClicked( ), 240
worldToScreen( )

G

game boards in Chess, 428-430
game code, Chess, 417-418
game files, using to start and play a game of Chess, 414-417
game genres, 13-14
game icons, showing, 420
game logic. *See* logic
game pieces in Chess, 427-428
game views, 8-10
game.checkForWalls( ) method, 155
game.checkPaddleCollisions( ) method, 156
gameClicked( ) function, 193
games
501 dart game. *See* 501 Dart Challenge
bonuses, 33
challenge games, 35
competition. *See* competition
concept and flow of, 27-28
characters, 29
developing themes, 28-29
flow, 30-31
storylines, 29
Cone Crazy. *See* Cone Crazy
darts. *See* 501 Dart Challenge
Easter eggs, 34
joining Chess games, 420-421
length of play, 34
levels of difficulty, 32-33
lives, 33
logic. *See* logic, 419
MMRPGs, 359
power-ups, 33
saving, 36
local files, 38
server-side databases, 38
SharedObject class, 36-37
scoring, 31
starting Chess, 422-423
tile-based worlds. *See* tile-based worlds
turn-based games, 280
Word Search. *See* Word Search
gender, demographics, 24
generateXML( ), 204
generating grids, Word Search, 391-393
getFrame( ), circle-line collision detection, 139
getRoomList method, 420
getScore( ), 501 Dart Challenge, 446-449
GIF (Graphics Interchange Format), 316
graphical user interface (GUI), 250
graphics
bitmap graphics, 314-315
compression, 317-318
Flash's settings, 320
lossless compression, 318-322
lossy compression, 320
lossy JPEG compression, 321
disbitmap graphics, 315
file types, 315-317
loading at run-time, 326-327
optimizing, 322-323
and performance, 322-326
vector graphics, 312-313
vector versus bitmap, 312
Graphics Interchange Format (GIF), 316
gravity, 87-89
grids generating in Word Search, 391-393
GUI (graphical user interface), level editors, 250

H

heuristic, A*, 298
high score lists, 263, 268
cheaters, 264
competition, 36
UberScore Administrator, 265-267
user-interface frames, 268-269
HighScoreList class, 269-271
ActionScript, 271-274
hit detection. *See* collision detection
hits, 444

hitTest( ), 98-100, 189, 472
  limitations of, 110-111
  movie clip-movie clip collisions, 100-102
  movie clip-point collisions, 103-106
  shape-point collisions, 107-109
human element of multiplayer games, 360

I

icons, showing game icons, 420
identifying tiles, selective processing in tile-based worlds, 190-193
images. *See* graphics
implementing
  A*, 303-307
  mazes, AI, 295
inelastic collisions, 164
Init, 268
  ActionScript, HighScoreList class, 271-274
initializeBall( ) function, 198
initializing
  sounds, Cone Crazy, 455
  variables for Cone Crazy game, 458-459
installing ElectroServer 3, 368
intersecting lines, line-line collision detection, 129-131
inverse cosine, 57-58
inverse sine, 57-58
inverse tangent, 57-58
inverse trigonometric functions, 57-58
isometric, 9
Isometric class, 224
isometric view, 211, 213-215
isometric worlds
  characters, moving, 235, 237-245
  correlative cues, 223
  deconstructing, 234-245
  placing objects in, 220-228
  z-sorting. *See* z-sorting
isometrics, coordinate systems, 215-220

J

joinGame method, 421
joining games of Chess, 420-421
JPEG (Joint Photographic Experts Group), 316
  lossy compression, 321

K

Key class, 81
kinetic energy, 90, 163
kings, Chess, 412
knights, Chess, 411

L

language filters, 371
layered sounds, 348
laying out worlds, for Cone Crazy game, 457-458
leader boards. *See* high score lists
length of play, 34
level editors, 250
  class files, 255-256
  GUI, 250
  guidelines for, 254
  sample game, 251-254
level generation, 279
levels of difficulty in games, 32-33
limitations
  of Flash, 14-17
  of hitTest( ), 110-111
line of action, 159
line segments, 129
  determining if they intersect, 131-134
line-line collision detection, 126
  determining if line segments intersect, 131-134
  equation of lines, 126-129
  intersecting lines, 129-131
lines, intersecting lines, 129-131
linkage identifiers, attachMovie( ), 106
lives, 33
loading
  graphics at run-time, 326-327
  progress bars
    501 Dart Challenge, 439
    Cone Crazy, 455
local files, saving game data, 38
logic
  501 Dart Challenge, 438, 440
    after the game, 449
    aiming darts, 441
    before the game setup, 438-440
    flying darts, 443-446
    getScore( ), 446-449
    releasing darts, 441-443
  Chess, 426
    ChessBoard class, 428-430
    ChessPiece class, 427-428

frame actions, 431-433
Tile class, 426-427
for Cone Crazy. *See* Cone Crazy, game logic, 454
Chess
creating games, 418-420
joining a game, 420-421
moveReceived event, 423-426
showing game icons, 420
starting the game, 422-423
custom logic, 280
of Word Search
choosing categories, 387-391
detecting choices, 402-403, 405
generating grids, 391-393
logic games, 14
Login, 268
Login frame, 372
Login frame label, ElectroServer 3, 373
loops, drum loops, 350-351
lossless compression, 318-322
lossy compression, 320
JPEG, 321

M

magnitude, 72
managing
sound effects, 334
with ActionScript, 38-41
sound placed on frames, 334-338
tile-independent objects, 195
maps, 12
mapToScreen( ), 225
massively multiplayer role-playing games (MMRPGs), 359-360
math
collision detection, 99, 110-111
circle-circle collision detection, 115
circle-circle collision detection (frame dependent), 116-118
circle-circle collision detection (frame independent), 118-125
circle-line collision detection, 135-142
line-line collision detection, 126-129
point-circle collision detection, 112-115
point-rectangle collision detection, 142-144
rectangle-rectangle collision detection, 145-146
trigonometry. *See* trigonometry
mazes, AI, 288
ActionScript for, 290-294
rules for, 289-290
visual implementation of, 295
MDM (Multimedia Limited), 256
measurements
degrees, 49
radians, 50
Message, 269
methods, 155
attachMovie, , linkage identifiers, 106
calculateDepth( ), 225, 231
createMaze( ), 293
flush( ), 37
fromXML( ), 256
game.checkForWalls( ), 155
game.checkPaddleCollisions( ), 156
getRoomList, 420
hitTest( ). *See* hitTest( )
joinGame, 421
mapToScreen( ), 225
new Astar( ), 305
sendMove, 423
toXML( ), 255
MMRPGs, 360
MMRPGs (massively multiplayer role-playing games), 359-360
momentum, 163
conservation laws, 164-165
motion
Newton's first law of motion, 82
Newton's second law of motion, 83-85
Newton's third law of motion, 86-87
moveBall( ), 198-199
moveCharacter( ), 242
moveReceived event, 423-426
moves
in Chess, 425
for spectators, 426
movie clip-movie clip collisions, 100-102
movie clip-point collisions, 103-106
moving characters in isometric worlds, 235, 237-245
multi-user servers, 12
multiplayer games
Chess. *See* Chess
ElectroServer 3, 367, 369
installing, 368
email-based games, 361
human element of, 360
MMRPGs, 359-360

more than one player on the same computer, 361
playing, 375-376
real-time games, 364-367
real-time multiplayer games, 361
socket-servers, 361-363
turn-based games, 361, 363-364
multiplayer logic. *See* logic
multiplayer servers, 12
music loops, 332
creating, 350-351
editing and preparing audio loops, 352-355

N

naming files, 334
neural networks, 279
new Astar( ), 305
Newton's first law of motion, 82
Newton's second law of motion, 83-85
Newton's third law of motion, 86-87
Newton, Sir Isaac, 82
nodes, A*, 298
normalization, 339
Northcode, 256

O

object-wall collision reactions, 152
bouncing objects off of walls, 153-158
objects
collisions with walls, 153
circle-line collision reactions, 159-162
object-wall collision reactions, 153-158
Cone Crazy, playing the game, 464-468
controlling
sound based on factors other than speed, 340-341
sound based on object speed, 338-340
defining for Cone Crazy game, 455-457
placing in isometric worlds, 220-228
player, 459
screen, 458
Sound, 334
tile-independent objects, 194-196
world, 458
octants, 220
on/off toggles, for sound, 335-337
onComplete event, HighScoreList class, 271
onEnterframe function, 195
optimizing
code, 325-326
images, 322-323

P

panning, automatic panning, 474
pathfinding, 278, 295-296
A*, 296-303, 307
implementing, 303-307
pawns, Chess, 412
performance and graphics, 322
alpha channels, 324
anti-aliasing, 324
bitmap smoothing, 324
optimizing code, 325-326
optimizing images, 322-323
simplifying vectors, 323
perspective, 213
physics, 70-71
friction, 90
good-enough friction, 92-93
real friction, 90-92
gravity, 87-89
Newton's first law of motion, 82
Newton's second law of motion, 83-85
Newton's third law of motion, 86-87
speed, 72-73
acceleration, 78-81
applying with ActionScript, 73-77
velocity, 72-73
pictures. *See* graphics
placing objects in isometric worlds, 220-228
playAccel( ), 343
playback specifications, 24-25
Flash version, 25-26
screen size, 26-27
speed, 25
playDecel( ), 343
player cars, adding for Cone Crazy game, 462-463
player object, 459
players
Cone Crazy, playing the game, 468-473
possible moves in Chess, 425
playersArrived property, 419
playing multiplayer games, 375-376

playSound( ), 334-335, 338, 341
PNG (Portable Network Graphics), 316
point of view, 9
point-circle collision detection, 112-115
point-rectangle collision detection, 142-144
pointRectangleDetection( ), 144
Portable Network Graphics (PNG), 316
positionCharacter( ), 239
potential energy, 163
power-ups, 33
preparing audio loops, 352-355
progress bars, loading for
 501 Dart Challenge, 439
 Cone Crazy, 455
projection, trigonometry, 59-61
promotion, 412
properties
 allowSpectators, 419
 FloodingFilterEnabled, 420
 playersArrived, 419
puzzle games, 14
Pythagorean theorem, 52-55

Q-R

quadratic equations, solving, 121
queens, Chess, 411

radians, converting to degrees, 50
radius/sin(gamma), 136
real-time, 12
real-time calculations, limitations of Flash, 17
real-time multiplayer competition, 35
real-time multiplayer games, 361, 364-367
reasons for using Flash for game development, 15
recording sound effects, 347
rectangle-rectangle collision detection, 145-146
rectangle-rectangle collision reactions, 152, 167-168
RectangleRectangleDetection( ), 146
Register, 269
releasing darts, 501 Dart Challenge, 441-443
removeMovieClip( ), 229
rendering, 12
resolution, screens, 26
resolving, vectors, 63
restart( ), 392, 401
role-playing games (RPG), 14, 361
rooks, Chess, 411
rotation, 77
 vectors, 62
RPGs (role-playing games), 14, 361
Rubberduck, 256
rules
 of Chess, 410-413
 for mazes, AI, 289-290
run-time, loading graphics at, 326-327

S

saving
 game data, 36-38
 high scores, 501 Dart Challenge, 438
scalar value. *See* magnitude
scaling, design considerations for tile-based worlds, 184-185
scores, 269
 A*, 298
 saving high scores, 501 Dart Challenge, 438
 updating high scores, 501 Dart Challenge, 449
scoring, 31
 501 Dart Challenge, 437
scrambleWords( ), 392, 394-397
screen object, 458
screen size, playback specifications, 26-27
Screenweaver (Rubberduck), 256
seamless tiles
 design considerations, for tile-based worlds, 183-184
 designing tile-based worlds, 183-184
selected( ), 402-403
selective processing, tile-based worlds, 189
 getting positions within tiles, 193-194
 identifying tiles, 190, 192-193
sendMove, 423
sendStartMove function, 422
serialization, 419
server-side databases, saving game data, 38
servers
 authoritative servers, 365
 socket-servers, 361-363
setInterval function, 196
setup, 501 Dart Challenge, 439-440
shape-point collisions, 107-109

shapes
  collision detection with advanced shapes, 147-148
  triangles, 51-52
SharedObject class, saving game data, 36-37
showGameRooms function, 420
showing game icons, 420
showPopup, 375
showRooms function, 420
showUsers, 422
side view, 10
simplifying vectors, 323
sine, 55-57
slopes, graphical representation of, 127
socket servers, 12, 361-363
solutions for AI, 284
solving quadratic equations, 121
songs, 332
sound
  creating fake sounds, 347-349
  digital sound, 346
  importance of, 332-333
  initializing Cone Crazy, 455
  layered sounds, 348
  music loops. *See* music loops, 350
  on frames, 334
    on/off toggles, 335-337
    setting volume for, 337-338
  of objects, controlling sound, 338-340
  playback specifications, 25
sound effects, 332
  creating, 345-347
  managing, 334
    with ActionScript, 338
    controlling sound based on factors other than speed, 340-341
    controlling sound based on object speed, 338-340
    sound placed on frames, 334-338
    volume control through acceleration, 341-345
  recording, 347
Sound Forge, 353
Sound object, 334
sound offset, 345
source code, 12
spectators, moves, 426
speed, 72-73
  acceleration, 78
    applying with ActionScript, 79-81
  applying with ActionScript, 73-77
  frame rate, 75
splash screens, 383
sports games, 14
sprites, 12
stacking order, 212
stalemates, Chess, 413
starting a game of Chess, 422-423
storing information for tile grids, 185-189
storylines, developing, 29
strategy games, 14
swapDepths( ), 229
SWF Studio, 256
tangent, 55-57

T

TBW. *See* tile-based worlds
terminal velocity, 86
testing AI, 284
texture mapping, limitations of Flash, 17
themes, developing, 28-29
third person, 10
tile attributes, changing based on object impact, 196-197
Tile class, 426-427
tile-based games
  Cone Crazy. *See* Cone Crazy
  defining with XML, 203-207
tile-based worlds, 179-182
  adding characters, 197-203
  creating the grid and storing information, 185-189
  designing
    scaling tiles, 184-185
    views, 182
    with seamless tiles, 183-184
  selective processing, 189
    getting positions within tiles, 193-194
    identifying tiles, 190, 192-193
  tile-independent objects, 194-196
tile-independent objects, 194-196
tiles, 180
  changing attributes based on object impact, 196-197
  Chess, 426-427
  Cone Crazy, playing the game, 464
  creating, 232
    grids, 185-189
  defining for Cone Crazy game, 455-457
  depth, 231

getting positions withing tiles, selective processing in tile-based worlds, 193-194
identifying, selective processing in tile-based worlds, 190-193
scaling, designing tile-based worlds, 184-185
timers, Cone Crazy, 473-474
toggles, on/off (sound), 335-337
tools, UberScore Administrator, 265-267
top-down view, 10
toXML( ) method, 255
trace action, movie clip-movie clip collisions, 101
triangles, 51-52
trigonometric functions, 55-57
trigonometry, 43
angles, 48-50
cosine, 55-57
inverse trigonometric functions, 57-58
projection, 59-61
Pythagorean theorem, 52-55
reasons for learning, 44
sine, 55-57
tangent, 55-57
triangles, anatomy of, 51-52
vectors, 62-66
turn-based games, 13, 280
turn-based multiplayer games, 361-364

U

UberScore Administrator, 265-267
updating high scores, 501 Dart Challenge, 449
user-interface frames, high score lists, 268-269
users, autonumbered users, 421

V

variables, initializing for Cone Crazy games, 458-459
vector graphics, 13, 312-313
vectors
resolving, 63
simplifying, 323
trigonometry, 62-66
velocity, 72-73
terminal velocity, 86
views
design considerations for tile-based worlds, 182
game views. *See* game views
virtual pen, 129
visual implementation of mazes, AI, 295
voice, 332
volume, setting for frame-based sounds, 337-338

W-Z

Word Search, 381
logic of
choosing categories, 387-391
detecting choices, 402-403, 405
generating grids, 391-393
overview of, 382-386
world object, 458
worldClicked( ), 240
worlds, 13
constructing for Cone Crazy game, 460-462
laying out for Cone Crazy games, 457-458
tile-based worlds. *See* tile-based worlds
worldToScreen( ) function for Cone Crazy game, 459-460

XML, tile-based games, 203-207

Z-sorting, 17, 212, 221, 229-234